Fundamentals of Arabic grammar

Fundamentals of Arabic Grammar provides an authoritative guide to Modern Standard Arabic (MSA) grammar. It has been organised to promote a thorough understanding of MSA grammar and presents its complexities in a cohesive and user-friendly format, filling many gaps left by other textbooks. Explanations are clear, full and accessible and extensive cross-referencing, two generous indexes and six appendices provide users with easy access to the information they require. No prior knowledge of linguistic terminology is required.

Features include:

- Expert treatment of a full range of grammar topics and structures, including the case system, *IDhaafa*, the equational sentence, quantifiers and the vocative, generously spread across thirty-eight chapters
- Special attention to parts of speech, such as nouns, pronouns, adjectives, adverbs and prepositions, given at the beginning of the book to acquaint students with the basic units of Arabic and provide a solid foundation for further learning
- A wide range of contemporary examples drawn from real life to provide a solid context for grammar points, further supported by word glosses and idiomatic translations of sentences
- Grammatical terms given in both Arabic and English
- A wide variety of supplementary learning resources such as practice sheets, exercises and verb tables available to download free at http://www.routledge.com/books/details/9780415710046/
- A substantial bibliography incorporating primary Arabic grammar sources in addition to secondary sources in Arabic and in English.

Fundamentals of Arabic Grammar has been field tested over a number of years and has been written by a highly experienced teacher of Arabic. It will be an essential resource for students and teachers of Arabic at all university levels and is suitable for use both as a companion reference text in Arabic language courses and as a standalone text in independent grammar classes.

Mohammed Sawaie is Professor of Arabic in the Department of Middle Eastern and South Asian Languages and Cultures at the University of Virginia, USA.

Fundamentals of Arabic Grammar

Mohammed Sawaie

أُصُولُ النَّحْوَ العَرَبِي

محمّد سَوَاعِي

Routledge
Taylor & Francis Group

LONDON AND NEW YORK

First published 2014
by Routledge
2 Park Square, Milton Park, Abingdon, Oxon OX14 4RN

and by Routledge
711 Third Avenue, New York, NY 10017

Routledge is an imprint of the Taylor & Francis Group, an informa business

British Library Cataloguing in Publication Data
A catalogue record for this book is available from the British Library

Library of Congress Cataloging in Publication Data
A catalog record for this book has been requested

ISBN: 978-0-415-71003-9 (hbk)
ISBN: 978-0-415-71004-6 (pbk)
ISBN: 978-0-315-88180-8 (ebk)

Typeset in Calisto
by Graphicraft Limited, Hong Kong

إِنِّي رَأَيْتُ أَنَّهُ لَا يَكْتُبُ أَحَدٌ كِتَاباً في يَوْمِهِ إِلَّا قَالَ في غَدِهِ: لَوْ غُيِّرَ هذا لَكَانَ أَحْسَنَ. وَلَوْ زِيدَ هذا لَكَانَ يُسْتَحْسَنُ، وَلَوْ قُدِّمَ هذا لَكَانَ أَجْمَلَ. وهذا مِنْ أعظَمِ العِبَرِ، وهُوَ دَلِيلٌ عَلَى اِسْتِيلَاءِ النَّقْصِ عَلَى جُمْلَةِ البَشَرِ.

العِمَاد الإصفهاني

خَرِيدَة القَصر وجَريدة العَصر

I have observed that no one finishes the writing of a book who does not say afterwards: had this change been made, the book would have been better; had this item been added the book would have been better appreciated; had this item been moved forward the book would have been more beautiful. In this lies the most important lesson: it is proof of the inherent imperfection of all humans.

Al-ʿImad al-ʿIsfahani (died 1201 AD)
Kharidat al-Qasr wa Jaridat al-ʿASr

Contents

Acknowledgements

This work originated as notes on Arabic grammar made while teaching Arabic as a foreign language at various levels, from beginning to advanced, and independent courses on Arabic grammar in a university setting over many years. I am indebted to Vivian Bishara McCormack for her encouragement to write down this material, and for her contribution to the early drafts. Barbara A. Brothers was always supportive and encouraging. Omima El-Araby witnessed the completion of an early draft, read the manuscript and offered many suggestions for improvement during her tenure at the University of Virginia, while teaching a joint course with me for a number of years. Students who used this material and tolerated the often last-minute production of rough chapters deserve sincere thanks. Many thanks to Farzaneh Milani, current Chair of my department, for providing funds to have the book manuscript edited professionally.

Numerous colleagues, friends and former students from various regions of the world read this material in its varying stages and contributed to its improvement: Abdulkarim S. Ramadan, Adel S. Gamal, Medhat Credi, Omar H. Okasha, Ahmad Abu Dalu, Benjamin Smith, Thomas Wilson, Ellen Duthoy, and Mohammed Rabbaa. To them all, I offer sincere thanks. I also thank anonymous reviewers, some of whose comments were helpful. I cannot express in words my gratitude to Cecilia F. Blewer for her encouragement, support and constant probing for a better understanding of grammar, and for her deep interest in improving this work. Susan Dempsey was most helpful in offering technical support. To the Routledge team, Andrea Hartill, Geraldine Martin, Isabelle Cheng, and Helena Power, Copy Editor, I extend my gratitude for their efficiency and cooperation at all stages of bringing this work to publication. From those who contributed to this work and were not mentioned I ask forgiveness.

Introduction

The rise of the grammatical tradition among Arabs is tied closely to the rise of Islam and its holy book, the Qur'an. This book became a subject of study and linguistic analysis in the seventh century A.D. This is no different to the development of grammars of other nations that was stimulated by religious or other major works: the Vedas gave rise to the grammar of Sanskrit, Homer to the Greek grammar, the Biblical canons to Hebrew and the book of Confucius to Chinese.

The first book on Arabic grammar, *al-Kitaab*, was authored by Sibawayhi in the eighth century. Since then, many schools of Arabic grammar have developed, with various competing regional and intellectual paradigms resulting in a great number of books from various perspectives and for different purposes. Through such works, the Arabic language has been minutely and painstakingly analyzed and set out in countless descriptions by eminent scholars writing in Arabic as well as in major Eastern and Western languages.

This work is not intended to add one more book to the distinguished list of classics on the subject. Rather, it is intended for a special audience: students learning Arabic as a foreign language at university level. One of its major goals is to present the fundamentals of Arabic grammar to those in the process of acquiring the language in an easy-to-read format.

This material consists of topics essential to the mastery of Arabic as a foreign language, both orally and in its written form. It treats the grammatical issues integral to language learning at university level, both undergraduate as well as graduate. Various grammar details and innumerable complex exceptions to rules, endemic to classic Arabic grammar books and university-level grammar courses in Arab universities, were deliberately left out.

The first eight chapters cover the basic building blocks of language in a manner learners untrained in grammar in their high schools can find accessible.

These chapters present a general overview of how those elements interface with each other to form a system of communication, both orally and in writing, to foster accuracy in the linguistic output, the means of communication in a speech community. *Fundamentals of Arabic Grammar*, henceforth *Fundamentals*, presumes its users to have mastered the Arabic writing system, the names of letters of the alphabet and the sounds they represent. This is normally expected by the end of the first four weeks of the first semester of an introductory Arabic language course in any serious university program. That is why all examples are given in the Arabic orthography, and references are made to the Arabic names of the letters and basic notions such as *tanwiin*.

Fundamentals is not intended to replace instructional textbooks. It is intended to supplement and to reinforce them; to function as a resource book, a reference tool providing a holistic presentation of grammar rather than the disjointed approach often encountered in textbooks available on the market nowadays.

The arrangement of chapters attempts to relate relevant items to one another. Materials specific to nouns, their cases, derivation, numbers, etc., for example, are sequentially ordered in the interest of providing a comprehensive treatment of nouns. The same is to be said about verbs, their types, behaviors, tenses, and moods, etc. Instructors can enjoy leeway in determining which chapters, or sections of chapters, are essential to their students' immediate needs. They, therefore, can order the presentation of materials to their students according to the learners' levels, curricular requirements in a specific week, or their program priorities. The chapter on verbs, for example, is too detailed to present to a beginning-level class in one sitting. The assignment of such a chapter could be spread over a number of sessions, as need dictates. Similarly, to treat the grammar of numbers adequately instructors may choose to divide this topic for different presentations on different days.

Fundamentals is well suited for an independent grammar course at university level. Indeed, its origin lay in just such a course. In this case, it plays a different role. As a course textbook, it can serve as a desk reference for both the student and instructor and will enable them to clarify points of grammar in an organized fashion.

The pages of this work contain a large number of tables of verb conjugation spread out in the various chapters dealing with verbs, their tenses and moods. In addition, there are several supplementary tables, placed on the web, to which learners can refer to ensure mastery of the verb system and other derivations.

Learning the grammar contained in the pages of this book is supported by the accompanying exercises placed on the web. These exercises are intended for in-class practice as well as for homework assignments. Language learning is not different from any skill that can be mastered through practice only. As the saying goes, "practice makes perfect."

The Arabic introduced in this book is often referred to as Modern Standard Arabic (MSA), or Modern Literary Arabic (MLA), the language variety used in formal settings across the Arabic-speaking regions, both in print and, increasingly, in electronic media, especially in the last few decades. The Arabic term *fuS-Ha*, "refined, pure," is often employed in reference to this linguistic variety. Thus, the examples used in these pages to illustrate certain grammar points mirror those utterances delivered in formal settings by literate, educated native speakers, orally or in writing. Due to historical and other reasons, educated native speakers of MSA have not represented a majority in their societies. Their numbers, however, are increasing due to many factors: the spread of education, rising literacy levels, and the recent introduction of pan-Arab electronic media venues that employ the linguistic variety contained in this work.

Examples are provided only in the Arabic script with full vocalization, except for proper nouns where case markers have been left out. Some grammar books provide phonetic transcription of example sentences. This book deliberately avoids this practice in order to encourage learners to access the language in its own writing system. Word glosses and idiomatic translations of sentences are also provided.

Latinate nomenclature may not always be adequate to characterize the Arabic linguistic phenomena under discussion. There is a deliberate effort on our side to introduce Arabic grammar terminology, often side by side with commonly used Western terminology. Instead of using the designation "assimilative verbs" used by Western sources, for example, the term *waaw*-beginning verbs is employed, named after the letter *waaw*—a term favored by Arab grammarians, and more descriptive in the classification of those verbs. The linguistically savvy learner will find the Arabic labels more accurate than the Latinate ones, which are conventionally imposed from outside the language tradition to describe grammar categories belonging to a different language tradition and family.

To study Arabic grammar is to participate in Arab culture. In addition to facilitating precise communication in Arabic, the study of grammar opens doors to cultural production like theology, literature, songs, and even humor. Many a fine point turns on grammar, and in these Arabic speakers have always found much to enjoy and debate. It is hoped that students will learn to appreciate Arabic grammar as much as they do the music, food and other aspects of Arab culture.

Mohammed Sawaie
Charlottesville, Virginia
April 26, 2013

Symbols used

' = *hamza* ء
H = *Haa'* ح
kh = khaa' خ
dh = ذ
S = *Saad* ص
Dh = *Dhaad* ض
T = Taa' ط
Z = Zaa' ظ
ᶜ = ᶜayn ع
gh = *ghayn* غ
q = *qaaf* ق
a = *fat-Ha*
aa = 'alif ا
i = *kasra*
ii = yaa' ي
y = semi consonant
u = *Dhamma*
uu = *waaw* و
w = semi consonant

M = Masculine
F = Feminine
s.o. = someone
s.th. = something
Sg = singular
D = dual
Pl = plural
lit. = literally

CHAPTER 1

The verb system in Arabic الأَفعال

Verbs are that part of speech that express action or the occurrence of an event. Verbs are usually the first element in MSA sentences that contain verbs, followed by performers of actions, called فاعِل in Arabic. A sentence whose initial element is a verb is known as a *verbal sentence*. A sentence beginning with a noun is called a *nominal sentence*. There are grammatical consequences for the choice of placing the verb or the performer of action at the head of the sentence. Examples of verbal and nominal sentences follow:

وَصَلَ الصَّديقُ أَمْسِ.	The friend (M) arrived yesterday.
الصَّديقَةُ وَصَلَت أَمْسِ.	The friend (F) arrived yesterday.

1.1 THE PERFORMER OF ACTION فاعِل

All verbs have a فاعِل, the performer of action. This element could be expressed as a noun, or nouns, or as a pronoun, explicit or implied. An expressed noun functioning as a performer is always in the nominative case; it can be definite or indefinite. Definite singular nouns must end with a *Dhamma* in the writing system of formal Arabic, pronounced -*u*; indefinite singular nouns end with two *Dhamma*s in orthography, pronounced -*un*. Dual definite and indefinite nouns such as فاعِل must have ـان- at their ends; regular masculine plural nouns have ـونَ-; irregular plural nouns, like singular nouns, have either a *Dhamma* or two, depending on their determination (whether they are definite or indefinite). Finally, regular feminine plural nouns must have ـات- with either a *Dhamma* or two, depending on their determination.

1.2 VERB TENSES

Verbs can convey a sense of time frame: past, present, or future; whether the action happened in the past or was a single occurrence, or if one action happened before or after another, whether it happens regularly and habitually, or is happening at the present time, or whether it will happen at some future time. These time references of events expressed by verbs are called tenses. Verb tenses in Arabic are divided into the following:

1. Past tense is used to express a past, completed action (see Chapter 11), or an action which was ongoing in the past (see Chapter 18 on past continuous tense), or two actions which happened in the past with one action occurring before the other (see past perfect tense, Chapter 19).

2. Present tense is used to express actions in the present, either happening habitually or regularly, or to state a fact. Additionally, this tense can be used to express the future (see Chapter 14). Forms of the present tense are also used in imperatives and their negatives, and follow subjunctive particles.

3. Future tense employs verbs to express action that will happen at some point in the future (see Chapter 14).

1.3 INTRANSITIVE VERBS الأَفْعَالُ اللازِمَةُ VERSUS TRANSITIVE VERBS الأَفعال الـمُتَعَدِّية

1.3.1 Intransitive verbs الأَفْعَالُ اللازِمَةُ

Some verbs require only a performer of action, the فاعل, to make a complete sentence. For example, the verbs نامَ "he slept, to sleep" or اِبْتَسَمَ "he smiled, to smile" express actions that are unilaterally performed by one person, namely the person who slept or smiled. Such verbs are referred to as *intransitive verbs* (فِعل لازم / Pl أفعال لازِمَة), verbs that do not require direct objects as in كَبُرَ "to become bigger," ضَحِكَ "to laugh." Intransitive verbs are often used with prepositions which are learned as part and parcel of learning the verb itself and how it is used. Examples of intransitive verbs include: ذَهَبَ إلى "to go to," رَجَعَ مِنْ/ إلى "to return from/to," خَرَجَ مِنْ "to go out, exit," etc.

1.3.2 Transitive verbs الأَفْعَالُ الـمُتَعَدِّيَة

Some verbs express actions by a performer that extends explicitly or implicitly to something or someone else. Such verbs are called *transitive verbs* (فِعل مُتَعَدٍّ / Pl أفعال مُتَعَدِّيَة). A transitive verb not only has a فاعل, performer, but can take what is referred to as مَفْعولٌ بِهِ, a direct object. Examples of transitive verbs include دَرَسَ "to study," كَتَبَ "to write," فَهِمَ "to understand," شَرِبَ "to drink," etc. If the direct object is not mentioned, the speaker/writer is using a stylistic strategy called *truncation* and is leaving it to the listener/reader to fill it in. A limited number of verbs take two direct objects. Examples of such verbs include: أَعْطى "to give," عَيَّنَ "to appoint," اِنْتَخَبَ "to elect, select." Consider the following examples:

أَعْطى الرَّجُلُ الوَلَدَ ديناراً.   The man gave the boy a *dinar*.

عَيَّنَ الرَّئيسُ الأُستاذَ وزيراً.   The president appointed the professor as a minister.

1.4 NOUNS AS DIRECT OBJECTS

Direct objects are always in the accusative case (مَنْصوب); they can be definite or indefinite (see Chapter 3 on cases). Singular, definite nouns functioning as direct objects must end with a *fat-Ha* in formal spoken or scripted Arabic. On the other hand, if the direct object is indefinite masculine, it must end with an *'alif* bearing two *fat-Ha*s ا (*tanwiin*) in the orthography. Masculine, indefinite nouns as direct objects ending with *hamza* do not take this *'alif*-bearing two *fat-Ha*s, as in, for example, سَماءً "sky," ماءً "water," هواءً "air," etc. Feminine nouns functioning as direct objects end with two *fat-Ha*s placed above the feminine marker, the *taa' marbuuTa* ة. Consider the following:

الطالِبَةُ قَرَأَت كِتاباً.   The student (F) read a book.

حُسَين شَرِبَ قَهْوَةً.   Hussein drank coffee.

Dual masculine or feminine nouns must end with ـيْنِ when functioning as direct objects, as in the following examples:

قابلوا مُوَظَّفَيْنِ.   They met two employees.

دَعَوْنا صَديقتَيْنِ.   We invited two friends (F).

Regular masculine nouns end with ـينَ; irregular plural nouns as objects behave largely like singular nouns with respect to their accusative case endings; definite feminine regular plural nouns must have a *kasra* instead of *fat-Ha* or two *fat-Has* if they are indefinite. Consider the following examples:

وَظَّفَتِ الشَّرِكَةُ مُهَنْدِسينَ.   The company employed engineers (M).

قَابَلَتِ المُديرَةُ مُدَرِّساتٍ.   The director met teachers (F, Pl).

1.5 PRONOUNS AS DIRECT OBJECTS

If the direct object is a pronoun, this pronoun assumes a *cliticized*, shortened form that must attach to the end of the verb as a suffix (see Chapter 5 on pronouns). The direct object pronoun cannot stand independently and is under-stood to be in the accusative case. Consider the following:

الأَبُ قَابَلَنا أَمْس.   The father met us yesterday.

هَلْ شاهَدْتَها في المَكْتَبَة؟   Did you see her in the library?

عَرَفْتُهُم أَثْناءَ الدِّراسَةِ في الجامِعَة.   I knew them during the [my] university study.

1.6 GENDER

Verbs are inflected to first, second and third pronouns. They must reflect the gender of the فاعِل for the second أَنْتَ "you (M)," أَنْتِ "you (F)," their dual and plural forms (see Chapter 5 on pronouns) and third person pronouns هُوَ "he," هِيَ "she," and their dual and plural forms. The first person pronouns أَنا "I" and نَحْنُ "we" do not have gender markings in verb inflection/conjugation. If the فاعِل is a feminine noun, it is marked by suffixing ت-, as in the following:

الطّالِبَةُ أَكَلَتِ الخُبْزَ.   The student (F) ate the bread.

أَكَلَتِ الطّالِبَةُ الخُبْزَ.   The student (F) ate the bread.

Because verbs are specific to gender, person and number (below), no pronoun is necessary to represent the فاعِل. If a pronoun is used, it simply adds emphasis.

1.7 NUMBER IN VERBS

Singular nouns such as فَاعِل are used with singular verbs. If, however, the فَاعِل is a dual or plural noun placed before the verb, as in nominal sentences, the verb must reflect the number of the noun. (This matter is treated in detail in Chapter 11.) The following examples are illustrative:

شَرِبَ المُعَلِّمونَ القَهْوَةَ.   The teachers drank coffee.

المُعَلِّمونَ شَرِبوا القَهْوَةَ.   The teachers drank coffee.

1.8 VERB VOICE

1.8.1 The active voice

All verb tenses, past, present and future, discussed thus far are in the active voice. This means that the identity of the performer of the action, i.e. the فَاعِل, is known to interlocutors; it is easily identifiable by the presence of the noun indicating who carried out the action, as in the following examples:

كَسَرَ الطالِبُ الزُّجاجَ.   The student broke the glass.

يَكْتُبُ الصُّحُفِيُّ مَقالَةً كُلَّ أُسْبوعٍ.   The journalist writes an article every week.

1.8.2 The passive voice

In cases when the performer is not identified or is unknown, the verb is rendered in the passive voice. Passive verbs in Arabic in all tenses undergo internal vowel change(s) from the active. The two examples in the active voice above are rendered in the passive voice as follows:

كُسِرَ الزُّجاجُ.   The glass was broken.

تُكْتَبُ مَقالَةٌ كُلَّ أُسْبوعٍ.   An article is written every week.

Note that the performers of actions in these sentences are not identified, and that the accusative direct objects الزُّجاجَ "the glass," and مَقالَةً "essay, an article," in the active voice sentences changed their cases to the nominative. Accusative direct objects changing to the nominative case are labeled as نائِب الفاعِل "performer deputy" in Arabic grammar. Note that the verb يَكْتُبُ "he writes" in the second sentence changes gender into the feminine to agree with the feminine noun مَقالة "essay, article" when it becomes the فاعِل of the passive verb.

In addition to obscuring the identity of the performer in the preceding examples, the passive voice is sometimes used for stylistic variation, especially in writing (see Chapter 16 for detailed discussion).

1.9 VERB FORMS OR PATTERNS وَزْن OR صيغة

Arab grammarians describe Arabic verbs by using a standard verb, the verb فَعَلَ "to do," and rendering it into various forms or patterns with prefixes and infixes to describe how a particular verb fits into the general patterning of Arabic verbs. It is a device similar to how X, Y, and Z serve as templates for algebraic expressions. The three consonants of the verb فَعَلَ stand for the three consonants that comprise the root of most Arabic verbs. These tri-consonantal verbs are called أَفْعال ثُلاثِيّة Pl / فِعْل ثُلاثِيّ. The ف represents the first consonant, ع represents the second consonant, and ل represents the third consonant. Thus, from the three consonants د، ر، and س we obtain the verb دَرَسَ "he studied, to study"; it is in the فَعَلَ form, Form I. When the middle consonant is doubled phonetically (written with a *shadda* in the orthography), we obtain دَرَّسَ. This verb is said to be in the فَعَّلَ form, Form II; the newly formed verb means "he taught." Western writers on Arabic grammar refer to verb categories by the use of Roman numerals. A verb consisting of three consonants is referred to as a Form I verb. Other verb forms are assigned different Roman numerals, as we shall see below.

1.9.1 Form I verbs صيغة فَعَلَ

Verbs in the past tense in فَعَلَ form express the third person singular pronoun هُوَ. They always end in *fat-Ha*. The middle vowel may be a *fat-Ha* as in كَتَبَ / يَكْتُبُ "he wrote," or a *kasra* as in لَعِبَ / يَلْعَبُ "he played," or a *Dhamma* as in كَبُرَ / يَكْبُرُ "he grew up." Schooled native speakers memorize their verb patterns and internalize this information. Foreign learners are expected to do the same.

Tri-consonantal فَعَلَ verbs can be intransitive and transitive verbs (see above). فَعَلَ verbs (Form I) are generally viewed to have several subcategories, presented below under their respective titles:

1.9.1.1 waaw-beginning verbs اَلأَفْعال الواوِيَّة

فَعَلَ verbs include a list of verbs that begin with a *waaw* in the past tense, known as أَفْعال المِثال, or أَفْعال واوِيَّة "*waaw*-beginning verbs." The middle vowel in the past tense varies. Some of these verbs are intransitive, others are transitive. In the present tense, the *waaw* for the third person singular pronoun هُوَ "he" changes to *yaa'*, as we shall see in Chapter 12. Following are intransitive verbs in this category: وَجَبَ / يَجِبُ "to become necessary, to be incumbent," وَصَلَ / يَصِلُ "to arrive at, reach," وَقَفَ / يَقِفُ "to stand up, to stop." Transitive verbs in this category include وَجَدَ / يَجِدُ "to find, to locate," وَصَفَ / يَصِفُ "to describe," and وَهَبَ / يَهَبُ "to grant."

1.9.1.2 yaa'-beginning verbs اَلأَفْعالُ اليائِيَّة

فَعَلَ verbs include a list of verbs that begin with a *yaa'* in the past tense, known as أَفْعال يائِيَّة "*yaa'*-beginning verbs." These verbs tend to be intransitive, and their use is rather infrequent. Examples include يَئِسَ / يَيْأَسُ "to despair, to lose hope," يَبِسَ / يَيْبَسُ "to be/become dry."

1.9.1.3 Hollow verbs اَلأَفْعال الجَوْفاء

Hollow verbs in the past tense consist of two consonants separated by an *'alif* ا as in نامَ / يَنامُ "to sleep," قالَ / يَقولُ "to say," etc. They have roots that are either *waaw* or *yaa'*.

1.9.1.4 Defective verbs اَلأَفْعالُ المُعْتَلَّة الآخِر (الأَفْعال النّاقِصة)

Defective verbs الأَفْعال النّاقِصة or الأَفْعال المُعْتَلَّة الآخِر in the past tense end with either *'alif maqSuura* or *'alif*. Examples of verbs ending with *'alif maqSuura* are بَنى / يَبْني "to build," and رَمى / يَرْمي "to throw, to toss." Examples of verbs ending with regular *'alif* include عَلا / يَعْلو "to go up, to rise," and سما / يَسْمو "to become sublime."

1.9.1.5 Doubled verbs اَلأَفْعال الـمُضَعَّفَة

The last sub-category of فَعَلَ verbs is a group of verbs that have a final doubled, geminated consonant, as in عَدَّ / يَعُدُّ "to count, to consider," مَرَّ / يَمُرُّ "to pass through," and so on.

1.9.1.6 Verbs of beginning أَفعال الشُّروع

This is a group of verbs denoting the onset of an action. Such verbs must be followed by a noun forming an equational sentence whose predicate must be an indicative present tense verb. For that reason, Arab grammarians consider verbs of beginning members of كانَ and its sisters (see Chapter 10) . This structure is used to indicate actions that happened in the past. All these verbs have the meaning of "[he] began, started, initiated." Such a finite list of verbs includes the following examples: أَخَذَ / يَأْخُذُ "[he] took it upon himself," بَدَأَ / يَبْدَأُ "he began," شَرَعَ / يَشْرَعُ "he started," etc.

These verbs are generally followed by verbs in the present tense to express the notion that someone initiated an action. Note that the forms of verbs of beginning themselves are in the past tense; however, the verb following them must be in the present tense. Examine the following illustrative examples:

أَخَذَ يَدْرُسُ عِنْدَما شاهَدَني.	He started to study when he saw me.
هَبَّ يُدافِعُ عَن هذِه القَضِيَّة.	He rushed to defend this matter.
شَرَعَ يَتَكَلَّمُ عَنْ آرائِهِ السِّياسِيَّة.	He began talking about his political views.
صارَ يَصيحُ بِصَوْتٍ عالٍ.	He started shouting in a loud voice.
أَخَذَ يَتَكَلَّمُ عَنِ السِّياسَة.	He began talking about politics.
بَدَأَ يَكْتُبُ مُذَكِّراتِه.	He started writing his memoirs.

1.9.2 Augmented verbs الأَفْعال الـمَزيدَة (Forms II–X)

The فَعَلَ form can be manipulated by prefixes and/or infixes, or a combination of these to create other verb categories. These elements are represented in the orthography and include doubling of a consonant in the middle or end of a verb (Form II), as was mentioned previously. In addition, there are the long vowel *aa* represented by *'alif* in the orthography (Form III); a *hamza* written on an *'alif* (Form IV); a *taa'* prefixed to Form II verbs (Form V); or a combination of *taa'* as a prefix and *'alif* as an infix (Form VI); or a combination of *'alif* and *nuun* as a prefix (Form VII); or *'alif* as prefix and *taa'* as infix (Form VIII); an *'alif* and doubling of the final consonant (Form IX); and, finally, اسْتَـ as prefix (Form X). Discussion of the various verb categories follows.

1.9.2.1 Form II verbs صِيغَة فَعَّلَ

This verb form is derived from فَعَلَ verbs by doubling the middle consonant. In the Arabic orthography, this is represented by writing the *shadda* followed by a *fat-Ha* above the middle consonant. This doubling of the middle consonant results in new verbs with new special meanings. Since فَعَّلَ form verbs are derived from فَعَلَ verbs, a semantic link between the original form and the augmented one may exist. For example, دَرَسَ / يَدْرُسُ means "to study." دَرَّسَ / يُدَرِّسُ, on the other hand, means "to make someone study" or "to cause someone to study." دَرَّسَ is, therefore, used in the sense of "to teach." Verbs in this category tend to be transitive, i.e. they require a direct object.

Some فَعَّلَ form verbs indicate a level of intensity added to the original meaning of فَعَلَ forms. For example, كَسَّرَ / يُكَسِّرُ is augmented from كَسَرَ / يَكْسِرُ "to break." It conveys the meaning of "to break in an intensive fashion," i.e., "to smash."

1.9.2.2 Form III verbs صِيغَة فاعَلَ

This verb form is derived from the فَعَلَ form by phonetically elongating the *fat-Ha* sound; in the orthography by inserting an *'alif* ا after the first consonant, resulting in فاعَلَ. Some verbs in this category can be transitive, others intransitive. Intransitive verbs require a preposition. Many instances of فاعَلَ forms indicate reciprocity or mutuality and have a semantic relationship to فَعَلَ verb forms. This relationship, however, is sometimes tenuous. Examine the following examples:

ساعَدَ المُدَرِّسُ الطالِبَ.   The instructor helped the student.

قابَلَ المُديرُ الطَّبيبَةَ.   The director met with the physician.

1.9.2.3 Form IV verbs صيغة أَفْعَلَ

Verbs in this form are derived by the prefixation of a *hamza* at the beginning of the فَعَلَ form. In the orthography, the *hamza* at the beginning of a word must always have a "seat" in the form of an *'alif*; such augmentation results in change in the vowel pattern. Notice in this form that the first consonant is not followed by a vowel; a *sukuun* is provided in the orthography. Many verbs in this category are transitive, others intransitive. In many instances أَفْعَلَ forms have a causal semantic relationship to فَعَلَ verb forms. This relationship, however, is sometimes tenuous. Examine the following examples:

عَلِمَ بالخَبَرِ.	He knew of the news [item].
أَعْلَمَ صَديقَهُ بالخَبَرِ.	He informed his friend of the news [item].
فَهِمَ السُّؤالَ.	He understood the question.
أَفْهَمَني السُّؤالَ.	He explained the question to me.

1.9.2.4 Form V verbs صيغة تَفَعَّلَ

This form is obtained by the prefixation of the ت to فَعَّلَ Form II verbs. Whereas Form II has a causative effect, the addition of *taa'* at the beginning contributes to make تَفَعَّلَ Form V reflexive, as in قَطَّعَ "to cut intensively," تَقَطَّعَ "to be cut." In addition, Form V also conveys a sense of intensity. For example, افْتَرَقَ means "to separate," and تَفَرَّقَ conveys the meaning of "disperse." Examine the following examples:

تَفَرَّقَ المُتظاهرونَ في شَوارِعِ المَدينةِ.	The demonstrators dispersed in the streets of the city.
تَكَلَّمَ المُحاضِرُ عَنْ سوريا.	The lecturer spoke about Syria.
تَأَلَّمَتِ الأُمُّ لِمَرَضِ اِبْنِها.	The mother felt pain due to her son's illness.

1.9.2.5 Form VI verbs صيغة تَفاعَلَ

This form is derived by the prefixation of *taa'* to the فاعَلَ form, thus resulting in تَفاعَلَ—a form that conveys the sense of reciprocity or mutuality. فاعَلَ verb forms and those of تَفَاعَلَ share features of the same meaning. The difference between these two categories, however, is in their syntax. Whereas فَاعَلَ forms often tend to have a direct object, تَفَاعَلَ verbs, on the other hand, often require the use of a preposition, most commonly مَعَ.

تَسَاعَدَ مَعَ الطُّلّابِ.   He and the students cooperated.

تَقَابَلَ مَعَ الزُّوّارِ.   He met with the visitors.

1.9.2.6 Form VII verbs صِيغَة اِنْفَعَلَ

This form is derived from فَعَلَ verb forms by the prefixation of اِنْـ to فَعَلَ verbs. In general, this verb form expresses a reflexive or passive meaning, i.e. something that happens to the entity, a person or a thing, from within itself, without external agents. For example, كَسَرَ "to break," requires an agent to effect the action. On the other hand, اِنْكَسَر expresses that the thing broke by itself; it was not broken by an outside agent. All اِنْفَعَلَ form verbs are intransitive; some in this category require the use of a preposition, usually مِنْ "from," إِلَى "to," or مَعَ "with," but other prepositions are also possible.

اِنْسَحَبَ مِنَ الاِجْتِماعِ.   He withdrew from the meeting.

اِنْكَسَر الزُّجاجُ.   The glass broke.

1.9.2.7 Form VIII verbs صِيغَة اِفْتَعَلَ

This verb form is derived by two processes: the use of *hamza* as a prefix (in the orthography it is written as an *'alif* with a *kasra* underneath it), and the insertion of a *taa'* after the first consonant of فَعَلَ verbs. The first consonant is not followed by a vowel. This explains why in the orthography the *sukuun* is written above the first organic consonant of the verb. From the verb سَمِعَ / يَسْمَعُ "to hear," we obtain اِسْتَمَعَ / يَسْتَمِعُ "to listen." Some of the verbs in this pattern are transitive, requiring direct objects; others are intransitive and require the use of prepositions.

The inserted *taa'* in this pattern undergoes changes in the environment of voiced and/or emphatic sounds. Thus, in the verb زَحَمَ / يَزْحَمُ "to crowd, to push," the *taa'* changes to its voiced counterpart, namely *daal*. Instead of the expected اِزْتَحَمَ the actual verb in use is اِزْدَحَمَ / يَزْدَحِمُ "to become crowded."

Similarly, in the verb زَهَرَ / يُزْهِرُ "to bloom, flourish" the *taa'* is assimilated by the voiced consonant ز and changes to *daal*, thus creating the verb اِزْدَهَرَ / يَزْدَهِرُ "to flourish, prosper."

If *dhaal* is the first letter/sound of the tri-consonantal verb, the inserted *taa'* is assimilated by this first letter. From ذَخَرَ "to keep, preserve" we obtain اِدَّخَرَ "to save, preserve, amass, hoard."

If the first letter/sound of the فَعَلَ Form I verb is either ص or ض the inserted ت changes into ط. Similarly, if the first letter/sound of the فَعَلَ Form I verb is ط the inserted ت changes to ط; if the first letter/sound is ظ the inserted ت changes to ظ, as the following examples illustrate:

From صَلَحَ, one of whose meanings is "to be useful," we obtain اِصْطَلَحَ "to accept, to adopt"; from صَادَ "to catch, to trap," we obtain اِصْطَادَ "to catch, to hunt." From ضَجَعَ "to sleep, recline," we obtain the verb اِضْطَجَعَ "to recline, to sleep, to lie down"; from ضَرَبَ "to hit," we obtain اِضْطَرَبَ "to be in a state of turmoil, to agitate." From طَلَعَ "to appear, to rise, to become visible," we obtain اِطَّلَعَ "to behold a view"; from ظَلَمَ "to do injustice to someone," we obtain اِظَّلَمَ "to suffer injustice, to be wronged."

Consider the following examples:

اِزْدَحَمَتِ الشَّوارِعُ بِالزُّوّارِ.	The streets were crowded with tourists.
اِزْدَهَرَ اِقْتِصادُ البِلادِ.	The country's economy flourished.
اِصْطادَ الصَّيّادُ سَمَكَةً كَبِيرَةً.	The fisher caught a big fish.
اِدَّخَرَ المُسْتَثْمِرُ أَمْوالاً كَثِيرَةً.	The investor amassed huge amounts of money.
اِضْطَرَبَتِ الأَسْواقُ المالِيَّةُ أَثْناءَ الحَرْبِ.	The stock markets were in a state of turmoil during the war.

In *waaw*-beginning verbs the *waaw* is assimilated by the inserted *taa'*. From Form I verb وَصَلَ "to arrive at," we obtain اِتَّصَلَ "to contact, communicate with," of Form VIII. Similarly, from أَخَذَ "to take," the Form VIII verb is اِتَّخَذَ "to take up, to take on, to adopt." Examine the following:

اِتَّصَلَ بِي صَدِيقِي أَحْمَد مِن دِمَشْق.	My friend Ahmad contacted me from Damascus.
اِتَّخَذَ سامِي رَأْيَ أَبِيهِ.	Sami adopted his father's opinion.

1.9.2.8 Form IX verbs صِيغَة اِفْعَلَّ

This verb form is obtained by the use of *hamza* as a prefix to the فَعَلَ form (in the orthography it is written as an *'alif* with a *kasra* underneath it) and the doubling of the final consonant, represented in the writing system by a *shadda*. Note that the first consonant is not followed by a vowel. اِفْعَلَّ verbs tend to designate physical defects or change of color. For example, the triconsonantal verb عَرَجَ / يَعْرُجُ pertains to limping or lameness. Thus, the verb اِعْرَجَّ / يَعْرُجُّ is used to express the condition of someone who has become lame.

اِفْعَلَّ however is used more frequently to express a change of color. These verbs are always intransitive. From the adjective أَحْمَر "red," we obtain اِحْمَرَّ / يَحْمَرُّ "to become red, to change color into red," as in the following example:

اِحْمَرَّتِ السَّمَاءُ.   The sky turned red.

1.9.2.9 Form X verbs صِيغَة اِسْتَفْعَلَ

This form is derived by the prefixation of اِسْتَ to فَعَلَ verbs. Note the change in the vowel pattern, namely the dropping of the *fat-Ha* after the first consonant of فَعَلَ verbs. Thus, from عَلِمَ / يَعْلَمُ "to know," we derive اِسْتَعْلَمَ / يَسْتَعْلِمُ "to inquire." In this example, a connection in meaning between عَلِمَ and اِسْتَعْلَمَ can be discerned. In other words, اِسْتَعْلَمَ "to inquire," has something to do with wanting to know. The relationship in meaning between the فَعَلَ verb form and its derived counterpart اِسْتَفْعَلَ may not always obtain. Some verbs in this category are transitive, requiring a direct object; others are intransitive and require the use of prepositions.

اِسْتَقْبَلَتِ العَائِلَةُ الزَّائِرَ.   The family received the visitor.

اِسْتَفْسَرَ الطَّبِيبُ عَنِ المَرِيضِ.   The doctor inquired about the patient.

1.9.3 Quadriliteral verbs

A group of verbs in Arabic consist of four consonants, hence the name الأَفْعَال الرُّبَاعِيَّة /يُتَرْجِمُ "quadriliteral verbs." Examples of such include تَرْجَمَ /يُتَرْجِمُ "to translate," هَنْدَسَ / يُهَنْدِسُ "to engineer," سَيْطَرَ / يُسَيْطِرُ "to control," and طَمْأَنَ / يُطَمْئِنُ "to assure, to calm someone down."

A common form of quadriliteral verbs is what is referred to as duplicatives. These are verbs in which the same syllable is duplicated, often expressing movement or sound. Such verbs include يُزَلْزِلُ / زَلْزَلَ / وَسْوَسَ / يُوَسْوِسُ "to whisper," "to shake," يُبَلْبِلُ / بَلْبَلَ "to confound, confuse," عَشْعَشَ / يُعَشْعِشُ "to nest," يُقَلْقِلُ / قَلْقَلَ "to disturb." (See Chapter 25 for more details.)

1.10 VERB MOODS

Verbs reflect whether the sentence conveys a simple statement of fact; expresses a belief, ability, or desire; gives a direct command; or states a conditional situation. These different nuances are called moods. The moods of Arabic verbs pertain only to the present tense. The past tense does not have moods.

1.10.1 Indicative mood حالةُ الرَّفْع

Verbs in the indicative mood comprise the majority of verb usage in the language. The indicative mood expresses statements of facts or opinions, as in the following examples:

يُغَيِّرُ عُنْوانَهُ كُلَّ سَنَةٍ. He changes his address annually.

تَدْرُسُ الإسبانِيَّةَ. She is studying Spanish.

1.10.2 Subjunctive mood

This mood occurs in dependent clauses following verbs in the main clause using, among many others, verbs like رَغِبَ "wish," تَمَنَّى "want," أرادَ "hope," أمَلَ "desire," خاف "fear," أَحَبَّ "want, like, love," وَدَّ "desire," نَصَحَ "advise," اقْتَرَحَ "suggest." Such verbs must be followed by a finite set of particles, called أدَوات النَّصْب "subjunctive particles," that are in turn followed by verbs having endings different from those in the indicative mood. Discussion of this and the particles that cause this change in verb endings is in Chapter 13.

The subjunctive in Arabic is not dissimilar to changes in present tense verbs for the English third person singular pronouns, "he" and "she". In the environment of verbs like "suggest," "advise," "recommend," etc., the verbs following in the dependent clause have different endings from the indicative, as in the following examples:

I suggest that he change his address annually.

Her advisor recommends that she study Spanish.

1.10.3 Jussive mood

Verbs in this mood can occur in main and subordinate clauses and assume different endings from those in the indicative, with some similarity to those in the subjunctive. This includes the use of the imperative mood, conditionals (both in the main and conditional clauses), and the use of the negative particle لَمْ to negate past tense actions. (Jussive with conditionals is in Chapter 20, and with لِ is in Chapter 15.)

1.10.4 Imperative mood

The imperative mood expresses a direct command in either the affirmative or negative. It is generally addressed to the second person, i.e. the various forms of "you." (See Chapter 17 for a detailed discussion.)

CHAPTER 2

Nouns الأَسْماء

The definition of nouns by linguists faces controversy as one definition by certain criteria may not fit all languages in the world. We will nonetheless attempt to provide a working definition of nouns. A noun denotes a person, place, thing or abstract idea. As members of a lexical category nouns can perform certain functions in the language. For example, the Arabic word شَجَرَةٌ "tree," while referring to an entity known to all readers, can only function as a subject of a sentence, or a direct object of a transitive verb, or it can be preceded by a preposition like عَلَى "on," or تَحْتَ "under," and so on. This Arabic word can also vary its number as it can be put in dual or plural; in addition the definite article اَلـ "the" can attach to it. On the other hand, the English equivalent *tree* can do some but not all of the preceding functions of the Arabic noun; for example it cannot have a dual form morphologically by adding a suffix as in the Arabic case; yet the English *tree* can, albeit not commonly, be used as a verb, which the Arabic equivalent cannot.

2.1 TYPES OF NOUNS

Nouns in Arabic are generally derived from verbs. كِتَابٌ "book," for example, is derived from the verbs كَتَبَ "to write," and مِفْتَاحٌ "key," from فَتَحَ "to open," according to a certain pattern (see Chapter 28). A noun of this type is often referred to as اسْم مُشْتَق "derivative," extracted from a verb form. Other nouns such as عَيْنٌ "eye," فَرَسٌ "horse," or بَطَّةٌ "duck," are not derived from verbs; they are often labeled as اسْم جامِد "primitive," or "stationary." Other types of nouns that Arab grammarians recognize in their rich grammar tradition are nouns that express concrete objects such as حَجَرٌ "stone," or abstract ideas such as عِلْمٌ "knowledge," or جَهْلٌ "ignorance." These are grouped under اِسْم جِنْس "a generic or common noun." Contrasted with this, there exists a category of nouns known by the name اِسْم عَلَم "proper nouns," to refer to named entities, such as عُمَر "Omar," سوزان "Susanne," القاهِرَة "Cairo," and so on.

Nouns derived from verbal forms are of many types, including, among others, المَصادِر (plural of مَصْدَر) "verbal nouns or gerunds" (see Chapter 25); أَسْماء الفاعِل "agentive nouns," or "active participles" (see Chapter 23); أَسْماء المَفْعول "passive participles" (see Chapter 24). Plurals of noun أَسْماء المَكان "place nouns," أَسْماء المِهْنَة "nouns of profession," أَسْماء الوَحْدة "unit nouns," أَسْماء الآلة "instrument nouns," etc. are all discussed in Chapter 28.

It is necessary to mention here that Arabic categorizes plural nouns in two groups: human, such as مُوَظَّفونَ "employees," طُلّابٌ "students," مُديراتٌ "directors (F)," and non-human, as in كِلابٌ "dogs," مَدارِسُ "schools," طائراتٌ "airplanes." Non-human plural nouns are treated as feminine singular in all their behavior in the language. We turn now to discuss various features of nouns.

2.2 GENDER

Nouns in Arabic are grouped in three classes with respect to gender. A noun can be masculine مُذَكَّر, feminine مُؤَنَّث, or, as in the case of a few nouns, either masculine or feminine. There is no neuter in Arabic.

Feminine nouns can be most readily recognized by their form, ending with ة *taa' marbuuTa* as in قَرْيَةٌ "village," عاصِمَةٌ "capital." They can also be identified by three other endings: the long *'alif* ا as in دُنيا "life, world," or the *'alif maqSuura* ى as in حُمّى "fever," بُشْرى "good news," or, in some cases, *'alif hamza* ءا as in صَحْراء "desert," حِرْباء "chameleon." Moreover, feminine nouns can be recognized by what they signify, for instance a female entity such as أُمٌّ "mother," or عَروسٌ "bride." Feminine nouns can indicate a natural or real feminine entity such as اِمْرَأَةٌ "woman," or an assigned gender such as الشَّمْس "the sun," or الأَرْض "the earth, land."

We must also emphasize that all cities in Arabic are treated as feminine nouns. Countries, on the other hand, can be either feminine or masculine. Countries that are written with regular *'alif* or *taa' marbuuTa* are always feminine, as in أَمْريكا (written as أَمْريكة by some) or سوريا / سورية, etc. Some other countries are treated as masculine, for example السّودان or العِراق.

As a general rule, nouns can be changed into their feminine forms through the addition of *taa' marbuuTa* ة preceded by a *fat-Ha* at the end of the masculine noun. For example, طالِبٌ "student (M)," becomes طالِبَةٌ "student (F)." (Note that the *taa' marbuuTa* ة is represented in the orthography as a *taa' maftuuHa* ت when a suffix, such as a possessive suffix pronoun, is added to feminine nouns.) However, the feminine forms of the masculine أَوَّل "first," آخَر "other," and أَحَد "one of" end with 'alif maqSuura, as in أُولى "first (F)," أُخْرى "other (F)," and إِحْدى "one of," respectively, not to mention other phonological changes in these words that are beyond this discussion.

It is worthy of mention that there are a few masculine nouns that end with *taa' marbuuTa*. These include, among others, خَلِيفَة "caliph," also a man's name," أُسامَة "Osama," رَحّالَة "avid traveler," عَلّامَة "erudite scholar," etc.

Finally, there are a few instances where a noun can be used in either the masculine or the feminine. Such examples include سوقٌ "suq, market," دُكّانٌ "shop," سِكّينٌ "knife," طَريقٌ "way, path."

2.3 NUMBER

Nouns in Arabic can be in the singular, dual or plural. Plural nouns are treated in some detail in Chapter 28.

Dual formation, masculine or feminine, is accomplished by the suffixation of ان to the termination of singular nouns. The ة *taa' marbuuTa* of feminine nouns changes in this case to a regular *taa'* ت, *taa' maftuuHa* or *taa' Tawiila* (as it is called by some), as in the following examples:

Singular nominative	Dual nominative	
طالِبٌ	طالِبانِ	Two students (M)
مُعَلِّمٌ	مُعَلِّمانِ	Two teachers (M)

Singular nominative	Dual nominative	
طالِبَةٌ	طالِبَتانِ	Two students (F)
مُعَلِّمَةٌ	مُعَلِّمَتانِ	Two teachers (F)

The examples in the dual, masculine and feminine, in the preceding tables, are in the nominative case, known by the Arabic name مَرْفوع. Nouns, regardless of number, take different endings, depending on their function in the sentence. (See Chapter 3 for discussion of the Arabic case system.) By coincidence, dual nouns have the same ending in the accusative and genitive cases, namely يْنِ. In other words, ان changes to يْنِ as shown in the following tables:

Dual nominative	Dual accusative/genitive	
طالِبان	طالِبَيْنِ	Two students (M)
مُعَلِّمان	مُعَلِّمَيْنِ	Two teachers (M)

Dual nominative	Dual accusative/genitive	
طالِبَتان	طالِبَتَيْنِ	Two students (F)
مُعَلِّمَتان	مُعَلِّمَتَيْنِ	Two teachers (F)

Singular nouns that end with 'alif maqSuura require the insertion of yaa' ي before the dual marker ان is suffixed. Thus, مَلْهى "entertainment place," and فَتْوى "religious legal opinion," become مَلْهَيان and فَتْوَيان respectively. Similarly, singular nouns whose ending is yaa' elided with tanwiin kasra as in ماشٍ "a walker," and بانٍ "a builder," for example, require the insertion of yaa' before the dual suffix is added. Thus, we obtain ماشِيان and بانِيان respectively.

The dual of singular nouns which end with 'alif hamza اء as in صَحْراء "desert," and سَماء "sky," requires the insertion of waaw و before the dual suffix is attached. Thus, we obtain صَحْراوان "two deserts," and سَماوان "two skies." Similarly, أَبٌّ "father," and أَخٌّ "brother," and the others in this group (see الأَسْماءُ الخمسة at the end of this chapter) require the insertion of waaw before the dual suffix is attached, as in the following: أَبَوانِ "two fathers," and أَخَوانِ "two brothers."

2.4 DETERMINATION OF NOUNS

Arab grammarians follow the tradition of citing nouns in dictionaries or in glossary lists in their indefinite, nominative, masculine forms. For example, مُعَلِّمٌ "teacher (M)," ends with two Dhammas in its orthographic representation in a glossary list. The first Dhamma indicates that this noun is in the nominative case; the second indicates the noun is indefinite. The second Dhamma has the value of an -n sound, a process referred to as tanwiin in Arabic. The case system in Arabic is discussed in some detail in Chapter 3.

There are four different ways of changing nouns (and adjectives for that matter) from indefinite to definite, i.e. unknown or unspecified entity to known, specified. This process is known by the name of determination, or تَعْريف الاِسْم in Arabic.

1. Nouns are made definite by the pre-fixation of the definite article الـ "the" to common nouns. By placing الـ in front of the common noun, the indefinite marker, i.e. the second -*n* sounding *Dhamma* mentioned above is dropped and the noun remains with only one *Dhamma* at its end. Thus, مُعَلِّمٌ "teacher" becomes المُعَلِّمُ "the teacher."

    The use of the definite article الـ is common in Arabic to indicate general categories or to make categorical statements. Thus, one speaks of السَّيَّارَة "car" in Arabic without a reference to a specific car but to the means of transportation in general. In addition, الـ is commonly used with plural nouns to indicate categories. For example, الطلّاب "students" expresses a categorical statement without specifying particular individuals.

2. Nouns become definite by suffixing a possessive pronoun (see Chapter 5). If we take مُعَلِّمٌ "teacher," and add the possessive suffix نا "our," we obtain مُعَلِّمُنا "our teacher." Notice that the second *Dhamma* in مُعَلِّمٌ, the marker of indefiniteness, is dropped, whereas the nominative case marker is maintained.

3. Nouns become definite in *IDhaafa*-constructs whose terminal noun is definite. In the example كِتابُ المُعَلِّم "*lit.* the book of the teacher; the teacher's book," the first noun كِتاب does not carry الـ "the," yet it is interpreted as specified, known to readers or speakers by virtue of the definite noun المُعَلِّم. Thus, while the initial noun is not carrying the definite article الـ it can be interpreted as definite by virtue of the terminal definite noun in such structures. However, if the second noun in *IDhaafa*-constructs is indefinite, then both elements in the construct are not specified, they are indefinite. Thus, كِتابُ مُعَلِّم would refer to an unspecified book belonging to some unspecified teacher, "book of a teacher, a teacher's book." (See Chapter 8 for a detailed discussion.)

4. Abstract nouns such as الحُرِّيَّةُ "freedom," الصَّداقَةُ "friendship," التَّعليمُ "learning, education," الحُبُّ "love," etc. are always definite and are used with the definite article الـ or as a part of *IDhaafa*.

5. Finally, a noun is definite, i.e. اِسْم مُعَرَّف by virtue of its being a proper noun. Thus, names of people or other entities such as عَلِي "Ali" or مَرْيَم "Maryam" or دِمَشْق "Damascus" or نيويورك "New York" are known entities and recognized to be definite by virtue of their being known to those involved in interlocution.

2.5 FUNCTION OF NOUNS

Nouns can play the following functions which are subject to certain requirements, conditions and/or constraints, as will be seen below:

1. Subjects of nominal or equational sentences: As subjects of this sentential structure, nouns must be definite (see the preceding section). In addition, common nouns must be in the nominative case (see Chapter 3). Nouns in the subject position can be singular, dual or plural, as in the following examples:

    المُعَلِّمُ جَديدٌ.   The teacher (M, Sg) is new.

    الصَّديقانِ مِن سوريا.   The two friends (M, D) are from Syria.

    البَناتُ في المَلْعَبِ.   The girls (F, Pl) are on the playground.

2. Predicates of nominal or equational sentences: Nouns as predicates are placed after subjects have been introduced. Predicates of equational/nominal sentences can be common or proper nouns. Common nouns in the predicate position must be indefinite and also nominative, as illustrated below:

    هِيَ مُديرَةٌ.   She is a director.

    هُم طُلّابٌ.   They are students.

Predicate nouns can also be definite. In this case, the subject and predicate must be separated by a third person pronoun, depending on the number and gender of the subject. In other words, it can be the third person singular pronouns هُوَ or هِيَ, the dual pronoun هُما, or the plural pronouns هُنَّ or هُم as in the following examples:

محْمود هُوَ المُديرُ.
Mahmoud is the director.

ساميَة وليَلى هُما المُوَظَّفتانِ.
Samia and Leila are the employees (F, D).

جورج وموسى ومُحَمَّد هُم المُدَرِّسونَ.
George, Musa and Mohammed are the teachers (M, Pl).

3. Predicate nouns of equational sentences preceded by one of the members of كانَ and its "sisters" (its verb group) must change into the accusative (see Chapter 10 on *kaana*). The subject of such sentences must remain nominative, as in the following:

كانَ الرَّجُلُ مُوَظَّفاً.   The man was an employee.

لَيْسَت المَرْأَةُ مُديرَةً.   The woman is not a director.

4. Nouns in subject positions preceded by one of the members of إنَّ and its "sisters" must be in the accusative case. The noun or adjective predicate of such sentences must maintain its nominative case, as in the following:

إنَّ الطَّقْسَ جَميلٌ.   Indeed the weather is beautiful.

5. Verbal sentences are those in which verbs are in initial positions in sentence structures. Nouns following verbs in these sentences can be performers of actions expressed by the verbs and are known as the فاعل in Arabic grammar terminology. In such cases, the فاعل must be in the nominative case. The فاعل can be definite or indefinite. However, the فاعل gender determines the gender of the verb. In other words, if the فاعل is a masculine noun, the verb must also exhibit this gender; similarly, if it is feminine, the verb must also be marked for feminine. Examine the following:

نامَ الطِّفْلُ.   The baby (M) went to sleep.

ضَحِكَت الأُستاذَةُ.   The teacher (F) laughed.

وَصَلَت سَيّارَةٌ.   A car arrived.

The فاعل following the verb could be in the singular, dual or plural. However, the verb in verbal sentences when it occupies its usual initial position must always be singular. The verb needs only to be marked for gender, i.e. masculine or feminine determined by the gender of the فاعل, as in the following:

عادَ الصَّديقانِ.   The friends (M, D) returned.

زارَتِ البَناتُ مصر.   The girls (F, Pl) visited Egypt.

6. Nouns can be direct objects of transitive verbs (see Chapter 11). Direct objects of transitive verbs must be in the accusative case. In singular nouns, direct objects end with one *fat-Ha* if they are definite. Indefinite, direct objects end with two *fat-Has*. Dual nouns in the direct object position must end with يْنَ ـ. Regular plural masculine nouns end with ينَ; regular feminine plural nouns in object position end with one *kasra* if they are definite or two if they are indefinite. Examine the following examples:

أَكَلَت هِند الخُبْزَ.	Hend ate the bread.
شاهَدَ صديقي فِلمَيْن.	My friend saw two films.
قابَلْنا المُهَنْدسينَ.	We met the engineers.
دَرَّسَ سامي الطالباتِ.	Sami taught the girls.
سامي دَرَّسَ طالباتٍ.	Sami taught girls.

Some transitive verbs like أَعْطى "to give," انْتَخَبَ "to elect," عَيَّنَ "to appoint," take two direct objects. Note that in English this operation would be accomplished either with an indirect object, or the object of a preposition such as "to" or "as." Examine the following:

أَعْطى الأَبُ البِنْتَ كِتاباً.	The father gave the girl a book.
عَيَّنَتِ الشَّرِكَةُ المُوَظَّفَ مُديراً.	The company appointed the employee as director.

7. Nouns can be preceded by prepositions. In this case, nouns must be in the genitive case (see Chapter 3), ending with one *kasra* if they are singular and definite, or two *kasras* if they are singular and indefinite. In pronunciation, the *kasra* is pronounced *-i*; the two *kasras* are pronounced *-in*; this phenomenon is called *tanwiin* in Arabic. In Modern Standard Arabic, proper nouns are usually not marked for case unless the text is of a very formal quality, as in formal reading of the news, or in scripted speeches delivered on highly formal occasions. Examine the following:

في البيْتِ	in the house
في بيْتٍ	in a house

Dual nouns preceded by prepositions end with ‍ـَيْنِ as in:

مَعَ صَديقَيْنِ   with two friends (M, D)

مَعَ صَديقَتَيْنِ   with two friends (F, D)

Regular masculine plural nouns end with ‍ـِينَ when preceded by prepositions:

مَعَ مُديرينَ   with directors (M, Pl)

Regular feminine plural nouns end with one *kasra* if they are definite, or two *kasra*s if they are indefinite:

مَعَ الطالِباتِ   with the students (F, Pl)

مَعَ طالِباتٍ   with students (F, Pl)

8. Finally, nouns can be constituents of *IDhaafa*-constructs (see Chapter 8). If a noun is the first element of such a construct, its case varies depending on its function in the sentence. The first noun in such a construct can never have a definite article. Nor can it have *tanwiin*, the -*n* sounding orthographic symbol. A noun in the second position in *IDhaafa*-constructs must always be in the genitive. It can be either definite or indefinite. If definite, it ends only with one *kasra*; if indefinite, it ends with two *kasra*s, as illustrated below:

صَديقَةُ الأُستاذِ   the teacher's friend (F) (*lit.* "the friend
of the teacher")

صَديقَةُ أُسْتاذٍ   a friend (F) of a teacher

مَعَ صَديقَةِ الأُستاذِ   with the teacher's friend (F)

IDhaafa-constructs may contain more than two nouns. All nouns in such a construct, except the first one, must be in the genitive case, ending in only one *kasra*. The terminal noun can only be either definite, carrying the article الـ for example, or indefinite, thus ending with two *kasra*s, as in the examples below:

كِتابُ طالِبِ الجامِعَةِ   the book of the university student

كِتابُ طالِبِ جامِعَةٍ   a book of a student of (some) university

2.6 THE FIVE NOUNS

The following nouns, known by the Arabic name الأَسْماءُ الخَمْسَة "the five nouns,"
form a special category; some grammarians speak of a sixth noun. They are
marked by *waaw* in the nominative case, *'alif* in the accusative, and *yaa'* in the
genitive. (See Chapter 3 for the case system in Arabic.) Further discussion of
these nouns will be in Chapter 28, section 28.6.

Nominative	*Accusative*	*Genitive*	
أَبو	أَبا	أَبي	father
أَخو	أَخا	أَخي	brother
حَمو	حَما	حَمي	father-in-law
فو	فا	في	mouth
ذو	ذا	ذي	owner of

The case system in Arabic

إِعْرابُ الأَسْماء

A brief word about case systems in languages is necessary. How nouns, pronouns, or adjectives are understood in their different functions in sentences is a matter of precision and clarity. In Arabic, as well as in German, Latin, Greek and Russian, among others, nouns and pronouns assume different forms or endings when performing specific functions in a sentence. A noun functioning as the subject of an equational/nominal sentence, or as the performer of an action in a verbal sentence, for example, may exhibit a different ending from that used when that noun is the object of a transitive verb. Different languages employ different cases; the number of cases varies from one language to another. The three cases that Arabic uses—nominative, accusative and genitive—are among the most common.

3.1 THE CASE SYSTEM IN ENGLISH

Only pronouns observe a case system in English. The pronoun "he," for example, can only be used as the subject of a sentence. Such a pronoun is said to be in the nominative case, because of its function. This same pronoun changes to "him" when the pronoun is used after a verb that requires a direct object, such as in the sentence "I saw him." In this case, he is the recipient of the verb "saw," and is said to be in the accusative case. Finally, to express possession, "he" changes into a third form, namely "his," as in "This is his book." "His" is in the genitive case, used, in this instance, to express possession. English nouns and adjectives have lost case markers that at one time existed in the language. One residue of cases in English nouns appears in the possessive system in the language, expressed in the writing system by the 's (apostrophe s) as in "the King's English." As the cases dropped, word order in the sentence structure became a determining factor in conveying the intended meaning. Thus, the words "boy" and "teacher" in the following two sentences convey different functions expressed only by the order of words. The "teacher" in the first sentence is the performer of action, and the "boy" the recipient; the roles are reversed in the second sentence:

1. The teacher saw the boy.
2. The boy saw the teacher.

3.2 THE CASE SYSTEM IN ARABIC

Pronouns and their cases in Arabic are introduced in Chapter 5. In this section the case system for nouns and adjectives is examined. While word order is important in Modern Standard Arabic, the language employs three cases to express relationships among words in sentences. These three cases are marked by different vowel sounds at the end of nouns and adjectives to express the various functions of these elements. The cases in Arabic are also marked in the orthography by various devices outlined below. It should be emphasized that adjectives used to modify nouns exhibit the same cases as those nouns, both in their phonological representation as well as in the orthography. The three cases in Arabic apply to singular, dual and plural nouns and adjectives. Pronouns as direct objects are explained when we examine verbal sentences in Chapter 11.

It is necessary to mention that the case system is a feature of classical as well as Modern Standard Arabic. The use of cases, however, is observed primarily in formal situations like public speeches, news broadcasts, university and public lectures, and scripted texts. We shall now turn to discuss briefly the three cases governing Arabic nouns. Adjectives and their cases are discussed in Chapter 4.

3.3 THE NOMINATIVE CASE

In general, the nominative case is used in the following instances:

1. when a noun is in the subject position of an equational/nominal sentence,
2. when a noun or adjective is the predicate of an equational/nominal sentence (see Chapter 3), and
3. when it is performer of an action, i.e., فاعِل in a verbal sentence (see Chapter 11).

Cases apply to singular, dual and plural nouns. In addition, adjectives modifying nominative nouns must also be marked for this same case. Nouns in the singular, dual and/or plural are marked by different endings for this case, as illustrated below.

3.3.1 Nominative singular nouns

In singular indefinite common nouns, the nominative case is marked by the sound -un at their end. The noun in this case is referred to as اِسْم مَرْفوع in the Arabic. In the orthography, this is generally marked by the writing of two terminal *Dhamma*s. On the other hand, a singular definite noun in the nominative case has at its end one *Dhamma*, pronounced -u. Let us illustrate this by using a common noun such as بَيْت "house." If بَيْت is the subject of an equational/ nominal sentence, it must be definite, pronounced with terminal -u, represented by one terminal *Dhamma* in the orthography, as in البَيْتُ كَبيرٌ "The house is big." Adjectives functioning as predicates in equational/nominal sentences in the affirmative must also be in the nominative but indefinite. This explains why كَبيرٌ in the preceding sentence ends with two *Dhamma*s in the writing system, pronounced -un.

Similarly, if بَيْت is the predicate of an equational/nominal sentence, it must be indefinite, pronounced with -un, represented by two *Dhamma*s at its end, as in هذا بَيْتٌ "This is a house." The adjective modifying بَيْتٌ must also be indefinite, nominative, written with two *Dhamma*s above its terminal consonant, as in: هذا بَيْتٌ كَبيرٌ "This is a big house."

3.3.2 Nominative dual nouns

Dual nouns, masculine or feminine, are marked for the nominative case by -ان suffixed to singular nouns. ان is part and parcel of this nominative marker that always remains the same, always indivisible. In other words, the *kasra* in ان is not a marker of the genitive case in singular nouns. Nouns such as صَديقان "two friends (M)," or صَديقَتان "two friends (F)," are to be used only as subjects or predicates of affirmative equational/nominal sentences, or as فاعِل performers of actions in verbal sentences (see Chapter 11).

3.3.3 Nominative plural nouns

Regular masculine plural nouns in the nominative case are marked by suffixing the indivisible suffix ‑وَن to singular nouns. Thus, مُعَلِّمونَ "teachers," can only function as the subject of equational/nominal sentences, or as the predicate of affirmative equational/nominal sentences, or فاعِل, i.e. performer of verbs in verbal sentences. In the latter case, this plural noun can be either definite or indefinite, depending on the intended meaning, as in the following:

وَصَلَ مُعَلِّمونَ.   [Some] teachers arrived.

وَصَلَ المُعَلِّمونَ.   The teachers arrived.

Irregular plural masculine nouns, on the other hand, demonstrate behavior similar to that of singular nouns in taking either the definite marker (one *Dhamma*) or the indefinite *nunation* (two *Dhamma*s). An example is the plural طُلّابٌ "students." As the subject of an equational sentence, this noun must be definite, written with only one *Dhamma*, as in الطُّلّابُ مُجْتَهِدونَ "The students are hard-working." On the other hand, when طُلّابٌ is used as the predicate of an affirmative equational sentence, it must be indefinite, written with two *Dhamma*s, as in هُم طُلّابٌ "They are students." As فاعِل or performer of verbs in verbal sentences it could be either definite or indefinite, depending on the intended meaning.

Regular feminine plural nouns in the nominative case are marked by the suffix ‑اتٌ added to singular nouns. Thus, مُديراتٌ "directors" can function as the subject of equational sentences, the predicate of affirmative equational sentences, or فاعِل, i.e. the performer of verbal sentences. In the latter case, it could be either definite with one *Dhamma*, or indefinite, written with two *Dhamma*s, as in the following:

خَضَرتِ المُديراتُ.   The directors came.

حَضَرَت مُديراتٌ.   [Some] directors came.

3.4 THE ACCUSATIVE CASE

The second case of nouns or adjectives is referred to as النَّصْب in Arabic, accusative. A noun in this case is labeled اسْم مَنصوب. Following is a partial list of situations where nouns or adjectives can be in the accusative case:

1. Direct objects of transitive verbs (see Chapter 11);
2. Predicates of equational/nominal sentences preceded by one of the members of كانَ and its sisters (see Chapter 10);
3. When preceded by إنَّ and any of its sisters (see Chapter 21);
4. Cognate objects (see Chapter 25);
5. Objects of purpose (see Chapter 25);
6. *Haal* clauses (see Chapter 32);
7. *Tamyiiz* (accusative of specification) (see Chapter 33);
8. Adjectives modifying accusative nouns (see Chapter 4);
9. Some adverbs (see Chapter 7).

3.4.1 Accusative singular nouns

Singular definite nouns functioning as direct objects of transitive verbs such as the verb بَنى "to build," for example, must end with one *fat-Ha* at the end of the noun, as in:

جورج بَنى البَيْتَ.   George built the house.

If بَيْت in the preceding example is indefinite, it must end with two *fat-Has* placed on an *'alif,* which, in this case, has no phonetic value, i.e., it is not pronounced but used as a carrier of the two *fat-Has,* as in the following:

جورج بَنى بَيْتاً.   George built a house.

In feminine nouns, the two *fat-Has* are written above ة, the *taa'marbuuTa,* as in:

جورج شاهَدَ سَيّارةً.   George saw a car.

3.4.2 Accusative dual nouns

Accusative dual nouns, masculine or feminine, are marked by ـيْن suffixed to singular nouns. ـيْن always remains the same, is always indivisible. Nouns such as صَديقَيْن "two friends (M)," or صَديقَتَيْن "two friends (F)," are to be used only as objects of transitive verbs, or predicates of equational/nominal sentences preceded by a member of كانَ and its "sisters," or in some other environments (see Chapter 3).

3.4.3 Accusative plural nouns

Regular masculine plural nouns in the accusative case are marked by adding the indivisible suffix ـينَ. Thus, مُعَلِّمينَ "teachers" can only function as object of transitive verbs, or predicate of equational/nominal sentences when preceded by كانَ or any of its "sisters," or in some other environments.

Irregular plural masculine nouns, on the other hand, generally demonstrate behavior similar to that of singular nouns in the accusative case. Take, for example, the plural طُلّاب "students." As the object of a transitive verb, this noun can be definite, written with only one *fat-Ha* الطلّابَ "the students," as in:

سامي دَرَّسَ الطلّابَ.   Sami taught the students.

Or it can be indefinite, written with two *fat-Ha*s طُلّاباً "students." The two *fat-Ha*s are written on a regular *'alif* that has no phonetic value, as in:

سامي دَرَّسَ طُلّاباً.   Sami taught students.

Regular indefinite feminine plural nouns in the accusative case are marked by the suffix ـاتِ. Thus, مُديراتٍ "directors" can function as the object of transitive verbs, or the predicate of affirmative equational sentences preceded by كانَ or any of its "sisters." In the latter case, it could be either definite with one *kasra*, or indefinite, written with two *kasra*s. Adjectives modifying accusative nouns must assume the same cases as the nouns they modify.

3.5 THE GENITIVE CASE

The genitive case جَرّ is used for nouns following prepositions and for the second and subsequent terms of the *IDhaafa*-construct. The *IDhaafa*-construct is discussed in some detail in Chapter 8.

3.5.1 Genitive singular nouns

Singular indefinite nouns are marked by two *kasras* at their end, pronounced
-in. Definite singular nouns in the genitive case end with one *kasra*.

3.5.2 Genitive dual nouns

Dual nouns, masculine or feminine, are marked for the genitive case by ـَيْن,
which is one indivisible unit. This form is identical to the accusative dual form.
Nouns such as صَدِيقَيْن "two friends (M)," or صَدِيقَتَيْن "two friends (F)," are to
be used after prepositions, or as the second noun of an *IDhaafa*-construct, as in:

بَيْتُ صَدِيقَيْن / صَدِيقَتَيْن   a house of two friends (M/F)

3.5.3 Genitive plural nouns

Regular masculine plural nouns in the genitive case are marked by adding
the indivisible suffix ـِينَ. Thus, مُعَلِّمِينَ "teachers" assumes this form after
prepositions, or if it is used as a second noun in an *IDhaafa*-construct, as
in مَكْتَبُ مُعَلِّمِينَ "teachers' office."

Irregular plural masculine nouns demonstrate behavior similar to that of
singular nouns in taking definite or indefinite markers. Let us take as an example
the plural طُلَّابٌ "students." When preceded by a preposition, this noun can
be definite, written with only one *kasra* مَعَ الطُّلَّابِ "the students," as in
"with the students." Or it can be indefinite as in طُلَّابٍ "students," written with
two terminal *kasras*, as in:

مَعَ طُلَّابٍ   with students

Regular indefinite feminine plural nouns in the genitive case are marked by the
suffix ـَات, identical to feminine plural nouns in the accusative case. Thus,
مُدِيرَاتٍ "directors" assumes this form when preceded by a preposition, or when
used as a second noun in an *IDhaafa*-construct. In the latter case, it could be
either definite, written with one *kasra*, as in مَكَاتِبُ الْمُدِيرَاتِ "the offices of the
directors," or it could be indefinite, written with two *kasras*, as in مَكَاتِبُ مُدِيرَاتٍ
"offices of directors."

CHAPTER 4

Adjectives النُّعوت or الصِّفات

Adjectives are elements in the language that modify nouns, adding more information about them. Adjectives can also function as nouns in that they can be subjects of sentences, objects of verbs, governed by prepositions, etc. Regular adjectives such as كَبيرٌ "big, large" or جَديدٌ "new" are commonly used as predicates of equational sentences (see Chapter 9). For the comparative and superlative forms of adjectives, see Chapter 27.

4.1 COMMON FORMS OF ADJECTIVES

4.1.1 Regular adjectives

Like many nouns in Arabic, adjectives can be derived from verbs according to particular patterns. A common adjectival form is of the فَعيلٌ pattern, producing, for example, كَبيرٌ "big, large," from كَبُرَ "to become big," or جَديدٌ "new," from جَدُدَ "to become new."

4.1.2 Color words and traits as adjectives

4.1.2.1 Color words

Words for basic colors: red, blue, yellow, etc. can function both as nouns and adjectives. Many of the color words in Arabic follow the pattern of أَفْعَلُ when used to modify masculine nouns (see Chapter 27). The feminine form of color words is formed from أَفْعَلُ words according to the pattern فَعْلاءُ as illustrated in the following table:

أَفْعَلُ	فَعْلاءُ	*Meaning*
أَحْمَرُ	حَمْراءُ	red
أَسْوَدُ	سَوْداءُ	dark [skinned]
أَسْوَدُ	سَوْداءُ	black
أَصْفَرُ	صَفْراءُ	yellow
أَبْيَضُ	بَيْضاءُ	white
أَزْرَقُ	زَرْقاءُ	blue
أَخْضَرُ	خَضْراءُ	green
أَشْقَرُ	شَقْراءُ	blond

The intensity or degree of color is gauged by either غامِق "deep, dark" or فاتِح "light," as in, for example, أَخْضَر غامِق "deep green," or أَخْضَر فاتِح "light green." Some color words collocate with certain adjectives: أَبْيَضُ ناصِعٌ "snow white," أَحْمَرُ قانٍ "blood red," and أَصْفَر فاقِع "intense/bright yellow." أَسْوَدُ قاتِمٌ "pitch black,"

The masculine dual of color adjectives is formed by the dual marker ان, as in بَيْتانِ أَبْيَضانِ "two white houses," and رَجُلانِ أَشْقَرانِ "two blond men." The feminine dual however is formed by dropping the *hamza*, inserting a *waaw* and adding the suffix ان, as in بِنْتانِ شَقْراوانِ "two blond girls," and سَيَّارَتانِ حَمْراوانِ "two red cars."

The plurals of the colors in the above table for human masculine nouns follow the فُعْلٌ pattern, as in the following: حُمْرٌ، سودٌ، صُفْرٌ، بيضٌ، زُرْقٌ، خُضْرٌ، شُقْرٌ. The case of these plural colors changes according to the case of the nouns they modify. Of these plural adjectives only two are actually used for humans, namely سودٌ "black," and بيضٌ "white," as in the following: رجالٌ سودٌ "black men," and رجالٌ بيضٌ "white men." The plural adjective حُمْرٌ "red" is used, despite its current political unacceptability, at least in English, to refer to native American citizens as in الهنودُ الحُمْرُ "Red Indians."

On the other hand, the plural adjectives for human feminine nouns follow the pattern فَعْلاوات. Thus, according to this pattern, we obtain حَمْراوات، سَوْداوات، صَفْراوات، بَيْضاوات، زَرْقاوات، خَضْراوات، شَقْراوات. Of these plural adjectives, only two can be used for humans, namely بَيْضاواتٌ "white," and

شَقْراوَاتٌ "blond," as in, for example, بَناتٌ شَقْراوَاتٌ "blond young women,"
بَناتٌ بَيْضاوَاتٌ "white women," سَيِّداتٌ سَمْراوَاتٌ "dark [skinned] ladies," نِساءٌ بَيْضاوَاتٌ
سَوْداوَاتٌ "black young women."

Non-human plural nouns take singular feminine adjectives, as in, for example, سَيّاراتٌ حَمْراءُ "red cars," حَقائِبُ سَوْداءُ "black bags." One is likely to encounter, for example, وُرودٌ بيضٌ "white roses," وُرودٌ حُمْرٌ and so on with other colors for roses.

4.1.2.2 Traits

Words denoting inherent characteristics or defects, often related to humans, comply with the pattern أَفْعَلُ in the masculine, and فَعْلاءُ in the feminine in the singular. Consider the examples in the table below:

أَفْعَلُ	فَعْلاءُ	Meaning
أَعْمى	عَمْياءُ	blind
أَطْرَشُ	طَرْشاءُ	deaf
أَحْمَقُ	حَمْقاءُ	foolish
أَصَمُّ	صَمّاءُ	deaf, solid
أَبْلَهُ	بَلْهاءُ	stupid
أَبْكَمُ	بَكْماءُ	dumb
أَبْرَصُ	بَرْصاءُ	leprous

Some of these adjectives exhibit two plurals, one adhering to the فُعْلٌ pattern, and another to the فُعْلان pattern. Thus we obtain عُمْيٌ and عُمْيان "blind," and بُكْمٌ "deaf," صُمٌّ "deaf." We also see حُمْقٌ and حَمْقى and طُرْشان and طُرْشٌ "foolish." ... "dumb," and بُلْهٌ "stupid," are the only plural forms used.

4.1.3 *Nisba* adjectives

The word نِسْبَة denotes "with relation to." A very common adjective form is the *nisba* adjective. Such forms are derived from place names such as a country, city, locality, or tribe, and from common nouns by the simple process of suffixing the *nisba* adjective marker ـِيّ (doubled *yaa'* that carries a *shadda* in the writing system). The consonant preceding the doubled *yaa'* must end with one *kasra*. Thus, from the name of the city of Damascus دِمَشْق we derive دِمَشْقِيٌّ "Damascene," from بَيْروت "Beirut," we derive بَيْروتيٌّ "Beiruti," and from تَغْلِب, a famous Arab tribe, we derive تَغْلِبيٌّ "taghlibi, member of the Taghlibs," from the common noun رَمْل "sand," we derive رَمْلِيٌّ "sandy," and so on.

If the noun ends with regular *'alif*, the *'alif* is dropped before adding the *nisba yaa'*. For example, from أَمْريكا "America," we derive أَمْريكِيٌّ "American," and from فَرَنْسا / فَرَنْسا "France," we derive فَرَنْسِيٌّ "French." If the place name carries the definite article الـ as in العِراق "Iraq," and الـمَغْرب "Morocco," the definite article is dropped before we add the *nisba yaa'*. Thus, from العِراق we derive the *nisba* adjective عِراقِيٌّ "Iraqi," and from المَغْرب we obtain مَغْرِبيٌّ "Moroccan." *Nisba*-adjectives derived from proper nouns are adjectives like any other. When used as predicates of equational sentences, they must be indefinite and in the nominative case. However, when such adjectives are used to modify definite nouns, the definite article is retrieved to modify definite nouns as in الطّالِبُ العِراقِيُّ "the Iraqi student."

Nisba adjectives are made feminine by the addition of the feminine marker, the *taa' marbuuTa* ة. The masculine adjective أَمْريكيٌّ becomes أَمْريكِيَّةٌ in the feminine.

4.1.3.1 Nisba *adjectives of color words*

Nisba adjectives produce the names of all secondary colors. These adjectives derive from the names of fruits, flowers, metals, household or consumable items. Thus from بُرْتُقال "oranges," we obtain بُرْتُقاليٌّ "orange color." The feminine form of this color adjective is obtained by the addition of the feminine marker, the *taa'-marbuuTa* بُرْتُقاليَّةٌ. Examine the list of such non-basic colors below:

Noun	*Adjective*	*Meaning*
لَيْمونٌ	لَيْمونيٌّ	lemon-yellow
بُنٌّ	بُنّيٌّ	brown
زَهْرٌ	زَهْريٌّ	pink
بَنَفْسَجٌ	بَنَفْسَجيٌّ	violet
وَرْدٌ	وَرْديٌّ	rose color

Noun	Adjective	Meaning
رَمادٌ	رَماديٌّ	gray
خَمْرٌ	خَمْريٌّ	burgundy color
أُرْجُوانٌ	أُرْجُوانيٌّ	deep red
فَيْروزٌ	فَيْروزيٌّ	turquoise
ذَهَبٌ	ذَهَبيٌّ	gold, golden
فِضّةٌ	فِضّيٌّ	silver
نُحاسٌ	نُحاسيٌّ	copper color
فَحْمٌ	فَحْميٌّ	coal color

Nisba adjectives can also have dual and plural forms, as in مِصْريّان "two Egyptians (M)," or فَرَنْسِيّونَ/ فِرَنْسِيّونَ "French (M, Pl)," سوريّاتٌ "Syrians (F, Pl)."

4.1.4 Other types of adjective

An active participle اِسْم الفاعِل and a passive participle اِسْم المَفعول can also serve as adjectives. These adjectives are referred to in the Arab grammatical tradition as صِفات مُشَبَّهة باسْم الفاعِل واسم المَفعول "adjectives like the active and passive participle forms." اِسْم الفاعِل "active participles" are discussed in detail in Chapter 23; passive participle اِسْم المَفعول forms are discussed in Chapter 24.

4.2 NOUN–ADJECTIVE AGREEMENT

4.2.1 Noun–adjective agreement in the singular

Adjectives modifying nouns in the singular assume the form of nouns in gender, number, determination (definite/indefinite) and case. If a noun is masculine, singular, indefinite and nominative, the adjective modifying it must have all these features, as in the following:

كاتِبٌ مَشْهورٌ   a famous writer

المُديرَةُ السُّوريَّةُ   the Syrian director

مَعَ طالِبَةٍ جَديدَةٍ   with a new student

4.2.2 Noun–adjective agreement in the dual

Dual masculine nouns in the nominative case, definite or indefinite, end with ان-. Accusative and genitive dual masculine nouns, definite or indefinite, end with يْنِ-. Dual masculine nouns look like the following in their various cases:

Dual nominative	Dual accusative/genitive	Meaning
طالبان	طالِبَيْنِ	two students
مُعَلِّمان	مُعَلِّمَيْنِ	two teachers

Dual nouns require dual adjectives that must agree with them in number, case and gender. In other words, adjectives used to modify dual masculine nouns must end with ان- in the nominative or يْنِ- in the accusative and genitive, as in the following:

Dual nominative	Dual accusative/genitive	Meaning
طالبانِ مُمْتازانِ	طالِبَيْنِ مُمْتازَيْنِ	excellent students (D, M)
مُعَلِّمانِ مَشْهورانِ	مُعَلِّمَيْنِ مَشْهورَيْنِ	famous teachers (D, M)

Dual feminine nouns in the nominative case, definite or indefinite, also end with ان. Recall that the feminine suffix *taa' marbuuTa* in singular feminine nouns changes to open ت before the addition of ان. Accusative and genitive dual feminine nouns end with يْنِ-. Dual feminine nouns look like the following in their various cases:

Dual nominative	Dual accusative/genitive	Meaning
طالبَتان	طالِبَتَيْنِ	two students (F)
مُعَلِّمَتان	مُعَلِّمَتَيْنِ	two teachers (F)

Adjectives used to modify dual nouns must end with ان- in the nominative and يْنِ- in the accusative and genitive, as in the following:

Dual nominative	Dual accusative/genitive	Meaning
طالِبَتانِ جَديدَتانِ	طالِبَتَيْنِ جَديدَتَيْنِ	two new students (F)
مُعَلِّمَتانِ مَشْهورَتانِ	مُعَلِّمَتَيْنِ مَشْهورَتَيْنِ	two famous teachers (F)

4.2.3 Human noun–adjective agreement in the plural

Plural human nouns are generally modified by plural adjectives that carry the regular plural marker for nouns. Thus, masculine human nouns that terminate with the nominative suffix ونَ - are modified by adjectives ending with ونَ -. Masculine human nouns in the accusative and genitive that end with ينَ are modified by adjectives ending in ينَ also, as in the following table:

Plural nominative	Plural accusative/genitive	Meaning
مُعَلِّمونَ مَشْهورونَ	مُعَلِّمينَ مَشْهورينَ	famous teachers (M)

There are irregular plural forms of adjectives that tend to collocate with plural human nouns in set phrases. These include, among a few others, جُدُدٌ "new," كِبارٌ "famous, big," عِظامٌ or عُظَماءُ "great, big," فُقَراءُ "poor," أَغْنِياءُ "rich, wealthy," صِغارٌ "young," أجانِبُ "foreign," يَهودٌ "Jews," عَرَبٌ "Arabs," etc. Thus, the adjective عَظيمونَ is acceptable in مُدَرِّسونَ عَظيمونَ "great teachers;" the use of عُظَماءُ or عِظامٌ instead, however, would be more acceptable, more idiomatic. In general there is a tendency among speakers to regularize forms in languages. It is not unlikely to encounter غَنِيّونَ "rich," in place of أَغْنِياء or فَقيرونَ "poor," in place of فُقَراء. However, plural nouns like عَرَبٌ "Arabs," يَهودٌ "Jews," and أجانِبُ "foreigners" never tolerate a plural form ending with the suffix ونَ or its accusative/genitive form ينَ.

    Feminine human nouns ending with ات- are modified by adjectives that terminate with the suffix اتٌ- i.e., ending with two *Dhamma*s in the nominative, and with two *kasra*s in the accusative and genitive, as in the following tables:

Plural nominative	Plural accusative/genitive	Meaning
مُعَلِّماتٌ مَشْهوراتٌ	مُعَلِّماتٍ مَشْهوراتٍ	famous teachers (F)

4.2.4 Non-human noun–adjective agreement in the plural

Non-human plural nouns must be modified by regular feminine singular adjectives. In the nominative, such adjectives carry one *Dhamma* when the noun is definite, and two *Dhamma*s when the noun is indefinite, as in the following:

الكُتُبُ الجَديدَةُ   the new books

كُتُبٌ جَديدَةٌ   new books

If the noun is in the accusative, the adjective carries one *fat-Ha* if the noun is definite, and two *fat-Ha*s if it is indefinite. In the writing system indefinite accusative masculine nouns require the use of *'alif* to carry the two *fat-Ha*s. The two *fat-Ha*s are written above the *taa' marbuuTa* in indefinite accusative feminine nouns.

الكُتُبَ الجَديدَةَ   the new books

كُتُباً جَديدةً   new books

If the noun is in the genitive, the adjective must carry one *kasra* if the noun is definite, and two *kasra*s if it is indefinite:

الكُتُبِ الجَديدَةِ   the new books

كُتُبٍ جَديدَةٍ   new books

CHAPTER 5

Pronouns الضَّمائِر

Pronouns are a finite set of words in languages that take the place of nouns or refer to them. Pronouns function in similar ways to nouns: they can be subjects of equational/nominal sentences and objects of transitive verbs. Some pronoun forms can indicate possession. In addition, pronouns can be preceded by prepositions, or a group of words Arab grammarians call ظُروف (Pl of ظَرْف) that are similar to prepositions in their behavior. A list of ظُروف "adverbs" will be provided in Chapter 7. Pronouns in Arabic are of different types and have singular, dual and plural forms.

5.1 PERSONAL PRONOUNS الضَّمائِر

There are three main categories of personal pronouns: (1) those used to indicate the speaker, such as أنا "I" and نَحْنُ "we," referred to as first person pronouns, ضَمير المُتَكَلِّم in Arabic; (2) those that indicate the addressee, as in أنْتَ "you," for example, referred to as second person pronouns, ضَمير المُخاطَب in Arabic; and (3) those that refer to someone other than the speaker or addressee, such as هُوَ "he," for example, referred to as third person pronouns, ضَمير الغائِب in Arabic.

The meaning of pronouns, especially the third person pronouns (هُوَ or هِيَ and their dual and plural forms), often involves a referent, an antecedent, i.e. an entity that has already been introduced in the discourse.

5.1.1 Singular independent personal pronouns

الضَّمائِرُ المُنْفَصِلة في المُفْرَد

Independent personal pronouns stand alone and function as subjects of sentences, as will be discussed in Chapter 9. In the singular they are:

Independent pronoun	Meaning
أَنا	I
أَنْتَ	you (M)
أَنْتِ	you (F)
هُوَ	he/it
هِيَ	she/it

5.1.2 Singular suffixal personal pronouns

الضَّمائِرُ المُتَّصِلة في المُفْرَد

Personal pronouns performing functions other than as subjects of sentences are expressed as suffixes in Arabic. These pronouns must be attached to other elements in the language: nouns, prepositions, or verbs.

1. By suffixing *possessive pronouns* to nouns, the nouns become definite. Consequently, nouns with suffixal pronouns attached to their endings function as subjects of equational sentences. Nouns cannot combine the definite article الـ and the possessive pronoun simultaneously. What follows is a list of suffixal possessive pronouns in the singular and their respective meanings:

Suffix pronoun form	Meaning
ي	my
كَ	your (M)
كِ	your (F)
هُ	his/its
ها	her/its

Attached to nominative nouns such as كِتاب "a book," the singular possessive pronouns appear as follows:

Suffix pronoun form	Meaning
كِتابِي	my book
كِتابُكَ	your (M) book
كِتابُكِ	your (F) book
كِتابُهُ	his book
كِتابُها	her book

The suffixes are invariable, except for هُ "his." Nouns in Arabic decline, i.e. they assume different endings according to their function in sentences (see Chapter 3). If هُ "his" is attached to a noun ending with *yaa'* or *kasra*, it changes to ه. The reason for the change of هُ to ه in this case is physiologically motivated. As the vocal tract produces the vowel /i/ in the *kasra* or the *yaa'* it is natural to continue in the same mode for the production of a following vowel, thus causing the *Dhamma* to change to an identical *kasra*.

2. The suffixal pronoun forms can be attached to prepositions, as in the table below:

Suffix pronoun form	Meaning
معي	with me
مَعَكَ	with you (M)
مَعَكِ	with you (F)
مَعَهُ	with him
مَعَها	with her

3. In addition, the suffixal pronoun forms can be attached to the end of verbs, thus functioning as direct objects of transitive verbs (see Chapter 11), as in the following table:

Suffix pronoun form	Meaning
ني	me
كَ	you (M)
كِ	you (F)
هُ	him
ها	her

Note that the first-person singular suffixal pronoun ي assumes the form ني when attached to transitive verbs as a direct object. In other words, the change from ي to ني involves the insertion of ن. Arabic does not allow two different vowels in sequence. As verbs in the past end with a *fat-Ha*, the ن is inserted to bridge the transition from the *fat-Ha* of the verb to ي, i.e. the *kasra* of the pronoun. This ن is known in Arabic grammar as نون الوقايَة "guarding or preventive *nuun*," i.e. it prevents the vowel at the end of the verb from being absorbed by the long vowel ي. This also applies to verbs in the present tense ending with a *Dhamma*.

With prepositions that end with a *yaa'*, the first person singular suffix pronoun ي is followed by a *fat-Ha*. The combination of the original *yaa'* ي of the preposition and the suffix pronoun *yaa'* sounds like a geminated *yaa'*, i.e. doubled, followed by a *fat-Ha*. Examine the following table:

Preposition	Suffix		Meaning
في	ي	فيَّ	in me
عَلى	ي	عَليَّ	on me
إلى	ي	إليَّ	to me

The *Dhamma* of the suffix pronoun هُ changes to a *kasra*, resulting in فيهِ. The *Dhamma* in all third person pronouns, singular as in هُ, dual as in هُما (M, F) and plural as in هُمْ and هُنَّ (see below) changes to a *kasra* when preceded by a *yaa'* or a *kasra*. In addition to فيهِ "in him," we obtain فيهِما "in them (D)," فيهِم "in them (M, Pl)" and فيهِنَّ "in them (F, Pl)".

5.1.3 Dual independent personal pronouns ضَمائِرُ الـمُثَنَّى الـمُنْفَصِلَة

نَحْنُ   we two (M, F)

أَنْتُما   you two (M, F)

هُما   they two (M, F)

There is not an independent dual pronoun in Arabic; instead the plural pronoun نَحْنُ is used to represent two people, as well as more than two.

5.1.4 Dual suffixal personal pronouns ضَمائِرُ الـمُثَنَّى الـمُتَّصِلَة

1.   The following dual suffix pronouns are suffixed to nouns to indicate possession:

-نا   our

-كُما   your (M, F)

-هُما   their (M, F)

These pronouns are attached to nominative nouns as follows:

Suffix pronoun form	Meaning
كِتابُنا	our (M, F) book
كِتابُكُما	your (M, F) book
كِتابُهُما	their (M, F) book

Note that -هُما "their (M, F)" changes to هِما when it is attached to a noun ending with a *kasra* or *yaa'*.

2. The following dual suffix pronouns also attach to prepositions or adverbs, as with مَعَ "with" or إلى "to, for," respectively:

مَعَنا	with us	إلَيْنا	to us, for us (M/F)
مَعَكُما	with you (M, F)	إلَيْكُما	to you (M/F)
مَعَهُما	with them (M, F)	إلَيْهِما	to them (M/F)

Note the change of the 'alif maqSuura إلى into yaa'. Often 'alif maqSuura changes to yaa' when suffixes are attached to it.

3. These dual suffixal pronouns can attach to verbs functioning as direct objects. This will be discussed further in Chapter 11.

5.1.5 Plural independent personal pronouns
ضَمائِر الجَمْع المُنْفَصِلَة

Independent pronoun	Meaning
نَحْنُ	we (M/F, Pl)
أَنْتُم	you (M, Pl)
أَنْتُـنَّ	you (F, Pl)
هُم	they (M, Pl)
هُنَّ	they (F, Pl)

5.1.6 Plural suffixal personal pronouns ضَمائِر الجَمْع المُتَّصِلَة

1. The following plural suffix pronouns must be suffixed to nouns to indicate possession:

Suffix pronoun form	Meaning
نا	our
كُم	your (M)
كُنَّ	your (F)
هُم	their (M)
هُنَّ	their (F)

When attached to nominative nouns, the plural possessive pronouns look like the following:

Example	Meaning
كِتابُنا	our book
كِتابُكُم	your (M) book
كِتابُكُنَّ	your (F) book
كِتابُهُم	their (M) book
كِتابُهُنَّ	their (F) book

2. The suffix pronouns can also attach to prepositions or adverbs, as in the following:

مَعَنا	with us
مَعَكُم	with you (M, Pl)
مَعَكُنَّ	with you (F, Pl)
مَعَهُم	with them (M, Pl)
مَعَهُنَّ	with them (F, Pl)

When the suffixal pronouns هُم "their (M)" and هُنَّ "their (F)" are preceded by a *kasra* or *yaa'*, the *Dhamma* at the beginning of these pronouns changes to a *kasra*, as in the following:

في كِتابِهِم	in their (M) book
في كِتابِهِنَّ	in their (F) book
عَلَيْهِنَّ	on them (F)

3. The suffixal plural pronouns can also attach to verbs, thus functioning as direct objects with meanings similar to those in the preceding sections 1 and 2.

5.2 DEMONSTRATIVE PRONOUNS

Demonstrative pronouns point to nouns and indicate whether they are near or far in time and space. The use of demonstrative pronouns in equational sentences is discussed in Chapter 9.

5.2.1 Singular demonstrative pronouns أَسْماءُ الإِشارَة - الـمُفْرَد

Singular demonstrative pronouns are invariable with respect to case. In other words, they exhibit the same endings in the nominative, accusative and genitive cases.

هذا / ذا	this (M)
هذِه	this (F)
ذلِكَ / ذاكَ	that (M)
تِلْكَ	that (F)

هذا "this (M)" and هذِه "this (F)" are used to indicate objects in close proximity to the speaker; ذلِكَ "that (M)" and تِلْكَ "that (F)" are used for entities distant from the speaker. ذلِكَ has other forms which are not commonly used but are likely to appear in writing, namely ذاكَ and ذ.

Non-human plural nouns are treated grammatically as feminine singular nouns in Arabic, whether reference to such nouns is made by demonstrative pronouns, or by the use of adjectives to modify them, or verbs. Reference to non-human plural nouns such as كُتُبٌ "books," سَيَّاراتٌ "cars," or كِلابٌ "dogs" is accomplished by the use of the singular demonstrative pronouns هذِه "this" or تِلْكَ "that" (see Chapter 5).

5.2.2 Dual demonstrative pronouns أسماءُ الإِشارة - الـمُثَنّى

هذان	these two (M)
هاتان	these two (F)

These two nouns are used to demonstrate dual nouns that are close to the speaker. They are in the nominative case, used when they are subjects or parts of subjects of equational sentences (see Chapter 9). In addition, they assume the same forms when they function as *faaʿil* فاعِل "performer of action" in verbal sentences (see Chapter 11).

هذانِ and هاتانِ assume different endings when they are direct objects of transitive verbs (see Chapter 11), or when preceded by prepositions or ظُروف "adverbs." The accusative and genitive forms are هذَيْنِ and هاتَيْنِ.

ذلكَ and تلْكَ have the following archaic dual nominative forms to demonstrate items distant from the speaker, namely ذانكَ and تانكَ. Their accusative and genitive forms are ذَيْنكَ and تَيْنكَ respectively. However, they are rarely used in Modern Standard Arabic (MSA). They are restricted to grammar books and extremely erudite writers/speakers. Instead of those obsolete forms, MSA uses the plural forms for these demonstratives, as we shall see below.

5.2.3 Plural demonstrative pronouns أَسْماءُ الإِشارة - الجَمْع

هؤُلاءِ   These (M, F)

أُولئِكَ   Those (M, F)

Both demonstrative pronouns are used to demonstrate *human* plural nouns. هؤُلاءِ is used to demonstrate persons that are close to the speaker; أُولئِكَ on the other hand is used to indicate persons distant from the speaker. They are invariable with respect to case, assuming the same form regardless of their function in sentences. Demonstrative pronouns for non-human plural nouns are always هذِه "this" or تلْكَ "that."

CHAPTER 6

Prepositions and adverbs functioning as prepositions
حُروفُ الجَرّ والظُّروف

Arabic has a limited set of words known by the Arabic name حُروف الجَرّ "prepositions." These always precede nouns and cause them to end in formal writing with two *kasra*s if they are indefinite, or with one if definite. (See Chapter 3 for discussion of the genitive case.) Prepositions may also precede pronouns, and they are of two types: bound and independent, free.

6.1 BOUND PREPOSITIONS

Bound prepositions consist of one consonant followed by a vowel. In the writing system, bound prepositions are represented by one orthographic symbol for the consonant followed by a vowel, usually a *kasra* or *fat-Ha*. In the writing system, these bound prepositions must attach to the following noun or pronoun, as in the following examples:

بِ   at, with, by means of, in

e.g. بالبَيتِ "at the house," بِسَيّارَةٍ "by means of a car"

بِهِ   with/in him or it

كَ   like

e.g. كأُمِّها "like her mother." This specific preposition can only be followed by a noun, never by a pronoun.

لِ   to, for

This preposition is followed only by nouns and the suffix pronoun ي "my," for example, لِلْمُعَلِّم "for the teacher," لِي "for me."

لَ   to, for

This is a variant of the preceding لِ with the same meaning. This preposition, however, must be followed by other suffix pronouns, except ي, e.g. لَهُ "for him, to him," لَكَ "for you, to you (M, Sg)." It cannot be followed by the suffix ي.

6.2 INDEPENDENT PREPOSITIONS

Independent, or free, prepositions usually consist of either two or three letters in writing. As was stated above, prepositions always precede nouns that must obligatorily end in formal writing or speaking with one *kasra* if the noun is definite or with two (i.e. *tanwiin*, pronounced -*in*) if it is indefinite. Examples of these prepositions include:

إلى	to, for	في	in, at
بَيْنَ	between, among	مَعَ	with
حَتّى	until	مِنْ	from, of
عَلى	on	لَدى	with, at
عَنْ	about		

Traditionally, Arab grammarians tended to include بَيْنَ "between, among" and مُنْذُ "since, for, from" in the list of adverbs, الظُروف. The above independent pronouns may be classified into three groups:

6.2.1 Prepositions that precede nouns or pronouns

This group includes إلى "to, for," بَيْنَ "between," عَلى "on," عَنْ "about," في "in, at," مَعَ "with," مِنْ "from, of." The *'alif maqSuura* in إلى "to," or عَلى "on," changes into a *yaa'* ي when a suffix pronoun is attached, as in عَلَيْهِ "on him,"

إِلَيْكِ "to you (F, Sg)." Suffixal pronouns attach to prepositions and/or adverbs as illustrated below, using مَعَ "with" and أَمَام "in front of," respectively:

مَعِي	with me	أَمَامِي	in front of me
مَعَكَ	with you (M, Sg)	أَمَامَكَ	in front of you (M, Sg)
مَعَكِ	with you (F, Sg)	أَمَامَكِ	in front of you (F, Sg)
مَعَهُ	with him/it	أَمَامَهُ	in front of him/it
مَعَها	with her/it	أَمَامَها	in front of her/it

Note that all suffixal pronouns remain unchanged. However, with the prepositions عَلَى "on" and إِلَى "to," three changes take place:

1. When the pronoun suffixes attach to these prepositions, the *'alif maqSuura* ى at the end of these prepositions is shortened and then a semi-consonant -y- phonetically, represented as a ي in the writing system, is introduced, as illustrated below:

عَلى	إِلى
عَلَيَّ	إِلَيَّ
عَلَيْكَ	إِلَيْكَ
عَلَيْكِ	إِلَيْكِ
عَلَيْهِ	إِلَيْهِ
عَلَيْها	إِلَيْها

2. The pronoun suffix ي for the pronoun أَنا carries a *shadda* followed by *fat-Ha* in the writing system، as in عَلَيَّ "on me," and إِلَيَّ "to me, toward me."

3. The pronoun suffix هُ for the pronoun هُوَ changes to ه for the physiological reason mentioned in Chapter 5. Similarly, the dual masculine and feminine suffixal pronoun هُما "them, their" changes to هِما, and the plural masculine suffixal pronoun هُم "them, their" and the plural feminine suffixal pronoun هُنَّ "them, their" change to هِم and هِنَّ, respectively, when suffixed to prepositions ending with *'alif maqSuura* like عَلَى "on" or إِلَى "to, for." The *'alif maqSuura* in these prepositions changes to *yaa'*, which causes the

Dhamma of such suffixes to change to *kasra* as in the following illustrative examples:

عَلَيْهِ   on him

إِلَيْهِم   to them

عَلَيْهِنَّ   on them (F, Pl)

6.2.2 Prepositions that precede nouns but not pronouns

This group includes حَتَّى "until" and, as mentioned above, the bound preposition كَ "like."

6.2.3 Prepositions that can precede nouns signaling time reference

This includes مُنْذُ "since, for, from," or its variation مُذْ "since, for, from," as in the following:

مُنْذُ ساعَةٍ   an hour ago

مُنْذُ زِيارَتِهِ الأخيرةِ   since his last visit

مُنْذُ can be followed by verbs in the same meaning.

وَصَلْنَ مُنْذُ يَوْمَيْنِ.   They (F, Pl) arrived two days ago.

6.3 وَ AND تَ IN OATH-MAKING

There are two one-letter prepositions used in oath-making: وَ "by" and تَ "by" The first is commonly used as in واللّٰه "by God." تَ on the other hand is practically obsolete and rarely used in Modern Standard Arabic. It is used only with the name of God, as in تَاللّٰه "by God."

6.4 PARTICLES FUNCTIONING AS PREPOSITIONS

The particles حاشا, عَدا, خَلا, and سِوى, all meaning "except," are followed by nouns in the genitive, thus functioning as prepositions. For a detailed discussion of these particles see Chapter 34.

6.5 ADVERBS FUNCTIONING AS PREPOSITIONS

Unlike the connotation of "adverb" in English grammar, the following list of Arabic words, labeled adverbs of place and time, function like prepositions: they make the nouns following them genitive. This class of adverbs was categorized by traditional Arab grammarians as nouns because they can be preceded by prepositions, attach to the definite article الـ and be part of *IDhaafa*-constructs (see Chapter 8). Definite nouns following them must end with one *kasra*; indefinite nouns must end with two *kasra*s.

أَمامَ	in front of	فَوْقَ	above, on
خَلْفَ	behind, at the back of	أَسْفَلَ	below, underneath
وَراءَ	behind, at the back of	تَحْتَ	below, underneath
داخِلَ	inside	حَسَبَ or حَسْبَ	according to
خارِجَ	outside		
جانِبَ	at the side of	قَبْلَ	before
ناحِيَةَ	in the direction of	بَعْدَ	after
نَحْوَ	in the direction of, toward	مُنْذُ	since, for, from
		عِنْدَ	at, with, for (possession)
خِلالَ	during		
أَثْناءَ	during	لَدى	at (place), with, by, for (possession)
بَيْنَ...وَبَيْنَ	between x and y	لَدُن	at (place or time), with, by
دونَ	without		

6.6 INTERROGATIVE PARTICLES أَدَوَاتُ الاِسْتِفْهَام

Interrogative particles in Arabic are of two types: (1) a group that is used with nouns to form equational/nominal sentences, and (2) those that are used with verbs in verbal sentences.

Interrogative particles restricted in their use to nouns include ما "what?" أَيُّ "which, he who (M)," and أَيَّةُ "she who (F)". Interrogative particles that appear before verbs include ماذا "what?," مِـمَّ "from what?," لِماذا "why, what for?," لِمَ "why?." Some of these particles are used with both nouns and verbs: مِنْ أَيْنَ "who?," مِـمَّنْ "from whom?," مَعَ مَنْ "with whom?," أَيْنَ "where?," مَن "where from?," إِلى أَيْنَ "where to?," كَيْفَ "how?," كَم "how much, how many?," بِكَم "for how much?" Finally, هَلْ or أ. The answer expected to questions beginning with هَلْ or أ must begin with yes or no.

CHAPTER 7

Adverbs الظُّروف

Adverbs are parts of speech that modify verbs, adding information with respect to time or manner, or indicating intensity, limitation, or repetitiveness. Generally, adverbs are derived from several word categories: nouns or adjectives, or formed by the use of prepositions plus nouns. Chapter 6 presents elements that Arab grammarians classify as adverbs, although in fact they function like prepositions in causing nouns that follow them to be in the genitive case. Many adverbs are invariable in the accusative case, written with *tanwiin*. A few end with a *Dhamma*; a small number end in a *kasra* or a *fat-Ha*.

Adverbs are divided into three types: adverbs of time, adverbs of place, and adverbs of degree.

7.1 ADVERBS OF TIME ظُروفُ الزَّمان

Adverbs and adverbial phrases of time indicate a particular action's time of occurrence, duration, or sequence. Several categories belong to this group:

1. Accusative nouns of units of time: Adverbs of time can be nouns denoting units of time like ساعةٌ "hour," يَوْمٌ "day," أُسْبوعٌ "week," شَهْرٌ "month," سَنَةٌ "year." These time nouns, when used as adverbs, must always be indefinite and accusative, thus ending in *tanwiin*, as in the following examples:

   دَرَسَ ساعةً.
   He studied for an hour.

   أقامَ في هذِهِ المَدينةِ سَنَةً.
   He resided a year in this city.

Below is a list of time adverbs derived from nouns:

صَباحاً	in the morning	عادَةً	usually
مَساءً	in the evening	أَحْياناً	sometimes
ظُهْراً	at noon	نَهاراً	day time
عَصْراً	in the afternoon	يَوْماً	some day
لَيْلاً	at night	أَبَداً	never
فَجْراً	at dawn	أَخيراً	lately, finally
غَداً	tomorrow		

The following examples illustrate the use of some of these adverbs in sentences:

رَجَعَ الـمُعَلِّمُ صَباحاً.   The teacher returned in the morning.

اِجْتَمَعَ مَعَنا لَيْلاً.   He met with us at night.

2. Adverbs of time derived from accusative adjectives:

قَديماً	in the past, formerly	دائِماً	always
حَديثاً	recently	باكِراً	early
حالِيّاً	presently, now	مُتَأَخِّراً	late
غالِباً	mostly		

The following examples illustrate the use of some of these adverbs in sentences:

وَصَلَ الأُستاذُ مُتَأَخِّراً.   The teacher arrived late.

دَرَسَ الطالِبُ الدَّرْسَ كَثيراً.   The student read the lesson many times.

3. Adverbs derived from ordinal numbers:

أَوَّلاً	first, firstly	ثالثاً	third, thirdly
ثانياً	second, secondly	رابعاً	fourth, fourthly

4. Prepositional phrases: this category consists of a preposition and a noun indicating time. Examples of prepositions include في "in, at" or قَبْلَ "before," or its diminutive form قُبَيْلَ "a little bit before," or بَعَدَ "after," or its diminutive form بُعَيْدَ "a little bit after."

في الصَّباح	in the morning	في الفَجْرِ	at dawn
في الـمَساءِ	in the evening	في الغَدِ	tomorrow
في الظُّهْرِ	at noon	في العادَةِ	usually
في العَصْرِ	in the late afternoon	في الغالِبِ	mostly
في النَّهارِ	during day time	في الـماضي	in the past
في اللَّيْلِ	at night		

Such prepositional phrases expressing the time of actions in this section are synonymous with adverbs of time listed in the first category. For example, في الصَّباح is synonymous with صَباحاً and so on. The choice is personal preference and carries a certain register in the sense that صَباحاً carries an educated speech register.

قَبْلَ ساعَةٍ	an hour ago	بَعْدَ الظُّهْرِ	in the afternoon
قَبْلَ أُسْبوعٍ	a week ago	بَعْدَ العَصْرِ	in the late afternoon
قَبْلَ شَهْرٍ	a month ago	بُعَيْدَ الفَجْرِ	a little bit after dawn
قَبْلَ سَنَةٍ	a year ago	بَعْدَ الصَّفِّ	after the class
قَبْلَ عام	a year ago	بَعْدَ أُسْبوعٍ	in a week's time
قَبْلَ الصَّفِّ	before the class	بَعْدَ شَهْرٍ	in a month's time
قَبْلَ الظُّهْرِ	before noon	بَعْدَ سَنَةٍ	in a year's time
قُبَيْلَ الظُّهْرِ	a little bit before noon	بَعْدَ عام	in a year's time

Some adverbs of time in this category include, in addition to the prepositional phrase, an adjective indicating a reference to past, present, or future times. Examine the following:

في الأُسْبوع الـماضي	last week
في الشَّهْر الـماضي	last month
في السَّنَةِ الـماضِيَة	last year
في العام الـماضي	last year
في يَوْمِ (الـجُمْعَةِ) الـماضي	last Friday
في نِهايةِ الأُسْبوعِ الـماضي	this past weekend
في الشِّتاءِ الـماضي	last winter
في الرَّبيع الـماضي	last spring
في الصَّيْفِ الـماضي	last summer
في الـخَريفِ الـماضي	last autumn
في الأسبوع الحالي/ الـجاري	in this [current] week
في السَّنَةِ الـحالِيَّةِ / الـجارِيَة	in this [current] year
في الأُسْبوعِ القادِم / التّالي	next week
[يَوْمَ] السَّبْتِ القادِمِ	next Saturday
[يَوْمَ] الـجُمْعَةِ القادِمِ	next Friday
في نِهايةِ الأُسْبوعِ القادِمِ	next weekend

5. Invariable adverbs whose endings remain unchanged:

صَباحَ...مَساءً	every morning and evening	الآنَ	now
بَيْنَ...بَيْنَ	so...so, between good and bad	اليَوْمَ	today
		بَعْدُ	yet
أَمْسِ	yesterday	مِنْ بَعْدُ	afterwards
		مِنْ قَبْلُ	before

6. One group of such invariable adverbs ends with the relative particle ما, as in the following:

أَيْنَما	wherever	طالَما	as long as
عِنْدَما	when	بَيْنَما	while
حينَما	when	رَيْثَما	until
حالَما	as soon as		

The following sentences illustrate the use of some of these adverbs:

تَكَلَّمَ مَعَ الـمُدير عِنْدَما وَصَلَ.

He spoke with the director when he arrived.

حينَما كانَ في دِمَشْق، دَرَسَ العَرَبِيَّةَ.

When he was in Damascus, he studied Arabic.

7. A quantifier plus a noun indicating a reference to time: this structure forms the *IDhaafa*-construct. As adverbial phrases, the first element of this construct is in the accusative. The second element of this *IDhaafa*-construct is in the genitive case (see Chapter 8).

كُلَّ يَوْم	every day	غالِبَ الأَحْيان	mostly
كُلَّ سَنَةٍ	every year	جَميعَ الأَيّام	all days
مُعْظَمَ الوَقْتِ	most of the time		

The following sentences illustrate the use of some of these adverbs:

كانَ يَجْلِسُ في مَكْتَبِهِ مُعْظَمَ الوَقْتِ.

He sat in his office most of the time.

كانَ يَزورُ القاهِرَةَ كُلَّ سَنَةٍ.

He used to visit Cairo every year.

8. A noun denoting time with the invariable suffix ئِذ "that" attached to it. The noun is always in the accusative, as in the following:

وَقْتَئِذٍ	at that time	يَوْمَئِذٍ	on that day
حِينَئِذٍ	then	بَعْدَئِذٍ	after that
عِنْدَئِذٍ	then	سَاعَتَئِذٍ	at that time, at that hour
آنَئِذٍ	then		

The following sentence illustrates the use of these adverbs:

دَرَّسَ صَفَّ التَّارِيخ وَبَعْدَئِذٍ رَجَعَ إِلى بَيْتِهِ.

He taught the history class and after that he returned home.

9. A noun denoting time with ذَاكَ "that," a form of the demonstrative ذلِكَ suffixed to the noun. The noun is always in the accusative, as in the following:

آنَذَاكَ	then, at that time	وَقْتَذَاكَ	then, at that time
حِينَذَاكَ	then, at that time	يَوْمَذاكَ	then, on that day

Examine the following sentence illustrating the use of such adverbs:

دَرَّسَ في الجَامِعَة وَحِينَذاكَ كانَ يَسْكُنُ في بَيْتٍ كَبِيرٍ.

He taught at the university and then he lived in a big house.

7.2 ADVERBS OF PLACE ظُروف المَكان

This group of adverbs and prepositional phrases modifies a verb by indicating its location or direction. This includes words like حَيْثُ "in the place where." حَيْثُ always ends with *Dhamma*, as the following sentence illustrates:

سَكَنَ حَيْثُ سَكَنَ أَبوهُ.   He resided where his father did.

The following categories belong to this group:

1. Words for directions like شَرْقٌ "east," غَرْبٌ "west," جَنوبٌ "south" and شَمالٌ "north." As adverbs, these are always indefinite, accusative, thus ending in *tanwiin*:

شَرْقاً	eastward	جَنوباً	southward
غَرْباً	westward	يَميناً	to the right
شَمالاً	northward	يَساراً	to the left

Examine the following sentence illustrating the use of such adverbs:

سارَ شَرْقاً.   He walked eastward.

مَشى شَمالاً.   He walked northward.

It is also possible to use prepositional phrases with the direction words as in

مَشى إلى الشَّمالِ.   He walked northward.

The use of شَمالاً as a synonym conveys a speech register revealing a more educated usage.

2. Words which are invariable in form, mostly ending with a *fat-Ha*. Note that a limited number end with a *Dhamma* or *kasra*. Nouns following them are always in the genitive case, ending with one *kasra* if the noun is definite, or with two *kasras* if it is indefinite:

أَمامَ	in front of	بَيْنَ...وَبَيْنَ	between X and Y
خَلْفَ	behind, at the back of	دونَ	without
وَراءَ	behind, at the back of	فَوْقَ	above, on
داخِلَ	inside	أَسْفَلَ	below, underneath
خارِجَ	outside	تَحْتَ	below, underneath, under
جانِبَ	at the side of, beside		
ناحِيَةَ	in the direction of	قَبْلَ	before
نَحْوَ	in the direction of, toward	بَعْدَ	after
		عِنْدَ	at, with
خِلالَ	during	لَدُنْ	at (place or time), with, by
أَثْناءَ	during		

The following sentences illustrate the use of such pronouns:

شَرِبَ القَهْوَةَ خارِجَ البَيْتِ.   He drank coffee outside the house.

جَلَسَت الأُسْتاذَةُ أمامَ الصَّفِّ.   The teacher sat in front of the class.

7.3 ADVERBS OF DEGREE

These adverbs modify the verb by indicating its degree or extent. They include:

1. Adverbs derived from adjectives. Masculine, indefinite, and accusative adjectives function as adverbs, for example كَثيراً "a lot," قَليلاً "a little," بَعيداً "distantly," as in:

أكَلَ كَثيراً.   He ate a lot.

نامَ قَليلاً.   He slept a little.

2. Adverbs of degree denoting or delimiting intensity. Such adverbs include فَقَط "only," جِدّاً "very, to a large extent," قَطُّ "ever, never," فَحَسْبُ "only," and البَتَّةَ or بَتاتاً "definitely, absolutely." قَطُّ and البَتَّةَ or بَتاتاً are used with past tense verbs often in the negative, or with jussive verbs. They are also in interrogative sentences. Consider the following examples:

ما رَأَيْتُهُ قَطُّ.   I never saw it/him.

هَلْ قابَلْتَها قَطُّ؟   Have you ever met her?

لَمْ أُدَخِّن في حَياتي البَتَّةَ.   I never smoked in my life.

3. Prepositional phrases of degree:

إلى حَدٍّ كَبيرٍ	to a large extent	بالضَّبْط	exactly
إلى حَدٍّ قَليلٍ	to a small extent	عَلى الأَقَلِّ	at least
لِلغايَةِ	to a large extent, extremely	عَلى الأَكْثَرِ	at most

Consider the following examples:

أَحَبَّتِ مَرْيم الـمَدينةَ إلى حَدٍّ كَبير.

Maryam liked the city a lot.

حَضَرَ الصَّفَّ خَمْسَةُ طُلَّابٍ على الأَكْثر.

At most five students attended the class.

4. Adverbs derived from *maSdars*. Prepositions like بِ "by, by means of," عَلى "on," with indefinite nouns or *maSdars* (see Chapter 25 on *maSdars*) function as adverbs modifying the manner of verbs. Examine the following:

مَشى بِسُرعَةٍ.   He walked in a hurry.

وَصَلَ عَلى عَجَلٍ.   He arrived in a hurry.

نامَتْ بِعُمْقٍ.   She slept deeply.

تَكَلَّمَتْ بِوُضوحٍ.   She spoke clearly.

We must mention also other types of adverbs that will be discussed separately in this book, namely adverbs of specification, "*tamyiiz*" (Chapter 33), adverbs of manner that include adverbs of circumstance, "*Haal*" (Chapter 32), and the cognate accusative/object "*al-maf'uul al-muTlaq*" in the *maSdar* chapter (Chapter 25).

7.4 PLACEMENT OF ADVERBS

As a general rule, adverbs are often placed after the verb they modify, or as close to it as possible. This part of speech, however, enjoys a degree of mobility with respect to its position in sentences. Adverb mobility is used for stylistic variation, or to highlight and emphasize a certain element. To illustrate this statement, examine the following sentence:

بِسُرعَةٍ كَبيرَةٍ انْطَلَقَت سَيّارَةُ الشُّرْطَةِ.

The police car set out at high speed.

The placement of بِسُرْعَة "at high speed, fast," at the beginning of the sentence lends emphasis to how the car set out. Adverbial phrases such as بِسُرْعَة "at high speed," can be modified by the use of adjectives as this example illustrates.

Adverbs of degree and time can be used in the same sentence, clearly modifying verbs in their different ways, as in the example below:

دَرَسَتِ الطَّالِبَةُ كثيراً أَمْسِ.

The student (F) studied a lot yesterday.

CHAPTER 8

The *IDhaafa*-construct الإضافة

The *IDhaafa*-construct consists of nouns bound together into an indivisible unit, generally indicating either possession or that one entity is related to another. Two nouns in an *IDhaafa*-construct are used to express the relationship between two nouns, for example, X noun of Y [noun]. As an illustration, صُعودُ الجَبَل "mountain climbing" or مُشاهَدَةُ الرِّياضَة "sport watching" do not convey a sense of ownership, or possession, as does كِتابُ الطّالِب "the student's book," literally, "the book of the student."

When nouns are used to form the *IDhaafa*-construct, the first noun indicates the possessed item, or the related item. The second indicates the possessor, or the entity to which another one is related. The *IDhaafa*-construct is generally formed by placing two nouns (in some cases adjectives, as we shall see in the Quasi- or Pseudo-*IDhaafa* section below) or more, in sequence. The second and any following nouns must always be in the genitive case. In Arabic, the first noun is called مُضاف *muDhaaf*; the second مُضاف إلَيْه *muDhaaf ilayhi*.

The *IDhaafa*-construct can also be formed by having a masculine or feminine adjective in the first position followed by a noun in the second position. This kind of construct is called in Arabic إضافة غَير حَقيقيَّة "Quasi or Pseudo *IDhaafa*." This will be discussed in a separate section below. There are certain conditions on each of the *IDhaafa* nouns to maintain grammaticality, correctness, as will be detailed below.

8.1 THE FIRST NOUN IN *IDHAAFA*

1. The first noun in the *IDhaafa*-construct can never carry the definite article الـ. Its definiteness is determined by the second or final noun of the construct. For example: كِتابُ الطّالِب "the student's book," literally, "the book of the student."
2. It can never carry *nunation*, the *n*-sound that marks indefinite nouns.

3. The case of the first noun may vary, depending on its function in the sentence. If it is the subject of a sentence, the noun must be in the nominative case, as in the following example:

كِتابُ الطّالِبِ جَديدٌ.   The student's book is new.

Similarly, if the first noun is predicate, it must be in the nominative case, as in the following example:

هذا هُوَ كِتابُ الطّالِبِ.   This is the student's book.

Or, if the first noun is the direct object of a transitive verb, it must bear only one *fat-Ha*, as in the following:

قَرَأْتُ كِتابَ الطّالِبِ.   I read the student's book.

Or, if it is governed by a preposition, it must end with only one *kasra*, as in the following:

هذا في كِتابِ الطّالِبِ.   This is in the student's book.

4. If the first noun in the *IDhaafa* is feminine, the *taa' marbuuTa* at the end of the noun *must* be pronounced explicitly, as in:

سَيّارَةُ الطّالِبِ جَديدَةٌ.   The student's car is new.

8.2 THE SECOND NOUN IN *IDHAAFA*

1. The second noun in the *IDhaafa*-construct must always be in the genitive case.

2. It can be a definite noun, marked by one *kasra*. This definite noun makes the first noun definite but without it having the definite article الـ. Thus, in كِتابُ الأُستاذِ "the teacher's book" the first noun كِتاب becomes definite, although it cannot, and does not, carry the definite article. It is definite by virtue of the presence of the definite article الـ in the second noun الأُستاذ.

3. It may be indefinite. In this case, the second noun must end with two *kasras*. The fact that the second noun is indefinite makes the whole *IDhaafa*-construct indefinite, both nouns are unspecified. Consider:

كِتابُ أُستاذٍ

lit. "a book of a professor" or
"a professor's book"

8.3 *IDHAAFA* FUNCTION IN SENTENCES

IDhaafa-constructs form a single indivisible nominal ("noun") unit. Let us examine the construct صَديقُ الطّالِب "the student's friend," to see how this indivisible unit can play the various functions of a single noun:

1. Subject of equational sentence: مُبْتَدَأ

صَديقُ الطّالِبِ أمريكِيٌّ.

The student's friend is American.

2. Predicate of equational sentence: خَبَر

هذا هُوَ صَديقُ الطّالِبِ.

This is the student's friend.

3. Performer of an action of a verb: فاعِل

سافَرَ صَديقُ الطّالِبِ إلى لُبنان.

The student's friend traveled to Lebanon.

4. Direct object of verb: مَفعول بِه

شاهَدْتُ صَديقَ الطّالِبِ.

I saw the student's friend.

5. Governed by a preposition: جار وَمَجْرور

سافَرَ مَعَ صَديقِ الطّالِبِ.

He traveled with the student's friend.

8.4 MULTIPLE FIRST NOUNS IN *IDHAAFA*

A new development has taken place in Modern Standard Arabic where the first noun of an *IDhaafa*-construct is conjoined by another noun, or more in some instances. This is perhaps becoming common due to translations from foreign languages, as in the following:

مَكْتَبَةٌ وَمُخْتَبَرَاتُ الجامعةِ

the library and laboratories of the university

مُوَظَّفو وَأَساتِذَةُ وَطُلاّبُ الجامعةِ

the employees, professors and students of the university

Traditional Arabic grammar does not sanction such structures. The preceding two *IDhaafa* structures are expressed, according to traditional grammar rules, in the following fashion:

مَكْتَبَةُ الجامعةِ وَمُخْتَبَرَاتُها

the university library and its laboratories

مُوَظَّفو الجامعةِ وَأَساتِذَتُها وَطُلاّبُها

the university employees, its professors and students

8.5 ADJECTIVE *IDHAAFA* (QUASI- OR PSEUDO-*IDHAAFA*) الإضافةُ غَيْرُ الحقيقِيَّة

The preceding examples of the *IDhaafa*-construct are formed by two or more nouns. It is possible to form a type of *IDhaafa* by having a masculine or feminine adjective in the position of the first noun of an *IDhaafa*-construct, as in, for example: طَيِّبَةُ القَلْبِ / طَيِّبُ القَلْبِ "good-hearted."

1. The case of the adjective can vary depending on its function in the sentence. The noun in the second position in this *IDhaafa*-construct must be definite. Examine the three sentences below:

وَصَلَت جَميلَةُ الوَجهِ.
The beautiful-faced [woman] arrived.

قابَلْتُ أَمسِ جَميلَةَ الوَجهِ.
I met the beautiful-faced [woman] yesterday.

حَضَرَ مَعَ جَميلةِ الوَجهِ.
He came with the beautiful-faced [woman].

2. The adjective *IDhaafa*-construct can function as an adjective. If the antecedent noun is definite, the adjective must be definite, as in the following examples:

يُحِبُّ السَّيَّاراتِ اليابانِيَّةَ الصُّنْعِ.

He likes Japanese-made cars.

تُغْرَسُ في شَوارِعِ المَدِينَةِ الأَشْجارُ الدّائِمَةُ الخُضْرَةِ.

Evergreen trees are planted in the city streets.

On the other hand, if the antecedent is indefinite, the quasi-*IDhaafa* must begin with an indefinite adjective. Consider the following examples:

جاءَت امْرَأَةٌ جَمِيلَةُ الوَجهِ.

A woman with a beautiful face arrived.

أَلْقَت الشُّرْطَةُ القَبْضَ عَلى قاتِلٍ كَثِيرِ الإِجْرامِ.

The police arrested a perpetrator of many crimes.

8.6 MODIFICATION OF *IDHAAFA*

Both nouns of an *IDhaafa*-construct may be modified by demonstrative pronouns and regular adjectives.

1. Modification by demonstrative pronouns (see Chapter 5): Only a demonstrative pronoun can intervene between the first noun in *IDhaafa*-constructs and the second. In this case, the demonstrative modifies the second noun in this structure. The modification of the second noun forms a single unit called the demonstrative phrase. Examine the following examples:

كِتابُ هذِه الطّالِبَةِ   *lit.* "the book of this student (F)"

أُستاذَةُ هذا الطّالِبِ   *lit.* "the teacher (F) of this student (M)"

2. The first noun in *IDhaafa* can also be modified by a demonstrative pronoun.
    However, it must be placed at the end of the *IDhaafa*-construct, as in the
    following examples:

    كِتابُ الطّالِبَةِ هذا   this book of the student (F)

    أُستاذَةُ الطّالِبِ هذِهِ   this teacher (F) of the student (M)

3. Modifying an *IDhaafa* with regular adjectives:
    As the two nouns in the *IDhaafa*-construct can only be split apart by a
    demonstrative pronoun, regular adjectives must occur at the end of the
    construct, as in the following:

    كِتابُ الطّالِبِ الجَديدُ ضَخْمٌ.   The new book of the student is big.

    Note that الجَديدُ in the preceding example carries the nominative marker
    functioning as modification of كِتابُ. Since كِتابُ is definite by virtue of the
    definite noun الطّالِبِ the adjective for this noun must also be definite. To
    illustrate how important the case is in Arabic, compare the following examples:

    كِتابُ الطّالِبِ الجَديدُ ضَخْمٌ.   The new book of the student is big.

    كِتابُ الطّالِبِ الجَديدِ ضَخْمٌ.   The book of the new student is big.

    It goes without saying that in spoken Arabic, the context plays a major role
    in eliminating ambiguity. Usually, interlocutors are aware of what they are
    talking about, and what adjectives go with what nouns. If interlocutors are
    not clear, clarification is requested. In written Arabic, however, the marking
    of case can remove ambiguity and facilitate communication.

4. Suffixal possessive pronouns may attach to the second noun in an *IDhaafa*-
    construct. Consider the following examples:

    هذا كِتابُ طالِبي.   This is my student's book.

    هذا كِتابُ طالِبِكَ.   This is your (M) student's book.

    Any adjective modifying كِتاب in the preceding examples must occur at the
    end of the *IDhaafa*-construct. In this case, the adjective must be in the

nominative case to agree with the noun it is modifying, as in the following example:

هذا كِتابُ طالبي الجَديدُ. This is my student's new book.

Any adjective modifying طالِبي must be in the genitive case and also definite, as in the following:

هذا كِتابُ طالِبي الجَديدِ. *lit.* "This is the book of my new student."

8.7 ـل CONSTRUCT FOR CLARIFICATION OF *IDHAAFA* ELEMENTS

An *IDhaafa* may consist of multiple nouns. As was mentioned, the placement of regular adjectives in any *IDhaafa* is restricted to the end of the construct. Sorting out which adjective applies to which noun can constrain processing of information as well as result in syntactically awkward structures. The solution to this grammatical clutter is to separate the nouns and their modifiers with the use of ـل. The following sentence in which the two nouns forming *IDhaafa* are modified by two sequential adjectives verges on unacceptability:

هذا كِتابُ الأُستاذِ العَرَبيُّ الجَديدِ
*This is the Arabic book of the new teacher.

Instead of stacking adjectives sequentially, as above, the language provides an alternative, simpler structure. The possessive preposition ـل "for, of, belonging to," is used to convey the function of *IDhaafa*. A simpler, more common structure of the above sentence is expressed as follows:

هذا الكِتابُ العَرَبيُّ للأُستاذِ الجَديدِ.
lit. "This Arabic book is for [belongs to] the new professor."

8.7.1 Multiple noun *IDhaafa* and ـل construct

In theory, the number of nouns in this construct can be large. However, real language usage dictates that only a small number of nouns can be sequentially allowed in *IDhaafa*. For example, the following four-noun string is easy to process, and, therefore, an acceptable utterance:

هذا هُوَ كِتابُ أُستاذِ جامِعَةِ القاهِرَة.

        4   3   2   1

lit. "This is the book of the professor of the University of Cairo."

Similarly, the following five-noun *IDhaafa* string is acceptable, and the information can be processed relatively easily:

هذا هُوَ عُنْوانُ كِتابِ أُستاذِ جامِعَةِ القاهِرَة.

     5   4   3   2   1

lit. "This is the title of the book of the professor of the
University of Cairo."

If one continues expanding the string of nouns forming the *IDhaafa*-construct as in the previous examples, the processing of information eventually becomes constrained. It follows, therefore, that the major criterion for determining the number of nouns forming *IDhaafa* is the ability to process information with some facility.

Another factor that determines the number of nouns in *IDhaafa* is the placement of adjectives modifying the nouns in the construct. Examine the following:

هذا هُوَ عُنْوانُ كِتابِ أُستاذِ جامِعَةِ القاهِرَةِ الجَديدُ.

lit. "This is the new title of the book of the professor of the
University of Cairo."

الجَديدُ "the new" in the preceding sentence modifies عُنْوانُ "the title," as can be determined by the nominative case marker of both the noun and adjective, despite the rather extensive separation between the two elements. As adjectives tend to be placed in closer proximity to the nouns they modify, لِـ provides a simpler alternative to cumbersome an *IDhaafa*-constructs. The above sentence can be expressed more elegantly and more easily as follows:

هذا هُوَ العُنْوانُ الجَديدُ لِكِتابِ أُستاذِ جامِعَةِ القاهِرَة.

lit. "This is the new title of the book of the professor of the
University of Cairo."

Thus, the use of the لِ construct becomes more expedient when more than one adjective is used to modify more than one noun in an *IDhaafa*-construct. Examine the following example:

هذا هُوَ العُنْوانُ الجَديدُ لِكِتابِ أُستاذِ جامِعَةِ القاهِرَةِ الجَديد.

This is the new title of the new book of the professor of the
  University of Cairo.

The adjective الجَديد in the *IDhaafa* component لِكِتابِ أُستاذِ جامِعَةِ القاهِرَةِ الجَديد. is ambiguous. The masculine adjective الجَديد "[the] new," in the genitive case, could, in fact, modify either كِتاب "book" or أُسْتاذ "professor," as both masculine nouns are in the genitive case. However, interlocutors involved in such a discourse know whether the discussion is about "the new book" or "the new professor." In other words, the pragmatics of the discourse eliminate such ambiguity.

8.8 USE OF مِنْ INSTEAD OF لِ

In some instances, the preposition مِن "from, of" is used instead of لِ. Examine the following examples:

أَصْدَرَتِ الشَّرِكَةُ الجيلَ الجَديدَ مِنْ سَيّاراتِ تويوتا.

The company produced the new model of Toyota cars.

أَعْلَنَتِ الحُكومَةُ القَراراتِ الرَّسْمِيَّةَ مِنَ القَراراتِ المُتَعَلِّقَةِ بِحُقوقِ العُمّالِ الوافِدينَ.

The government issued the official regulations pertaining to the
  rights of migrant laborers.

8.9 THE NEGATIVE NOUN غَير

The negative noun غَيْرُ can be used in forming *IDhaafa*-constructs to produce the meaning of "non-," "not," or "without." غَيْرُ remains invariable with respect to gender. Its case can vary depending on its function. It can be followed by a noun, pronoun, *'ism faaʿil* "active participle," *'ism mafʿuul* "passive participle," or adjective. Additionally, it can be preceded by a preposition, thus causing it to be put into the genitive case. Consider the following:

غَيْرُ الطُّلّابِ	non-students	غَيْرُ مَفْهومٍ	unintelligible
غَيْرُ قادِمٍ	not coming, arriving	غَيْرُ مَعْقولٍ	unreasonable
غَيْرُ مَدْروسٍ	unstudied, un-researched	غَيْرُهُم	other than them
غَيْرُ قَديمٍ	not old	مِنْ غَيْرِنا	without us
غَيْرُ صَحيحٍ	untrue		

8.9.1 غَيْر with nouns

The noun following غَيْر must always be in the genitive. Examine the following examples:

وَفَدَ الطُّلّابُ وَغَيْرُ الطُّلّابِ إلى الـمَدينةِ.

Students and non-students flocked to the city.

يَأْكُلونَ الجُبْنَةَ وَغَيْرَ الجُبْنَةِ.

They eat cheese and [foods] other than cheese.

يَنْتَقِلُ الـحُجّاجُ بِالسَّيّاراتِ وَغَيْرِ السَّيّاراتِ.

The pilgrims travel in cars and other means of transportation.

Note that غَيْرُ in the preceding examples agrees with the case of the noun to which it is conjoined.

8.9.2 غَيْرُ with pronouns

The nouns following غَيْر in the preceding section can be replaced by the appropriate pronoun to produce the meaning of "other than," as in the following:

وَفَدَ الطُّلّابُ وَغَيْرُهُم إلى الـمَدينةِ.

Students and others [other than them] flocked to the city.

يَأْكُلونَ الجُبْنَةَ وَغَيْرَها.

They eat cheese and other [food items].

يَنْتَقِلُ الـحُجّاجُ بِالسَّيّاراتِ وَغَيْرِها.

Pilgrims travel in cars and by other [means of transportation].

8.9.3 غَيْر with adjectives

غَيْر can function as a negative particle of adjectives to produce the meaning of "not" or "un-." As a first term in an *IDhaafa*-construct, the adjective following it must always be in the genitive case. Examine the following examples:

غَيْرُ بَعِيدٍ   not far

غَيْرُ صَعْبَةٍ   not difficult

غَيْرُ أَمرِيكِيٍّ   un-American

The preceding can also be expressed by the use of لَيْسَ, conveying the same meaning:

لَيْسَ بَعيداً

لَيْسَ صَعْباً

لَيْسَ أَمرِيكِيّاً

The following sentences illustrate غَيْرُ with adjectives:

المَطْعَمُ غَيْرُ بَعيدٍ مِنْ هُنا.
The restaurant is not far from here.

يَقولُ هذا الرَّجُلُ قَوْلاً غَيْرَ حَكيمٍ.
This man says an unwise thing.

ناقَشَ الوَزيرُ المَسائِلَ الصَّعْبَةَ وَغَيْرَ الصَّعْبَةِ.
The minister discussed the difficult and not difficult issues.

Note that in the first sentence the phrase beginning with غَيْر is in the nominative, functioning as the predicate of the sentence. In the second sentence, the phrase beginning with غَيْر is an adjective of the direct object قَوْلاً, which explains why غَيْر is in the accusative. غَيْر in the third sentence is conjoined to the direct object and its adjective المَسائِلَ الصَّعْبَةَ, which explains why غَيْر is in the accusative case.

8.9.4 غَير after prepositions

غَير can attach to a preposition such as بِ or be preceded by مِن, conveying the meaning of "without," or "other than," as in the following:

يَشْرَبُ القَهْوَةَ مِنْ غَيْرِ سُكَّرٍ.

He drinks coffee without sugar.

واجَهَ خُصومَهُ بِغَيْرِ أفكارِهِم.

He faced his adversaries with ideas other than theirs.

8.9.5 غَير with the definite article

غَير can support the prefixing of the definite article الـ in limited usages. This is frowned upon by purists who consider this structure ungrammatical. One may, however, encounter examples like the following in the press, or other media:

يُفَضِّلُ الغَيْرَ عَلى نَفْسِه.

He places others before himself.

تُسَبِّبُ الضَّوْضاءُ الإِزْعاجَ لِلْغَيْرِ.

Loud noise causes disturbance to others.

8.9.6 لَيْسَ غَيْرُ and لا غَيْرُ

Thus far, غَير has been shown to behave as a declinable noun showing three cases: the nominative, accusative and genitive. غَيْرُ can be preceded by the negative particles لا or لَيْسَ to function as an adverb in the sense of "only." In this case, it must always be in the nominative, as in the following examples:

أَشْرَبُ القَهْوَةَ لا غَيْرُ.

I only drink coffee.

أُريدُ فَقَط هذا الكِتابَ لَيْسَ غَيْرُ.

I want only this book, not any other.

8.10 *IDHAAFA* USING ELEMENTS OTHER THAN غَير

Finally, we should add that there are elements other than غَير which are used in forming *IDhaafa*-constructs. سِوى, synonymous to غَير for example, functions in the same way as غَير in making *IDhaafa*-constructs. Discussion of these two elements will be detailed in Chapter 34. Furthermore, the quantifiers كُلّ "all of," بَعْض "some of," جَميع "all of," مُعْظَم "most of," and كِلا and كِلْتا "both of" are also used to form *IDhaafa*s. Discussion of these quantifiers is presented in some detail in Chapter 31.

CHAPTER 9

The equational sentence
الجُمْلَة الاِسْمِيَّة

The equational sentence الجُمْلَة الاِسْمِيَّة is a basic sentence structure in Arabic and expresses propositions in the present tense. Young children first learn such utterances when speaking stretches longer than a single word. It is not surprising, therefore, that learners of Arabic as a foreign language are introduced to this structure first.

The basic equational sentence in Arabic consists of two components: *mubtada'* مُبْتَدَأ "subject," often placed at the beginning of the sentence, and *khabar* خَبَر "predicate," the element that states something about the subject. Both the subject and predicate are governed by rules to maintain sentence acceptability.

Unlike English or other European languages, equational sentences in Arabic are constructed without the verb "to be" in the *present* tense. The absence of the verb "to be" is not unique to Arabic, however; other languages, such as Russian and Hebrew share this feature as well. We present below several patterns in which the equational sentence is constructed:

9.1 PERSONAL PRONOUNS AS SUBJECTS

Personal pronouns can act as subjects of equational sentences with proper nouns, common nouns, adjectives and prepositional phrases as their predicates. (See Chapter 5 for discussion of personal pronouns.)

9.1.1 Personal pronouns (as subjects) + proper nouns (as predicates)

· **Singular:**

أَنا أَحْمَد. I am Ahmad.   هِيَ مَرْيَم. She is Maryam.

أَنْتِ لَيْلى. You are Leila.

Dual:

نَحْنُ أَحْمَد وَلَيْلَى.   We are Ahmad and Leila.

هُما سَميرَة وَسَليم.   They are Samira and Salim.

هُما فاطِمَة وسامي.   They are Fatima and Sami.

Plural:

أَنْتُنَّ هِنْد وَسَلْمَى وَلَيْلَى.   You are Hind, Salma and Leila.

هُم خالِدْ وَعامِر وفُؤَاد.   They are Khaled, Aamir and Fuoad.

هُم علي وسَلمى ومَرْيَم.   They are Ali, Salma and Maryam.

هُنَّ فاطِمَة وَيُسْرَى وَسِهام.   They are Fatima, Yusra and Siham.

9.1.2 Personal pronouns + common nouns

The predicate must agree with the subject pronoun in gender and number. The predicate noun must be indefinite, hence the two *Dhamma*s at its end.

Singular:

أَنا طالِبٌ.   I am a student.

هُوَ أُسْتاذٌ.   He is a teacher.

هِيَ مُعَلِّمَةٌ.   She is a teacher.

Dual:

Predicate nouns of sentences containing dual pronouns (or nouns) as subjects must be dual, indefinite and nominative, and must agree with the subject in gender.

أَنْتُما مُعَلِّمَتان.   You are teachers (F).

هُما طالِبَتان.   They are students (F).

هُما مُعَلِّمان.   They are teachers (M).

نَحْنُ مُوَظَّفان.   We (D, M) are employees.

Plural:

Predicate nouns of sentences containing plural pronouns or nouns as subjects must be plural, indefinite and nominative. Predicate nouns must also agree with the subject in gender.

نَحْنُ طُلاّبٌ.   We are students.

هُنَّ مُعَلِّماتٌ.   They (F) are teachers.

9.1.3 Personal pronouns + adjectives

Adjective predicates must be nominative. In addition, they must agree with the subject in number and gender, as in the following:

Singular:

هُوَ جَديدٌ.   He is new.

هِيَ مَشْهورَةٌ.   She is famous.

Dual:

هُما جَميلَتانِ.   They (F) are beautiful.

هُما مَشْهورانِ.   They (M) are famous.

هَلْ أَنْتُما مَغْرِبيّانِ؟   Are you (M) Moroccan?

Plural:

هُمْ أَمريكيّونَ.   They (M) are Americans.

أَنْتُمْ مُسْتَعِدّونَ.   You (M) are ready.

هُنَّ كَريماتٌ.   They (F) are generous.

9.1.4 Proper nouns or personal pronouns + prepositional phrases or adverbs

Nouns following prepositions end with one *kasra* if they are definite, and with two *kasra*s if they are indefinite. Proper nouns like واشِنْطُن "Washington" are not marked for case.

Singular:

أَنا في البَيْتِ.   I am in the house.

هِي في الجامِعَةِ.   She is at the university.

سَعيد في البَيْتِ.   Said is in the house.

Dual:

هُما مِن واشِنْطُن.   They are from Washington.

هُما في مَطْعَم.   They are in a restaurant.

هَلْ أَنْتُما في البَيْتِ؟   Are you at home?

سَليم وسَلْمى في المَدْرَسَةِ.   Salim and Salma are at school.

هِنْد وَلَيْلى في القاهِرَة.   Hind and Leila are in Cairo.

أَنا وحُسَين مِنْ سوريا.   Hussein and I are from Syria.

Plural:

هُم مَعَ المُدير.

They (M) are with the director.

هُنَّ في مَطْعَم.

They (F) are in a restaurant.

سَلْمى وَشَريفَة وَأَحْمَد في الشَّرِكاتِ.

Salma, Sharifa and Ahmad are at the companies.

مَرْيَمْ وَهالَة وَسَحَر أَمامَ الصَّفِّ.

Maryam, Hala and Sahar are at the front of the classroom.

9.2 DEMONSTRATIVE PRONOUNS

Demonstrative pronouns can function both as subjects of equational sentences and as modifiers of nouns in the subject position. (See Chapter 5 for a discussion of demonstrative pronouns.) They can also follow prepositions, as in وَمِثالٌ على هذا "and an example of this," وَمِثالٌ على ذلِكَ "and an example of that," etc.

9.2.1 Demonstrative pronouns + proper nouns

In Modern Standard Arabic, proper nouns in the predicate position, as well as in the subject position, are often used without the nominative case marker.

Singular:

هذا مَحْمود.   This is Mahmoud.

هذِهِ سَميرَة.   This is Samira.

Dual:

هذانِ أَحْمَد وَمَحْمود.   These are Ahmad and Mahmoud.

هاتانِ فِرْدَوْس وَسُوزان.   These are Firdaws and Suzanne.

Plural:

أُولئِكَ لَيْلى وَسامِيَة وَهادِيَة.   Those are Leila, Samia and Hadia.

هؤُلاءِ عَدْنان وَلَيْلى وَزَيْنَب.   These are Adnan, Leila and Zainab.

9.2.2 Demonstrative pronouns with common nouns as predicates

When the subjects of equational sentences are demonstrative pronouns, the predicate must be indefinite and agree in gender and number, as in the following examples:

Singular:

هذِهِ أُسْتاذَةٌ.   This (F) is a teacher (F).

هذا كِتابٌ.   This (M) is a book (M).

Dual:

هذان طالِبان.   These (M) are students.

هاتان مُعَلِّمَتان.   These (F) are teachers.

Plural:

هؤُلاءِ مُدَرِّسونَ.   These are teachers (M).

اولئكَ مُوَظَّفاتٌ.   Those are employees (F).

9.2.3 Demonstrative pronouns modifying subjects of equational sentences

If the noun following the demonstrative is definite, the construct is not a sentence. Thus هذا الكتابُ is equivalent to "this book" in English. To turn such a structure into a sentence, a third person pronoun must be inserted between the subject and the definite noun to form a predicate and an equational sentence. This intervening pronoun, known in Arabic as ضَمير الفَصْل "the pronoun of separation," must agree with the demonstrative subject in number and gender. Compare the following pairs in which the first is a phrase, the second a sentence:

Singular:

هذا الطّالبُ   this student (M)

هذا هُوَ الطّالبُ.   This is the student (M).

هذه الجَريدَةُ   this newspaper

هذه هِيَ الجَريدَةُ.   This is the newspaper (F).

Dual:

هاتان البِنْتان   these girls

هاتان هُما البِنْتانِ.   These are the girls.

Plural:

هؤُلاءِ المُعَلِّمونَ   these teachers

هؤُلاءِ هُمُ المُعَلِّمونَ.   These are the teachers (M).

9.3 COMMON NOUNS AS SUBJECTS

A common noun beginning equational sentences in Arabic must be definite, by having either a definite article الـ, a possessive pronoun suffix such as ي "my," ها "her," for example, or the first noun of an *IDhaafa*-construct whose terminal noun is definite, as in مُديرُ الشَّرِكَةِ "the company's manager." (See Chapter 2 for a discussion of determination of nouns.) Consider the following examples:

الكِتابُ عَلى الطاوِلَةِ.   The book is on the table.

كِتابي عَلى الطاوِلَةِ.   My book is on the table.

كِتابُ المُعَلِّم عَلى الطاوِلَةِ.   The teacher's book is on the table.

9.3.1 Common nouns + prepositional phrases or adverbs

Singular:

الأُسْتاذُ في البَيْتِ.   The teacher (M) is in the house.

الطالِبُ في الصَّفِّ.   The student (M) is in the classroom.

Dual:

الطَّالِبانِ مِنَ المَغْرِب.   The students (M) are from Morocco.

الكُرْسِيّانِ أمامَ الصَّفِّ.   The chairs (M) are at the front of the classroom.

المَدينَتانِ في مِصر.   The cities (F) are in Egypt.

Plural:

الطُّلّابُ في الصُّفوفِ.   The students (M/F) are in the classrooms.

الـمُوَظَّفونَ في مَكاتِبِهم.   The employees (M/F) are in their offices.

المُعَلِّمونَ خارِجَ الصَّفّ.   The teachers (M/F) are outside the classroom.

9.3.2 Common nouns + adjectives

Regardless of the number of the subject, the predicate adjective must be in the nominative, indefinite, and it must agree with the subject in gender and number.

Singular:

بَيْتُكِ جَمِيلٌ.   Your (F, Sg) house is beautiful.

سَيَّارَتُكَ جَمِيلَةٌ.   Your (M) car is beautiful.

Dual:

الصَّدِيقَتانِ جَمِيلَتانِ.   The two friends (F) are beautiful.

الكِتابانِ مُمْتِعانِ.   The two books (M) are enjoyable.

Plural:

Note that irregular plural nouns can be human or non-human. Adjectives used with human nouns must agree with the nouns they modify in number and gender. Furthermore, they must agree in case.

الـمُوَظَّفونَ نَشيطونَ.   The employees are energetic.

الطَّالِباتُ عِراقِيّاتٌ.   The students (F) are Iraqis.

Adjectives used with non-human plural nouns, on the other hand, must be in the feminine singular. Examine the following:

الكُتُبُ جَديدَةٌ.   The books are new.

الـمُدُنُ جَميلَةٌ.   The cities are beautiful.

Non-human plural nouns are treated grammatically in all facets of the language as feminine singular.

9.4 SUBJECT-PREDICATE INVERSION

Subjects usually occur at the beginning of equational sentences and are followed by their predicates. There are instances, however, when the subject and predicate of the equational sentence switch positions. This can be called either subject–predicate inversion or a fronted predicate. This condition occurs in two cases:

(a) When using the interrogative particles أَدَواتُ الاِسْتِفْهام at the beginning of the sentence, and

(b) when using prepositional or adverbial phrases at the beginning of the sentence.

9.4.1 Interrogative particles

Interrogative particles in Arabic occur at the beginnings of sentences, thus causing the inversion of subject and predicate. The inverted subject could be a personal pronoun, a demonstrative pronoun, or a proper noun. These possibilities are illustrated with the interrogative particle مَنْ "who" below:

مَنْ أَنْتَ؟	Who are you?
مَنْ هُوَ؟	Who is he?
مَنْ هُما؟	Who are they (M/F, D)?
مَنْ أَنْتُمْ؟	Who are you (M, Pl)?

Or:

A demonstrative pronoun, which remains unchanged, as in the following examples:

مَنْ ذلِكَ؟	Who is that (M)?
مَنْ تِلْكَ؟	Who is that (F)?
مَنْ هذانِ؟	Who are these (M, D)?
مَنْ هؤُلاءِ؟	Who are these (M/F, Pl)?

Or:

A nominative definite common noun. In the singular, the noun ends with one *Dhamma*. If the noun is in the dual, the noun ends with انِ. Regular masculine plural nouns end with ونَ-. Irregular plural nouns end with one *Dhamma*. Regular feminine plural nouns end with only one *Dhamma*.

Inverted subjects could be definite when prefixed by the definite article الـ or by a possessive pronoun, or by an *IDhaafa*-construct. Consider the following examples:

Singular:

مَنِ الأُسْتاذَةُ؟   Who is the teacher (F)?

مَنِ الطّالِبُ؟   Who is the student?

مَنْ صَديقُهُ؟   Who is his friend?

مَنْ مُديرُ المَكْتَبِ؟   Who is the office manager?

Dual:

مَنِ الـمُديرَتانِ؟   Who are the directors (F, D)?

مَنِ الصَّديقانِ؟   Who are the friends (M, D)?

Plural:

مَنِ الـمُوَظَّفونَ؟   Who are the employees (M, Pl)?

مَنِ الـمُوَظَّفاتُ؟   Who are the employees (F, Pl)?

Note that the definite article in the non-initial position loses the *hamza* sound, thus creating the possibility of having three consonants in a row. To avoid this possibility, a *kasra* is inserted at the end of مَنْ in the previous examples that begin with the definite article الـ.

9.4.1.1 ما *"What?"*

This particle is commonly used with the demonstrative pronouns هذا، هذِهِ، ذلِكَ، or تِلْكَ. Unlike مَنْ mentioned above, ما generally solicits information about non-human entities, as in the following examples:

ما هذا؟   What is this?

ما هذِهِ؟   What is this/are those?

ما هذانِ؟   What are those (M, D)?

Since ما has a definitional function, the predicates of sentences in answers to questions having ما tend to be indefinite. Note again that the use of ما, unlike مَن, is restricted to non-human entities. As a reminder, non-human plural entities are treated as feminine singular nouns. In answer to the second question, هذه can conceivably refer to "books," "tables," or some other non-human plural noun, as in the following:

ما هذِهِ الكُتُبُ؟   What are these books?

9.4.1.2 أَيْنَ "Where?"

This particle inquires about the location of an entity, a person or a thing. Examine the following sentences:

أَيْنَ هُوَ؟   Where is he?

أَيْنَ الطالِبُ؟   Where is the student?

أَيْنَ هُما؟   Where are they (M/F, D)?

أَيْنَ هُنَّ؟   Where are they (F, Pl)?

أَيْنَ الـمُعَلِّمونَ؟   Where are the teachers (M, Pl)?

Predicates in answers to such questions must be prepositional phrases comprising a preposition indicating location or place, followed by a noun. The following prepositions في "in" and عَلى "on" indicate location. There are adverbs like أمامَ "in front of," بجانب "to the side of," and a few others that can answer questions with أَيْنَ. Note that nouns following prepositions or adverbs must end with one *kasra* if the noun is definite, or with two *kasras* if it is indefinite.

9.4.1.3 مِنْ أَيْنَ "Where from?" or "from where?"

In an equational sentence this particle inquires about where the person or entity in question is from. The inverted subject in this case can be a pronoun, a proper noun, or a common noun, as in the following examples:

مِنْ أَيْنَ هُوَ؟   Where is he from?

مِنْ أَيْنَ سُلَيْمان؟   Where is Sulaiman from?

مِنْ أَيْنَ الأُسْتاذُ؟ Where is the teacher from?

مِنْ أَيْنَ هُما؟ Where are they (M/F, D) from?

مِنْ أَيْنَ هؤُلاءِ؟ Where are these (M/F, Pl) from?

Note that the common noun in the third sentence is in the definite and nominative. An indefinite noun would result in an ungrammatical sentence. The reason for this is perhaps that the entity in question is known to both interlocutors. We should also mention that as a question word, مِنْ أَيْنَ can also be used with verbs, as in, for example:

مِنْ أَيْنَ حَصلوا عَلى المالِ؟ Where did they get the money from?

Answers to questions with مِنْ أَيْنَ must always have مِنْ, in addition to a place or location, as in the following:

مِنْ أَيْنَ أَنْتَ؟ Where are you from?

أَنا مِن سوريا. I'm from Syria.

9.4.1.4 كَيْفَ *"How?"*

This particle solicits information about a condition, or how someone or something is. It can be followed by a proper noun or a common noun. If the noun following كَيْفَ is a common noun, it must be both definite and nominative, as in the following examples:

كَيْفَ مَرْيَـم؟ How is Maryam?

كَيْفَ الحالُ؟ How are you? (*lit.* "How is the condition?")

كَيْفَ الطَّقْسُ؟ How is the weather?

كَيْفَ الطُّلاّبُ؟ How are the students?

كَيْفَ can also be followed by an independent pronoun, as in the following:

كَيْفَ هِيَ؟ How is she?

كَيْفَ أنتِ؟ How are you (F)?

كَيْفَ هُمْ؟ How are they (M, Pl)?

As with مِنْ أَيْنَ above, كَيْفَ can also be followed by verbs as in the following examples:

كَيْفَ وَصَلْتَ إلى هُنا؟   How did you arrive here?

كَيْفَ حَصَلْتَ عَلى هذا الكِتابِ؟   How did you obtain this book?

9.4.2 Prepositional or adverbial phrases

Subject–predicate inversion also occurs when using prepositional or adverbial phrases indicating location, possession, or ownership. The subject must be indefinite and nominative. Examine the following example:

في السَّيّارَةِ حَقيبةٌ.   There is a bag in the car.

Note that subjects of equational sentences in initial position must always start with a known entity, i.e., definite. Contrast the preceding sentence in which the subject is in the indefinite with the following, where the subject is definite:

الحَقيبَةُ في السَّيّارَةِ.   The bag is in the car.

9.4.2.1 Prepositional phrases جارٌّ وَمَجْرورٌ

1. The prepositions في "in" and عَلى "on" indicate location, as in the following examples:

    عَلى الطّاولَةِ وَرَقةٌ.   There is a paper on the table.

    في البَيْتِ كِتابٌ.   There is a book in the house.

    في المُدُنِ مَكْتَباتٌ.   There are libraries (bookshops) in cities.

    في البَيْتَيْنِ سَيّارَتانِ.   There are cars (D) in the houses (D).

2. لِ indicates possession in the sense of "for" or "to," and attaches to suffix pronouns only, as in the following example:

    لَنا مُدَرِّساتٌ مَشْهوراتٌ.   We have famous instructors (F, Pl).

This preposition also has the variant ـِل which attaches to proper or common nouns, as in the following:

لِعَلِي بَيْتٌ.	Ali has a house.
لِلطّالِبَيْنِ صَديقانِ.	The students (M, D) have friends (M, D).

3. The preposition مَعَ "with" indicates possession, and also accompaniment. Examine the following example:

مَعي كِتابٌ.	I have a book. (*lit.* "A book is with me.")
مَعي أَصْدِقاءُ في البَيْتِ.	I have friends in the house.
مَعي جَريدَتانِ.	I have two newspapers.

9.4.2.2 Adverbial phrases الظروف

Arab grammarians classify a group of words indicating location as ظُروف مَكان "adverbs of place." This group includes أَمامَ "in front of," وَراءَ "behind, at the back of," خَلْفَ "behind, at the back of," بِجانِب "beside, to the side of," عِنْدَ "at, with," فَوْقَ "over," تَحْتَ "under," etc.

Nouns following prepositions or ظُروف "adverbs" must be in the genitive case, as in the following examples:

أَمامَ البَيْتِ مَكْتَبَةٌ.	There is a bookstore/library in front of the house.
عِنْدَ الأَسْتاذِ كِتابٌ.	The professor has a book.
خَلْفَ الـمَكْتَبَةِ بِناءٌ كَبيرٌ.	There is a big building behind the library.

9.5 MODIFYING SUBJECTS AND PREDICATES الصِّفات

When the subject of the equational sentence is a common noun, it is possible to provide additional information about this noun. This can be done in several ways. In this section, we shall discuss only two of these: adjectives and prepositions.

9.5.1 Modifying subjects by adjectives

Adjectives add extra information in the form of epithets, attributes or descriptions. This process is subject to several restrictions. Adjectives modifying subject nouns must be definite and nominative. In addition, they must agree with nouns in gender and number. If the subject is feminine, the adjective must also be feminine, and *vice versa*. Examine the following sentences:

الطالِبُ الجَديدُ في البَيْتِ.

The new student (M) is in the house.

الأُستاذَةُ الجَميلَةُ مِنَ العِراق.

The beautiful teacher (F) is from Iraq.

الطّالِبَتان الطّويلَتان مِنْ أمريكا.

The tall students (F, D) are from America.

المُدَرِّسونَ المَشهورونَ حَصلوا عَلى جائِزَةٍ.

The famous instructors (M, Pl) won a prize.

Note that the adjectives in the above examples agree with their subjects in determination (definiteness/indefiniteness), case (nominative), number and gender.

If the subject is a non-human plural, the adjective must be feminine singular, as in the following example. (See Chapter 2, section 2.1 for discussion of non-human plurals.)

السَّيّاراتُ الجَديدَةُ وَصَلَت أَمْسِ.   The new cars arrived yesterday.

A legitimate question can be raised: how many adjectives can be combined to modify a particular noun? The answer to this question is not clear-cut. In theory, there is no limit to the number. However, if too many adjectives are stacked up it presents processing problems to the reader or listener. Generally, it would be safe to state that two to three consecutive adjectives following a noun will be tolerated, as in the following examples:

الأُستاذَةُ الجَميلَةُ الطويلَةُ مِن المَغرِبِ.
2   1

The tall, beautiful teacher is from Morocco.

الطالِبُ الأَمْريكيُّ الجَديدُ مِنْ كاليفورنيا.
2   1

The new American student is from California.

الطّالِبُ الأَمريكِيُّ الجَديدُ الطّويلُ مِن كاليفورنيا.
3   2   1

The tall, new American student is from California.

If more than two or three adjectives are used, there is a tendency to conjoin adjectives by the conjunctive particle و. Examine the example below:

الطالبُ الأَمريكيُّ الجَديدُ والجَميلُ مِن كاليفورنيا.

The new, handsome American student is from California.

(Note that و attaches to the word following it in the writing system.)

Nouns with possessive pronoun suffixes are definite by virtue of the possessive suffixes attached to them. Adjectives modifying such subjects must be definite and also nominative. Examine the following examples:

كِتابي الجَديدُ عَلى الطّاولةِ. My new book is on the table.

سَيّارَتُها الجَديدَةُ في البَيتِ. Her new car is at home.

9.5.2 Modifying predicates by adjectives

Nouns functioning as predicates of equational sentences can also be modified by adjectives or prepositional/adverbial phrases. Recall that adjectives must exactly mirror the noun in four features: determination; number; case; and gender.

The conditions of subject modification illustrated in the previous section can be generalized to apply to predicate modification. In other words, the number of adjectives used to modify a predicate noun should be limited. If more adjectives are used, the conjoining particle و will be used to conjoin these adjectives, as in the following examples:

روبَرْت طالِبٌ أَمْريكيٌّ جَديدٌ ومُمْتازٌ.
Robert is a new and excellent American student.

هذِهِ طالِبَةٌ أَمْريكيَّةٌ جَديدَةٌ وجَميلَةٌ.
This is a new, beautiful American student (F).

هذانِ كِتابانِ جَديدانِ مُمْتِعانِ.
These are new, interesting books (D).

هؤُلاءِ مُدَرِّساتٌ مِصْريّاتٌ مَشْهوراتٌ ومُدَرَّباتٌ في أَمريكا.
These are famous Egyptian teachers (F, Pl) and well-trained in
America.

Nouns with possessive pronoun suffixes functioning as predicates can also be modified by adjectives. Since these nouns are definite by virtue of the possessive suffixes attached to them, adjectives modifying such predicates must also be definite. Examine the following examples:

هذا كِتابِي الجَديدُ.　　This is my new book.

هذِهِ سَيّارَتُها القَديمَةُ.　　This is her old car.

الآنِسَةُ بْراوْن مُديرَتُنا الجَديدَةُ.　　Miss Brown is our new director.

Note that the adjectives in the above sentences are definite because the nouns they modify are definite by virtue of the possessive pronouns attached to the predicate nouns. Also, note that the adjectives in these sentences are in the nominative because of the case of the nouns they modify.

9.6 هَل

هَل is used to solicit confirmation about the truth value of the proposition in question, i.e. whether the information in the sentence is true or not.

Technically, هَل is not like the preceding interrogative particles. It does not cause the inversion of subject and predicate. Sentences containing هَل maintain their normal order, i.e., the subject initiates the sentence and the predicate occupies the second position. The placement of هَل must be directly in front of the subject. Examine the following examples:

هَل هُوَ طالِبٌ؟　　Is he a student?

هَل هُمْ أَمْريكِيّونَ؟　　Are they (M, Pl) Americans?

هَل أَنْـتُـنَّ طالِباتٌ؟　　Are you (F, Pl) students?

The questions in these examples require either a نَعَم "yes" or لا "no" response.

9.7 CATEGORICAL NEGATION لا النّافِيَة لِلجِنْس

لا negates the existence of entities in absolute terms. It is followed by indefinite nouns or *maSdar*s in the accusative without *tanwiin*. In equational sentences, the predicate, noun or adjective, must be in the nominative, as in the following:

لا طالبَ نائمٌ. No student is asleep.

If a regular feminine plural noun follows لا, a *kasra* terminates the noun, as in the following:

لا مُعَلِّماتٍ حَضَرْنَ اليَوْمَ. No teachers came today.

Some grammarians tolerate the use of a *fat-Ha* to terminate a regular feminine plural. The preceding sentences can appear as follows:

لا مُعَلِّماتَ حَضَرْنَ اليَوْمَ. No teachers came today.

لا سَيّاراتَ في الشَّوارِعِ. There are no cars on the streets.

This negative particle forms certain sentential expressions commonly used in discourse, as in the following:

لا بَأْسَ عَلَيْكَ! No harm will befall you.

لا حَوْلَ ولا قُوَّةَ إلاّ بِاللهِ! There is no power or might save in God.

لا شَكَّ في ذَلِكَ. There is no doubt in that.

Expressions such as the following are used to introduce sentences, as illustrated below:

لا بُدَّ مِن It is absolutely necessary that

لا غَرْوَ أَنَّ There is no wondering that

لا بُدَّ مِن العَمَلِ الجادّ! Serious work is necessary!

لا غَرْوَ أَنَّ الحَرْبَ سَبَّبَت خَسائِرَ في الأرْواحِ. There is no question that the war caused the loss of many lives.

Equational sentences are negated by the use of the negative particle لَيْسَ, which will be discussed in detail in Chapter 10.

Kaana and its sisters كَانَ وَأَخَواتُها

There is a small group of verbs in Arabic that are used with equational sentences to express meanings related to being, becoming or their negation. Traditional Arabic grammarians labeled this group أَفْعال ناقِصَة "incomplete or defective verbs," primarily because of their form. Their use is restricted to certain domains. A commonly used member of this group is the verb كانَ "to be," which is employed in equational sentences to state a proposition in the past tense. It can also be used to form the future tense. Arab grammmarians call these verbs كانَ وَأَخَواتُها "*kaana* and its sisters." The name assigned to this group as sisters is premised on the identical behavior that these verbs exhibit when used in equational/nominal sentences. The most striking grammatical feature of كانَ and its sisters is that they turn common nouns and adjectives functioning as predicates into the accusative case. كانَ is used with verbs in the present tense to express an action that happened at a point of time in the past (see Chapter 18 on past continuous).

In the following list, we present these verbs in the past and present tenses for the third person singular pronoun هُوَ. Out of the list, all but لَيْسَ exhibit a present tense form:

كانَ / يَكونُ	to be	أَمْسى / يُـمْسي	to become
لَيْسَ	is not	باتَ / يَبيتُ	to become
صارَ / يَصيرُ	to become	ما زالَ / لا يَزالُ	to remain, still is
أَصْبَحَ / يُصْبِحُ	to become	ظَلَّ / يَظَلُّ	to remain
أَضْحى / يُضْحي	to become		

We should note that some of these verbs etymologically pertain to different times of day. For example, أَصْبَحَ / يُصْبِحُ "to become" pertains to صَباح "morning;"

أَضْحى / يُضْحي / أَمْسى / يُـمْسي "to become" pertains to مَساء "evening," يُضْحي / أَضْحى "to become" pertains to ضُحى "mid-morning, before noon" and بات / يَبيتُ "to remain" pertains to sleeping overnight, overnighting.

Furthermore, some of these verbs share the same meaning although they are derived from different roots. For example, أَصْبَحَ / يُصْبِحُ and صارَ / يَصيرُ and, in addition to أَمْسى / يُـمْسي, all mean "to become."

The frequency with which these verbs are used varies. For example, أَمْسى / يُـمْسي and صارَ / يَصيرَ and أَصْبَحَ / يُصْبِحَ are more frequently used than أَضْحى / يُضْحي despite their shared meaning. On the other hand, ما زالَ / لا يَزالُ and بات / يَبيتُ, in addition to ظَلَّ / يَظَلُّ, all mean "to remain." ما زالَ / لا يَزالُ and ظَلَّ / يَظَلُّ and ما دامَ are more commonly used than بات / يَبيتُ. We should also mention that one hears or sees in writing the forms لا زالَ and ما يَزالُ, which are considered by purists to be wrong usages. They consider ما زالَ and its present form لا يَزالُ to be the only correct forms since ما is restricted to past tense verbs, and لا to the present tense.

There are other verbs that belong to this list of *kaana* and its sisters, including ما انْفَكَّ، ما بَرِحَ، ما فَتِئَ. These verbs are characterized by the past tense negative particle ما in front of them; however, these verbs are not commonly used in Modern Standard Arabic. They all convey the meaning of ما زالَ / لا يَزالُ introduced in the list above. Some of these verbs have functions outside of equational sentences.

It was stated at the outset of this chapter that all these elements are used with equational sentences and exhibit an identical behavior, despite differences in their functions. General statements about their behavior in equational sentences can be made:

1. The gender of the subject must be marked in the verb.
2. If subjects optionally precede any *kaana* and any of its sisters, these verbs must mark the number and gender of the subject.
3. Subjects of equational sentences remain unchanged with respect to case; they always remain in the nominative.
4. Prepositional phrases as predicates remain unchanged.
5. Adjectives functioning as predicates must change their case from the nominative into the accusative case.
6. Nouns functioning as predicates must also change from the nominative to the accusative case.

10.1 NEGATION OF EQUATIONAL SENTENCES
نَفْي الجُملةِ الاِسْمِيَّة

لَيْسَ is treated as a verb in Arabic, subject to conjugation only in the past tense.
It conjugates with singular, dual and plural pronouns.

10.1.1 Negation of the equational sentence in the singular

The singular pronouns are listed in the table below, along with the ending
associated with each pronoun:

Independent pronoun	Suffix pronoun form	لَيْسَ form	Meaning
أَنا	تُ	لَسْتُ	I am not
أَنْتَ	تَ	لَسْتَ	you (M) are not
أَنْتِ	تِ	لَسْتِ	you (F) are not
هُوَ	—	لَيْسَ	he/it is not
هِيَ	تْ	لَيْسَتْ	she/it is not

Note that the *yaa'* of لَيْسَ is dropped for the first person singular pronoun أَنا
and for the second person pronoun أَنْتَ and أَنْتِ. As the table illustrates, if the
subject of the equational sentence is a pronoun, لَيْسَ changes its ending to
express that pronoun in its suffix. This is accomplished by having a suffixal
form attached to the end of لَيْسَ as in any verb. In addition to the singular,
لَيْسَ conjugates in the dual and plural as we shall see below.

Equational sentences are negated by لَيْسَ in the present tense. Compare the
following examples in the affirmative, followed by the negative:

الأُستاذُ في الصَّفِّ.	The teacher (M) is in the classroom.
لَيْسَ الأُستاذُ في الصَّفِّ.	The teacher (M) is not in the classroom.
الأُستاذَةُ في الصَّفِّ.	The teacher (F) is in the classroom.
لَيْسَتِ الأُستاذَةُ في الصَّفِّ.	The teacher (F) is not in the classroom.

The use of لَيْسَ as a negative particle is restricted to written and formal spoken Arabic only.

The position of لَيْسَ in the sentence has some flexibility. It can either precede the subject or follow it immediately, as in the following.

الطَّالِبُ فِي الـمَكْتَبَةِ. The student is in the library.

الطَّالِبُ لَيْسَ فِي الـمَكْتَبَةِ. The student is not in the library.

لَيْسَ الطَّالِبُ فِي الـمَكْتَبَةِ. The student is not in the library.

The repetition of the pronoun with the conjugated لَيْسَ is redundant; however, its repetition adds emphasis, as in the following:

هِيَ مِن بَيْروت. She is from Beirut.

هِيَ لَيْسَت مِن بَيْروت. She is not from Beirut.

لَيْسَت مِن بَيْروت. She is not from Beirut.

If, in discourses, a noun has been previously mentioned, the repetition of the noun or pronoun becomes redundant.

Mention should be made that لَيْسَ can be preceded by the interrogative أَ to corroborate or to seek information, as in the following:

أَلَيْسَ محمّد أُسْتاذاً؟ Isn't Mohammed a teacher?

Additionally, أَلَيْسَ could be used in a question tag format following an equational sentence, also to corroborate the statement in the sentence. Consider the following:

الطَّقْسُ جَميلٌ اليَوْمَ. أَلَيْسَ كَذلِك؟ The weather is good today. Isn't it?

10.1.2 Negation of the equational sentence in the dual
نَفْي الـجُمْلَة الاسْمِيَّة - الـمُثَنَّى

The following table shows the conjugation of لَيْسَ in the dual with the suffixal forms attached to the end of لَيْسَ.

Independent pronoun	Suffix pronoun form	لَيْسَ form	Meaning
نَحْنُ	نا	لَسْنا	we (D) are not
أَنْتُما	تُما	لَسْتُما	you (M, D) are not
أَنْتُما	تُما	لَسْتُما	you (F, D) are not
هُما	ا	لَيْسا	they (M, D) are not
هُما	تا	لَيْسَتا	they (F, D) are not

As in the singular, subjects of equational sentence negated by لَيْسَ remain unchanged. لَيْسَ must indicate the subject's gender. If the dual subject precedes لَيْسَ its number must also be marked in the verb. Consider the following examples:

لَيْسَ الْمُوَظَّفانِ في الْمَكْتَبِ.   The employees (M, D) are not in the office.

الْمُوَظَّفانِ لَيْسا في الْمَكْتَبِ.   The employees (M) are not in the office.

الْمُوَظَّفَتانِ لَيْسَتا في الْمَكْتَبِ.   The employees (F) are not in the office.

10.1.3 Negation of the equational sentence in the plural
نَفْي الْجُمْلَة الاِسْمِيَّة - ١ الْجَمْع

The following table shows the conjugation of لَيْسَ in the plural. Suffixal plural pronouns are attached to the end of لَيْسَ.

Independent pronoun	Suffix pronoun form	لَيْسَ form	Meaning
نَحْنُ	نا	لَسْنا	we (M/F) are not
أَنْتُم	تُم	لَسْتُم	you (M) are not
أَنْتُنَّ	تُنَّ	لَسْتُنَّ	you (F) are not
هُم	وا	لَيْسوا	they (M) are not
هُنَّ	نَ	لَسْنَ	they (F) are not

Examine the following:

هُم في البَيْتِ.   They (M, Pl) are in the house.

لَيْسوا (هُم) في البَيْتِ.   They (M, Pl) are not in the house.

هُنَّ في البَيْتِ.   They (F, Pl) are in the house.

لَسْنَ (هُنَّ) في البَيْتِ.   They (F, Pl) are not in the house.

10.2 NOUNS OR ADJECTIVES AS PREDICATES

10.2.1 Singular nouns and adjectives as predicates

Nouns or adjectives functioning as predicates of equational sentences negated by لَيْسَ must change into the accusative case. In formal spoken Arabic, this is marked by the sound *-an*. In the orthography, the predicate must end with an *'alif* with two *fat-Has* ا if the negated predicate noun or adjective is masculine, as in the following examples:

أَحْمَد طالبٌ في الجامِعَة.   Ahmad is a student at the university.

لَيْسَ أَحْمَد طالباً في الجامِعَة.   Ahmad is not a student at the university.

الطّالبُ جَديدٌ في الـمَدْرَسَة.   The student is new at school.

لَيْسَ الطّالبُ جَديداً في الـمَدْرَسَةِ.   The student is not new at school.

If the predicate noun or adjective is feminine, the two *fat-Has* are placed above the *taa' marbuuTa* ة of the feminine noun or adjective, as in the following examples:

مَرْيَم طالبَةٌ.   Maryam is a student.

لَيْسَت مَرْيَم طالبَةً.   Maryam is not a student.

السّيّارَةُ جَديدَةٌ.   The car is new.

لَيْسَتِ السّيارَةُ جَديدَةً.   The car is not new.

If the predicate is an *IDhaafa*-construct, only the first noun of the *IDhaafa* is in the accusative case, as in the following example:

سوزان هِيَ مُديرَةُ المَكْتَب.   Suzanne is the office director.

لَيْسَت سوزان مُديرَةَ المَكْتَب.   Suzanne is not the office director.

10.2.2 Dual nouns and adjectives as predicates

Predicate adjectives or nouns must change into the accusative. The accusative case of the dual noun or adjective is يْنِ for the masculine and تَيْنِ for the feminine. لَيْسَ must indicate the gender of the feminine subject. The following pairs, in which the first sentence is in the affirmative, the second in the negative, illustrate the point:

مَحمود وعَلي طالِبانِ. Mahmoud and Ali are students (M, D).

لَيْسَ محمود وَعَلي طالِبَيْنِ. Mahmoud and Ali are not students (M, D).

الـمُديرَتانِ جَديدَتانِ. The directors (F, D) are new.

لَيْسَتِ الـمُديرَتانِ جَديدَتَيْنِ. The directors (F, D) are not new.

If لَيْسَ follows the subject, it must express the number of the subject as well as its gender, as in the following:

الـمُديرَتانِ جَديدَتانِ. The directors (F, D) are new.

الـمُديرَتانِ لَيْسَتا جَديدَتَيْنِ. The directors (F, D) are not new.

مَحمود وَعَلي طالِبانِ. Mahmoud and Ali are students (M, D).

محمود وَعَلي لَيْسا طالِبَيْنِ. Mahmoud and Ali are not students (M, D).

10.2.3 Plural nouns and adjectives as predicates

Adjectives or nouns as predicates of equational sentences must change into the accusative. The accusative case of a regular plural noun or adjective is ـينَ for the masculine and ـاتِ for the feminine. Consider the following:

سَليم وعلي وجورج مُوَظَّفونَ.
Salim, Ali and George are employees.

لَيْسَ سَليم وعلي وجورج مُوَظَّفينَ.
Salim, Ali and George are not employees.

سوزان ولَيْلى وسَلمى طالِباتٌ.
Susanne, Laila and Salma are students.

لَيْسَت سوزان ولَيْلى وسَلمى طالباتٍ.

Susanne, Laila and Salma are not students.

الـمُديرونَ مَعروفونَ.

The directors (M, Pl) are well known.

لَيْسَ الـمُديرونَ مَعروفينَ.

The directors (M, Pl) are not well known.

الطَّالباتُ نَشيطاتٌ.

The students (F, Pl) are active.

لَيْسَتِ الطَّالباتُ نَشيطاتٍ.

The students (F, Pl) are not active.

Consider the following examples that illustrate the verb's gender and number when subjects precede لَيْسَ or any of the members of كانَ:

الـمُديرونَ مَعْروفونَ.

The directors (M, Pl) are well known.

الـمُديرونَ لَيْسوا مَعْروفينَ.

The directors (M, Pl) are not well known.

الأُسْتاذاتُ عِراقِيّاتٌ.

The teachers (F, Pl) are Iraqis.

الأُسْتاذاتُ لَسْنَ عِراقِيّاتٍ.

The teachers (F, Pl) are not Iraqis.

10.3 THE EQUATIONAL SENTENCE IN PAST TENSE
الجُملة الاسمِيَّة في الماضي

Equational sentences express propositions in the present time without the use of a verb (see Chapter 9 on the equational sentence). The use of the verb كانَ is required to put equational sentences into the past tense. As with لَيْسَ in the preceding section, كانَ has some flexibility with respect to its placement in the equational sentence. Regardless of its position, كانَ has no impact on the case of the sentence subject. Prepositional or adverbial phrase predicates remain unchanged. Noun or adjective predicates must change into the accusative.

10.3.1 The equational sentence in past tense in the singular الجُمْلَة الاِسْمِيَّة في الـماضي - الـمُفْرَد

كانَ is conjugated like any other Form I hollow verb, as illustrated in the table below. The singular pronouns are listed below, along with the ending associated with each pronoun:

Independent pronoun	Suffix pronoun form	كانَ form	Meaning
أَنا	تُ	كُنْتُ	I was
أَنْتَ	تَ	كُنْتَ	you (M) were
أَنْتِ	تِ	كُنْتِ	you (F) were
هُوَ	—	كانَ	he was
هِيَ	تْ	كانَتْ	she was

This internal morphological change by the use of *Dhamma* can be explained by considering the present tense form of كانَ for هُوَ, which is يَكونُ. (See the detailed discussion of hollow verbs in Form I in Chapter 11).

10.3.1.1 Nouns or adjectives as predicates

أَحْمَد طالِبٌ.	Ahmad is a student.
كانَ أَحْمَد طالِباً.	Ahmad was a student.
الطّالِبُ جَديدٌ.	The student is new.
كانَ الطّالِبُ جَديداً.	The student was new.

If the predicate is a feminine noun or adjective, two *fat-IIas* are placed above the *taa' marbuuTa* ة of the feminine noun or adjective. Compare the following sentences in the present and in the past:

مَرْيَم طالِبَةٌ.	Maryam is a student.
كانَت مَرْيَم طالِبَةً.	Maryam was a student.
السَّيّارَةُ جَديدَةٌ.	The car is new.
كانَتِ السَّيّارَةُ جَديدَةً.	The car was new.

10.3.2 The equational sentence in past tense in the dual

الجُمْلَة الاِسْمِيَّة في الـماضي - الـمُثَنَّى

The dual pronouns are listed below, along with the endings associated with each pronoun and the conjugation of كانَ in the dual:

Independent pronoun	Suffix pronoun form	كانَ form	Meaning
نَحْنُ	نا	كُنّا	we were
أَنْتُما	تُما	كُنتُما	you (M) were
أَنتُما	تُما	كُنتُما	you (F) were
هُما	ا	كانا	they (M) were
هُما	تا	كانَتا	they (F) were

10.3.2.1 Nouns or adjectives as predicates

Examine the following pairs of sentences in which the first expresses present time, the second past:

مَحْمود وعَلي طالِبانِ.
Mahmoud and Ali are students (M, D).

كانَ مَحْمود وعَلي طالِبَيْنِ.
Mahmoud and Ali were students (M, D).

الـمُديرَتانِ جَديدَتانِ.
The directors (F, D) are new.

كانَتِ الـمُديرَتانِ جَديدَتَيْنِ.
The directors (F, D) were new.

10.3.3 The equational sentence in past tense in the plural الـجُمْلَة الاِسْمِيَّة في الـمـاضي - الـجَمْع

The plural pronouns are listed below, along with the endings associated with each pronoun and the conjugation of كانَ in the plural:

Independent pronoun	Suffix pronoun form	كانَ form	Meaning
نَحْنُ	نا	كُنّا	we (M/F) were
أنْتُمْ	تُمْ	كُنْتُمْ	you (M) were
أنْتُنَّ	تُنَّ	كُنْتُنَّ	you (F) were
هُمْ	وا	كانوا	they (M) were
هُنَّ	نَ	كُنَّ	they (F) were

10.3.3.1 Nouns or adjectives as predicates

Examine the following pairs in which the first sentence is in the present tense, the second in the past:

الـمُديراتُ جَديداتٌ.

The directors (F, Pl) are new.

كانَتِ اَلـمُديراتُ جَديداتٍ.

The directors (F, PL) were new.

مَحْمود وَعَلي وَسامي مُهَنْدِسونَ.

Mahmoud, Ali and Sami are engineers (M, Pl).

كانَ مَحْمود وَعَلي وَسامي مُهَنْدِسينَ.

Mahmoud, Ali and Sami were engineers (M, Pl).

10.4 NEGATION OF **KAANA**

Equational sentences can be negated in two ways: by the use of the negative particle ما placed immediately before the verb كانَ, and by the negative particle لَمْ followed by the jussive form of the verb (see Chapter 15 on jussive).

10.4.1 ما + past tense of كانَ

10.4.1.1 Singular

Examine the following two pairs of sentences in which the first is in the affirmative, the second in the negative:

كُنْتُ في البَيْتِ. I was in the house.

ما كُنْتُ في البَيْتِ. I was not in the house.

كانَ علي طالباً. Ali was a student.

ما كانَ علي طالباً. Ali was not a student.

10.4.1.2 Dual

كانَ الأُسْتاذانِ في الجامعَةِ.
The professors (M, D) were at the university.

ما كانَ الأُسْتاذانِ في الجامعَةِ.
The professors (M, D) were not at the university.

Or, by placing the subject initially:

الأُسْتاذانِ كانا في الجامعَةِ.
The professors (M, D) were at the university.

الأُسْتاذانِ ما كانا في الجامعَةِ.
The professors (M, D) were not at the university.

10.4.1.3 Plural in a verbal sentence

كانَتِ الأُسْتاذاتُ في الـمَطْعَمِ.
The professors (F, Pl) were in the restaurant.

ما كانَتِ الأُسْتاذاتُ في الـمَطْعَمِ.
The professors (F, Pl) were not in the restaurant.

Or, in a nominal sentence:

الأُسْتاذاتُ كُنَّ في الـمَطْعَمِ.

The professors (F, Pl) were in the restaurant.

الأُسْتاذاتُ ما كُنَّ في الـمَطْعَمِ.

The professors (F, Pl) were not in the restaurant.

10.4.2 لَمْ + Jussive of كانَ

كانَ can be negated by the negative particle لَمْ, which requires a present tense form in the jussive to follow it. As shown in Chapter 15, the use of لَمْ with hollow verbs results in the shortening of the long vowel of the present tense form into its counterpart. In other words, if the present tense form of the hollow verb has *waaw*, the short counterpart vowel is *Dhamma*; if it is *yaa'*, the short counterpart vowel is *kasra*; and, finally, if it is *'alif* the counterpart vowel is *fat-Ha*. In the case of كانَ the verb form following لَمْ must have a *Dhamma* due to the fact that the present tense of this verb has a *waaw*, namely يَكونُ. The following table illustrates كانَ after لَمْ in the singular, dual and plural:

Singular	Dual	Plural
أنا لَمْ أَكُنْ	نَحْنُ لَمْ نَكُنْ	نَحْنُ لَمْ نَكُنْ
أَنْتَ لَمْ تَكُنْ	أَنْتُما لَمْ تَكونا	أَنْتُم لَمْ تَكونوا
أَنْتِ لَمْ تَكوني	أَنْتُما لَمْ تَكونا	أَنْتُنَّ لَمْ تَكُنَّ
هُوَ لَمْ يَكُنْ	هُما لَمْ يَكونا	هُم لَمْ يَكونوا
هِيَ لَمْ تَكُنْ	هُما لَمْ تَكونا	هُنَّ لَمْ يَكُنَّ

10.5 OTHER SISTERS OF كانَ

Like لَيْسَ and كانَ, the other verbs of this group require that nouns and adjectives functioning as their predicates be in the indefinite accusative.

In the following tables we provide the conjugation of أَصْبَحَ "to become" and ظَلَّ "to remain," in the singular, dual and plural, and some sample sentences using various members of كانَ sisters:

Singular	Dual	Plural
أنا أَصْبَحْتُ	نَحْنُ أَصْبَحْنا	نَحْنُ أَصْبَحْنا
أَنْتَ أَصْبَحْتَ	أَنْتُما أَصْبَحْتُما	أَنْتُم أَصْبَحْتُم
أَنْتِ أَصْبَحْتِ	أَنْتُما أَصْبَحْتُما	أَنْتُنَّ أَصْبَحْتُنَّ
هُوَ أَصْبَحَ	هُما أَصْبَحا	هُم أَصْبَحوا
هِيَ أَصْبَحَت	هُما أَصْبَحَتا	هُنَّ أَصْبَحْنَ

Singular	Dual	Plural
أنا ظَلَلْتُ	نَحْنُ ظَلَلْنا	نَحْنُ ظَلَلْنا
أَنْتَ ظَلَلْتَ	أَنْتُما ظَلَلْتُما	أَنْتُم ظَلَلْتُم
أَنْتِ ظَلَلْتِ	أَنْتُما ظَلَلْتُما	أَنْتُنَّ ظَلَلْتُنَّ
هُوَ ظَلَّ	هُما ظَلّا	هُم ظَلّوا
هِيَ ظَلَّت	هُما ظَلَّتا	هُنَّ ظَلَلْنَ

Examples of sentences using various members of كانَ sisters in the singular, dual, and plural:

ظَلَّت سُعاد في الـمَتْحَفِ.	Suad stayed in the museum.
ما زالَ الطَّقْسُ بارِداً.	The weather is still cold.
صارَ الطُّلابُ مُعَلِّمِينَ.	The students became teachers.
أَمْسَتِ الحَرْبُ وَشيكَةً.	The war became imminent.
ظَلَلْنا جالِسينَ في الـمَطارِ.	We remained sitting at the airport.

Finally, it should be mentioned that كانَ and its sisters except لَيْسَ، ما زالَ، ما فَتِئَ، ما بَرِحَ can be put in the future by using either of the two future particles سَوْفَ and سَـ plus the present tense of the verb, as in, for example: سَوْفَ يَكونُ "he will be," سَيُصْبِحُ "he will become". (The future tense and its negation is presented in Chapter 14.)

CHAPTER 11

Verbal sentences: past tense
الجُمْلَةُ الفِعْلِيَّة

The second type of sentence structure in Arabic, the verbal sentence, is introduced in this chapter. Following that, verbs in the past tense in the singular are presented, followed by verbs in the dual and the plural, respectively. Other tenses will be discussed in subsequent chapters. We now turn to examine how verbal sentences are constructed with these two types of verbs.

11.1 SENTENCE STRUCTURE بِناء الجُملَة

Verbal sentences are formed by placing the verb at the beginning of the sentence, followed by the فاعِل noun in the nominative. Recall that the verb at the beginning of a sentence is always singular, regardless of the number of the subject. Verbs must indicate gender, however. Examine the following verbal sentences in which the subject is a plural noun:

سافَرَ الطُّلّابُ إلى حَلَب.   The students traveled to Aleppo.

سافَرَتِ الطّالِباتُ إلى حَلَب.   The students (F) traveled to Aleppo.

As has been mentioned elsewhere, the subject can occur before the verb, thus adding emphasis to the subject. The verb must indicate number and gender, as in the following examples of nominal sentences:

الطُّلّابُ سافَروا إلى تونِس.   The students (M) traveled to Tunisia.

الطّالِباتُ سافَرْنَ إلى تونِس.   The students (F) traveled to Tunisia.

Arab grammarians emphasize and encourage the placement of verbs at the beginning of sentences.

11.2 SENTENCES WITH INTRANSITIVE VERBS
الأَفْعالُ اللازِمَةُ

As a general rule, sentences are constructed in the following sequential format: A verb occurs at the beginning of the sentence, followed by the فاعِل, i.e. agentive noun, the doer, and, optionally, there may be additional information that is provided by the speaker to the addressee, or reader. This additional information could be expressed by the use of prepositional or adverbial phrases expressing place, time, or manner. Schematically, a verbal sentence in Arabic looks like the following in its sequential order from right to left:

←——————————————————————————

(Additional information) + (Agentive noun) + Verb

Note that the use of parentheses in the string in the schema above indicates that this information is optional. The following sentences are generated according to this schema:

نامَ عَلي.   Ali slept.

اِبْتَسَمَ الطّالِبُ.   The student smiled.

If one chooses to add extra information as to where, when, or how Ali slept in the first sentence above, this is usually done by the use of prepositional or adverbial phrases, as in the examples below:

نامَ عَلي في البَيْتِ.   Ali slept in the house.

نامَ عَلي صَباحاً.   Ali slept in the morning.

اِبْتَسَمَ عَلي كَثيراً.   Ali smiled a lot.

Thus the phrases في البَيْتِ "in the house," صَباحاً "in the morning," and كَثيراً "a lot" provide additional, optional information. Lists of adverbs of time, as well as adverbs of place, in addition to adverbs of degree are provided in Chapter 7.

11.3 SENTENCES WITH TRANSITIVE VERBS
الأَفْعالُ الـمُتَعَدِّية

Sentences with transitive verbs are structured in the following linear sequence: a verb occurs at the beginning of the sentence, followed by the فاعِل performer of action, the doer, followed by the direct object (مَفعول بِهِ), followed by any other additional information that the speaker or writer wishes to provide to his/her listener or reader. مَفعول بِهِ is a person or a thing that undergoes or receives the action expressed in the verb. The direct object is always in the accusative case (مَنْصوب), and it can be definite or indefinite. If the direct object noun is singular and definite, it must end with a *fat-Ha* in formal spoken or scripted Arabic. On the other hand, if the direct object is indefinite, it must end with an *'alif* bearing two *fat-Has* اً (*tanwiin*) in the orthography if the noun is masculine. Some masculine nouns ending with *hamza* do not take this *'alif*-bearing two *fat-Has* when such nouns are indefinite and accusative, as in, for example, سَماءً "sky," ماءً "water," هواءً "air," etc. If the direct object is a feminine noun, it ends with two *fat-Has* placed above the feminine marker, the *taa' marbuuTa* ةً.

Any additional information can be expressed through the use of prepositional or adverbial phrases that express place, time, manner, or degree. Schematically, this looks like the following right-to-left order:

←─────────────────────────────────────

(additional information) + direct object + (agentive noun) + verb

The parentheses in the string indicate that such items are optional. Examine the following sentences in which the direct object nouns are definite:

أَكَلَ عَلي الخُبْزَ.   Ali ate the bread.

دَرَّسَ الأُسْتاذُ الطّالِبَ.   The teacher taught the student.

The direct objects in the following sentences are indefinite nouns. Hence the use of اً with the masculine noun in the first example, and ةً with the feminine noun in the second:

دَرَّسَ الأُسْتاذُ طالِباً.   The teacher taught a student (M).

دَرَّسَ الأُسْتاذُ طالِبَةً.   The teacher taught a student (F).

If one chooses to add extra information as to where, when, or how Ali ate the bread in the first sentence above, or where, how, or when the teacher taught the student in the second sentence above, this information can be provided most readily through the use of prepositional or adverbial phrases, as in the examples below:

أَكَلَ علي الخُبْزَ في البَيْتِ.   Ali ate the bread in the house.

دَرَّسَ الأُستاذُ الطّالبَ أَمْس.   The teacher taught the student yesterday.

Thus in the sentences above, في البَيْتِ "in the house" and أَمْسِ "yesterday" provide added optional information.

Arabic provides some flexibility in the order of elements in verbal sentences. This pertains to two elements: (1) the فاعِل "agentive noun," and (2) the prepositional or adverbial phrase.

The فاعِل can precede the verb optionally. This changes the status of the sentence from a verbal to a nominal sentence. Placing a word at the beginning of a sentence adds emphasis to that word. The sentence below, for instance, emphasizes that the bread eater was the student, not anyone else:

الطّالبُ أَكَلَ الخُبْزَ.   The student ate the bread.

If the فاعِل is a feminine noun, gender agreement must be marked in the verb by suffixing ت- to the verb. Examine the following examples:

الطّالبَةُ أَكَلَتِ الخُبْزَ.   The student (F) ate the bread.

أَكَلَتِ الطّالبَةُ الخُبْزَ.   The student (F) ate the bread.

The verb أَكَلَتِ "she ate" in the preceding two examples ends with an epenthetic *kasra*. The insertion of this vowel is to break the consonant cluster for easier pronunciation.

There is another condition pertaining to number that must apply. Singular nouns do not present any further requirements. If, however, the فاعِل is a dual or plural noun placed before the verb, the verb must reflect the number of the agentive noun. This matter will be taken up when we discuss duals and plurals, and verb conjugation with dual and plural nouns in this chapter.

Prepositional or adverbial phrases have more flexibility in word order in verbal sentences. They can occur at the beginning or at the end of a sentence.

The location of these phrases is linked to the degree of emphasis desired. Compare the following two examples:

في البَيْتِ أَكَلَ عَلي الخُبْزَ. At home, Ali ate the bread.

أَكَلَ عَلي الخُبْزَ في البَيْتِ. Ali ate the bread at home.

In the first sentence, the prepositional phrase في البَيْتِ highlights the location of the action. In the second, emphasis is on أَكَلَ "he ate," as opposed to another action Ali might have performed.

11.4 PAST TENSE SINGULAR الفِعْل الـماضي مَعَ الـمُفْرَد

Verbs in the past tense conjugate according to the pronoun used. This is manifested in suffixes at the end of the verb. These suffixes for the singular pronouns in the past tense are presented in the table below:

Independent pronoun	Suffix pronoun form	Meaning
أَنا	تُ	I
أَنْتَ	تَ	you (M)
أَنْتِ	تِ	you (F)
هُوَ		he
هِيَ	تَ	she

11.4.1 Form I verbs صيغَة فَعَلَ

The verb دَرَسَ "he studied, to study," conjugates in the past tense as follows:

Independent pronoun	Past tense form	Meaning
أَنا	دَرَسْتُ	I studied
أَنْتَ	دَرَسْتَ	you (M) studied
أَنْتِ	دَرَسْتِ	you (F) studied
هُوَ	دَرَسَ	he studied
هِيَ	دَرَسَتْ	she studied

Arabic verbs in the past tense for the third person singular pronoun هُوَ always end with a *fat-Ha*. The middle vowel may be a *fat-Ha* as in كَتَبَ "he wrote," or a *kasra* as in لَعِبَ "he played," or a *Dhamma* as in كَبُرَ "he grew up." It is difficult to make generalizations about the middle vowel of فَعَلَ verbs. Schooled native speakers memorize their verb patterns and internalize this information. Foreign learners are expected to do the same.

Below is a list of tri-consonantal فَعَلَ verbs that are commonly used. The list is divided into intransitive and transitive verbs. As a general tendency, intransitive verbs are often used with prepositions which are learned as part and parcel of learning the verb itself and how it is used.

Intransitive verbs:

Middle *fat-Ha*:

ذَهَبَ   to go جَلَسَ   to sit

رَجَعَ   to return نَهَضَ   to rise, get up

خَرَجَ   to go out, exit

Middle *Dhamma*:

كَبُرَ   to become bigger جَمُلَ   to become pretty

صَغُرَ   to become smaller قَبُحَ   to become ugly

حَسُنَ   to become better

Middle *kasra*:

ضَحِك   to laugh فَرِحَ   to become happy

خَجِلَ   to become shy طَرِبَ   to be moved by music, song

يَئِسَ   to despair, to lose hope سَعِدَ   to become happy

يَبِسَ   to become dry

Transitive verbs:

Middle *fat-Ha*:

دَرَسَ	to study	شَكَرَ	to thank
كَتَبَ	to write	طَبَخَ	to cook
فَتَحَ	to open	بَعَثَ	to send, dispatch
أَكَلَ	to eat	حَضَرَ	to attend
عَرَفَ	to know	تَرَكَ	to leave
قَرَأَ	to read	غَسَلَ	to wash

Middle *kasra*:

فَهِمَ	to understand	لَعِبَ	to play
شَرِبَ	to drink	عَمِلَ	to make, to do, to work
سَمِعَ	to hear	صَعِدَ	to ascend, to climb

No matter what the middle vowel is, or whether they are transitive or intransitive, the above verbs are conjugated in the past tense like the verb دَرَسَ introduced above. For further illustration, the conjugation of the verb شَرِبَ is provided below:

Independent pronoun	Past tense form	Meaning
أَنا	شَرِبْتُ	I drank
أَنْتَ	شَرِبْتَ	you (M) drank
أَنْتِ	شَرِبْتِ	you (F) drank
هُوَ	شَرِبَ	he drank
هِيَ	شَرِبَتْ	she drank

فَعَلَ verbs (Form I) include several subcategories that we shall discuss at some length in the following pages.

11.4.1.1 Waaw-*beginning verbs* الأَفْعال الواوِيَّة

In the present tense, the *waaw* for the third person singular pronoun هُوَ "he" changes to *yaa'*, as we shall see in Chapter 12. Below is a list of أفْعال الــمثال or أفْعال واوِيَّة "*waaw*-beginning verbs," grouped as intransitive and transitive according to their middle vowel:

Intransitive verbs:

Middle *fat-Ha*:

وَثَبَ to jump, to leap	وَصَلَ to arrive at, to reach
وَجَبَ to become necessary, to be incumbent	وَفَدَ to come, to visit, to arrive
	وَقَعَ to fall, to be located
وَرَدَ to come, to appear	وَقَفَ to stand up, to stop

Transitive verbs:

Middle *fat-Ha*

وَجَدَ to find, to locate	وَضَعَ to put, to place
وَزَنَ to weigh, to balance	وَعَدَ to promise
وَسَمَ to brand, to mark, to stamp	وَعَظَ to preach
	وَقَدَ to light a fire
وَصَفَ to describe, to depict, to portray	وَلَدَ to give birth to a child
وَصَمَ to disgrace, to tarnish	وَهَبَ to grant

Middle *kasra*

وَرِثَ to inherit	وَثِقَ to trust, to put faith in
وَسِعَ to be wide, to accommodate	

---

waaw-beginning verbs are conjugated in the past tense like دَرَسَ and شَرِبَ introduced above. The following table is illustrative:

Independent pronoun	Past tense form	Meaning
أَنا	وَصَفْتُ	I described
أَنْتَ	وَصَفْتَ	you (M) described
أَنْتِ	وَصَفْتِ	you (F) described
هُوَ	وَصَفَ	he described
هِيَ	وَصَفَتْ	she described

11.4.1.2 Yaa'-*beginning verbs* الأَفْعالُ اليائِيَّة

أَفْعال يائِيَّة "*yaa'*-beginning verbs tend to be intransitive, and their use is rather infrequent. Below is a list of some of these verbs:

يَئِسَ	to lose hope
يَبِسَ	to be / become dry
يَتَمَ / يَتِمَ / يَتُمَ	to become orphaned
يَسَرَ	"to be / become easy
يَسُرَ	to be / become easy; also to become less
يَفَعَ	to reach adolescence, to come of age
يَقِظَ	to be awake
يَقِنَ	to be sure
يَنَعَ	to be / become ripe

yaa'-beginning verbs are conjugated in the past tense like دَرَسَ and شَرِبَ introduced above, as in the following illustrative table:

Independent pronoun	Past tense form	Meaning
أَنا	يَئِسْتُ	I despaired
أَنْتَ	يَئِسْتَ	you (M) despaired
أَنْتِ	يَئِسْتِ	you (F) despaired
هُوَ	يَئِسَ	he despaired
هِيَ	يَئِسَت	she despaired

11.4.1.3 Hollow verbs الأَفْعال الجَوْفاء

Hollow verbs in the past tense consist of two consonants separated by an *'alif* ا as in نامَ "to sleep," قالَ "to say," etc.

All hollow verbs maintain the past tense suffixes in their conjugation in the past tense. The only noticeable difference is the change in the vowel following the first consonant. This vowel can be a *Dhamma* or a *kasra*.

The *Dhamma* is a reflex of the long vowel *waaw* in its present tense form of the verb. For example, the present tense of the verb زارَ "to visit" is يَزورُ. In conjugating this verb in the past tense, a *Dhamma*, a short version of the *waaw*, is used. Examine the following table:

Independent pronoun	Past tense form	Meaning
أَنا	زُرْتُ	I visited
أَنْتَ	زُرْتَ	you (M) visited
أَنْتِ	زُرْتِ	you (F) visited
هُوَ	زارَ	he visited
هِيَ	زارَتْ	she visited

If the middle vowel in the present tense form of the verb is an *'alif* ا or a *yaa'* ي the vowel following the first consonant in the past tense must be a *kasra* for the pronouns أنا "I," أَنْتَ "you (M)," and أنتِ "you (F)." For example, the present tense form of the verb نامَ "to sleep" is يَنامُ and سارَ / يَسيرُ is "to walk." Examine the conjugation of the verb نامَ "to sleep," in the past tense, followed by the conjugation of سارَ "to walk":

[handwritten margin note: Q: All alift-present hollow verbs take kasra as the default short vowel?]

Independent pronoun	Past tense form	Meaning
أنا	نِمْتُ	I slept
أَنْتَ	نِمْتَ	you (M) slept
أَنْتِ	نِمْتِ	you (F) slept
هُوَ	نامَ	he slept
هِيَ	نامَتْ	she slept

Independent pronoun	Past tense form	Meaning
أَنا	سِرْتُ	I walked
أَنْتَ	سِرْتَ	you (M) walked
أَنْتِ	سِرْتِ	you (F) walked
هُوَ	سارَ	he walked
هِيَ	سارَتْ	she walked

Hollow verbs can be transitive or intransitive, commonly followed by a preposition. Following is a list of commonly used hollow verbs in the past tense with their present tense forms indicated, along with their meanings.

Waaw hollow verbs:

جاعَ / يَجوعُ	to get hungry	عادَ / يَعودُ	to return
جالَ / يَجولُ	to wander around, to roam	فازَ / يَفوزُ	to succeed, to win
دارَ / يَدورُ	to rotate, to evolve	قادَ / يَقودُ	to lead
دامَ / يَدومُ	to last	قالَ / يَقولُ	to say
ذاقَ / يَذوقُ	to taste	قامَ / يَقومُ	to stand up
ساقَ / يَسوقُ	to drive	كانَ / يَكونُ	to be
صامَ / يَصومُ	to fast	داسَ / يَدوسُ	to step on

Yaa' hollow verbs:

باعَ / يَبيعُ	to sell	صارَ / يَصيرُ	to become
جاءَ / يَجيءُ	to come, to arrive	طارَ / يَطيرُ	to fly
زادَ / يَزيدُ	to increase, to surpass	عاشَ / يَعيشُ	to live, to dwell, to survive

'Alif hollow verbs:

خافَ / يَخافُ	to be afraid
نالَ / يَنالُ	to obtain, to acquire
نامَ / يَنامُ	to sleep

More hollow verbs are listed in Appendix A.

11.4.1.4 Defective verbs (الأَفْعال النّاقِصَة) الأَفْعال الـمُعْتَلَّة الآخِر

Verbs that end with 'alif maqSuura exhibit a shortening of this vowel sound, and a compensatory semi-consonant yaa' is added following this short fat-Ha. In the orthography, this yaa' is written on a seat. This is true for the conjugation of such verbs for the pronouns أنا "I," أَنْتَ "you (M)," and أَنْتِ "you (F)." The 'alif maqSuura is simply shortened to a fat-Ha in the conjugation of such verbs for the pronoun هِيَ. but no yaa' is added. Examine the following conjugation of بَنَى / يَبْني "to build":

Independent pronoun	Past tense form	Meaning
أَنا	بَنَيْتُ	I built
أَنْتَ	بَنَيْتَ	you (M) built
أَنْتِ	بَنَيْتِ	you (F) built
هُوَ	بَنَى	he built
هِيَ	بَنَتْ	she built

Below is a list of verbs that end with 'alif maqSuura and their meanings:

بَكى / يَبْكي	to cry, to weep
جَرى / يَجْري	to run, to occur
حَكى / يَحْكي	to tell, to say, to speak
دَرى / يَدْري	to know, to be aware of
رَثى / يَرْثي	to eulogize, to lament the death of s.o.
رَمى / يَرْمي	to throw, to toss
شَوى / يَشْوي	to grill, to roast
غَلى / يَغْلي	to boil
قَضى / يَقْضي	to spend time, to judge
قَلى / يَقْلي	to fry
كَفى / يَكْفي	to suffice
مَشى / يَمْشي	to walk
مَضى / يَمْضي	to depart, to elapse
نَفى / يَنْفي	to deny, to refute
هَدى / يَهْدي	to guide, to lead on the right way

What about هم & duals?

The verbs رَأَى / يَرى "to see, view" and سَعَى / يَسْعى "to move quickly, to strive" conform to the preceding list in their past tense form. Nouns derived from such verbs exhibit a *yaa'*, as in رَأْيٌ "opinion, view" and سَعْيٌ "effort, hard work." However, in the present tense they end with *'alif maqSuura* for the pronoun هُوَ as in يَرى and يَسْعى respectively. Examine the conjugation of the verb رَأَى "to see" in the past tense:

Independent pronoun	Past tense form	Meaning
أَنا	رَأَيْتُ	I saw
أَنْتَ	رَأَيْتَ	you (M) saw
أَنْتِ	رَأَيْتِ	you (F) saw
هُوَ	رَأَى	he saw
هِيَ	رَأَتْ	she saw

The following small group of defective verbs end in a *yaa'* followed by a *fat-Ha* in the past tense. The present tense of this group ends in *'alif maqSuura*. We list some of these verbs, followed by the conjugation of بَقِيَ "to stay" in the past tense:

بَقِيَ / يَبْقى	to stay, to remain, to last
خَفِيَ / يُخْفى	to be hidden, to be concealed
قَوِيَ / يَقْوى	to become strong
لَقِيَ / يَلْقى	to meet, to encounter, to find
نَسِيَ / يَنْسى	to forget

Independent pronoun	Past tense form	Meaning
أَنا	بَقيتُ	I stayed
أَنْتَ	بَقيتَ	you (M) stayed
أَنْتِ	بَقيتِ	you (F) stayed
هُوَ	بَقِيَ	he stayed
هِيَ	بَقِيَتْ	she stayed

Verbs that end with regular long *'alif* in the orthography in the past tense have *waaw* both in their conjugation in the past tense and also in the present tense, as will be discussed in Chapter 12. The conjugation of دَعا / يَدعو "to invite" in the past tense is presented below:

Independent pronoun	Past tense form	Meaning
أَنا	دَعَوْتُ	I invited
أَنْتَ	دَعَوْتَ	you (M) invited
أَنْتِ	دَعَوْتِ	you (F) invited
هُوَ	دَعا	he invited
هِيَ	دَعَتْ	she invited

For the pronouns أَنْتِ، أَنا and أَنْتَ the *waaw* appears in the conjugation before attaching the suffixes. The *'alif* is dropped in the conjugation of such verbs for the pronoun هِيَ.

Following is a list of commonly used defective verbs that end with regular long *'alif* and their meanings.

بَدا / يَبْدو   to appear

دَعا / يَدْعو   to invite, to call

رَجا / يَرْجو   to request

شَكا / يَشْكو   to complain

عَدا / يَعْدو   to run

عَلا / يَعْلو   to rise, to go up

غَزا / يَغْزو   to invade

مَحا / يَمْحو   to erase, to obliterate

More defective verbs are listed in Appendix B.

11.4.1.5 Doubled verbs اَلأَفْعال الـمُضَعَّفة

In conjugating such verbs in the past tense, the geminated consonants get separated, usually by a *fat-Ha*, when the personal suffix is attached, as in the following conjugation of عَدَّ:

Independent pronoun	Past tense form	Meaning
أَنا	عَدَدْتُ	I counted
أَنْتَ	عَدَدْتَ	you (M) counted
أَنْتِ	عَدَدْتِ	you (F) counted
هُوَ	عَدَّ	he counted
هِيَ	عَدَّتْ	she counted

Some of these verbs have a *Dhamma* as their middle vowel in the present tense. Below is a list of commonly used verbs and their meanings.

> **Doubled verbs: middle *Dhamma***
>
> حَلَّ / يَحُلُّ   to solve
>
> دَلَّ / يَدُلُّ   to guide
>
> رَدَّ / يَرُدُّ   to reply, to respond
>
> شَكَّ / يَشُكُّ   to pierce, to doubt
>
> ضَمَّ / يَضُمُّ   to bring together, to join, to embrace
>
> ظَنَّ / يَظُنُّ   to think, to assume
>
> عَدَّ / يَعُدُّ   to count, to enumerate
>
> مَرَّ / يَمُرُّ   to pass through

Another group of these verbs has a *kasra* or *fat-Ha* as their middle vowel in the present tense. Below are lists of such verbs:

Doubled verbs: middle *kasra*		Doubled verbs: middle *fat-Ha*	
تَمَّ / يَتِمُّ	to come to completion, to end	ظَلَّ / يَظَلُّ	to remain
جَفَّ / يَجِفُّ	to dry up	وَدَّ / يَوَدُّ	to want, to desire
رَنَّ / يَرِنُّ	to ring	مَلَّ / يَمَلُّ	to become bored
قَلَّ / يَقِلُّ	to become less/few		

More doubled verbs are listed in Appendix C.

11.4.2 Augmented verbs الأَفْعال الـمَزيدَة (Forms II–X)

11.4.2.1 Form II verbs صيغة فَعَّلَ

Verbs in this category convey a sense of intensity, and also a meaning of causativity in the sense that they are transitive, requiring direct objects. كَسَرَ, for example, means "to break." Form II of this verb, كَسَّرَ, conveys the meaning of "to break in an intensive fashion," i.e., "to smash."

The conjugation of the verb دَرَّسَ "to teach" follows. The suffixes indicating the past tense for the singular pronouns in فَعَّلَ verbs are the same as those with فَعَلَ verb forms.

Independent pronoun	Past tense form	Meaning
أنا	دَرَّسْتُ	I taught
أَنْتَ	دَرَّسْتَ	you (M) taught
أَنْتِ	دَرَّسْتِ	you (F) taught
هُوَ	دَرَّسَ	he taught
هِيَ	دَرَّسَتْ	she taught

Below is a table of some verbs with their meanings to illustrate the semantic relationship between فَعَّلَ verbs (Form II) and فَعَلَ (Form I). Note that the vowel following the doubled consonant (marked in the orthography by *shadda*) is always a *fat-Ha* in the past tense, and a *kasra* in the present tense:

فَعَلَ		فَعَّلَ	
دَرَسَ / يَدْرُسُ	to study	دَرَّسَ / يُدَرِّسُ	to teach
عَلِمَ / يَعْلَمُ	to learn	عَلَّمَ / يُعَلِّمُ	to teach
دَخَلَ / يَدْخُلُ	to enter	دَخَّلَ / يُدَخِّلُ	to insert
خَرَجَ / يَخْرُجُ	to exit	خَرَّجَ / يُخَرِّجُ	to send out, to expel
عَرَفَ / يَعْرِفُ	to know	عَرَّفَ / يُعَرِّفُ	to introduce, to define
كَسَرَ / يَكْسِرُ	to break	كَسَّرَ / يُكَسِّرُ	to smash
فَهِمَ / يَفْهَمُ	to understand	فَهَّمَ / يُفَهِّمُ	to explain
سَمِعَ / يَسْمَعُ	to hear	سَمَّعَ / يُسَمِّعُ	to make s.o. hear s.th.
حَسُنَ / يَحْسُنُ	to improve	حَسَّنَ / يُحَسِّنُ	to make s.th. better
جَمُلَ / يَجْمُلُ	to become pretty	جَمَّلَ / يُجَمِّلُ	to beautify
كَبُرَ / يَكْبُرُ	to grow	كَبَّرَ / يُكَبِّرُ	to enlarge
صَغُرَ / يَصْغُرُ	to become small	صَغَّرَ / يُصَغِّرُ	to reduce in size

In addition to the verbs in the preceding table, we provide below more commonly used فَعَّلَ verbs and their meanings:

أَسَّسَ / يُؤَسِّسُ	to establish, to found	طَوَّلَ / يُطَوِّلُ	to lengthen
بَعَّدَ / يُبَعِّدُ	to distance	عَبَّرَ / يُعَبِّرُ	to express
حَضَّرَ / يُحَضِّرُ	to prepare	فَرَّقَ / يُفَرِّقُ	to separate
دَرَّبَ / يُدَرِّبُ	to train	قَرَّبَ / يُقَرِّبُ	to bring nearer
دَمَّرَ / يُدَمِّرُ	to destroy	قَسَّمَ / يُقَسِّمُ	to divide
رَتَّبَ / يُرَتِّبُ	to arrange, to tidy up	قَصَّرَ / يُقَصِّرُ	to shorten, to abbreviate
سَلَّمَ / يُسَلِّمُ	to greet, to hand	كَسَّرَ / يُكَسِّرُ	to smash
شَجَّعَ / يُشَجِّعُ	to encourage	مَرَّنَ / يُمَرِّنُ	to train, to drill
صَوَّرَ / يُصَوِّرُ	to depict, to photograph	نَظَّمَ / يُنَظِّمُ	to organize
طَوَّرَ / يُطَوِّرُ	to develop		

The فَعَّلَ form (Form II) includes defective verbs that end with 'alif maqSuura in the orthography in the past tense, as in سَمَّى / يُسَمِّي "to name." In conjugating such verbs in the past tense, the 'alif maqSuura turns into yaa' for some pronouns, as in the following:

Independent pronoun	Past tense form	Meaning
أنا	سَمَّيْتُ	I named
أَنْتَ	سَمَّيْتَ	you (M) named
أَنْتِ	سَمَّيْتِ	you (F) named
هُوَ	سَمَّى	he named
هِيَ	سَمَّتْ	she named

Below is a list of such verbs:

بَكَّى / يُبَكِّي	to cause s.o. to weep / cry
ثَنَّى / يُثَنِّي	to second
رَقَّى / يُرَقِّي	to elevate, to develop, to promote
عَزَّى / يُعَزِّي	to console, to comfort
عَلَّى / يُعَلِّي	to lift, to raise
غَلَّى / يُغَلِّي	to raise the price, to elevate
غَنَّى / يُغَنِّي	to sing

It is of interest to note that the verb حَيَّا / يُحَيِّي "to greet" that belongs to this group is written with regular long 'alif: an example of imperfect orthography. Perhaps this is done to avoid the writing of two adjacent yaa's (one with the two integral dots, followed by the 'alif maqSuura that resembles yaa' but without the dots.)

The following are examples of فَعَّلَ verbs used in sentences:

أَسَّسَ جَفَرْسون جامِعَةَ فرجينيا.	Jefferson established the University of Virginia.
حَسَّنَتِ الأُسْتاذَةُ الكِتابَ.	The teacher (F) improved the book.
غَنَّتِ الصَّديقَةُ أُغْنِيَةً جَميلَةً.	The friend sang a beautiful song.

11.4.2.2 Form III verbs صيغَة فاعَلَ

Form III is made by inserting *'alif* after the first consonant of the verb; it conveys the notion that effort is made to carry out the action of the verb upon the recipient, the direct object (in the case of transitive verbs). It also conveys the idea of reciprocity.

Below is the conjugation of كاتَبَ / يُكاتِبُ "to correspond with" as an illustration.

Independent pronoun	Past tense form	Meaning
أَنا	كاتَبْتُ	I corresponded
أَنْتَ	كاتَبْتَ	you (M) corresponded
أَنْتِ	كاتَبْتِ	you (F) corresponded
هُوَ	كاتَبَ	he corresponded
هِيَ	كاتَبْتْ	she corresponded

Following is a list of commonly used verbs in this category and their meanings.

تابَعَ / يُتابِعُ	to pursue
حادَثَ / يُحادِثُ	to converse with
حافَظَ عَلى / يُحافِظُ عَلى	to protect, to defend, to keep
راسَلَ / يُراسِلُ	to correspond with
ساعَدَ / يُساعِدُ	to assist, to help, to aid
سافَرَ إلى / يُسافِرُ إلى	to travel
شارَكَ في / يُشارِكُ في	to participate
شاهَدَ / يُشاهِدُ	to view, to see
عالَجَ / يُعالِجُ	to treat medically, to discuss a topic
عاوَنَ / يُعاوِنُ	to aid, to assist, to help
غادَرَ / يُغادِرُ	to depart
قابَلَ / يُقابِلُ	to encounter, to meet
كاتَبَ / يُكاتِبُ	to correspond with
ناقَشَ / يُناقِشُ	to debate, to discuss

A group of فاعَلَ form (Form III) verbs ends with *'alif maqSuura*, as in the following list. In conjugating these verbs in the past tense, the *'alif maqSuura* changes to a *yaa'* before the suffix is added, similar to the defective verbs ending with *'alif maqSuura* presented in an earlier section. Examine the conjugation of the verb نادى / يُنادي "to call":

Independent pronoun	Past tense form	Meaning
أَنا	نادَيْتُ	I called
أَنْتَ	نادَيْتَ	you (M) called
أَنْتِ	نادَيْتِ	you (F) called
هُوَ	نادى	he called
هِيَ	نادَتْ	she called

The present tense of such a group has a *yaa'* at this end, as in نادى / يُنادي "to call someone's attention." Here is a sample list:

باری / يُباري	to compete with (in sports)
حابى / يُحابي	to favor, to side with s.o.
داری / يُداري	to cajole, to coax
داوى / يُداوي	to treat medically
عادى / يُعادي	to antagonize, to make an enemy of s.o.
قاسى / يُقاسي	to suffer
قاضى / يُقاضي	to take s.o. to court
لاقى / يُلاقي	to meet, to encounter
ماشى / يُماشي	to walk with, to accompany

The following are illustrative examples of how such verbs are used in sentences:

تابَعَتِ الطّالِبَةُ الدِّراسَةَ في الجامِعَةِ.

The student (F) pursued [her] studies at the university.

حافَظَ صَديقي عَلى الهَديَّةِ.
My friend kept the gift.

داوَتِ الطَّبيبةُ الـمَريضَ.
The doctor (F) treated the patient.

More فاعَلَ (Form III) verbs are listed in Appendix D.

11.4.2.3 Form IV verbs صيغَة أَفْعَلَ

These are formed by the prefixation of *'alif*, causing the first consonant to lose
its vowel. Verbs in this category can be transitive or intransitive. Some of these
verbs are declarative, stating a fact, often derived from nouns. For example,
أَمْطَرَ "to rain" is derived from the noun مَطَرٌ "rain," and أَثْلَجَ "to snow" is
derived from ثَلْجٌ "snow."

In the table below, we provide the conjugation of the verb أَكْمَلَ "to complete,"
as an example of the conjugation of this group in the past tense:

Independent pronoun	Past tense form	Meaning
أَنا	أَكْمَلْتُ	I completed
أَنْتَ	أَكْمَلْتَ	you (M) completed
أَنْتِ	أَكْمَلْتِ	you (F) completed
هُوَ	أَكْمَلَ	he completed
هِيَ	أَكْمَلَتْ	she completed

The following is a list of commonly used verbs in أَفْعَلَ form (Form IV) and
their meanings.

أَحْضَرَ / يُحْضِرُ	to bring	أَرْسَلَ / يُرْسِلُ	to send, to dispatch
أَخْبَرَ / يُخْبِرُ	to inform	أَعْجَبَ / يُعْجِبُ	to please
أَخْرَجَ / يُخْرِجُ	to expel, to bring out	أَعْلَمَ / يُعْلِمُ	to inform
أَدْخَلَ / يُدْخِلُ	to let in, to insert	أَكْمَلَ / يُكْمِلُ	to complete, to finish

A limited number of augmented hollow verbs can be derived according to this pattern (Form IV), as in the following examples:

أَبادَ / يُبيدُ	to obliterate, to annihilate
أَجابَ / يُجيبُ	to reply, to respond
أَخافَ / يُخيفُ	to scare
أَدارَ / يُديرُ	to manage, to administer
أَساءَ / يُسيءُ	to cause harm/damage to s.o.
أَضافَ / يُضيفُ	to add, to increase
أَعادَ / يُعيدُ	to return s.th.
أَفادَ / يُفيدُ	to benefit s.o.
أَقامَ / يُقيمُ	to establish, to found, to make s.o. or s.th. stand up
أَماتَ / يُميتُ	to cause s.o. or s.th. to die
أَنامَ / يُنيمُ	to put s.o. to sleep

In conjugating these verbs in the past tense, the 'alif gets shortened to a fat-Ha when the verb suffix is a consonant; otherwise it remains unchanged. Examine the following:

Independent pronoun	Past tense form	Meaning
أَنا	أَجَبْتُ	I answered
أَنْتَ	أَجَبْتَ	you (M) answered
أَنْتِ	أَجَبْتِ	you (F) answered
هُوَ	أَجابَ	he answered
هِيَ	أَجابَتْ	she answered

In addition, a limited number of augmented defective verbs can be derived according to Form IV, as in the following:

أَبْقى / يُبْقي	to retain, to preserve
أَعْطى / يُعْطي	to give
أَغْنى / يُغْني	to enrich
أَفْنى / يُفْني	to annihilate, to ruin
أَلْغى / يُلْغي	to cancel, to abolish
أَلْقى / يُلْقي	to throw, to deliver a poem or speech
أَمْسى / يُـمْسي	to become, to while away the evening

In conjugating these verbs in the past tense, the *'alif maqSuura* changes to a *yaa'* when the verb suffix is a consonant; otherwise it remains unchanged. Examine the following verb أَعْطى "to give":

Independent pronoun	Past tense form	Meaning
أَنا	أَعْطَيْتُ	I gave
أَنْتَ	أَعْطَيْتَ	you (M) gave
أَنْتِ	أَعْطَيْتِ	you (F) gave
هُوَ	أَعْطى	he gave
هِيَ	أَعْطَتْ	she gave

Additionally, a few doubled verbs can be derived according to this pattern, as in the following:

أَتَمَّ / يُتِمُّ	to complete, to finish
أَحَبَّ / يُحِبُّ	to love, to like
أَحَلَّ / يُحِلُّ	to make legal/legitimate
أَسَرَّ / يَسَرُّ	to confide in
أَضَرَّ / يُضِرُّ	to cause harm to
أَعَدَّ / يُعِدُّ	to prepare
أَمَدَّ / يُـمِدُّ	to supply

In conjugating these verbs in the past tense, the doubled consonant gets separated by a *fat-Ha* when the verb suffix is a consonant; otherwise, it remains unchanged. Examine the following verb أَحَبَّ "to like, to love":

Independent pronoun	Past tense form	Meaning
أَنا	أَحْبَبْتُ	I liked
أَنْتَ	أَحْبَبْتَ	you (M) liked
أَنْتِ	أَحْبَبْتِ	you (F) liked
هُوَ	أَحَبَّ	he liked
هِيَ	أَحَبَّتْ	she liked

The following are examples of how verbs in this category are used in sentences:

أَرْسَلَ صَديقي رسالَةً إلى أُمِّه أَمْس.

My friend sent a letter to his mother yesterday.

أَكْمَلَتِ الطّالِبَةُ واجِبَها.

The student completed her homework.

أَعْطَيْتُ قَلَمي لِلطّالِبِ.

I gave my pen to the student.

More أَفْعَلَ (Form IV) verbs are listed in Appendix E.

11.4.2.4 Form V verbs صيغة تَفَعَّلَ

This form is obtained by the prefixation of تَ to Form II verbs and conveys a reflexive notion and also a degree of intensity as in Form II. تَفَعَّلَ verbs share features of the same meaning with verbs in فَعَّلَ forms. However, the difference between these two categories is in the way they are used in sentence construction, i.e. syntax. Whereas فَعَّلَ forms often tend to have a direct object, تَفَعَّلَ verbs often require the use of a preposition. Examine the following pair of sentences:

عَلي كَلَّمَ أَحْمد.   Ali spoke to Ahmad.

عَلي تَكَلَّمَ مَعَ أَحْمد.   Ali spoke with Ahmad.

As has been the case with verbs in the other categories, some تَفَعَّلَ form verbs can be transitive, others intransitive. Below is the conjugation of تَعَلَّمَ as an illustration:

Independent pronoun	Past tense form	Meaning
أَنا	تَعَلَّمْتُ	I learned
أَنْتَ	تَعَلَّمْتَ	you (M) learned
أَنْتِ	تَعَلَّمْتِ	you (F) learned
هُوَ	تَعَلَّمَ	he learned
هِيَ	تَعَلَّمَتْ	she learned

The following list contains some تَفَعَّلَ verb forms and their meanings:

تَجَدَّدَ / يَتَجَدَّدُ	to be renewed
تَحَدَّثَ / يَتَحَدَّثُ	to talk (to)
تَحَسَّنَ / يَتَحَسَّنُ	to improve
تَخَرَّجَ / يَتَخَرَّجُ	to graduate (from)
تَزَعَّمَ / يَتَزَعَّمُ	to lead, to set oneself up as leader
تَزَوَّجَ / يَتَزَوَّجُ	to get married
تَسَرَّعَ / يَتَسَرَّعُ	to act hurriedly, to be hasty
تَطَوَّرَ / يَتَطَوَّرُ	to progress, to advance, to develop
تَعَلَّمَ / يَتَعَلَّمُ	to learn
تَفَهَّمَ / يَتَفَهَّمُ	to act in an understanding manner
تَقَبَّلَ / يَتَقَبَّلُ	to accept s.th. (an idea)
تَقَدَّمَ / يَتَقَدَّمُ	to develop, to move forward
تَقَلَّصَ / يَتَقَلَّصُ	to decrease, to shrink
تَكَبَّرَ / يَتَكَبَّرُ	to be haughty
تَكَلَّمَ / يَتَكَلَّمُ	to speak with, to speak

A limited number of defective verbs can be derived according to this pattern, as in the following:

تَبَنَّى / يَتَبَنَّى	to adopt s.o. or s.th. (such as an idea, religion)
تَرَجَّى / يَتَرَجَّى	to appeal to, to beseech
تَرَقَّى / يَتَرَقَّى	to be promoted/developed
تَسَمَّى / يَتَسَمَّى	to adopt a name
تَشَكَّى / يَتَشَكَّى	to complain
تَعَدَّى / يَتَعَدَّى	to infringe upon, to violate
تَعَشَّى / يَتَعَشَّى	to dine, to eat dinner
تَغَدَّى / يَتَغَدَّى	to eat lunch
تَغَنَّى / يَتَغَنَّى	to sing the praises
تَلَقَّى / يَتَلَقَّى	to receive
تَمَطَّى / يَتَمَطَّى	to stretch oneself
تَمَنَّى / يَتَمَنَّى	to wish

11.4.2.5 *Form VI verbs* صيغَة تَفاعَلَ

This form is obtained by adding تَـ to the beginning of Form III فاعَلَ verbs. It carries a notion of reflexivity and also reciprocity. تَفاعَلَ verbs share features of the same meaning with فاعَلَ verb forms. The difference between these two categories, however, lies in syntax. Whereas فاعَلَ forms tend to have a direct object; تَفاعَلَ verbs, on the other hand, often require the use of a preposition, most commonly مَعَ. Examine the following pair of sentences:

عَلِي قابَلَ أَحْمَد.	Ali met Ahmad.
عَلِي تَقابَلَ مَعَ أَحْمد.	Ali met with Ahmad.

Below is the conjugation of تَقابَلَ "to meet, encounter":

Independent pronoun	Past tense form	Meaning
أَنا	تَقابَلْتُ	I met with
أَنْتَ	تَقابَلْتَ	you (M) met with
أَنْتِ	تَقابَلْتِ	you (F) met with
هُوَ	تَقابَلَ	he met with
هِيَ	تَقابَلَتْ	she met with

Below is a list of verbs in تَفاعَلَ form and their meanings. Some of these verbs require the use of the preposition مَعَ "with" to indicate another participant involved in the action expressed by the verb. Others are transitive and thus require the presence of a direct object:

تَحادَثَ (مَعَ) / يَتَحادَثُ (مَعَ)	to converse with
تَحارَبَ (مَعَ) / يَتَحارَبُ (مَعَ)	to wage war with
تَراسَلَ (مَعَ) / يَتَراسَلُ (مَعَ)	to correspond with
تَساعَدَ (مَعَ) / يَتَساعَدُ (مَعَ)	to aid one another
تَشارَكَ (مَعَ) / يَتَشارَكُ (مَعَ)	to take part in
تَصارَعَ (مَعَ) / يَتَصارَعُ (مَعَ)	to struggle with
تَصافَحَ (مَعَ) / يَتَصافَحُ (مَعَ)	to shake hands with
تَعارَفَ (مَعَ) / يَتَعارَفُ (مَعَ)	to get acquainted with
تَعاوَنَ (مَعَ) / يَتَعاوَنُ (مَعَ)	to cooperate with
تَفاوَضَ (مَعَ) / يَتَفاوَضُ (مَعَ)	to negotiate with
تَفاهَمَ (مَعَ) / يَتَفاهَمُ (مَعَ)	to come to an understanding with
تَقابَلَ (مَعَ) / يَتقابَلُ (مَعَ)	to meet with/encounter
تَقاسَمَ (مَعَ) / يَتقاسَمُ (مَعَ)	to divide s.th. with
تَكاتَبَ (مَعَ) / يَتكاتَبُ (مَعَ)	to correspond with

تَنافَسَ (مَعَ) / يَتَنافَسُ (مَعَ)   to compete with

تَناقَشَ (مَعَ) / يَتَناقَشُ (مَعَ)   to discuss with, to debate with

تَناوَلَ / يَتَناوَلُ   to treat a topic, to receive, to take in

تَعالَجَ / يَتَعالَجُ   to be treated medically

A limited number of defective verbs can be derived according to this pattern, as in the following list. We should note that these verbs require the use of prepositions or adverbs. Such elements are learned as a part of the verb and the intended meaning, as the use of one preposition or another may result in different meanings, as illustrated below:

تَباكى / يَتَباكى	to bemoan
تَداوى / يَتَداوى	to be treated medically
تَسامى / يَتَسامى	to be sublime, to rise above (morally)
تَعافى / يَتَعافى	to convalesce, to recover from illness
تَعالى / يَتَعالى	to be haughty, to be sublime
تَفادى / يَتَفادى	to avoid
تَقاضى / يَتَقاضى	to litigate
تَلاقى / يَتَلاقى	to meet
تَنادى / يَتَنادى	to call one another

Examine the following sentences and the various prepositions/adverbs used with the verb تَداوى "to receive treatment," to convey different meanings:

تَداوى عِنْدَ طَبيبٍ ماهِرٍ.   He received treatment by a skillful doctor.

تَداوى بِالأعشابِ.   He received treatment by the use of herbs.

تَداوى مِنْ مَرَضٍ خَطيرٍ.   He received treatment for a serious illness.

11.4.2.6 Form VII verbs صيغَة اِنْفَعَلَ

This form is composed of Form I verbs with the prefix اِنْ attached to them. All اِنْفَعَلَ form verbs are intransitive and convey a reflexive meaning. Below is a list of verbs in this category with their meanings.

اِنْبَعَثَ / يَنْبَعِثُ	to be sent/resurrected
اِنْسَحَبَ / يَنْسَحِبُ	to withdraw
اِنْصَرَفَ / يَنْصَرِفُ	to go away
اِنْعَزَلَ / يَنْعَزِلُ	to isolate oneself
اِنْعَقَدَ / يَنْعَقِدُ	to be held
اِنْفَجَرَ / يَنْفَجِرُ	to explode, to implode
اِنْقَسَمَ / يَنْقَسِمُ	to be divided
اِنْقَلَبَ / يَنْقَلِبُ	to be turned over
اِنْكَسَرَ / يَنْكَسِرُ	to get broken

A limited number of augmented hollow verbs can be derived according to this pattern, as in the following:

اِنْقادَ / يَنْقادُ	to be led, to follow
اِنْدارَ / يَنْدارُ	to be managed
اِنْحازَ / يَنْحازُ	to align oneself with

Additionally, a few defective verbs can be derived according to this pattern, as in the following:

اِنْبَنى / يَنْبَنِي	to be built, to be established	اِنْعَدى / يَنْعَدِي	to be infected
اِنْشَوى / يَنْشَوِي	to be grilled/roasted	اِنْغَلى / يَنْغَلِي	to be boiled
اِنْطَوى / يَنْطَوِي	to be folded	اِنْقَضى / يَنْقَضِي	to elapse, to pass

A few doubled verbs can be derived according to this pattern, as in the following:

اِنْبَلَّ / يَنْبَلُّ	to get wet
اِنْـجَرَّ / يَنْجَرُّ	to be swept along
اِنْحَلَّ / يَنْحَلُّ	to be dissolved
اِنْدَسَّ / يَنْدَسُّ	to infiltrate, to sneak between/among
اِنْسَرَّ / يَنْسَرُّ	to be pleased, to be happy
اِنْضَمَّ إلى / يَنْضَمُّ إلى	to join
اِنْفَضَّ / يَنْفَضُّ	to come to an end, to adjourn

11.4.2.7 Form VIII verbs صيغَة اِفْتَعَلَ

These are formed by the prefixation of *'alif* أ إ, causing the first consonant to lose its vowel, and the insertion of a *taa'* after the first consonant. Verbs in this category have reflexive and reciprocal notions. Some of the verbs in this pattern are transitive and require direct objects; others are intransitive and require the use of prepositions, but not a direct object. Below, we list a number of verbs in this category and their meanings:

اِحْتَفَلَ بِـ / يَحْتَفِلُ بِـ	to celebrate
اِرْتَجَعَ / يَرْتَجِعُ	to retrieve
اِسْتَمَعَ إلى / يَسْتَمِعُ إلى	to listen to
اِشْتَرَكَ بِـ / يَشْتَرِكُ بِـ	to partake in
اِعْتَرَفَ بِـ / يَعْتَرِفُ بِـ	to recognize, to admit, to confess
اِعْتَقَدَ بِـ / يَعْتَقِدُ بِـ	to believe in
اِعْتَمَدَ عَلى / يَعْتَمِدُ عَلى	to depend on
اِغْتَسَلَ / يَغْتَسِلُ	to wash oneself
اِفْتَتَحَ / يَفْتَتِحُ	to inaugurate
اِقْتَرَبَ مِنْ / يَقْتَرِبُ مِنْ	to get closer to
اِقْتَسَمَ / يَقْتَسِمُ	to partake, to share
اِقْتَصَرَ عَلى / يَقْتَصِرُ عَلى	to be restricted to

Recall that the ت of اِفْتَعَلَ Form VIII verbs is assimilated by particular consonants that precede it (see Chapter 1).

A limited number of augmented hollow verbs can be derived according to this pattern, as in the following:

اِبْتَاعَ / يَبْتَاعُ	to buy
اِحْتَاجَ إلى / يَحْتَاجُ إلى	to be in need of, to need
اِخْتَارَ / يَخْتَارُ	to select, to choose
اِزْدَادَ / يَزْدَادُ	to become larger, to increase
اِرْتَاحَ إلى / يَرْتَاحُ إلى	to be comfortable with
اِعْتَادَ عَلى / يَعْتَادُ عَلى	to get used to
اِغْتَالَ / يَغْتَالُ	to assassinate
اِمْتَازَ بِ / يَمْتَازُ بِ	to be distinguished by

Additionally, a few doubled verbs can be derived according to this pattern, as in the following:

اِحْتَلَّ / يَحْتَلُّ	to occupy
اِرْتَدَّ / يَرْتَدُّ	to retreat, to fall back
اِشْتَدَّ / يَشْتَدُّ	to increase in intensity
اِعْتَدَّ بِ / يَعْتَدُّ بِ	to be proud of
اِلْتَفَّ / يَلْتَفُّ	to go around, to encircle
اِمْتَدَّ / يَـمْتَدُّ	to stretch, to extend
اِمْتَصَّ / يَـمْتَصُّ	to absorb
اِهْتَمَّ بِ / يَهْتَمُّ بِ	to take an interest in

11.4.2.8 Form IX verbs صيغَة اِفْعَلَّ

This form is obtained by the prefixation of *'alif* followed by a *kasra* ا and the doubling of the last consonant, represented by a *shadda* in the writing. Form IX verbs are not commonly used and are reserved for the basic colors and for defects. A notion of intensiveness is detected in verbs of this category. Below is a list of Form IX, verbs and their meanings:

اِبْيَضَّ / يَبْيَضُّ	to become white
اِحْوَلَّ / يَحْوَلُّ	to become cross-eyed
اِخْضَرَّ / يَخْضَرُّ	to turn green
اِزْرَقَّ / يَزْرَقُّ	to turn blue
اِسْوَدَّ / يَسْوَدُّ	to become black
اِصْفَرَّ / يَصْفَرُّ	to turn yellow
اِعْرَجَّ / يَعْرَجُّ	to become lame

11.4.2.9 Form X verbs صيغَة اِسْتَفْعَلَ

These are formed by the prefixation of اِسْتـ to Form I verbs. Verbs in this category convey a reflexive notion. Some verbs are transitive, requiring a direct object; others are intransitive, requiring the use of prepositions. Below is a list of verbs in this category and their meanings:

اِسْتَخْدَمَ / يَسْتَخْدِمُ	to employ, to utilize
اِسْتَرْجَعَ / يَسْتَرْجِعُ	to retrieve
اِسْتَعْمَلَ / يَسْتَعْمِلُ	to use, to utilize
اِسْتَفْسَرَ / يَسْتَفْسِرُ	to inquire
اِسْتَفْهَمَ / يَسْتَفْهِمُ	to inquire
اِسْتَقْبَلَ / يَسْتَقْبِلُ	to welcome

A limited number of hollow verbs can be derived according to this pattern, as in the following:

اِسْتَراحَ / يَسْتَرِيحُ	to rest
اسْتَطاعَ / يَسْتَطِيعُ	to be able to
اسْتَعادَ / يَسْتَعِيدُ	to retrieve
اسْتَفادَ / يَسْتَفِيدُ	to benefit from
اسْتَقامَ / يَسْتَقِيمُ	to become straight
اسْتَنامَ / يَسْتَنِيمُ	to let oneself be lulled to sleep, to accede

Moreover, a few doubled verbs can be derived according to this pattern:

اِسْتَجَدَّ / يَسْتَجِدُّ	to come newly into existence
اسْتَحَلَّ / يَسْتَحِلُّ	to seize unlawfully, to regard s.th. as permissible
اسْتَرَدَّ / يَسْتَرِدُّ	to retrieve
اسْتَعَدَّ / يَسْتَعِدُّ	to be ready or prepared
اسْتَفَزَّ / يَسْتَفِزُّ	to provoke
اسْتَقَلَّ / يَسْتَقِلُّ	to become independent
اسْتَمَدَّ / يَسْتَمِدُّ	to derive
اسْتَمَرَّ / يَسْتَمِرُّ	to continue, to pursue

Additionally, a few defective verbs can be derived according to this pattern:

اِسْتَبْقى / يَسْتَبْقِي	to ask s.o. to stay
اسْتَثْنى / يَسْتَثْنِي	to exclude, to except
اسْتَدْعى / يَسْتَدْعِي	to call, to beckon
اسْتَعْلى / يَسْتَعْلِي	to become haughty
اسْتَغْلى / يَسْتَغْلِي	to consider s.th. expensive
اسْتَغْنى / يَسْتَغْنِي	to become rich, wealthy
اسْتَغْنى عَنْ / يَسْتَغْنِي عَنْ	to do without

11.4.3 Quadriliteral verbs

Another group, فَعْلَلَ, is derived from nouns originally assimilated into Arabic from foreign languages. These include, among others, فَلْسَفَ "to philosophize," derived from فَلْسَفَة "philosophy," جَلْبَبَ "to dress s.o. with a garment," from جِلْباب "a garment, a dress," and تَلْمَذَ "to make someone a pupil," from تِلْميذ "a student."

The quadriliteral verb pattern فَعْلَلَ is used in Modern Standard Arabic to derive verbs from borrowed European nouns, such as names of modern apparatuses imported from the West. Thus, the verb تَلْفَنَ "to telephone" was derived from the commonly used European noun تِلْفون "telephone." Similarly تَلْفَزَ "to televise" was derived from the borrowed European noun تِلْفزيون "television." Quadriliteral verbs can also be derived from some country names. For example, from امريكا "USA," we obtain the verb أَمْرَكَ "to americanize;" from لُبْنان "Lebanon," we obtain لَبْنَنَ "to lebanize;" from الأُرْدُنّ "Jordan," we obtain أَرْدَنَ "to jordanize."

It is worth noting that some of these verbs are transitive, requiring direct objects, such as هَنْدَسَ "to engineer" and دَحْرَجَ "to roll something out"; some others are intransitive and require the use of prepositions such as سَيْطَرَ عَلى "to have control over someone or something," وَشْوَشَ إلى "to whisper to someone." Examine the following examples:

دَحْرَجَ اللاعِبُ كُرَةَ القَدَم.   The player rolled the football.

سَيْطَرَتِ الشَّرِكَةُ عَلى الأَسْواقِ.   The company had control over all markets.

It should be mentioned that from the verb form فَعْلَلَ other verbs can be derived according to the pattern تَفَعْلَلَ to signify a reflexive meaning. Thus from the transitive verb دَحْرَجَ "to roll s.th." we obtain تَدَحْرَجَ "to roll oneself;" from أَمْرَكَ "to Americanize," we obtain تَأَمْرَكَ "to become American;" and from بَلْبَلَ "to confuse someone," we obtain تَبَلْبَلَ "to become confused, confounded."

11.5 SINGULAR SUFFIX PRONOUNS: DIRECT OBJECT
ضَمائِر الـمُفْرَد الـمُتَّصِلَة - الـمَفعول بِه

In Chapter 5, we introduced the suffixal forms of personal pronouns to indicate possession when attached to nouns. These same suffixal forms of personal pronouns have a second function in Arabic. They can be suffixed to transitive verbs to function as direct objects. The suffix form of a pronoun cannot stand alone; it must be attached to the verb. There is a minor difference, however, in the suffixal form of أَنا. When ي is suffixed to verbs it changes to نِ by inserting a *nuun* to avoid having two vowels in sequence. Let us now examine the suffix pronouns as direct objects of the transitive verb شاهَدَ in the past tense:

عُمَر شاهَدَني.	Omar saw me.
عُمَر شاهَدَكَ.	Omar saw you (M).
عُمَر شاهَدَكِ.	Omar saw you (F).
عُمَر شاهَدَهُ.	Omar saw him.
عُمَر شاهَدَها.	Omar saw her.

11.6 DUAL VERB CONJUGATION: THE PAST TENSE
تَصريف الـمُثَنّى في الـماضي

Verbs in the dual conjugate in the past tense by attaching the personal suffixes at the end in a similar fashion to the conjugation of verbs in the singular. In a table format, the dual suffixes that attach to past tense verbs look like the following:

Independent pronoun	Past tense suffix pronoun form	Meaning
نَحْنُ	نا	we
أَنْتُما	تُما	you (M, D)
أَنْتُما	تُما	you (F, D)
هُما	ا	they (M, D)
هُما	تا	they (F, D)

Examine the conjugation of the verbs شَرِبَ "to drink," دَرَّسَ "to teach, instruct," and سافَرَ "to travel" in the dual past tense in the following tables:

Independent pronoun	Past tense form	Meaning
نَحْنُ	شَرِبْنا	we drank
أَنْتُما	شَرِبْتُما	you (M) drank
أَنْتُما	شَرِبْتُما	you (F) drank
هُما	شَرِبا	they (M) drank
هُما	شَرِبَتا	they (F) drank

Independent pronoun	Past tense form	Meaning
نَحْنُ	دَرَّسْنا	we taught
أَنْتُما	دَرَّسْتُما	you (M) taught
أَنْتُما	دَرَّسْتُما	you (F) taught
هُما	دَرَّسا	they (M) taught
هُما	دَرَّسَتا	They (F) taught

Independent pronoun	Past tense form	Meaning
نَحْنُ	سافَرْنا	we traveled
أَنْتُما	سافَرْتُما	you (M) traveled
أَنْتُما	سافَرْتُما	you (F) traveled
هُما	سافَرا	they (M) traveled
هُما	سافَرَتا	they (F) traveled

11.6.1 Hollow verbs الأَفْعال الجَوْفاء

Hollow verbs show a change in their middle vowels when suffixes beginning with consonants as in نا and تُمْ are attached to past tense verbs. Past tense verbs for هُما (M) end with a regular *'alif* ١. Past tense verbs for هُما (F) end with تا.

The middle vowel in the past tense is always either a *Dhamma*, as in زارَ / يَزورُ "to visit," or a *kasra*, as in سارَ / يَسيرُ "to walk." The choice of *Dhamma* or *kasra* is related to the vowel in the present tense form of the verb. If the vowel in the present tense is a *waaw*, the vowel in the past tense is a *Dhamma*. For example, the present tense of the verb زارَ "to visit" is يَزورُ. Therefore, a *Dhamma* is used in the conjugation of this verb in the past, as in the following table:

Independent pronoun	Past tense form	Meaning
نَحْنُ	زُرْنا	we visited
أَنْتُما	زُرْتُما	you (M) visited
أَنْتُما	زُرْتُما	you (F) visited
هُما	زارا	they (M) visited
هُما	زارَتا	they (F) visited

On the other hand, if the vowel in the present tense of the verb is an *'alif* or a *yaa'*, the short vowel in the past tense is a *kasra*. The verb سارَ "to walk" has a *yaa'* in its present tense, and the verb نامَ "to sleep" has an *'alif* in its present tense. A *kasra* is used in the conjugation of these two verbs in the past tense. Examine the following table:

Independent pronoun	Past tense form	Meaning
نَحْنُ	سِرْنا	we walked
أَنْتُما	سِرْتُما	you (M) walked
أَنْتُما	سِرْتُما	you (F) walked
هُما	سارا	they (M) walked
هُما	سارَتا	they (F) walked

Independent pronoun	Past tense form	Meaning
نَحْنُ	نِـمْنا	we slept
أَنْتُما	نِـمْتُـما	you (M) slept
أَنْتُما	نِـمْتُـما	you (F) slept
هُما	ناما	they (M) slept
هُما	نامَتـا	they (F) slept

11.6.2 Defective verbs الأَفْعال الـمُعْتَلَّة الآخِر

Verbs that end with *'alif maqSuura* in the past tense have *yaa'* in the conjugation of such verbs in the dual past tense as in بَنَى / يَبْني "to build." The only exception is the form for the pronoun هُما (F, D). This *yaa'* appears in the conjugation of verbs in the dual for the following pronouns: نَحْنُ and أَنْتُما (M, F) and هُما (M). Examine the conjugation of بَنَى / يَبْني "to build" in the table below:

Independent pronoun	Past tense form	Meaning
نَحْنُ	بَنَيْنـا	we built
أَنْتُما	بَنَيتُـما	you (M) built
أَنْتُما	بَنَيتُـما	you (F) built
هُما	بَنَيـا	they (M) built
هُما	بَنَتـا	they (F) built

Verbs that end with regular long *'alif* in the past tense have *waaw* in the conjugation of these verbs in the past tense. This *waaw* appears in the conjugation of verbs for the following pronouns: نَحْنُ and أَنْتُما (M, F). For هُما (F), only تا is suffixed. The conjugation of دَعا / يَدعو "to invite" in the dual in the past tense is provided below:

Independent pronoun	Past tense form	Meaning
نَحْنُ	دَعَوْنا	we invited
أَنْتُما	دَعَوْتُـما	you (M) invited
أَنْتُما	دَعَوْتُـما	you (F) invited
هُما	دَعَـوا	they (M) invited
هُما	دَعَتـا	they (F) invited

11.6.3 Doubled verbs الأَفْعال المُضَعَّفة

In conjugating verbs that have a doubled, geminated consonant, the geminated consonants become separated when the dual suffix that marks the pronoun is added. The only exceptions are the verb forms for هُما (M) and هُما (F). Examine the conjugation of عَدَّ / يَعُدُّ "to count" below:

Independent pronoun	Past tense form	Meaning
نَحْنُ	عَدَدْنا	we counted
أَنْتُما	عَدَدْتُما	you (M) counted
أَنْتُما	عَدَدْتُما	you (F) counted
هُما	عَدّا	they (M) counted
هُما	عَدَّتا	they (F) counted

11.7 SENTENCE STRUCTURE بِناء الجُمْلة

The verb at the beginning of a sentence is always singular, regardless of the number of the subject. The only condition placed on initial verbs is gender agreement between the verb and the subject, as in the following examples:

دَرَسَ الطَّالِبانِ العَرَبِيَّةَ.
The students (M, D) studied Arabic.

دَرَسَتِ الطَّالِبَتانِ العَرَبِيَّةَ.
The students (F, D) studied Arabic.

If the dual subject precedes the verb, the verb must express the number and gender of the subject noun. Examine the following examples:

الطَّالِبانِ سافَرا إلى تونِس.
The two students (M) traveled to Tunisia.

الطَّالِبَتانِ سافَرَتا إلى تونِس.
The two students (F) traveled to Tunisia.

When the dual pronouns أَنْتُمَا and هُمَا precede the verb in the past tense, the verb must be marked for the dual by the presence of an *'alif* at the end of the verb, as in the following sentences:

أَنْتُمَا دَرَسْتُمَا في الجامعَة.   You studied at the university.

هُمَا دَرَسا في الجامعَة.   They studied at the university.

هُمَا دَرَسَتا في الجامعَة.   They studied at the university.

11.8 DUAL SUFFIX PRONOUNS: DIRECT OBJECT

ضَمائِرُ المُثَنَّى المُتَّصِلَة: المَفعول بِهِ

Suffix pronoun	Independent pronoun
نا	نَحْنُ
كُمَا	أَنْتُمَا
كُمَا	أَنْتُمَا
هُمَا	هُمَا
هُمَا	هُمَا

Parallel to the singular suffix pronouns used as direct objects when suffixed to transitive verbs, the dual suffix pronouns نا "us," كُمَا "you (D, M/F)," and هُمَا "them (D, M/F)" are also used to perform a similar function. Examine the suffix pronouns as direct objects of the transitive verb شاهَدَ in the past tense:

عُمَر شاهَدَنا.   Omar saw us.

عُمَر شاهَدَكُمَا.   Omar saw you (M/F).

عُمَر شاهَدَهُمَا.   Omar saw them (M/F).

11.9 PLURAL VERB CONJUGATION: THE PAST TENSE

تَصْريف الأَفْعال الجَمْع في الـماضي

Verbs conjugate in the plural in the past tense by attaching the personal plural pronoun suffixes to the end of the verb. This process is similar to the conjugation of verbs in the singular and dual, presented earlier. Put in a table format, the following are the personal plural pronoun suffixes:

Past tense verb suffix	Independent pronoun
نا	نَحْنُ
تُـم	أَنـتُـم
تُـنَّ	أَنـتُـنَّ
وا	هُـم
نَ	هُنَّ

Note the following:

1. The phonetic similarity between the second syllables of أَنْتُمْ and أَنْتُـنَّ and the suffixes that attach to verbs in the past tense;

2. For هُمْ "they (M)," the verb suffix in the past tense is represented in the writing system by *waaw* followed by a dummy *'alif* that has no phonetic value, i.e., it is not pronounced. The writing of the *'alif* is simply an aid to the reader to indicate that this element is a verb. Examine the conjugation of the verbs شَرِبَ "to drink," دَرَّسَ "to teach, instruct," and سافَرَ "to travel" in the following tables:

Independent pronoun	Past tense form	Meaning
نَحْنُ	شَرِبْنا	we drank
أَنْتُم	شَرِبْتُـم	you (M) drank
أَنْتُـنَّ	شَرِبْتُـنَّ	you (F) drank
هُـم	شَرِبوا	they (M) drank
هُنَّ	شَرِبْنَ	they (F) drank

Independent pronoun	Past tense form	Meaning
نَحْنُ	دَرَّسْنـا	we taught
أَنْتُمْ	دَرَّسْتُـمْ	you (M) taught
أَنْتُـنَّ	دَرَّسْتُـنَّ	you (F) taught
هُمْ	دَرَّسوا	they (M) taught
هُنَّ	دَرَّسْنَ	they (F) taught

Independent pronoun	Past tense form	Meaning
نَحْنُ	سافَرْنا	we traveled
أَنْتُمْ	سافَرْتُـمْ	you (M) traveled
أَنْتُـنَّ	سافَرْتُـنَّ	you (F) traveled
هُمْ	سافَروا	they (M) traveled
هُنَّ	سافَرْنَ	they (F) traveled

11.9.1 Hollow verbs الأفْعال الجَوْفاء

Hollow verbs show a change in their middle vowels when suffixes beginning with consonants as in نا and تُمْ, in addition to تُنَّ and نَ, are attached to past tense verbs.

When conjugating these verbs in the past tense, the middle vowel is always either a *Dhamma*, as in زارَ / يَزورُ "to visit," or a *kasra*, as in سارَ / يَسيرُ "to walk."

The choice between the *Dhamma* or *kasra* is determined by the vowel in the present tense form of the verb. If the vowel is a *waaw* in the present tense, the vowel in the past tense is a *Dhamma*, as in زارَ "to visit," whose present tense for the pronoun هُوَ "he" is يَزورُ.

On the other hand, if the vowel in the present tense of the verb is an *'alif* or a *yaa'*, the short vowel in the past tense is a *kasra*. The verb نامَ "to sleep" has an *'alif* in its present tense for the pronoun هُوَ, as in يَنامُ, and the verb سارَ "to walk" has a *yaa'* in its present tense, as in يَسيرُ. A *kasra*, therefore, is used in the conjugation of these two verbs in the past tense. Examine the conjugation of the hollow verbs in the following tables:

Independent pronoun	Past tense form	Meaning
نَحْنُ	زُرْنا	we visited
أَنْتُم	زُرْتُمْ	you (M) visited
أَنْتُنَّ	زُرْتُنَّ	you (F) visited
هُمْ	زاروا	they (M) visited
هُنَّ	زُرْنَ	they (F) visited

Independent pronoun	Past tense form	Meaning
نَحْنُ	سِرْنا	we walked
أَنْتُم	سِرْتُمْ	you (M) walked
أَنْتُنَّ	سِرْتُنَّ	you (F) walked
هُمْ	ساروا	they (M) walked
هُنَّ	سِرْنَ	they (F) walked

Independent pronoun	Past tense form	Meaning
نَحْنُ	نِمْنا	we slept
أَنْتُم	نِمْتُمْ	you (M) slept
أَنْتُنَّ	نِمْتُنَّ	you (F) slept
هُمْ	ناموا	they (M) slept
هُنَّ	نِمْنَ	they (F) slept

11.9.2 Defective verbs الأَفعَال الـمُعْتَلَّة الآخِر

Verbs ending with 'alif maqSuura in the past tense have a *yaa'* before the plural suffix is attached. The only exception to this is the form of the pronoun هُمْ in which the *yaa'* is dropped before the addition of the suffix و and a dummy *'alif*. The reason for the dropping of the *yaa'* is to avoid having two vowels in sequence. The conjugation of بَنَى / يَبْني "to build" in the past plural is provided below:

Independent pronoun	Past tense form	Meaning
نَحْنُ	بَنَيْنا	we built
أَنْتُم	بَنَيْتُمْ	you (M) built
أَنْتُنَّ	بَنَيْتُنَّ	you (F) built
هُمْ	بَنَوْا	they (M) built
هُنَّ	بَنَيْنَ	they (F) built

In the conjugation of verbs ending with a regular long *'alif* in the orthography in the past tense, they are written with a *waaw* before the suffix is attached. The conjugation of دَعا / يَدْعو "to invite" in the plural in the past tense is provided below:

Independent pronoun	Past tense form	Meaning
نَحْنُ	دَعَوْنا	we invited
أَنْتُم	دَعَوْتُمْ	you (M) invited
أَنْتُنَّ	دَعَوْتُنَّ	you (F) invited
هُمْ	دَعَوْا	they (M) invited
هُنَّ	دَعَوْنَ	they (F) invited

11.9.3 Doubled verbs الأفْعال الـمُضَعَّفَة

In conjugating verbs that have a doubled, geminated consonant at their end in the past tense, as in عَدَّ "to count, to consider" or مَرَّ "to pass through," the geminated consonants are separated when the plural past tense suffix is added. The only exception is the form for the pronoun هُمْ "they (M, Pl)." Examine the following conjugation of عَدَّ / يَعُدُّ "to count":

Independent pronoun	Past tense form	Meaning
نَحْنُ	عَدَدْنـا	we counted
أَنْتُم	عَدَدْتُـمْ	you (M) counted
أَنْتُـنَّ	عَدَدْتُنَّ	you (F) counted
هُمْ	عَدّوا	they (M) counted
هُنَّ	عَدَدْنَ	they (F) counted

11.10 PLURAL SUFFIX PRONOUNS: DIRECT OBJECT

ضَمائِرِ الـجَمْع الـمُتَّصِلة: الـمَفعول بِهِ

The plural suffix pronouns are used as direct objects when suffixed to transitive verbs. Let us now examine the suffix pronouns as direct objects of the transitive verb شاهَدَ in the past tense:

Suffix pronoun	Independent pronoun
نا	نَحْنُ
كُم	أَنْتُـم
كُنَّ	أَنْتُـنَّ
هُم	هُمْ
هُنَّ	هُنَّ

عُمَر شاهَدَنا.	Omar saw us (M/F).
عُمَر شاهَدَكُم.	Omar saw you (M).
عُمَر شاهَدَكُنَّ.	Omar saw you (F).
عُمَر شاهَدَهُم.	Omar saw them (M).
عُمَر شاهَدَهُنَّ.	Omar saw them (F).

11.11 PAST TENSE NEGATION

Verbs in the past tense are negated by the negative particle ما placed immediately in front of the verb. The verb form remains unchanged, as in the following examples:

ما دَرَسَ الطّالِبُ دَرْسَهُ.

The student did not read his lesson.

ما سافَرَ الـمُعَلِّمونَ إلى بيْروت.

The teacher did not travel to Beirut.

ما كَتَبَتِ الطّالِبَتانِ الواجبَ.

The two students (F) did not write the homework.

ما شَرِبَتِ البَناتُ القَهْوَةَ.

The girls did not drink the coffee.

If the فاعِل precedes the verb, ما is placed immediately before the verb, as in the following examples:

الطّالِبَةُ ما رَجَعَت مِنْ بَيْتِها.

The student (F) did not return from her house.

الـمُعَلِّمانِ ما حَضَرا الـمُحاضَرَةَ.

The teachers (M, D) did not attend the lecture.

الـمُوَظّفونَ ما شاركوا في الاحْتِفال.

The employees did not participate in the celebration.

الطَّبيباتُ ما اسْتَقْبَلْنَ الـمَرْضى اليَوْمَ.

The doctors (F, Pl) did not receive patients today.

There is a second negative particle used to negate past tense verbs, namely لَمْ. The use of لَمْ requires change in the verb that follows it. This negative particle will be presented in detail in Chapter 15.

CHAPTER 12

Present tense indicative
الفِعْل المُضارِع المَرْفوع

The present tense indicative is used to express actions occurring in the present time as statements of fact or opinion. The actions can be a singular occurrence, as in:

يَعْمَلُ اِبْني واجِبَهُ الآنَ.

My son is doing his homework now.

Or they can be habitual, as in:

يَرْكُضُ عَزيز كُلَّ صَباحٍ قَبْلَ المَدْرَسَة.

Aziz runs every morning before school.

The present tense indicative can also express actions that will happen in the future, particularly the very near future, as in:

تَرْجِعُ المُديرَةُ غَداً.

The director (F) returns tomorrow.

Other moods of the present tense are covered in Chapter 13 (subjunctive); Chapter 15 (jussive); and Chapter 17 (imperative).

12.1 PRESENT TENSE SINGULAR الفِعْل الـمُضارِع الـمُفْرَد

The present tense of verbs in the singular is indicated by the use of prefixes in the form of consonants followed by vowels. The vowel following the prefix, written above it in the orthography, is either a *fat-Ha* or a *Dhamma*, depending on the verb form, called وَزْن or صيغة in Arabic. The present tense verb form for the feminine singular pronoun أنْتِ requires a prefix and a suffix. The prefixes (and suffix for the أنْتِ) for the singular pronouns are represented in the table below:

Singular pronoun	Suffix	Prefix
أَنا		أَ
أَنْتَ		تَ
أَنْتِ	ينَ	تَ
هُوَ		يَـ
هِيَ		تَ

Present tense indicative verbs in the singular end with a *Dhamma*. The only exception is the verb form for the pronoun أَنْتِ, which ends with ينَ.

12.1.1 Form I verbs صيغة فَعَلَ

The prefixes in the conjugation of this verb pattern are followed by a *fat-Ha*, which is used throughout the فَعَلَ verbs (Form I). Thus, the conjugation of the verb دَرَسَ "to study" in the present tense looks like the following:

Singular pronoun	Present tense form	Meaning
أَنا	أَدْرُسُ	I study
أَنْتَ	تَدْرُسُ	you (M) study
أَنْتِ	تَدْرُسِينَ	you (F) study
هُوَ	يَـدْرُسُ	he studies
هِيَ	تَدْرُسُ	she studies

In فَعَلَ verbs (Form I) the middle vowel is largely unpredictable. It can be a *fat-Ha*, a *Dhamma*, or a *kasra*. It is difficult to make a definitive rule about which verbs in فَعَلَ form (Form I) take which vowel in their middle, except for one group of verbs. Verbs that have a *kasra* in their middle in the past tense always have a *fat-Ha* in the present tense, as in the following illustrative examples:

سَمِعَ / يَسْمَعُ to hear

شَرِبَ / يَشْرَبُ to drink

عَمِلَ / يَعْمَلُ to make, to do

فَهِمَ / يَفْهَمُ   to understand

لَعِبَ / يَلْعَبُ   to play

The following may help manage this phenomenon. Schoolchildren in the Arab world are introduced to the past tense of a particular verb for the third person singular pronoun هُوَ when they begin learning verbs in Arabic, and they simultaneously learn the present tense for that verb. For example, they learn the past tense verb هُوَ كَتَبَ "to write; *lit.* he wrote," and its present form: هُوَ يَكْتُبُ. The middle vowel in the present for the verb كَتَبَ is therefore a *Dhamma*. It must be strongly emphasized that the *Dhamma* is specific in this case to the verb كَتَبَ and some others. Other verbs may have different vowels in their middle. For example, the middle vowel of the verb ذَهَبَ "to go" in the present tense is a *fat-Ha*, i.e. يَذْهَبُ. Therefore, foreign learners, following the tradition practiced by schooled native speakers, are expected to memorize the middle vowel of the past and the present tense of verb forms to be able to use them correctly.

Below is a list of Form I verbs صِيغَة فَعَلَ with their meanings, grouped together according to the middle vowel in the present tense:

Dhamma

أَخَذَ / يَأْخُذُ   to take

أَكَلَ / يَأْكُلُ   to eat

تَرَكَ / يَتْرُكُ   to leave s.th., to depart

حَصَلَ عَلى / يَحْصُلُ عَلى   to obtain

حَضَرَ / يَحْضُرُ   to attend

دَرَسَ / يَدْرُسُ   to study

كَتَبَ / يَكْتُبُ   to write

شَكَرَ / يَشْكُرُ   to thank

دَخَلَ / يَدْخُلُ   to enter

In conjugating the verb أَكَلَ / يَأْكُلُ "to eat" the *hamza* is maintained on its *'alif* for all prefixes except for the pronoun أنا. The combination of the two *hamzas* in أَأْكُلُ and أَأْخُذُ is replaced by *madda*, as in أَنا آكُلُ "I eat" and أَنا آخُذُ "I take."

> **Fat-Ha**
>
> ذَهَبَ / يَذْهَبُ   to go
>
> فَعَلَ / يَفْعَلُ   to do
>
> قَرَأَ / يَقْرَأُ   to read
>
> نَهَضَ / يَنْهَضُ   to rise, to wake up
>
> سَأَلَ / يَسْأَلُ   to ask, to inquire

In writing, the *hamza* of قَرَأَ / يَقْرَأُ "to read" is written above the *'alif* as in أَنا أَقْرَأُ "I read" and so on. For the pronoun أَنتِ "you (F)," the verb form in the present can be written in one of two ways: أَنْتِ تَقْرَئِينَ or أَنْتِ تَقْرَئِينَ "you (F) read."

> **Kasra**
>
> جَلَسَ / يَجْلِسُ   to sit   عَرَفَ / يَعْرِفُ   to know
>
> رَجَعَ / يَرْجِعُ   to return   غَسَلَ / يَغْسِلُ   to wash

12.1.1.1 Waaw-*beginning verbs* الأفعال الواويَّة

The initial *waaw* of such verbs in the present tense for the third person singular pronoun هُوَ, i.e. يَوْجَدُ, is dropped. Instead, we obtain a *yaa'* for this pronoun; the correct form is يَجِدُ "he finds." This *yaa'* is dropped for the other pronouns before the addition of their respective prefixes, as in the table below:

Independent pronoun	Present tense form	Meaning
أَنا	أَجِدُ	I find
أَنْتَ	تَجِدُ	you (M) find
أَنْتِ	تَجِدِينَ	you (F) find
هُوَ	يَجِدُ	he finds
هِيَ	تَجِدُ	she finds

12.1.1.2 Hollow verbs اَلأَفْعال الجَوْفاء

Hollow verbs have a long vowel in their middle in the past tense, namely
'alif l. This *'alif* is realized as a *waaw* in the present tense of some verbs; in
other verbs it is realized as a *yaa'*. In the following table, we present the conjugation of زارَ "to visit" in the present tense:

زارَ / يَزورُ

Independent pronoun	Present tense form	Meaning
أَنا	أَزورُ	I visit
أَنْتَ	تَزورُ	you (M) visit
أَنْتِ	تَزورينَ	you (F) visit
هُوَ	يَزورُ	he visits
هِيَ	تَزورُ	she visits

By way of comparison, we present below the conjugation of نامَ / يَنامُ "to sleep,"
followed by سارَ / يَسيرُ "to walk":

نامَ / يَنامُ

Independent pronoun	Present tense form	Meaning
أَنا	أَنامُ	I sleep
أَنْتَ	تَـنامُ	you (M) sleep
أَنْتِ	تَـنامينَ	you (F) sleep
هُوَ	يَـنامُ	he sleeps
هِيَ	تَـنامُ	she sleeps

سارَ / يَسيرُ

Independent pronoun	Present tense form	Meaning
أنا	أَسيرُ	I walk
أنْتَ	تَسيرُ	you (M) walk
أنْتِ	تَسيرينَ	you (F) walk
هُوَ	يَسيرُ	he walks
هِيَ	تَسيرُ	she walks

12.1.1.3 Defective verbs اَلأفْعال المُعْتَلَّة الآخِر

Verbs that end with 'alif maqSuura in the orthography in the past tense exhibit a yaa' in their conjugation in the present tense, as in the following for بَنى / يَبْني "to build":

Independent pronoun	Present tense form	Meaning
أنا	أَبْني	I build
أنْتَ	تَبْني	you (M) build
أنْتِ	تَبْنينَ	you (F) build
هُوَ	يَبْني	he builds
هِيَ	تَبْني	she builds

An exception to the above is the verb رَأَى / يَرى "to see, to view, to witness." The present tense for the pronoun هُوَ ends with 'alif maqSuura يَرى, which is also maintained for the pronouns أنا، أنْتَ and هِيَ. The present tense form for the pronoun أنْتِ ends with يْنَ. Examine the following:

Independent pronoun	Present tense form	Meaning
أنا	أرى	I see
أنْتَ	تَرى	you (M) see
أنْتِ	تَرَيْنَ	you (F) see
هُوَ	يَرى	he sees
هِيَ	تَرى	she sees

Verbs that end with regular long *'alif* in the orthography in the past tense have *waaw* in their conjugation in the present tense except for أَنْتِ, as in the following for دَعا / يَدعو "to invite":

Independent pronoun	Present tense form	Meaning
أَنا	أَدعو	I invite
أَنْتَ	تَدْعو	you (M) invite
أَنْتِ	تَدْعيـنَ	you (F) invite
هُوَ	يَدْعو	he invites
هِيَ	تَدْعو	she invites

12.1.1.4 Doubled verbs الأَفْعال الـمُضَعَّفة

Verbs in this category maintain two identical consonants at their end, which are not separated by a vowel in the present tense. The vowel following the first consonant in some of these verbs can be a *Dhamma* or a *kasra* and, in a few cases, a *fat-Ha*. Examine the conjugation of the verb شَكَّ / يَشُكُّ "to doubt" in the table below:

Independent pronoun	Present tense form	Meaning
أَنا	أَشُكُّ	I doubt
أَنْتَ	تَشُكُّ	you (M) doubt
أَنْتِ	تَشُكّينَ	you (F) doubt
هُوَ	يَشُكُّ	he doubts
هِيَ	تَشُكُّ	she doubts

The only exception in the preceding table is the ending of indicative verbs for the pronoun أَنْتِ "you (F)," which ends with يـنَ.

12.1.2 Augmented verbs (Forms II–X) الأَفْعالُ المَزيدَة

We present below a list of the remaining nine verb forms that were introduced in Chapters 1 and 11. In the heading of each form, we provide its present tense pattern. While فَعَلَ Form I verbs generally tend to be unpredictable with respect to their middle vowels, Form II (فَعَّلَ)–Form X (اسْتَفْعَلَ) verbs are entirely predictable with respect to the vowels that follow the prefixes, and also with respect to their penultimate vowels.

The present tense prefix for the respective pronouns is followed by *Dhamma* in the verb forms فَعَّلَ (Form II), فاعَلَ (Form III) and أفْعَلَ (Form IV). In a chart format, the present tense indicative in the singular is as follows:

Form	Indicative mood final vowel	Middle consonant vowel	Subject prefix
Form II	*Dhamma*	*kasra*	*Dhamma*
Form III	*Dhamma*	*kasra*	*Dhamma*
Form IV	*Dhamma*	*kasra*	*Dhamma*

As in فَعَلَ (Form I) verbs, the only exception in the preceding table is the ending of indicative verbs for the pronoun أنْتِ "you (F)," which end with ينَ.

12.1.2.1 *Form II verbs* فَعَّلَ / يُفَعِّلُ

Examine the following conjugation of دَرَّسَ / يُدَرِّس "to teach, to instruct" in the present tense:

دَرَّسَ

Independent pronoun	Present tense form	Meaning
أَنا	أُدَرِّسُ	I teach
أَنْتَ	تُدَرِّسُ	you (M) teach
أَنْتِ	تُدَرِّسينَ	you (F) teach
هُوَ	يُدَرِّسُ	he teaches
هِيَ	تُدَرِّسُ	she teaches

12.1.2.2 Form III verbs فاعَلَ / يُفاعِلُ

Sample conjugations in the present tense of شاهَدَ / يُشاهِد "to see, to view, to witness" and نادى / يُنادي "to call," as an example of defective verbs in فاعَلَ (Form III), are presented below:

شاهَدَ

Independent pronoun	Present tense form	Meaning
أَنا	أُشاهِدُ	I see
أَنْتَ	تُشاهِدُ	you (M) see
أَنْتِ	تُشاهِدينَ	you (F) see
هُوَ	يُشاهِدُ	he sees
هِيَ	تُشاهِدُ	she sees

نادى

Independent pronoun	Present tense form	Meaning
أَنا	أُنادي	I call
أَنْتَ	تُنادي	you (M) call
أَنْتِ	تُنادينَ	you (F) call
هُوَ	يُنادي	he calls
هِيَ	تُنادي	she calls

12.1.2.3 Form IV verbs أَفْعَلَ / يُفْعِلُ

We provide below sample conjugations of regular augmented, hollow, defective and doubled augmented verbs:

أَرْسَلَ

Independent pronoun	Present tense form	Meaning
أَنا	أُرْسِلُ	I send
أَنْتَ	تُرْسِلُ	you (M) send
أَنْتِ	تُرْسِلينَ	you (F) send
هُوَ	يُرْسِلُ	he sends
هِيَ	تُرْسِلُ	she sends

أَجابَ

Independent pronoun	Present tense form	Meaning
أَنا	أُجيبُ	I reply
أَنْتَ	تُجيبُ	you (M) reply
أَنْتِ	تُجيبينَ	you (F) reply
هُوَ	يُجيبُ	he replies
هِيَ	تُجيبُ	she replies

أَعْطى

Independent pronoun	Present tense form	Meaning
أَنا	أُعْطي	I give
أَنْتَ	تُعْطي	you (M) give
أَنْتِ	تُعْطينَ	you (F) give
هُوَ	يُعْطي	he gives
هِيَ	تُعْطي	she gives

أَتَمَّ

Independent pronoun	Present tense form	Meaning
أَنا	أُتِمُّ	I finish
أَنْتَ	تُتِمُّ	you (M) finish
أَنْتِ	تُتِمِّينَ	you (F) finish
هُوَ	يُتِمُّ	he finishes
هِيَ	تُتِمُّ	she finishes

The present tense prefix for the respective pronouns is followed by *Dhamma* in the verb forms فَعَّلَ (Form II), فاعَلَ (Form III) and أَفْعَلَ (Form IV). The only exception is the ending of the indicative verb for the dual pronoun نَحْنُ, which ends with a *Dhamma*.

The present tense prefix for the respective pronouns is followed by a *fat-Ha* in the augmented verb forms تَفَعَّلَ (Form V), تَفاعَلَ (Form VI), اِنْفَعَلَ (Form VII), اِفْتَعَلَ (Form VIII), اِفْعَلَّ (Form IX), and, finally, اِسْتَفْعَلَ (Form X).

Form	Indicative mood final vowel	Middle consonant vowel	Subject prefix
Form V	Dhamma	fat-Ha	fat-Ha
Form VI	Dhamma	fat-Ha	fat-Ha
Form VII	Dhamma	fat-Ha	fat-Ha
Form VIII	Dhamma	fat-Ha	fat-Ha
Form IX	Dhamma	fat-Ha	fat-Ha
Form X	Dhamma	fat-Ha	fat-Ha

12.1.2.4 Form V verbs تَفَعَّلَ / يَتَفَعَّلُ

We provide below sample conjugations of verbs in this category. A sample of defective verbs in this pattern is also provided:

تَكَلَّمَ

Independent pronoun	Present tense form	Meaning
أَنا	أَتَـكَلَّـمُ	I speak
أَنْتَ	تَتَكَلَّـمُ	you (M) speak
أَنْتِ	تَتَكَلَّمِينَ	you (F) speak
هُوَ	يَتَكَلَّـمُ	he speaks
هِيَ	تَتَكَلَّـمُ	she speaks

تَبَنَّى / يَتَبَنَّى

Independent pronoun	Present tense form	Meaning
أَنا	أَتَـبَنَّى	I adopt (an idea)
أَنْتَ	تَتَبَنَّى	you (M) adopt
أَنْتِ	تَتَبَنَّينَ	you (F) adopt
هُوَ	يَتَـبَنَّى	he adopts
هِيَ	تَتَبَنَّى	she adopts

12.1.2.5 *Form VI verbs* تَفاعَلَ / يَتَفاعَلُ

A sample conjugation of تَفاعَلَ / يَتَفاعَلُ (Form VI) in addition to defective verbs in this category is provided below:

تَقابَلَ مَع / يَتَقابَلُ مَع

Independent pronoun	Present tense form	Meaning
أَنا	أَتَقابَلُ مَع	I meet
أَنْتَ	تَتَقابَلُ مَع	you (M) meet
أَنْتِ	تَتَقابَلينَ مَع	you (F) meet
هُوَ	يَـتَقابَلُ مَع	he meets
هِيَ	تَتَقابَلُ مَع	she meets

تَداوى / يَتَداوى

Independent pronoun	Present tense form	Meaning
أَنا	أَتَداوى	I receive treatment
أَنْتَ	تَتَداوى	you (M) receive treatment
أَنْتِ	تَتَداوينَ	you (F) receive treatment
هُوَ	يَتَداوى	he receives treatment
هِيَ	تَتَداوى	she receives treatment

12.1.2.6 Form VII verbs اِنْفَعَلَ / يَنْفَعِلُ

A sample of conjugations of various verbs in اِنْفَعَلَ / يَنْفَعِلُ (Form VII) and its various subcategories of hollow, defective, and doubled follows:

اِنْسَحَبَ / يَنْسَحِبُ

Independent pronoun	Present tense form	Meaning
أَنا	أَنْسَحِبُ	I withdraw
أَنْتَ	تَنْسَحِبُ	you (M) withdraw
أَنْتِ	تَنْسَحِبينَ	you (F) withdraw
هُوَ	يَنْسَحِبُ	he withdraws
هِيَ	تَنْسَحِبُ	she withdraws

اِنْقادَ / يَنْقادُ

Independent pronoun	Present tense form	Meaning
أَنا	أَنْقادُ	I get led
أَنْتَ	تَنْقادُ	you (M) get led
أَنْتِ	تَنْقادينَ	you (F) get led
هُوَ	يَنْقادُ	he gets led
هِيَ	تَنْقادُ	she gets led

اِنْدَعَى / يَنْدَعِي

Independent pronoun	Present tense form	Meaning
أَنا	أَنْدَعِي	I get invited
أَنْتَ	تَنْدَعِي	you (M) get invited
أَنْتِ	تَنْدَعِينَ	you (F) get invited
هُوَ	يَنْدَعِي	he gets invited
هِيَ	تَنْدَعِي	she gets invited

اِنْبَلَّ / يَنْبَلُّ

Independent pronoun	Present tense form	Meaning
أَنا	أَنْبَلُّ	I get wet
أَنْتَ	تَنْبَلُّ	you (M) get wet
أَنْتِ	تَنْبَلِّينَ	you (F) get wet
هُوَ	يَنْبَلُّ	he gets wet
هِيَ	تَنْبَلُّ	she gets wet

12.1.2.7 Form VIII verbs اِفْتَعَلَ / يَفْتَعِلُ

A sample conjugation of اِفْتَعَلَ / يَفْتَعِلُ (Form VIII) and its various subcategories of hollow, doubled, and defective verbs is provided below:

اِسْتَمَعَ / يَسْتَمِعُ

Independent pronoun	Present tense form	Meaning
أَنا	أَسْتَمِعُ	I listen
أَنْتَ	تَسْتَمِعُ	you (M) listen
أَنْتِ	تَسْتَمِعينَ	you (F) listen
هُوَ	يَسْتَمِعُ	he listens
هِيَ	تَسْتَمِعُ	she listens

اِعْتادَ / يَعْتادُ

Independent pronoun	Present tense form	Meaning
أَنا	أَعْتادُ	I get used to
أَنْتَ	تَعْتادُ	you (M) get used to
أَنْتِ	تَعْتادينَ	you (F) get used to
هُوَ	يَعْتادُ	he gets used to
هِيَ	تَعْتادُ	she gets used to

اِحْتَلَّ / يَحْتَلُّ

Independent pronoun	Present tense form	Meaning
أَنا	أَحْتَلُّ	I occupy
أَنْتَ	تَحْتَلُّ	you (M) occupy
أَنْتِ	تَحْتَلّينَ	you (F) occupy
هُوَ	يَحْتَلُّ	he occupies
هِيَ	تَحْتَلُّ	she occupies

اِرْتَوَى / يَرْتَوي

Independent pronoun	Present tense form	Meaning
أَنا	أَرْتَوي	I get enough water
أَنْتَ	تَرْتَوي	you (M) get enough water
أَنْتِ	تَرْتَوينَ	you (F) get enough water
هُوَ	يَرْتَوي	he gets enough water
هِيَ	تَرْتَوي	she gets enough water

12.1.2.8 Form IX verbs اِفْعَلَّ / يَفْعَلُّ

A sample conjugation of اِفْعَلَّ / يَفْعَلُّ (Form IX) is provided below. Recall that verbs in this category often express colors and/or physical defects:

اِصْفَرَّ / يَصْفَرُّ

Independent pronoun	Present tense form	Meaning
أَنا	أَصْفَرُّ	I turn yellow
أَنْتَ	تَصْفَرُّ	you (M) turn yellow
أَنْتِ	تَصْفَرِّينَ	you (F) turn yellow
هُوَ	يَصْفَرُّ	he turns yellow
هِيَ	تَصْفَرُّ	she turns yellow

اِعْوَجَّ / يَعْوَجُّ

Independent pronoun	Present tense form	Meaning
أَنا	أَعْوَجُّ	I bend
أَنْتَ	تَعْوَجُّ	you (M) bend
أَنْتِ	تَعْوَجِّينَ	you (F) bend
هُوَ	يَعْوَجُّ	he bends
هِيَ	تَعْوَجُّ	she bends

12.1.2.9 *Form X verbs* اِسْتَفْعَلَ / يَسْتَفْعِلُ

A sample conjugation of اِسْتَفْعَلَ / يَسْتَفْعِلُ (Form X) and its various subcategories derived from hollow, defective, and doubled follows:

اِسْتَقْبَلَ / يَسْتَقْبِلُ

Independent pronoun	Present tense form	Meaning
أَنا	أَسْتَقْبِلُ	I receive
أَنْتَ	تَسْتَقْبِلُ	you (M) receive
أَنْتِ	تَسْتَقْبِلينَ	you (F) receive
هُوَ	يَسْتَقْبِلُ	he receives
هِيَ	تَسْتَقْبِلُ	she receives

اِسْتَراحَ / يَسْتَريحُ

Independent pronoun	Present tense form	Meaning
أَنا	أَسْتَريحُ	I rest
أَنْتَ	تَسْتَريحُ	you (M) rest
أَنْتِ	تَسْتَريحينَ	you (F) rest
هُوَ	يَسْتَريحُ	he rests
هِيَ	تَسْتَريحُ	she rests

اِسْتَثْنَى / يَسْتَثْني

Independent pronoun	Present tense form	Meaning
أَنا	أَسْتَثْني	I exclude
أَنْتَ	تَسْتَثْني	you (M) exclude
أَنْتِ	تَسْتَثْنينَ	you (F) exclude
هُوَ	يَسْتَثْني	he excludes
هِيَ	تَسْتَثْني	she excludes

اِسْتَعَدَّ / يَسْتَعِدُّ

Independent pronoun	Present tense form	Meaning
أَنا	أَسْتَعِدُّ	I prepare
أَنْتَ	تَسْتَعِدُّ	you (M) prepare
أَنْتِ	تَسْتَعِدّينَ	you (F) prepare
هُوَ	يَسْتَعِدُّ	he prepares
هِيَ	تَسْتَعِدُّ	she prepares

12.2 PRESENT TENSE DUAL الفِعْل الـمُضارِع الـمُثَنّى

Verbs in the present tense for the different pronouns in the dual have prefixes and suffixes attached to them to indicate the person involved in the act. There is no dual pronoun form for the first person. Instead, the plural pronoun نَحْنُ and its prefixes are used to represent the plural. We list below the prefixes and suffixes for the different pronouns that are used in the conjugation of the present tense in the dual.

Independent dual pronoun	Suffix	Prefix
نَحْنُ		ـن
أَنْتُـما (M)	ان	ت
أَنْتُـما (F)	ان	ت
هُما (M)	ان	ـيـ
هُما (F)	ان	ت

The only exception is the ending of indicative verbs for the pronoun نَحْنُ, which ends with a *Dhamma* for all categories of tri-consonantal verbs except defective verbs ending with either a *yaa'* or *waaw*.

The vowels following these prefixes are the same as those presented in the singular section above. Form I verbs always have a *fat-Ha*; Forms II, III and IV have a *Dhamma*. Forms V, VI, VII, VIII, IX and X have a *fat-Ha*. Examine the conjugation of the verb شَرِبَ / يَشْرَبُ "to drink" in the following table:

Independent dual pronoun	Present tense form	Meaning
نَحْنُ	نَشْرَبُ	we (M/F, D) drink
أَنْتُما	تَشْرَبانِ	you (M, D) drink
أَنْتُما	تَشْرَبانِ	you (F, D) drink
هُما	يَشْرَبانِ	they (M, D) drink
هُما	تَشْرَبانِ	they (F, D) drink

12.2.1 Hollow verbs الأفْعال الجَوْفاء

Hollow verbs maintain their middle vowel in the present tense. If the middle vowel is a *yaa'* in the present tense verb for هُوَ, this *yaa'* is maintained throughout the paradigm, as in the following example of the verb سارَ / يَسيرُ "to walk, to run":

Independent dual pronoun	Present tense form	Meaning
نَحْنُ	نَسيرُ	we (M/F, D) walk
أَنْتُما	تَسيرانِ	you (M, D) walk
أَنْتُما	تَسيرانِ	you (F, D) walk
هُما	يَسيرانِ	they (M, D) walk
هُما	تَسيرانِ	they (F, D) walk

On the other hand, if the middle vowel is a *waaw* in the present tense verb for هُوَ, this *waaw* is maintained throughout the paradigm, as in the following example of the verb زارَ / يَزورُ "to visit":

Independent dual pronoun	Present tense form	Meaning
نَحْنُ	نَزورُ	we (M/F, D) visit
أَنْتُما	تَزورانِ	you (M, D) visit
أَنْتُما	تَزورانِ	you (F, D) visit
هُما	يَزورانِ	they (M, D) visit
هُما	تَزورانِ	they (F, D) visit

If the middle vowel is an *'alif* in the present tense verb for هُوَ, this *'alif* is maintained throughout the paradigm, as in the following example of the verb نامَ / يَنامُ "to sleep":

Independent dual pronoun	Present tense form	Meaning
نَحْنُ	نَنامُ	we (M/F, D) sleep
أَنْتُما	تَنامانِ	you (M, D) sleep
أَنْتُما	تَنامانِ	you (F, D) sleep
هُما	يَنامانِ	they (M, D) sleep
هُما	تَنامانِ	they (F, D) sleep

12.2.2 Defective verbs الأفْعال الـمُعْتَلَّة الآخِر

Defective verbs that end with *yaa'* in their present tense such as شَوَى / يَشْوي "to grill, roast" maintain the final *yaa'* in the present tense, as illustrated in the following table:

Independent dual pronoun	Present tense form	Meaning
نَحْنُ	نَشْوي	we (M/F, D) grill
أَنْتُما	تَشْويانِ	you (M, D) grill
أَنْتُما	تَشْويانِ	you (F, D) grill
هُما	يَشْويانِ	they (M, D) grill
هُما	تَشْويانِ	they (F, D) grill

On the other hand, verbs containing a regular long *'alif* in the orthography and a *waaw* in their present tense, as in دَعا / يَدْعو "to invite," maintain the final *waaw* in the present tense, as illustrated in the following table:

Independent dual pronoun	Present tense form	Meaning
نَحْنُ	نَدْعو	we (M/F, D) invite
أَنْتُما	تَدْعُوانِ	you (M, D) invite
أَنْتُما	تَدْعُوانِ	you (F, D) invite
هُما	يَدْعُوانِ	they (M, D) invite
هُما	تَدْعُوانِ	they (F, D) invite

12.2.3 Doubled verbs الأَفْعال الـمُضَعَّفَة

When conjugating doubled verbs (الأَفْعال الـمُضَعَّفَة) in the present tense, the geminated consonants remain in their geminated form.

As noted previously, the middle vowel in some of these verbs is sometimes a *Dhamma*, as in مَرَّ / يَمُرُّ "to pass through"; at other times it is a *kasra*, as in قَلَّ / يَقِلُّ "to become less, few," or a *fat-Ha*, as in ظَلَّ / يَظَلُّ "to remain." Examine the conjugation of the verb مَرَّ / يَمُرُّ "to pass through" in the following table:

Independent dual pronoun	Present tense form	Meaning
نَحْنُ	نَمُرُّ	we (M/F, D) pass through
أَنْتُما	تَمُرّانِ	you (M, D) pass through
أَنْتُما	تَمُرّانِ	you (F, D) pass through
هُما	يَمُرّانِ	they (M, D) pass through
هُما	تَمُرّانِ	they (F, D) pass through

12.3 PRESENT TENSE PLURAL الفِعْل الـمُضارِع الجَمْع

Verbs are conjugated in the plural in the present tense by attaching prefixes that represent the person involved in the action. In addition, suffixes are attached to the end of the verb form for all pronouns except نَحْنُ, as in the table below:

Independent plural pronoun	Suffix	Prefix
نَحْنُ (M/F)		نـ
أَنْتُمْ (M)	ونَ	تـ
أَنْتُنَّ (F)	نَ	تـ
هُمْ (M)	ونَ	يـ
هُنَّ (F)	نَ	يـ

The only exception is the ending of indicative verbs for the pronoun نَحْنُ, which ends with a *Dhamma* for all categories of verbs except defective verbs that end with either a *yaa'* or *waaw*. Examine the conjugation of the verb شَرِبَ "to drink" in the present tense in the plural in the following table:

12.3.1 Form I فَعَلَ verbs

شَرِبَ / يَشْرَبُ

Independent plural pronoun	Present tense form	Meaning
نَحْنُ	نَشْرَبُ	we (M/F) drink
أَنْتُم	تَشْرَبونَ	you (M) drink
أَنْتُنَّ	تَشْرَبْنَ	you (F) drink
هُمْ	يَشْرَبونَ	they (M) drink
هُنَّ	يَشْرَبْنَ	they (F) drink

The present tense prefixes of the preceding verb are always followed by a *fat-Ha*. This rule applies to Form V verbs, صيغَة تَفَعَّلَ, Form VI verbs, صيغَة تَفاعَلَ, Form VII verbs, صيغَة انْفَعَلَ, Form VIII verbs, صيغَة افْتَعَلَ, Form IX verbs, صيغَة افْعَلَّ, and, finally, Form X verbs, صيغَة اسْتَفْعَلَ, as we shall see below.

12.3.1.1 Hollow verbs الأفعال الجَوْفاء

In the conjugation of hollow verbs, the middle vowel is shortened when the suffix begins with a consonant. This applies to the suffixes for أَنْتُنَّ "you (F)" and هُنَّ "they (F)." The vowel following the prefix is always a *fat-Ha*, as in the following examples:

سارَ / يَسيرُ

Independent plural pronoun	Present tense form	Meaning
نَحْنُ	نَسيرُ	we (M/F) walk
أَنْتُم	تَسيرونَ	you (M) walk
أَنْتُنَّ	تَسِرْنَ	you (F) walk
هُمْ	يَسيرونَ	they (M) walk
هُنَّ	يَسِرْنَ	they (F) walk

عادَ / يَعودُ

Independent plural pronoun	Present tense form	Meaning
نَحْنُ	نَعودُ	we (M/F) return
أَنْتُم	تَعودونَ	you (M) return
أَنْتُنَّ	تَعُدْنَ	you (F) return
هُمْ	يَعودونَ	they (M) return
هُنَّ	يَعُدْنَ	they (F) return

نامَ / يَنامُ

Independent plural pronoun	Present tense form	Meaning
نَحْنُ	نَنامُ	we (M/F) sleep
أَنْتُم	تَنامونَ	you (M) sleep
أَنْتُنَّ	تَنَمْنَ	you (F) sleep
هُمْ	يَنامونَ	they (M) sleep
هُنَّ	يَنَمْنَ	they (F) sleep

12.3.1.2 *Defective verbs* الأَفْعال الـمُعْتَـلَّة الآخِرِ

Defective verbs whose present tense ends with *yaa'*, such as شَوَى / يَشْوي "to grill, roast," or *waaw*, as in دَعا / يَدعو "to invite," show some change in the conjugation in the present tense for some pronouns.

In verbs ending with *yaa'* such as شَوَى / يَشْوي "to grill, roast," for example, for the pronouns أَنْتُم and هُم the *yaa'* is dropped, a *waaw* is called up, and the plural suffix ونَ is added. In other words, the present tense of defective verbs for the pronouns أَنْتُم and هُم is represented in the orthography with two *waaw*s.

For the pronouns أَنْتُنَّ and هُنَّ the *yaa'* is maintained in the singular, and is followed by a *nuun*. Examine the conjugation of شَوَى / يَشْوي in the following table:

شَوَى / يَشْوي

Independent plural pronoun	*Present tense form*	*Meaning*
نَحْنُ	نَشْوي	we (M/F) grill
أَنْتُم	تَشْوونَ	you (M) grill
أَنْتُنَّ	تَشْوينَ	you (F) grill
هُم	يَشْوونَ	they (M) grill
هُنَّ	يَشْوينَ	they (F) grill

In verbs ending with a *waaw*, such as دَعا / يَدْعو "to invite," for example, for the pronouns أَنْتُم and هُم the *waaw* in the singular verb is dropped before attaching the plural suffix ونَ. In other words, the present tense of defective verbs for the pronouns أَنْتُم and هُم is written with one *waaw*. For the pronouns أَنْتُنَّ and هُنَّ the original *waaw* in the singular is maintained, followed by the suffix نَ as illustrated in the table above. Now examine the conjugation of دَعا / يَدْعو "to invite" in the following table:

دعا / يَدعو

Independent plural pronoun	Present tense form	Meaning
نَحْنُ	نَدعو	we (M/F) invite
أَنْتُم	تَدْعونَ	you (M) invite
أَنْتُنَّ	تَدعونَ	you (F) invite
هُمْ	يَدْعونَ	they (M) invite
هُنَّ	يَدعينَ	they (F) invite

12.3.1.3 Doubled verbs الأفْعال الـمُضَعَّفَة

When conjugating doubled verbs (الأَفْعال الـمُضَعَّفَة) such as مَرَّ / يَمُرُّ "to pass" in the present tense, geminated consonants (the doubled consonants marked by a *shadda* in the orthography) remain in their geminated form when the suffix begins with a vowel. This applies to the pronouns نَحْنُ، أَنْتُمْ and هُمْ as in the table below.

When the suffix begins with a consonant, e.g. نَ, the geminated consonants must be separated by a vowel. This is to prevent the clustering of three consonants. The separation of the geminated consonants, only applies to the pronouns أَنْتُنَّ and هُنَّ.

As noted previously, the middle vowel in some of these verbs is sometimes a *Dhamma*, as in مَرَّ / يَمُرُّ "to pass through"; in other verbs it is a *kasra*, as in قَلَّ / يَقِلُّ "to become less, few," or a *fat-Ha*, as in ظَلَّ / يَظَلُّ "to remain." In the majority of verbs the middle vowel is a *Dhamma*. Examine the conjugation of the verb مَرَّ / يَمُرُّ "to pass" in the following table:

مَرَّ / يَمُرُّ

Independent plural pronoun	Present tense form	Meaning
نَحْنُ	نَمُرُّ	we (M/F) pass through
أَنْتُمْ	تَمُرّونَ	you (M) pass through
أَنْتُنَّ	تَمْرُرْنَ	you (F) pass through
هُمْ	يَمُرّونَ	they (M) pass through
هُنَّ	يَمْرُرْنَ	they (F) pass through

We turn now to present the conjugation of the present tense indicative of various verb forms in the plural:

12.3.2 Form V verbs تَفَعَّلَ

تَكَلَّمَ / يَتَكَلَّمُ

Independent plural pronoun	Present tense form	Meaning
نَحْنُ	نَتَكَلَّمُ	we (M/F) speak
أَنْتُم	تَتَكَلَّمونَ	you (M) speak
أَنْتُنَّ	تَتَكَلَّمْنَ	you (F) speak
هُمْ	يَتَكَلَّمونَ	they (M) speak
هُنَّ	يَتَكَلَّمْنَ	they (F) speak

12.3.3 Form VI verbs تَفاعَلَ

تَعاوَنَ / يَتَعاوَنُ

Independent plural pronoun	Present tense form	Meaning
نَحْنُ	نَتَعاوَنُ	we (M/F) cooperate
أَنْتُم	تَتَعاوَنونَ	you (M) cooperate
أَنْتُنَّ	تَتَعاوَنَّ	you (F) cooperate
هُمْ	يَتَعاوَنونَ	they (M) cooperate
هُنَّ	يَتَعاوَنَّ	they (F, Pl) cooperate

12.3.4 Form VII verbs اِنْسَحَبَ

اِنْسَحَبَ / يَنْسَحِبُ

Independent plural pronoun	Present tense form	Meaning
نَحْنُ	نَنْسَحِبُ	we (M/F) withdraw
أَنْتُم	تَنْسَحِبونَ	you (M) withdraw
أَنْتُنَّ	تَنْسَحِبْنَ	you (F) withdraw
هُمْ	يَنْسَحِبونَ	they (M) withdraw
هُنَّ	يَنْسَحِبْنَ	they (F) withdraw

12.3.5 Form VIII verbs اِحْتَفَلَ

اِحْتَفَلَ / يَحْتَفِلُ

Independent plural pronoun	Present tense form	Meaning
نَحْنُ	نَحْتَفِلُ	we (M/F) celebrate
أَنْتُم	تَحْتَفِلونَ	you (M) celebrate
أَنْتُنَّ	تَحْتَفِلْنَ	you (F) celebrate
هُمْ	يَحْتَفِلونَ	they (M) celebrate
هُنَّ	يَحْتَفِلْنَ	they (F) celebrate

12.3.6 Form IX verbs اِفْعَلَّ

اِحْمَرَّ / يَحْمَرُّ

Independent plural pronoun	Present tense form	Meaning
نَحْنُ	نَحْمَرُّ	we (M/F) turn red
أَنْتُم	تَحْمَرّونَ	you (M) turn red
أَنْتُنَّ	تَحْمَرِرْنَ	you (F) turn red
هُمْ	يَحْمَرّونَ	they (M) turn red
هُنَّ	يَحْمَرِرْنَ	they (F) turn red

12.3.7 Form X verbs اِسّتَقْبَلَ

اِسْتَقْبَلَ / يَسْتَقْبِلُ

Independent plural pronoun	Present tense form	Meaning
نَحْنُ	نَسْتَقْبِلُ	we (M/F) receive
أَنْتُمْ	تَسْتَقْبِلونَ	you (M) receive
أَنْتُنَّ	تَسْتَقْبِلْنَ	you (F) receive
هُمْ	يَسْتَقْبِلونَ	they (M) receive
هُنَّ	يَسْتَقْبِلْنَ	they (F) receive

On the other hand, in the following verb patterns a *Dhamma* must be used after the prefix, and a *kasra* following the penultimate consonant: فَعَّلَ / يُفَعِّلُ (Form II), فاعَلَ / يُفاعِلُ (Form III), and أَفْعَلَ / يُفْعِلُ (Form IV). The conjugation of examples of verbs in these patterns in the plural present tense is provided below:

دَرَّسَ / يُدَرِّسُ

Independent plural pronoun	Present tense form	Meaning
نَحْنُ	نُدَرِّسُ	we (M/F) teach
أَنْتُمْ	تُدَرِّسونَ	you (M) teach
أَنْتُنَّ	تُدَرِّسْنَ	you (F) teach
هُمْ	يُدَرِّسونَ	they (M) teach
هُنَّ	يُدَرِّسْنَ	they (F) teach

شاهَدَ / يُشاهِدُ

Independent plural pronoun	Present tense form	Meaning
نَحْنُ	نُشاهِدُ	we (M/F) see
أَنْتُمْ	تُشاهِدونَ	you (M) see
أَنْتُنَّ	تُشاهِدْنَ	you (F) see
هُمْ	يُشاهِدونَ	they (M) see
هُنَّ	يُشاهِدْنَ	they (F) see

أَرْسَلَ / يُرْسِلُ

Independent plural pronoun	Present tense form	Meaning
نَحْنُ	نُرْسِلُ	we (M/F) send
أَنْتُمْ	تُرْسِلونَ	you (M) send
أَنْتُنَّ	تُرْسِلْنَ	you (F) send
هُمْ	يُرْسِلونَ	they (M) send
هُنَّ	يُرْسِلْنَ	they (F) send

12.4 PRESENT TENSE NEGATION «لا» نَفْي الـمُضارِع

Verbs in the present tense in the singular, dual and plural are negated by the use of لا placed immediately in front of the verb. The verb remains unchanged, as in the examples below:

يَذْهَبُ الطالِبُ إلى الجامِعَةِ.
The student (M) goes to the university.

لا يَذْهَبُ الطّالِبُ إلى الجامِعَةِ.
The student (M) does not go to the university.

يُدَرِّسُ الـمُعَلِّمانِ العَرَبِيَّةَ.
The teachers (M, D) teach Arabic.

لا يُدَرِّسُ الـمُعَلِّمانِ العَرَبِيَّةَ.
The teachers (M, D) do not teach Arabic.

يَجْتَمِعُ الـمُوَظَّفونَ في مَكْتَبِ الـمُدير.
The employees (M, Pl) meet in the director's office.

لا يَجْتَمِعُ الـمُوَظَّفونَ في مَكْتَبِ الـمُدير.
The employees (M, Pl) do not meet in the director's office.

تُكْمِلُ الـمُعَلِّماتُ التَّدريسَ اليَوْمَ.
The teachers (F, Pl) finish teaching today.

لا تُكْمِلُ الـمُعَلِّماتُ التَّدريسَ اليَوْمَ.
The teachers (F, Pl) do not finish teaching today.

CHAPTER 13

Present tense subjunctive
الفِعْل الـمُضارِع الـمَنْصوب

When a verb in a main clause expresses a wish, doubt, desire, fear, obligation, etc. the verb in the subordinate clause takes the subjunctive mood. This situation applies in the context of certain elements called أَدَوات النَّصْب "subjunctive particles," which include حَتّى / لِـ / كَيْ and لِكَيْ, all meaning "so that" or "in order to," and express desire, reason, or a goal. Other subjunctive particles include أَنْ "so that" and the negative particle لَن. These particles must be immediately followed by a verb in the subjunctive. The difference between a verb in the present indicative and a verb in the subjunctive is a matter of their endings. A verb that undergoes this change is called فِعْل مَنصوب "subjunctive verb." A list of verbs that trigger the subjunctive is included in this chapter. Note that the verb in the main clause may be in the past, present or future tense.

13.1 SINGULAR SUBJUNCTIVE VERBS
الفِعْل الـمُضارِع الـمَنْصوب - الـمُفْرَد

Indicative present tense verbs in the singular always end with a *Dhamma* except in the verb form for the feminine pronoun أَنْتِ "you (F)," which ends with -*iina* يـنَ. However, when such verbs follow any of the subjunctive particles the *Dhamma* at the end must change to a *fat-Ha*. The suffix -*iina* -يـنَ for أَنْتِ changes into -*ii* ي. In other words, the *nuun* must be dropped. These subjunctive particles are presented in some detail below:

13.1.1 لِـ، لِكَيْ، كَيْ، حَتّى "in order to," "for the purpose of"

These particles must be followed immediately by a verb in the subjunctive mood. All forms of singular verbs in this mood end with a *fat-Ha* except the verb form for the pronoun أَنْتِ, which results in the dropping of the *nuun* نَ.

These four particles are always used in response to the question لِـماذا "why? what for?" or لِأَيِّ سَبَبٍ "for what reason?" Examine the sentences below:

لِـماذا ذَهَبَ الطَّالِبُ إلى الـمَكتَبَةِ؟

Why did the student go to the library?

ذَهَبَ الطَّالِبُ إلى الـمَكتَبَةِ حَتّى يَدْرُسَ.

The student went to the library to study.

In answering the question above, one could have used any of the four particles حَتّى or لِـ or لِكَيْ or كَيْ. They all convey the same meaning.

13.1.2 أَنْ

This particle is used after certain verbs that convey the notions of loving, liking, wishing, desiring, hoping, dreaming, deciding, being able to, etc. Broad categories of such verbs are listed below:

Verbs expressing loving, liking, wishing, desiring, hoping:

أَحَبَّ / يُحِبُّ	to love, to like
أَرادَ / يُريدُ	to want
أَمَلَ / يَأْمَلُ	to hope
تَـمَنّى / يَتَمَنّى	to wish
حَلَمَ / يَحْلُمُ	to dream
رَجا / يَرْجو	to request
رَغِبَ (في) / يَرْغَبُ (في)	to desire
فَضَّلَ / يُفَضِّلُ	to prefer
هَدَفَ / يَهْدُفُ	to target, to aim, to have an objective
وَدَّ / يَوَدُّ	to wish, to want

Verbs expressing ordering, requesting, agreeing / disagreeing, etc.:

اتَّفَقَ / يَتَّفِقُ	to agree
رَضِيَ / يَرْضى	to accept, to agree
قَبِلَ / يَقْبَلُ	to accept
وافَقَ / يُوافِقُ	to agree
أَمَرَ / يَأْمُرُ	to order, to command
دَعا / يَدْعو	to invite, to call for
طَلَبَ / يَطْلُبُ	to seek, to request, to order
طالَبَ / يُطالِبُ	to demand, to call for
ناشَدَ / يُناشِدُ	to appeal to, to request
حَرَّمَ / يُحَرِّمُ	to prohibit (religiously), to forbid
حَلَّلَ / يُحَلِّلُ	to allow (religiously), to allow
رَفَضَ / يَرْفُضُ	to refuse, to reject
سَمَحَ / يَسْمَحُ	to permit, to allow

Verbs expressing ability, capability, etc.:

أَتاح لِ / يُتيحُ لِ	to enable, to provide s.o. with opportunity
اسْتَطاعَ / يَسْتَطيعُ	to be able to
تَمَكَّنَ (مِنْ) / يَتَمَكَّنُ (مِنْ)	to be able to
طاقَ / يَطيقُ	to tolerate, to shoulder
قَدَرَ / يَقْدِرُ	to be able to
اِعْتادَ / يَعْتادُ	to become accustomed to, to get used to
جازَ / يَجوزُ	to become possible, to be allowed
أَدّى إلى / يُؤَدّي إلى	to result in, to lead to

Verbs expressing fear:

خَافَ / يَخَافُ	to be afraid of
خَشِيَ / يَخْشَى	to fear, to be afraid of

Verbs expressing enforcing, decision:

أَجْبَرَ / يُجْبِرُ	to force, to coerce
أَكْرَهَ / يُكْرِهُ	to force, to coerce
فَرَضَ / يَفْرِضُ	to impose, to decree
اُضْطُرَّ / يُضْطَرُّ	to be obliged to
أَصَرَّ / يُصِرُّ	to insist, to persist
حَتَّمَ / يُحَتِّمُ	to ascertain, to emphasize
أَوْصَى / يُوصِي	to recommend, to will
قَدَّرَ / يُقَدِّرُ	to estimate, to guess
قَرَّرَ / يُقَرِّرُ	to decide
صَمَّمَ / يُصَمِّمُ	to decide, to determine
عَزَمَ / يَعْزِمُ	to decide, to make up one's mind
حَاوَلَ / يُحَاوِلُ	to try, to attempt
هَمَّ / يَهُمُّ	to be at the point of starting s.th., to begin to
تَرَدَّدَ / يَتَرَدَّدُ	to hesitate
اِسْتَغْرَبَ / يَسْتَغْرِبُ	to find s.th. strange
اِسْتَحَقَّ / يَسْتَحِقُّ	to deserve, to be worthy of
اِسْتَأْهَلَ / يَسْتَأْهِلُ	to deserve, to be worthy of, to merit
اِسْتَحَالَ / يَسْتَحِيلُ	to become impossible

Verbs expressing remembering, forgetting, etc.

> تَذَكَّرَ / يَتَذَكَّرُ   to remember
>
> نَسِيَ / يَنْسى   to forget

An alternative to the subordinate clause after أَنْ is using the *maSdar*, the verbal noun, of the verb instead of the subjunctive. (See Chapter 25 on *maSdar*s.)

The following verbs convey an impersonal use. In other words, they cannot be conjugated with the various pronouns.

> أَمْكَنَ لِـ / يُـمْكِنُ لِـ   to become possible
>
> اِنْبَغى عَلى / يَنْبَغي عَلى   to become necessary
>
> سَهُلَ عَلى / يَسْهُلُ عَلى   to become easy
>
> صَعُبَ عَلى / يَصْعُبُ عَلى   to become difficult
>
> كَفى / يَكْفي   to suffice, to be sufficient
>
> لَزِمَ عَلى / يَلْزَمُ عَلى   to become necessary
>
> هالَ / يَهالُ   to be overwhelmed, to be overawed
>
> وَجَبَ عَلى / يَجِبُ عَلى   to become necessary

As an illustration, the verb وَجَبَ عَلى "to become necessary" requires the use of a designated noun to follow the preposition عَلَ as in the following example:

وَجَبَ عَلى الطّالِبِ أَنْ يَدْرُسَ.   It was necessary for the student to study.

Similarly, if a suffixal pronoun designating a person is used, the pronoun must attach to the preposition, as in the following:

يَجِبُ عَلَيْكَ أَنْ تَذْهَبَ.   It is necessary that you go.

يَجِبُ عَلَيَّ أَنْ أُسافِرَ.   I must travel.

يَجِبُ عَلَيْهِ أَنْ يَدْرُسَ.   He must study.

أَرَادَ صَدِيقِي أَنْ يَأْكُلَ.   My friend wanted to eat.

أُحِبُّ أَنْ أَزورَ الـمَتْحَفَ.   I like to visit the museum.

يَجِبُ عَلى الطّالِبِ أَنْ يَدْرُسَ.   It is necessary that the student study.

The *nuun* of the second person singular أَنْتِ must be dropped, as in the example below:

يَجِبُ عَلَيْكِ أَنْ تَدْرُسِي.   You (F) must study.

Note also in the above examples that the subjects of the verbs in the main clauses are the same as for the subjunctive verbs in the subordinate clauses. Subjects of verbs in the main clause can be different from those of the subjunctive verb in subordinate clauses, as in the following examples:

أَرَادَ صَدِيقِي أَنْ تَأْكُلَ سوزان مَعَهُ.
My friend (M) wanted Suzanne to eat with him.

أُحِبُّ أَنْ تَزورَ صَدِيقتي الـمَتْحَفَ.
I [would] like my friend (F) to visit the museum.

يُرِيدُ الأُسْتاذُ أَنْ يَدْرُسَ الطّالِبُ العَرَبِيَّةَ.
The teacher wants the student to study Arabic.

13.1.2.1 Expressions with 'an عِبارات مَعَ أَنْ

In addition to the verbs listed above, أَنْ is also used with certain fixed expressions, including, but not restricted to, the following:

مِنَ الأَحْسَن أَنْ it is better that		مِنَ اللازِم أَنْ it is obligatory that	
مِنَ الأَفْضَل أَنْ it is preferable that		مِنَ الـمُحْتَمَل أَنْ it is probable that	
مِنَ السَّهْل أَنْ it is easy to		مِنَ الـمُمْكِن أَنْ it is possible that	
مِنَ الصَّحيح أَنْ it is correct that		مِنَ الـمُناسِب أَنْ it is appropriate that	
مِنَ الصَّعْب أَنْ it is difficult to		مِنَ الـمُهِمِّ أَنْ it is important that	
مِنَ الضَّروري أَنْ it is necessary that		مِنَ الواجِبِ أَنْ it is incumbent that	
مِنَ الغَريب أَنْ it is strange that			

These phrases are invariable. The subjunctive verb following أَنْ, however, indicates the intended person(s). Examine the following:

مِنَ الضَّروري أَنْ يَذْهَبَ الطُّلّابُ إلى الـمَكتَبةِ.
It is necessary that students go to the library.

مِنَ اللازِم أَنْ نَذهَبَ إلى الـمَكتبةِ.
It is obligatory that we go to the library.

مِنَ الأَحْسَن أَنْ تَذْهَبي غَداً.
It is better that you (F) go tomorrow.

There are other phrases containing the absolute negative particle لا followed by a noun in the accusative, as in the following:

لا بُدَّ (مِن) أَنْ	it is necessary that, it is obligatory that
لا عَجَبَ أَنْ	it is not unusual that, it is not surprising that
لا غَرابَةَ أَنْ	it is not unusual that, it is not surprising that

Examine the following examples:

لا بُدَّ مِنْ أَنْ أزورَ أَصْدِقائي. It is necessary that I visit my friends.

لا عَجَبَ أَنْ يَعْمَلَ في الجامعةِ. It is not surprising that he works at
the university.

Some prepositions, prepositional phrases, adverbial phrases, conditional particles and others require the use of أَنْ and, consequently, the subjunctive verb form. Below is a partial list:

عَلى (الطّالِبِ) أَنْ	(the student) is obligated to	في العادَة أَنْ	it is customary that
دونَ أَنْ	without	بَدَلاً مِنْ أَنْ	in lieu of
بَعْدَ أَنْ	after	هَيْهاتَ أَنْ	it is absolutely out of the question that
قَبْلَ أَنْ	before	إِيَّاكَ أَنْ	beware of
مِنْ أَجلِ أَنْ	in order to		

13.1.2.1.1 The phrases in the negative

The negative of the preceding phrases is formed by the use of لَيْسَ, which remains invariable, regardless of the person intended, as in the following illustrative examples:

لَيْسَ مِنَ الأَحْسَنِ أَنْ   it is not better that

لَيْسَ مِنَ الأَفْضَل أَنْ   it is not preferable that

لَيْسَ مِنَ اللازم أَنْ   it is not necessary that

لَيْسَ مِنَ الضَّروري أَنْ   it is not obligatory/necessary that

13.1.2.1.2 The phrases in the past tense

The preceding phrases can be used to refer to time in the past by the use of كانَ, which remains invariable. The following examples are illustrative:

كانَ مِنَ الواجبَ أَنْ يَذهَبَ الطَّالبُ إلى الـمَكتَبَة.
It was incumbent upon the student (M) to go to the library.

كانَ مِنَ الضَّروريِّ أَنْ تَتَكَلَّمَ الأُسْتاذَةُ مَعَ الطُّلّابِ.
It was necessary for the teacher (F) to speak with the students.

13.1.2.1.3 The phrases in the future tense

The preceding phrases can also be used to express the future by سَوْفَ or سَـ "will, shall" followed by يَكونُ. The sequence of سَوْفَ يَكونُ is invariable. Examine the following examples:

سَوْفَ يَكونُ مِنَ الضَّروريِّ أَنْ تَذْهَبي.
It will be necessary that you (F) go.

سَوْفَ يَكونُ مِنَ اللازم أَنْ تُقابِلَ الـمُديرَ.
It will be necessary that you (M, Sg) meet the director.

13.2 DUAL SUBJUNCTIVE VERBS

الفِعْل الـمُضارِع الـمَنْصوب - الـمُثَنَّى

The final *nuun* of dual verbs in the present tense preceded by any of لِ، لِكَيْ،
كَيْ، حَتّى، لَن، أَنْ is dropped, as in the examples below.

ذَهَبَ الـمُعَلِّمانِ حَتّى يُدَرِّسا.
The teachers (M, D) went to teach.

أَنْتُما رَجَعْتُما حَتّى تُشاهِدا البَيْتَ.
You (M/F, D) returned to see the house.

أَرادَ الطّالِبانِ أَنْ يَدْرُسا.
The students (M, D) wanted to study.

البِنْتانِ لَنْ تَأْكُلا في هذا الـمَطعَمِ.
The two girls will not eat in this restaurant.

عادا إلى مِصر كَيْ يَدْرُسا في القاهِرَة.
They (M, D) returned to Egypt to study in Cairo.

خَرَجَتا مِنَ البَيْتِ لِكَيْ تُقابِلا صَديقَتَهُما.
They (F, D) went out of the house to meet their friend (F).

The following examples are in the negative:

أَرادَ الصَّديقانِ أَنْ لا يَدْرُسا.
The two friends (M) wanted not to study.

خَرَجَتا مِنَ البَيْتِ كَيْ لا تَسْتَقْبِلا الزّائِرَ.
They (F, D) left the house in order not to receive the visitor.

The *nuun* in أَنْ when followed by *laam* as in لا gets assimilated by *laam*. The
preceding first sentence can appear in the orthography as follows:

أَرادَ الصَّديقانِ أَلَّا يَدْرُسا.
The two friends (M, D) wanted not to study.

On the other hand, كَيْ and لا in the second sentence above can be conjoined in the writing system, appearing as كَيْلا, as in the following:

خَرَجَتا مِن البَيْتِ كَيْلا تَسْتَقْبِلا الزَّائِرَ.

They (F, D) left the house in order not to receive the visitor.

13.3 PLURAL SUBJUNCTIVE VERBS

الفِعْل المُضارِع المَنصوب - الجَمْع

The final *nuun* of plural verbs in the present tense only drops when preceded by a long vowel. This applies to the verbs for the pronouns أَنْتُمْ "you (M, Pl)" and هُمْ "they (M, Pl)", as in the examples below:

أَنْتُمْ رَجَعْتُم حَتّى تُشاهِدوا البَيْتَ.

You (M, Pl) returned (in order) to see the house.

سافَرَ المُعَلِّمونَ حَتّى يُدَرِّسوا.

The teachers (M, Pl) left (in order) to teach.

أَحَبّوا أَنْ يُسافِروا لِيُشاهِدوا الآثارَ القَديمَةَ.

They (M, Pl) wanted to travel to see the old antiquities.

أَرادَ الطُّلّابُ أَنْ يُشاهِدوا الفِلْمَ.

The students (M, Pl) wanted to see the film.

يُحِبُّ الطُّلّابُ أَنْ يَدْرُسوا.

The students like to study.

لَزِمَ عَلى المُوَظَّفينَ أَنْ يَعْمَلوا.

The employees (M, Pl) had to work. (*lit.*: "It was obligatory for the employees to work.")

In the orthography, when the *nuun* of the plural verb is dropped an *'alif* is added. This *'alif* is not pronounced but rather functions as a device to indicate that the word in question is a verb.

If the plural verb in the present tense ends with a *nuun* not preceded by a long vowel, the *nuun* is maintained. This applies to the verb forms for the pronouns أَنْتُنَّ "you (F, Pl)" and هُنَّ "they (F, Pl)," as in the following examples:

الطّالِباتُ ذَهَبْـنَ إلى الـمَكتَبَةِ حَتّى يَدرُسْنَ.

The students (F, Pl) went to the library to study.

البَناتُ رَجَعْنَ إلى الـمَلْعَبِ حَتّى يَلْعَبْـنَ.

The girls returned to the playground to play.

أَنْتُـنَّ رَجَعْتُـنَّ حَتّى تَدْرُسْنَ.

You (F, Pl) returned in order to study.

سَهُلَ عَلى الطّالِباتِ أَنْ يَدْرُسْنَ.

It was easy for the students (F, Pl) to study.

13.4 NEGATION OF THE SUBJUNCTIVE
نَفي الفِعْل الـمَنْصوب

Negation of the subjunctive verb is accomplished by placing لا between the subjunctive particle and the verb. Examine the following:

قَرَّرَ صَديقي أَنْ لا يَأْكُلَ.

My friend decided not to eat.

أُفَضِّلُ أَنْ لا أَزورَ الـمَتْحَفَ اليَوْمَ.

I prefer not to visit the museum today.

يَجِبُ عَلى الطّالِبِ أَنْ لا يُسافِرَ.

It is necessary that the student does not travel.

بَقِيَ في البَيْتِ حَتّى لا يَمْشيَ في المَطَر.

He stayed at home in order not to walk in the rain.

عَمِلْنا كُلَّ الواجِباتِ كَيْلا نُغْضِبَ الـمُعَلِّمَةَ.

We did all the homework in order not to anger the teacher.

The *nuun* in أَنْ gets assimilated by the *laam* of the negative particle thus obtaining أَلّا, as in the following:

مِنَ اللازِم عَلَيْكُم أَلّا تَرْجِعوا إلى هذا المَكَانِ.

It is incumbent upon you not to return to this place.

On the other hand, writing أَنْ and لا independently is quite acceptable, as we see below:

قَرَّرَ الصَّديقانِ أَنْ لا يُسافِرا.

The two friends (M, D) decided not to travel.

تُحِبُّ البِنتانِ أَنْ لا تَدْرُسا الطِّبَّ.

The two girls do not like to study medicine.

رَغِبوا أَنْ لا يُسافِروا.

They did not want to travel.

وَجَبَ عَلَيْهِم أَنْ لا يَرْجِعوا.

It was incumbent upon them not to return.

أَحَبَّت الطّالِباتُ أَنْ لا يُقابِلْنَ الأُسْتاذَةَ.

The students (F) did not want to meet the teacher.

CHAPTER 14

The future tense الـمُسْتَقْبَل

Putting a verb in Arabic into the future is a simple matter of using either of two particles, سَوْفَ and ـسَ, in front of a verb in the present indicative tense. These "auxiliary" elements are the same in singular, dual or plural verbs. The negative of a verb in the future requires لَنْ followed by the subjunctive.

14.1 FUTURE TENSE SINGULAR الفِعْل الـمُسْتَقْبَل - الـمُفْرَد

The two particles expressing the future, سَوْفَ and its shorter version ـس, must be followed immediately by a verb in the present tense indicative. In the orthography, سَوْفَ stands independent of the verb. However, ـسَ must attach to the verb following it, as in these examples:

سَوْفَ يُسافِرُ كَريم إلى الـمَغْرِب غَداً.
Kareem will travel to Morocco tomorrow.

سَيُسافِرُ كَريم إلى الـمَغْرِب غَداً.
Kareem will travel to Morocco tomorrow.

Classical Arabic grammarians belabored the difference between these two particles with respect to near future time when using ـسَ as opposed to distant future time when using سَوْفَ. In Modern Standard Arabic, however, the difference in meaning between these particles is blurred.

The main verb must be marked for gender, as in the following pairs of sentences:

سَوْفَ يَدْرُسُ سامي العَرَبِيَّةَ.	Sami will study Arabic.
سَيَدْرُسُ سامي العَرَبِيَّةَ.	Sami will study Arabic.
سَوْفَ تَدْرُسُ سامِية العَرَبِيَّةَ.	Samia will study Arabic.
سَتَدْرُسُ سامِية العَرَبِيَّةَ.	Samia will study Arabic.

The present tense could be used to express a future action or condition. This use holds especially when adverbs of time expressing the future are used, as in the following illustrative example:

يُسافِرُ كَريم إلى الـمَغْرِب غَداً.   Kareem will travel to Morocco tomorrow.

This new tendency in Arabic seems to be widely used in the media.

14.2 FUTURE TENSE DUAL الفِعْل الـمُسْتَقْبَل - الـمُثَنّى

The future tense dual is expressed by either سَوْفَ or سَـ followed by the verb in the present tense. This verb combination is treated as one indivisible unit. Examine the following examples:

سَوْفَ يُسافِرُ الطَّالِبانِ إلى سوريا غَداً.
The two students (M) will travel to Syria tomorrow.

The verb preceding the فاعِل, the performer, must always be in the singular. When the فاعِل precedes the verb, the verb must be conjugated to express the number and gender of the subject. سَوْفَ or سَـ in this case must precede the conjugated dual verb, as in the following two sentences:

الـمُوَظَّفَتانِ سَوْفَ تَرجِعانِ غَداً.
The two employees (F) will return tomorrow.

الـمُهَنْدِسانِ سَوْفَ يَبْنِيانِ البِناءَ الجَديدَ بَعْدَ سَنَةٍ.
The two engineers will build the new building in a year's time.

14.3 FUTURE TENSE PLURAL الفِعْل الـمُسْتَقْبَل - الجَمْع

The future tense plural is expressed by either سَوْفَ or سَـ plus a verb in the present tense. When the verbs precede the performer of action, the فاعِل must always be in the singular as required by verbal sentences. Consider the following examples:

سَوْفَ يُسافِرُ الطُّلَّابُ إلى سوريا غَداً.
The students will travel to Syria tomorrow.

سَيُسافِرُ الـمُعَلِّمونَ إلى القاهِرَة.
The teachers will travel to Cairo.

When the فاعِل precedes the verb, the verb must be conjugated to agree with the فاعِل in number and gender, as in the following examples:

الـمُوَظَّفاتُ سَوْفَ يَرْجِعْنَ غَداً.

The employees (F) will return tomorrow.

الـمُهَنْدِسونَ سَيَبْنونَ البِناءَ الـجَديدَ بَعْدَ سَنَةٍ.

The engineers will build the new building in a year's time.

As was stated elsewhere, Arabic strongly prefers to begin sentences with verbs. The preceding two sentences are preferably rendered as follows:

سَوْف تَرجِعُ الـمُوَظَّفاتُ غَداً.

The employees (F) will return tomorrow.

سَيَبْني الـمُهَنْدِسونَ البِناءَ الـجَديدَ بَعْدَ سَنَةٍ.

The engineers will build the new building in a year's time.

14.4 FUTURE TENSE NEGATION نَفْي الـمُسْتَقْبَل

14.4.1 Singular

Verbs in the future tense are negated by placing the particle لَنْ immediately in front of the present tense verb, thus changing it into the subjunctive. لَنْ is one of several particles that must be followed by present tense verbs in the subjunctive. These particles and the subjunctive are presented in Chapter 13. Singular verbs following لَنْ must end with a *fat-Ha*. The only exception is the verb form for the pronoun أنتِ "you (F)", which must end with a *yaa'*. Examine the following two pairs of examples in the singular, in which the first sentence is in the affirmative in the future, and the second is negated in the future:

سَوْفَ يَدْرُسُ كَريم العَرَبِيَّةَ.   Kareem will study Arabic.

لَنْ يَدْرُسَ كَريم العَرَبِيَّةَ.   Kareem will not study Arabic.

When the فاعِل is placed at the beginning, which one may encounter, the above sentences are rendered as follows:

كَريم سَوْفَ يَدْرُسُ العَرَبِيَّةَ.   Kareem will study Arabic.

كَريم لَنْ يَدْرُسَ العَرَبِيَّةَ.   Kareem will not study Arabic.

14.4.2 Dual

As in the singular, this is accomplished by the dropping of سَوْفَ or سَـ and placing لَنْ in front of the main verb. This results in the dropping of the final *nuun*, as in the following:

سَوْفَ يَدْرُسُ الطّالِبانِ العَرَبِيَّةَ.   The students (M, D) will study Arabic.

لَنْ يَدْرُسَ الطّالِبانِ العَرَبِيَّةَ.   The students (M, D) will not study Arabic.

By placing فاعِل at the beginning of the sentence, the main verb must express the gender and number of the dual noun, as in the following sexample:

الطّالِبانِ لَنْ يَدْرُسا العَرَبِيَّةَ.

The students (M, D) will not study Arabic.

المُوَظَّفتانِ لَنْ تَعْمَلا في هذِهِ الشَّرِكَةِ.

The employees (F, D) will not work in this company.

14.4.3 Plural

In the presence of لَنْ plural verbs lose their *-nuun* when the *nuun* is preceded by a long vowel. Consider the following:

سَوْفَ يَعْقِدُ المُوَظَّفونَ الاِجْتِماعَ.
The employees will hold the meeting.

لَنْ يَعْقِدَ المُوَظَّفونَ الاِجْتِماعَ.
The employees will not hold the meeting.

الـمُدَرِّسونَ سَيزورونَ الـمَدارِسَ غَداً.
The teachers (M, Pl) will visit the schools tomorrow.

الـمُدَرِّسونَ لَنْ يَزوروا الـمَدارِسَ غَداً.
The teachers (M, Pl) will not visit the schools tomorrow.

However, if the *nuun* is not preceded by a long vowel, as in the case of verbs for the pronouns أَنْتُنَّ and هُنَّ, the *nuun* is maintained, as in the following:

الـمُدَرِّساتُ سَيَزُرْنَ الـمَدارِسَ غَداً.

The teachers (F, Pl) will visit the schools tomorrow.

الـمُدَرِّساتُ لَنْ يَزُرْنَ الـمَدارِسَ غَداً.

The teachers (F, Pl) will not visit the schools tomorrow.

أَنْتُـنَّ سَوْفَ تُقابِلْنَ الـمُديرَةَ غَداً.

You (F, Pl) will meet the director tomorrow.

أَنْتُـنَّ لَن تُقابِلْنَ الـمُديرَةَ غَداً.

You (F, Pl) will not meet the director tomorrow.

CHAPTER 15

Jussive verbs الفِعْل المَجزوم

The jussive جَزْم is a mood of the present tense that performs a variety of functions in Arabic. It is used in negating the past tense with the negative particle لَـمْ, in conditional clauses, and in forming the imperative verb. This chapter will be devoted to لم and its impact on verbs. The imperative will be discussed in Chapter 17, and the conditionals in Chapter 20.

The verb in the jussive is referred to as فِعْل مَجزوم. It is a foreshortened version of the present tense. Present tense indicative verbs become jussive by dropping their final vowel in the singular and their final *nuun* when preceded by a long vowel such as *yaa'* in the singular (this mostly applies to the pronoun أَنْتِ), or *'alif* (in the dual), or *waaw* (in the plural).

15.1 NEGATION WITH *LAM* «لَمْ» بِـ النَّفْي

Past tense verbs can be negated by placing ما in front of them (see Chapter 11). The negative particle لم is used for the same purpose but requires that the verb be in the jussive mood of the present tense. There is a slight difference in register but not in meaning. The negative particle ما is used in formal written Arabic as well as everyday speech; لم on the other hand is used in written Arabic and formal speech only.

15.1.1 Verbs in the singular

Singular verbs in the present indicative ending with a *Dhamma* lose their *Dhamma* when they appear after لَمْ. A *sukuun* replaces the *Dhamma* in the orthography. Examine the following examples:

أَنا لَمْ أَدْرُسْ أَمْسِ.   I did not study yesterday.

هِيَ لَمْ تَرْجِعْ مِنَ العِراق.   She did not return from Iraq.

The present tense verb form for the singular feminine pronoun أُنْتِ loses its *nuun* after لَمْ, as in the following example:

أَنْتِ لَمْ تَكْتُبِي هٰذِهِ الكَلِمَاتِ.   You (F, Sg) did not write these words.

To illustrate the use of لَمْ with the various forms of verbs in the singular, examine the following tables. For the sake of comparison, we will provide similar tables illustrating the use of لَمْ with the same verbs in the dual and plural in the sections below:

فَعَلَ verbs

Example: شَرِبَ / يَشْرَبُ and its negative

Affirmative past tense	Negative with لَمْ	Meaning
أَنا شَرِبْتُ القَهْوَةَ.	أَنا لَمْ أَشْرَبِ القَهْوَةَ.	I did not drink the coffee.
أَنْتَ شَرِبْتَ القَهْوَةَ.	أَنْتَ لَمْ تَشْرَبِ القَهْوَةَ.	You (M) did not drink the coffee.
أَنْتِ شَرِبْتِ القَهْوَةَ.	أَنْتِ لَمْ تَشْرَبِي القَهْوَةَ.	You (F) did not drink the coffee.
هُوَ شَرِبَ القَهْوَةَ.	هُوَ لَمْ يَشْرَبِ القَهْوَةَ.	He did not drink the coffee.
هِيَ شَرِبَتِ القَهْوَةَ.	هِيَ لَمْ تَشْرَبِ القَهْوَةَ.	She did not drink the coffee.

An -*i* sound is heard when jussive verbs are followed by definite nouns. In the orthography, a *kasra* is inserted at the end of the verb.

15.1.1.1 Hollow verbs

The use of لَمْ before hollow verbs results in two things: (1) the shortening of the middle long vowel in the present tense form, and (2) the loss of the final *nuun*. The exceptions to this rule in the singular are the verb forms for the pronoun أَنْتِ. As verbs for أَنْتِ have long vowels (*yaa'* or *waaw* or *'alif*), the "organic" long vowels in the present tense of these verbs must be maintained. Examine the following tables.

Hollow verbs (present tense with *waaw*)

Example: زارَ / يَزورُ and its negative

Affirmative past tense	Negative with لَـمْ	Meaning
أَنا زُرْتَ عائلَتي.	أَنا لَمْ أَزُرْ عائِلَتي.	I did not visit my family.
أَنْتَ زُرْتَ عائِلَتَكَ.	أَنْتَ لَمْ تَزُرْ عائِلَتَكَ.	You (M) did not visit your family.
أَنْتِ زُرْتِ عائِلَتَكِ.	أَنْتِ لَمْ تَزوري عائِلَتَكِ.	You (F) did not visit your family.
هُوَ زارَ عَائِلَتَهُ.	هُوَ لَمْ يَزُرْ عائِلَتَهُ.	He did not visit his family.
هِيَ زارَت عائِلَتَها.	هِيَ لَمْ تَزُرْ عائِلَتَها.	She did not visit her family.

Hollow verbs (present tense with *yaa'*)

Example: سارَ / يَسيرُ and its negative

Affirmative past tense	Negative with لَـمْ	Meaning
أَنا سِرْتُ مِنَ البَيْتِ.	أَنا لَمْ أَسِرْ مِنَ البَيْتِ.	I did not walk from the house.
أَنْتَ سِرْتَ مِنَ البَيْتِ.	أَنْتَ لَمْ تَسِرْ مِنَ البَيْتِ.	You (M) did not walk from the house.
أَنْتِ سِرْتِ مِنَ البَيْتِ.	أَنْتِ لَمْ تَسيري مِنَ البَيْتِ.	You (F) did not walk from the house.
هُوَ سارَ مِنَ البَيْتِ.	هُوَ لَمْ يَسِرْ مِنَ البَيْتِ.	He did not walk from the house.
هِيَ سارَت مِنَ البَيْتِ.	هِيَ لَمْ تَسِرْ مِنَ البَيْتِ.	She did not walk from the house.

Hollow verbs (present tense with *'alif*)

Example: نامَ / يَنامُ and its negative

Affirmative past tense	Negative with لَـمْ	Meaning
أَنا نِـمْتُ في الفُنْدُقِ.	أَنا لَمْ أَنَمْ في الفُنْدُقِ.	I did not sleep in the hotel.
أَنْتَ نِـمْتَ في الفُنْدُقِ.	أَنْتَ لَمْ تَنَمْ في الفُنْدُقِ.	You (M) did not sleep in the hotel.
أَنْتِ نِـمْتِ في الفُنْدُقِ.	أَنْتِ لَمْ تَنامي في الفُنْدُقِ.	You (F) did not sleep in the hotel.
هُوَ نامَ في الفُنْدُقِ.	هُوَ لَمْ يَنَـمْ في الفُنْدُقِ.	He did not sleep in the hotel.
هِيَ نامَت في الفُنْدُقِ.	هِيَ لَـمْ تَنَـمْ في الفُنْدُقِ.	She did not sleep in the hotel.

15.1.1.2 Defective verbs

لَمْ before defective verbs in the singular results in the shortening of the final long vowel to its short counterpart. The exceptions are the verb forms for the pronoun أَنْتِ, where the long vowel is maintained. Examine the following tables:

Defective verbs (present tense with *yaa'*)

Example: مَشى / يَـمْشي and its negative

Affirmative past tense	Negative with لَـمْ	Meaning
أَنا مَشَيْتُ مِيلاً.	أَنا لَمْ أَمْشِ مِيلاً.	I did not walk a mile.
أَنْتَ مَشَيْتَ مِيلاً.	أَنْتَ لَمْ تَـمْشِ مِيلاً.	You (M) did not walk a mile.
أَنْتِ مَشَيْتِ مِيلاً.	أَنْتِ لَمْ تَـمْشي مِيلاً.	You (F) did not walk a mile.
هُوَ مَشى مِيلاً.	هُوَ لَمْ يَـمْشِ مِيلاً.	He did not walk a mile.
هِيَ مَشَتْ مِيلاً.	هِيَ لَمْ تَـمْشِ مِيلاً.	She did not walk a mile.

Defective verbs (present tense with *waaw*)

Example: دَعا / يَـدْعو and its negative

Affirmative past tense	Negative with لَـمْ	Meaning
أَنا دَعَوْتُ الأُسْتاذَ.	أَنا لَمْ أَدْعُ الأُسْتاذَ.	I did not invite the teacher.
أَنْتَ دَعَوْتَ الأُسْتاذَ.	أَنْتَ لَمْ تَدْعُ الأُسْتاذَ.	You (M) did not invite the teacher.
أَنْتِ دَعَوْتِ الأُسْتاذَ.	أَنْتِ لَمْ تَدْعي الأُسْتاذَ.	You (F) did not invite the teacher.
هُوَ دَعا الأُسْتاذَ.	هُوَ لَمْ يَدْعُ الأُسْتاذَ.	He did not invite the teacher.
هِيَ دَعَتِ الأُسْتاذَ.	هِيَ لَمْ تَدْعُ الأُسْتاذَ.	She did not invite the teacher.

15.1.1.3 Doubled verbs

لَمْ before doubled verbs in the singular results in the use of a *fat-Ha* at the end of the verb instead of the expected *sukuun*. The exceptions are the verb forms for the pronoun أَنْتِ, where the long vowel is maintained. Examine the following example and its negative meanings:

أَحَبَّ / يُحِبُّ

Affirmative past tense	Negative with لَمْ	Meaning
أَنا أَحْبَبْتُ الأَكْلَ.	أَنا لَمْ أُحِبَّ الأَكْلَ.	I did not like the food.
أَنْتَ أَحْبَبْتَ الأَكْلَ.	أَنْتَ لَمْ تُحِبَّ الأَكْلَ.	You (M) did not like the food.
أَنْتِ أَحْبَبْتِ الأَكْلَ.	أَنْتِ لَمْ تُحِبّي الأَكْلَ.	You (F) did not like the food.
هُوَ أَحَبَّ الأَكْلَ.	هُوَ لَمْ يُحِبَّ الأَكْلَ.	He did not like the food.
هِيَ أَحَبَّتِ الأَكْلَ.	هِيَ لَمْ تُحِبَّ الأَكْلَ.	She did not like the food.

15.1.2 Verbs in the dual

Present tense verbs in the dual lose their final *nuun* when the verb is preceded by لَمْ. Consider the following pairs of examples, in which the first sentence is in the past tense affirmative, the second in the negative:

الطَّالِبانِ دَرَسا الدَّرْسَ. The students (M, D) studied the lesson.

الطَّالِبانِ لَمْ يَدْرُسا الدَّرْسَ. The students (M, D) did not study the lesson.

هُما شَرِبَتا الماءَ. They (F, D) drank the water.

هُما لَمْ تَشْرَبا الماءَ. They (F, D) did not drink the water.

أَنْتُما شَرِبْتُما القَهْوَةَ. You (M/F, D) drank the coffee.

أَنْتُما لَمْ تَشْرَبا القَهْوَةَ. You (M/F, D) did not drink the coffee.

In dual verbs for the first person نَحْنُ the usual *Dhamma* at the end of the verb changes to *sukuun*, as in the following:

نَحْنُ عَمِلْنا في الشَّرِكَةِ. We (M/F, D) worked at the company.

نَحْنُ لم نَعْمَلْ في الشَّرِكَةِ. We (M/F, D) did not work at the company.

Note that the pronoun نَحْنُ is also used in the plural. In the preceding two sentences, the context clarifies that two persons are involved in the action.

To illustrate the use of لَمْ with the various forms of verbs in the dual, examine the following tables:

فَعَلَ verbs

Example: شَرِبَ / يَشْرَبُ and its negative

Affirmative past tense	Negative with لَـمْ	Meaning
نَحْنُ شَرِبْنا	نَحْنُ لَمْ نَشْرَبْ	we (M/F) did not drink
أَنْتُما شَرِبْتُما	أَنْتُما لَمْ تَشْرَبا	you (M, D) did not drink
أَنْتُما شَرِبْتُما	أَنْتُما لَمْ تَشْرَبا	you (F, D) did not drink
هُما شَرِبا	هُما لَمْ يَشْرَبا	they (M, D) did not drink
هُما شَرِبَتا	هُما لَمْ تَشْرَبا	they (F, D) did not drink

Note that the verb forms for the second person duals, male and female, are the same.

15.1.2.1 Hollow verbs

لَمْ before hollow verbs results in the shortening of the middle long vowel to its short counterpart and also in dropping the *nuun*. The exceptions to this rule in the dual are the verb forms for the pronouns أَنْتُما (M/F) and هُما (M/F), as in the following tables:

Hollow verbs with present tense *waaw*

Example: زارَ / يَزورُ and its negative

Affirmative past tense	Negative with لَـمْ	Meaning
نَحْنُ زُرْنا	نَحْنُ لَمْ نَزُرْ	we (M/F) did not visit
أَنْتُما زُرْتُما	أَنْتُما لَمْ تَزورا	you (M, D) did not visit
أَنْتُما زُرْتُما	أَنْتُما لَمْ تَزورا	you (F, D) did not visit
هُما زارا	هُما لَمْ يَزورا	they (M, D) did not visit
هُما زارَتا	هُما لَمْ تَزورا	they (F, D) did not visit

Hollow verbs (with present tense *yaa'*)

Example: سارَ / يَسيرُ and its negative

Affirmative past tense	Negative with لَمْ	Meaning
نَحْنُ سِرْنا	نَحْنُ لَمْ نَسِرْ	we (M/F) did not walk
أَنتُما سِرْتُما	أَنْتُما لَمْ تَسيرا	you (M, D) did not walk
أَنْتُما سِرْتُما	أَنْتُما لَمْ تَسيرا	you (F, D) did not walk
هُما سارا	هُما لَمْ يَسيرا	they (M, D) did not walk
هُما سارَتا	هُما لَمْ تَسيرا	they (F, D) did not walk

Hollow verbs (with present tense *'alif*)

Example: نامَ / يَنامُ and its negative

Affirmative past tense	Negative with لَمْ	Meaning
نَحْنُ نِـمْنا	نَحْنُ لَمْ نَنَمْ	we (M/F) did not sleep
أَنتُما نِمْتُما	أَنتُما لَمْ تَناما	you (M, D) did not sleep
أَنْتُما نِمْتُما	أَنْتُما لَمْ تَناما	you (F, D) did not sleep
هُما ناما	هُما لَمْ يَناما	they (M, D) did not sleep
هُما نامَتا	هُما لَمْ تَناما	they (F, D) did not sleep

15.1.2.2 Defective verbs

لَمْ before defective verbs in the dual results in the shortening of the final long vowel to its short counterpart for the pronoun نَحْنُ. The *nuun* is dropped when preceded by a long vowel. Examine the following tables:

Example: رَمى / يَرمي and its negative

Affirmative past tense	Negative with لَمْ	Meaning
نَحْنُ رَمَيْنا	نَحْنُ لَمْ نَرْم	we (M/F) did not throw
أَنْتُما رَمَيْتُما	أَنْتُما لَمْ تَرْمِيا	you (M, D) did not throw
أَنْتُما رَمَيْتُما	أَنْتُما لَمْ تَـرْمِيا	you (F, D) did not throw
هُما رَمَيا	هُما لَمْ يَـرْمِيا	they (M, D) did not throw
هُما رَمَتا	هُما لَمْ تَرْمِيا	they (F, D) did not throw

Defective verbs (present tense with *waaw*)

Example: دَعا / يَدْعو and its negative

Affirmative past tense	Negative with لَمْ	Meaning
نَحْنُ دَعَوْنا	نَحْنُ لَمْ نَدْعُ	we (M/F) did not invite
أَنْتُما .دَعَوْتُما	أَنْتُما لَمْ تَدْعُوا	you (M, D) did not invite
أَنْتُما دَعَوْتُما	أَنْتُما لَمْ تَدْعُوا	you (F, D) did not invite
هُما دَعَوا	هُما لَمْ يَـدْعُوا	they (M, D) did not invite
هُما دَعَتا	هُما لَمْ تَـدْعُوا	they (F, D) did not invite

15.1.2.3 Doubled verbs

لَمْ before doubled verbs in the dual results in the use of a *fat-Ha* at the end of the verb for the pronoun نَحْنُ and the dropping of *nuun* when preceded by a long vowel.

Example: أَحَبَّ / يُحِبُّ and its negative

Affirmative past tense	Negative with لَمْ	Meaning
نَحْنُ أَحْبَبْنا	نَحْنُ لَمْ نُحِبَّ	we (M/F) did not love/like
أَنْتُما أَحْبَبْتُما	أَنْتُما لَمْ تُـحِبّا	you (M, D) did not love/like
أَنْتُما أَحْبَبْتُما	أَنْتُما لَمْ تُحِبّا	you (F, D) did not love/like
هُما أَحَبّا	هُما لَمْ يُحِبّا	they (M, D) did not love/like
هُما أَحَبَّتا	هُما لَمْ تُحِبّا	they (F, D) did not love/like

15.1.3 Verbs in the plural

As in the dual, when plural verbs are used with لَمْ they lose their *nuun* when it is preceded by a long vowel. This applies to the pronouns أَنْتُمْ "you (M, Pl)" and هُمْ "they (M, Pl)." Examine the following pairs, in which the first is in the affirmative, the second in the negative:

الطُّلَّابُ دَرَسوا الدَّرْسَ.	The students read the lesson.
الطُّلَّابُ لَمْ يَدْرُسوا الدَّرْسَ.	The students (M, Pl) did not study the lesson.
أَنْتُمْ شَرِبْتُمُ القَهْوَةَ.	You drank the coffee.
أَنْتُمْ لَمْ تَشْرَبوا القَهْوَةَ.	You (M, Pl) did not drink the coffee.

Plural verbs that end with a *nuun* not preceded by a long vowel maintain the *nuun*. This applies only to two pronouns, namely أَنْتُنَّ "you (F, Pl)," and هُنَّ "they (F, Pl)," as in the following examples:

أَنْتُنَّ شَرِبْتُنَّ القَهْوَةَ.	You (F, Pl) drank the coffee.
أَنْتُنَّ لَمْ تَشْرَبْنَ القَهْوَةَ.	You (F, Pl) did not drink the coffee.
هُنَّ شَرِبْنَ القَهْوَةَ.	They (F, Pl) drank the coffee.
هُنَّ لَمْ يَشْرَبْنَ القَهْوَةَ.	They (F, Pl) did not drink the coffee.

The plural verb form for نَحْنُ "we (M/F, Pl)" ends with a *sukuun*, as in the following:

نَحْنُ أَكْمَلْنا الواجِباتِ.	We completed the homework assignments.
نَحْنُ لَمْ نُكْمِلِ الواجِباتِ.	We did not complete the homework assignments.

To illustrate the negative particle لَمْ and the various verb forms in the plural, examine the following table:

شَرِبَ / يَشْرَبُ

Affirmative past tense	Negative with لَمْ	Meaning
نَحْنُ شَرِبْنا	نَحْنُ لَمْ نَشْرَبْ	we (M/F, Pl) did not drink
أَنْتُمْ شَرِبْتُمْ	أَنْتُمْ لَمْ تَشْرَبوا	you (M, Pl) did not drink
أَنْتُنَّ شَرِبْتُنَّ	أَنْتُنَّ لَمْ تَشْرَبْنَ	you (F, Pl) did not drink
هُمْ شَرِبوا	هُمْ لَمْ يَشْرَبوا	they (M, Pl) did not drink
هُنَّ شَرِبْنَ	هُنَّ لَمْ يَشْرَبْنَ	they (F, Pl) did not drink

15.1.3.1 Hollow verbs

لَمْ before hollow verbs results in the shortening of the middle long vowel to its short counterpart. The exceptions to this rule are the verb forms for أَنْتُمْ and هُمْ in the plural. Examine the following tables:

زارَ / يَزورُ and its negative

Affirmative past tense	Negative with لَمْ	Meaning
نَحْنُ زُرْنا	نَحْنُ لَمْ نَزُرْ	we (M/F, Pl) did not visit
أَنْتُمْ زُرْتُمْ	أَنْتُمْ لَمْ تَزوروا	you (M, Pl) did not visit
أَنْتُنَّ زُرْتُنَّ	أَنْتُنَّ لَمْ تَزُرْنَ	you (F, Pl) did not visit
هُمْ زاروا	هُمْ لَمْ يَزوروا	they (M, Pl) did not visit
هُنَّ زُرْنَ	هُنَّ لَمْ يَزُرْنَ	they (F, Pl) did not visit

سارَ / يَسيرُ

Affirmative past tense	Negative with لَمْ	Meaning
نَحْنُ سِرْنا	نَحْنُ لَمْ نَسِرْ	we (M/F, Pl) did not walk
أَنْتُمْ سِرْتُمْ	أَنْتُمْ لَمْ تَسيروا	you (M, Pl) did not walk
أَنْتُنَّ سِرْتُنَّ	أَنْتُنَّ لَمْ تَسِرْنَ	you (F, Pl) did not walk
هُمْ ساروا	هُمْ لَمْ يَسيروا	they (M, Pl) did not walk
هُنَّ سِرْنَ	هُنَّ لَمْ يَسِرْنَ	they (F, Pl) did not walk

نامَ / يَنامُ

Affirmative past tense	Negative with لَــمْ	Meaning
نَحْنُ نِمْنا	نَحْنُ لَمْ نَنَمْ	we (M/F, Pl) did not sleep
أَنْتُم نِمْتُمْ	أَنْتُم لَمْ تَناموا	you (M, Pl) did not sleep
أَنْتُنَّ نِمْتُنَّ	أَنْتُنَّ لَمْ تَنَمْنَ	you (F, Pl) did not sleep
هُم ناموا	هُمْ لَمْ يَناموا	they (M, Pl) did not sleep
هُنَّ نِمْنَ	هُنَّ لَمْ يَنَمْنَ	they (F, Pl) did not sleep

15.1.3.2 Defective verbs

لَمْ before defective verbs in the plural results in the shortening of the final long vowel to its short counterpart for the pronoun نَحْنُ. The *nuun* is dropped when preceded by a long vowel. This applies on verbs for the pronouns أَنْتُمْ and هُمْ. The verb forms for أَنْتُنَّ and هُنَّ do not undergo any change since the *nuun* is not preceded by a long vowel. Examine the following tables:

رَمَى / يَرْمي

Affirmative past tense	Negative with لَــمْ	Meaning
نَحْنُ رَمَيْنا	نَحْنُ لَمْ نَرْمِ	we (M/F, Pl) did not throw
أَنْتُم رَمَيْتُمْ	أَنْتُم لَمْ تَرْموا	you (M, Pl) did not throw
أَنْتُنَّ رَمَيْتُنَّ	أَنْتُنَّ لَمْ تَرْمينَ	you (F, Pl) did not throw
هُم رَمَوْا	هُم لَمْ يَرْموا	they (M, Pl) did not throw
هُنَّ رَمَيْنَ	هُنَّ لَمْ يَرْمينَ	they (F, Pl) did not throw

دَعا / يَدْعو

Affirmative past tense	Negative with لَمْ	Meaning
نَحْنُ دَعَوْنا	نَحْنُ لَمْ نَدْعُ	we (M/F, Pl) did not invite
أَنْتُم دَعَوْتُمْ	أَنْتُم لَمْ تَدْعوا	you (M, Pl) did not invite
أَنْتُم دَعَوْتُنَّ	أَنْتُنَّ لَمْ تَدْعونَ	they (F, Pl) did not invite
هُم دَعَوْا	هُم لَمْ يَدْعوا	they (M, Pl) did not invite
هُنَّ دَعَوْنَ	هُنَّ لَمْ يَدْعونَ	they (F, Pl) did not invite

In plural doubled verbs, the doubled consonant is separated by a vowel when the attached suffix begins with a consonant. This applies to the pronouns أَنْتُنَّ and هُنَّ. When the suffix is a vowel, the double consonants remain geminated. This applies to the pronouns نَحْنُ and أَنْتُمْ on one hand, and هُمْ on the other. Verb forms for the plural pronoun نَحْنُ always end with a *fat-Ha*, as a way to break consonant gemination. Examine the following verb: أَحَبَّ / يُحِبُّ and its negative:

Affirmative past tense	Negative with لَمْ	Meaning
نَحْنُ أَحْبَبْنا	نَحْنُ لَمْ نُحِبّ	we (M/F, Pl) did not love
أَنْتُم أَحْبَبْتُمْ	أَنْتُم لَمْ تُحِبّوا	you (M, Pl) did not love
أَنْتُنَّ أَحْبَبْتُنَّ	أَنْتُنَّ لَمْ تُحْبِبْنَ	you (F, Pl) did not love
هُم أَحَبّوا	هُمْ لَمْ يُحِبّوا	they (M, Pl) did not love
هُنَّ أَحْبَبْنَ	هُنَّ لَمْ يُحْبِبْنَ	they (F, Pl) did not love

CHAPTER 16

Passive voice الـمَبْنيُّ لِلْـمَجْهول

16.1 PAST TENSE

We stated in Chapter 1 that verbs are of two types: (1) intransitive verbs أَفْعال لازِمَة, i.e. verbs which do not require direct objects; the singular of this form is called فِعْل لازِم. Examples of such verbs include ضَحِكَ "to laugh," عادَ "to come back," رَجَعَ "to come back," etc. And (2) transitive verbs أَفْعال مُتَعَدِّيَة, which require direct objects, مَفْعولٌ بِهِ. Examples include شَرِبَ "to drink," أَكَلَ "to eat," etc.

The forms of verbs presented thus far are said to be in the active voice. Verbs can also assume another form referred to as فِعْل مَبْنِيّ لِلْمَجْهول in Arabic, or the passive voice. The passive voice form of verbs in Arabic is obtained by internal change in the vowel pattern within the verb. Past and present tenses of these verbs follow different patterns to form their passive voice, as will be illustrated below.

Passive voice forms are generally derived from transitive verbs. Intransitive verbs that require the presence of prepositions can be put in the passive voice. Verbs in the passive voice, like verbs in the active voice, can be in the singular, dual or plural. This form of verbs is used for two possible reasons: (1) lack of knowledge about the agentive noun فاعِل, i.e. the performer of the action, and (2) stylistic variation in writing. It must be noted that the use of the passive voice is more common in written than in spoken Arabic. Examine the following pair of sentences:

كَتَبَ الأُستاذُ الكِتابَ.   The professor wrote the book.

كُتِبَ الكِتابُ.   The book was written.

In the first sentence above, the agentive noun, namely الأُستاذُ, is known, whereas in the second sentence, information about who wrote the book is lacking. Note also that in the two sentences above, الكِتاب in the first sentence is a direct object, ending with the accusative marker, a *fat-Ha* in singular nouns. In the second sentence, however, الكِتاب is in the nominative, ending with a *Dhamma*.

When transitive verbs are put in the passive voice, their direct objects must change their accusative endings into the nominative. In Arabic, the changed noun is referred to as نائِبُ الفاعِل *lit.* "deputy of the فاعِل، the agentive noun." In other words, the change in the status of the direct object entitles this changed noun to occupy the place of فاعِل. This explains why direct object nouns, when verbs are put in the passive, assume the nominative ending of the فاعِل indicated by the *Dhamma* in singular nouns.

In dual nouns, نائِب الفاعِل is marked by ان-. And in regular masculine plural nouns, نائِب الفاعِل is generally marked by ونَ-. Regular feminine plural nouns نائِب الفاعِل are marked by اتٌ-. In irregular plural nouns, the نائِب الفاعِل is marked orthographically by a *Dhamma* and phonetically by the sound -*u*.

The following sets of sentences in the past tense illustrate these points. In each set the first sentence is in the active voice, the second in the passive:

1. Singular:

كَسَرَ الطالِبُ الزُّجاجَ أَمْسِ.   The student broke the glass yesterday.

كُسِرَ الزُّجاجُ أَمْسِ.   The glass was broken yesterday.

شاهَدَ الطُّلابُ الأُستاذَ في الجامِعَةِ.   The students saw the professor at the university.

شُوهِدَ الأُسْتاذُ في الجامِعَةِ.   The professor was seen at the university.

2. Dual:

كَسَرَ الطالِبانِ الزُّجاجَ أَمْسِ.   The students (M, D) broke the glass yesterday.

كُسِرَ الزُّجاجُ أَمْسِ.   The glass was broken yesterday.

شاهَدَ الطُّلابُ الأُستاذَيْنِ في الجامِعَةِ.   The students saw the professors (M, D) at the university.

شُوهِدَ الأُسْتاذانِ في الجامِعَةِ.   The professors (M, D) were seen at the university.

شَاهَدَ الطُّلَّابُ الأُسْتَاذَتَيْنِ في الجَامِعَةِ.

The students saw the professors (F, D) at the university.

شُوهِدَتِ الأُسْتَاذَتَانِ في الجَامِعَةِ.

The professors (F, D) were seen at the university.

Recall that when the subject precedes the verb, the latter must indicate the number of the noun as well as its gender, as in the following examples:

الأُسْتاذانِ شُوهِدا في الجَامِعَةِ.

The professors (M, D) were seen at the university.

الأُسْتاذَتانِ شُوهِدَتا في الجَامِعَةِ.

The professors (F, D) were seen at the university.

In the preceding first sentence, the subject, a masculine, dual noun, is placed before the verb, thus making it necessary for the verb to agree with the noun in gender and number. On the other hand, the subject that begins the second sentence is feminine and dual, which explains why the verb شُوهِدَتا is feminine and dual.

3. Plural:

شَاهَدَ الطُّلَّابُ الـمُعَلِّمينَ في الجَامِعَةِ.
The students saw the teachers (M, Pl) at the university.

شُوهِدَ الـمُعَلِّمونَ في الجَامِعَةِ.
The teachers (M, Pl) were seen at the university.

شَاهَدَ الطُّلَّابُ الـمُعَلِّماتِ في الجَامِعَةِ.
The students saw the teachers (F, Pl) at the university.

شُوهِدَتِ الـمُعَلِّماتُ في الجَامِعَةِ.
The teachers (F, Pl) were seen at the university.

As in the dual above, when the subject precedes the verb, the verb must agree with the subject in number and gender, as in the following:

الـمُعَلِّمونَ شُوهِدوا في الجامِعَة.

The teachers (M, Pl) were seen at the university.

الـمُعَلِّماتُ شُوهِدْنَ في الجامِعَة.

The teachers (F, Pl) were seen at the university.

It should be mentioned that whereas فاعِل, the performer, is not expressed in passive structures, certain phrases are typically used to indicate the doer, or the agent who executed the action. Such phrases, which may have been introduced into Modern Standard Arabic due to translation from Western languages, include بِقَلَم "by the pen of" (restricted to verbs expressing writing), عَلى يَدِ "by/on the hand of," مِن قِبَل "by," or مِن طَرَف "by" (lit. "from the side of"), مِنْ جانِب "from the side of," and مِن لَدُنْ "by." Thus, one encounters examples like the following:

كُتِبَتِ الرِّسالةُ بِقَلَمِ الرَّئيس.

The letter was written by the president. (lit. "by the president's pen")

مُنِحَ الكاتِبُ الجائِزَةَ مِنْ طَرفِ الحُكومَةِ.

The writer was awarded the prize by the government.

We mentioned above that verbs in the passive voice undergo internal change in their vowel patterns. The passive voice in past tense verbs requires the initial consonant to always be followed by a *Dhamma*. If the verb has a long vowel as in فاعَل and تَفاعَل forms, a *waaw* is used instead of a *Dhamma*. The penultimate consonant must always be followed by a *kasra*. Examine the following lists of verbs in the past tense in the active and passive voice:

Verb form	Active voice	Passive voice	Meaning
فَعَل	كَتَبَ	كُتِبَ	was written
	زارَ	زيرَ	was visited
	سارَ	سيرَ	was walked
	نامَ	نيمَ	was put to sleep
	مَشى	مُشِيَ	was walked
	عَدَّ	عُدَّ	was counted

Verb form	Active voice	Passive voice	Meaning
فَعَّلَ	عَلَّمَ	عُلِّمَ	was taught
	سَمَّى	سُمِّيَ	was named
فاعَلَ	ساعَدَ	سوعِدَ	was helped
	نادَى	نُودِيَ	was called
أَفْعَلَ	أَرْسَلَ	أُرْسِلَ	was sent
	أَجابَ	أُجِيبَ	was answered
	أَعْطى	أُعْطِيَ	was given
	أَعَدَّ	أُعِدَّ	was prepared
تَفَعَّلَ	تَعَلَّمَ	تُعُلِّمَ	was learned
	تَحَدَّث	تُحُدِّث	was discussed
	تَبَنَّى	تُبُنِّيَ	was adopted
تَفاعَلَ	تَحارَبَ	تُحورِبَ	was battled
	تَنادى	تُنُودِيَ	was called
اِنْفَعَلَ	اِنْكَسَرَ		was broken
	اِنقادَ		was led
	اِنْبَنى		was built
	اِنْضَمَّ		was joined
اِفْتَعَلَ	اِحْتَفَلَ	اُحْتُفِلَ	was celebrated
	اِخْتارَ	اِخْتِيرَ	was chosen
	اِهْتَمَّ	اُهْتُمَّ	was paid attention to
اِفْعَلَّ	اِحْمَرَّ		turned red
اِسْتَفْعَلَ	اِسْتَعْمَلَ	اُسْتُعْمِلَ	was used
	اِسْتَطاعَ	اُسْتُطِيعَ	was enabled
	اِسْتَرَدَّ	اُسْتُرِدَّ	was retrieved
	اِسْتَثْنى	اُسْتُثْنِيَ	was excepted from

Note that اِنْفَعَلَ and اِفْعَلَّ verb forms cannot be put in the passive voice due to the fact that they are not transitive verbs. Additionally, some verbs are often, but not always, used in the passive voice. Examples include وُلِدَ "to be born," شُفِيَ "to recover from illness," and جُنَّ "to be or become insane, mad, madly excited," as in the following:

وُلِدَ أَحْمَد في مَرّاكِش.	Ahmad was born in the city of Marrakesh.
شُفِيَ الـمَريضُ مِنْ مَرَضِه.	The sick person recovered.
جُنَّ جنونُهُ عِنْدَما سَمِعَ الخَبَر.	He became madly upset when he heard the news.

Hollow verbs form their passive voice in the past tense by changing the middle *'alif* into a *yaa'*. The use of the *yaa'* instead of a *kasra* is to compensate for the missing third consonant. Thus, in the active voice زارَ "to visit" and قالَ "to say" become زِيرَ "he/it was visited," and قِيلَ "it was said," respectively. It must be noted that the active voice form of such verbs is commonly used. However, the passive voice form قِيلَ إِنَّ "it was said that" is rather common, especially when the source of "reporting" or "news" is not known. Examine the following example:

قيلَ إِنَّ الرَّئيسَ اِجْتَمَعَ مَعَ بَعْضِ الوُزَراءِ.
It was mentioned that the president met with some ministers.

16.1.1 Defective verbs

In the past tense, defective verbs form their passive voice by placing a *Dhamma* after the first consonant and a *kasra* before the final consonant which is changed into a *yaa'*. This causes some adjustment in the orthography. Instead of the regular *'alif* in verbs that are normally written with a final *'alif*, or an *'alif maySuura*, the passive voice of such verbs in the past tense is written with a *yaa'*, as in the following examples:

Active voice	Passive voice	Meaning
دَعا	دُعِيَ	was invited
قَضى	قُضِيَ	was judged
سَمّى	سُمِّيَ	was named

Examine the following sentences, which illustrate some of these passive verbs:

دُعِيَ الطُّلَّابُ إلى حَفْلَةِ الأُستاذِ.	The students were invited to the teacher's party.
سُمِّيَتِ البِنْتُ لَيْلى.	The girl was named Laila.
قُضِيَ في هذِهِ القَضِيَّةِ.	This case was decided.

16.1.2 Doubled verbs

In the past tense, doubled verbs, on the other hand, begin with a *Dhamma* after the first consonant; the final vowel in this case is a *fat-Ha*. For example, we obtain عُدَّ "he/it was counted, considered" from عَدَّ and شُكَّ في "he/it was doubted," from شَكَّ في and so on. Examine the following sentence:

شُكَّ في قَوْلِ هذا الرَّجُلِ.	The words of this man were doubted.
حُلَّت هَذِهِ المُشْكِلَةُ بِسُهولَةٍ.	This problem was easily solved.

16.2 PRESENT TENSE الـمُضارِع الـمَبْنيّ لِلمَجْهول

Present tense verbs form the passive voice by placing a *Dhamma* following the first consonant and a *fat-Ha* before the final consonant. Examine the following lists of verbs in the present, active, and passive voice:

Verb form	Active voice	Passive voice	Meaning
فَعَلَ	يَكْتُبُ	يُكْتَبُ	is written
	يَزورُ	يُزارُ	is visited
	يَسيرُ	يُسارُ	is walked
	يَنامُ	يُنامُ	is put to sleep
	يَمْشي	يُمْشى	is walked
	يَعُدُّ	يُعَدُّ	is counted
فَعَّلَ	يُعَلِّمُ	يُعَلَّمُ	is taught
	يُسَمّي	يُسَمّى	is named

Verb form	Active voice	Passive voice	Meaning
فاعَلَ	يُساعِدُ	يُساعَدُ	is helped
	يُنادي	يُنادى	is called
أَفْعَلَ	يُرْسِلُ	يُرْسَلُ	is sent
	يُجيبُ	يُجابُ	is answered
	يُعْطي	يُعْطى	is given
	يُعِدِّ	يُعَدُّ	is prepared
تَفَعَّلَ	يَتَعَلَّمُ	يُتَعَلَّمُ	is learned
	يَتَحَدَّثُ	يُتَحَدَّثُ	is discussed
	يَتَبَنَّى	يُتَبَنّى	is adopted
تَفاعَلَ	يَتَحارَبُ	يُتَحارَبُ	is battled
	يَتَنادَى	يُتَنادَى	is called
اِنْفَعَلَ	يَنْكَسِرُ		is broken
	يَنْقادُ		is led
	يَنْبَني		is built
	يَنْضَمُّ إلى	يُنْضَمُّ إلى	is joined
اِفْتَعَلَ	يَحْتَفِلُ	يُحْتَفَلُ	is celebrated
	يَخْتارُ	يُخْتارُ	is chosen
	يَهْتَمُّ بِ	يُهْتَمُّ بِ	is paid attention to
اِفْعَلَّ	يَحْمَرُّ		to turn red
اِسْتَفْعَلَ	يَسْتَعْمِلُ	يُسْتَعْمَلُ	is used
	يَسْتَطيعُ	يُسْتَطاعُ	is enabled
	يَسْتَرِدُّ	يُسْتَرَدُّ	is retrieved
	يَسْتَثْني	يُسْتَثْنى	is excepted

16.2.1 Hollow verbs

The passive voice of hollow verbs in the present tense is formed by placing a *Dhamma* after the first consonant, and instead of the penultimate *fat-Ha*, an *'alif* is used. The use of an *'alif* instead of a *fat-Ha* is to compensate for the absence of the third consonant. Examine the following table:

Active voice	Passive voice	Meaning
يَزورُ	يُزارُ	is visited
يَعودُ	يُعادُ	is returned
يَقولُ	يُقالُ	is said
يَقومُ	يُقامُ	is established

Examine the following sentences:

يُزارُ هذا الـمَكانُ كَثيراً.   This place is visited a lot.

The passive voice verb يُقالُ إنَّ "it is said that" is commonly used, especially when the source of "news" or "reporting" is not known. Examine the following example:

يُقالُ إنَّ الشِّتاءَ القادِمَ سَيَكونُ بارداً.   It is said that next winter will be cold.

16.2.2 Defective verbs

The passive voice of defective verbs in the present tense is formed by placing a *Dhamma* after the first consonant and a *fat-Ha* following the final consonant. These verbs end with an *'alif* sound. This necessitates an adjustment in the orthography. Instead of the final *waaw* or final *yaa'* in the present tense, the passive voice of such verbs is written with an *'alif maqSuura*, as in the following examples:

Active voice	Passive voice	Meaning
يَدْعو	يُدْعى	is called
يَقْلي	يُقْلى	is fried
يُسَمّي	يُسَمّى	is named
يَرْمي	يُرْمى	is thrown

Examine the following sentences:

تُقْلَى البَطاطا أَوَّلاً.

Potatoes are fried first.

تُسَمَّى مَدينةٌ نيويورك بـ «التُّفاحَة الكَبيرَة».

The City of New York is called 'The Big Apple'.

تُلْقى الأَوْساخُ في شَوارِع الـمَدينةِ.

Garbage is thrown onto the city streets.

16.2.3 Doubled verbs

Doubled verbs begin with a *Dhamma* after the first consonant in the present
tense verb form. The penultimate consonant is followed by a *fat-Ha*, as illustrated
in the following table:

Active voice	Passive voice	Meaning
يَعُدُّ	يُعَدُّ	is counted
يَشُكُّ بـِ / في	يُشَكُّ بـِ / في	is doubted
يَظُنُّ	يُظَنُّ	is thought that

Examine the following examples:

يُشَكُّ في صَحَّةِ هذا الخَبَرِ.

This news item is doubted.

يُعَدُّ هذا القائِدُ مُهِمّاً في التّاريخِ.

This leader is considered important in history.

16.3 SUBJUNCTIVE VERBS IN THE PASSIVE VOICE

Additionally, present tense verbs in the passive voice can also be preceded by
أَدَوات النَّصْب "accusative particles," such as أَنْ، كَيْ، حَتّى، لِكَيْ، لِـ، لَنْ, causing
these verbs to end with a *fat-Ha* in the singular, or to drop the *nuun* in the dual

and in the plural when they are preceded by a long vowel (see Chapter 13). Examine the following examples:

يَجِبُ أَنْ تُنْشَرَ هذِهِ المَقالةُ في الجَريدةِ.

This article must be published in the newspaper.

يا سَلْمى، هَلْ نُوديتِ حَتّى تُقابَلي؟

Salma, were you called for an interview (*lit.* to be interviewed)?

طُلِبَ أَحْمَد كَيْ يُوَظَّفَ في الشَّرِكةِ.

Ahmad was invited in order to be employed in the company.

دُعِيَ الطّالِبانِ كَيْ يُسْتَخْدَما في الجَيْشِ.

The two students were called in order to serve in the army.

دُعِيَ المُوَظَّفونَ لِيُدَرَّبوا عَلى الحاسوبِ.

The employees were assembled to be trained on the computer.

16.4 FUTURE TENSE المُسْتَقْبَل المَبْنيّ لِلمَجْهول

The passive voice can be put in the future tense simply by the use of the future particle سَوْفَ or سَـ plus the passive voice of verbs in the present tense, as in the following:

سَوْفَ يُؤْكَلُ هذا الطَّعامُ غَداً.

This food will be eaten tomorrow.

سَتُدَرَّسُ اللُغاتُ الأَجْنَبِيَّةُ في المَدْرسةِ الجَديدةِ.

Foreign languages will be taught in the new school.

سَوْفَ تُبْنى المَدينةُ مِن جَديدٍ.

The city will be rebuilt again.

سَيُعادُ الكِتابُ إلى المَكتَبَةِ غَداً.

The book will be returned to the library tomorrow.

سَوْفَ تُعادُ هذِهِ المَجَلَّةُ إلى المَكتَبَةِ.

This journal will be returned to the library.

CHAPTER 17

Imperative verbs فِعْل الأَمْر

The imperative form of verbs is used to give someone, an addressee, a command, an order, or a request to perform an act. There are two types of commands: (1) direct and (2) indirect.

The direct imperative is the form of a verb used to ask the addressee to perform an act. Imperative verb forms are generally used with the second person pronouns, singular, dual, or plural, as in the following for the verb كَتَبَ "to write":

$$كَتَبَ / يَكْتُبُ$$

Singular pronouns:

Independent pronoun	Imperative form	Meaning
أَنْتَ	اُكْتُبْ	[you (M)] write!
أَنْتِ	اُكْتُبِي	[you (F)] write!

Dual pronouns:

Independent pronoun	Imperative form	Meaning
أَنْتُمَا	اُكْتُبَا	[you (M)] write!
أَنْتُمَا	اُكْتُبَا	[you (F)] write!

Plural pronouns:

Independent pronoun	Imperative form	Meaning
أنتُم	اُكْتُبُوا	[you (M)] write!
أنْتُنَّ	اُكْتُبْنَ	[you (F)] write!

The indirect imperative conveys a suggestion, a request or a milder form of command directed to an addressee to perform an act. It is generally used with the third person singular, dual or plural pronoun. The indirect imperative can also be used with the first and second person pronouns. It is often translated as "had better" in English.

17.1 FORM I IMPERATIVE VERBS الأَمْر - صِيغَة فَعَل

Verbs of the فَعَل pattern such as دَرَسَ، كَتَبَ، شَرِبَ begin with أُ or اِ. The choice of أُ or اِ is determined by the penultimate vowel in the present tense form of the verb. It is therefore very necessary to learn the present tense form of verbs accurately. For example, the imperative of كَتَبَ / يَكْتُبُ is اُكْتُب.

If the middle vowel in the present tense of فَعَل verbs is a *fat-Ha* or a *kasra*, the imperative verb form must begin with a *kasra*. In the orthography, the expected *hamza* is not written; an *'alif* followed by a *kasra* اِ (*prosthetic 'alif*) is used, as in شَرِبَ / يَشْرَبُ:

17.1.1 Middle vowel *fat-Ha* or *kasra*

شَرِبَ / يَشْرَبُ

Singular:

Independent pronoun	Imperative form	Meaning
أَنْتَ	اِشْرَب	[you (M)] drink!
أَنْتِ	اِشْرَبِي	[you (F)] drink!

Dual:

Independent pronoun	Imperative form	Meaning
أَنْتُما	اِشْرَبا	[you (M)] drink!
أَنْتُما	اِشْرَبا	[you (F)] drink!

Plural:

Independent pronoun	Imperative form	Meaning
أَنْتُمْ	اِشْرَبوا	[you (M)] drink!
أَنْتُنَّ	اِشْرَبْنَ	[you (F)] drink!

Recall that the final *'alif* in the plural verb in the masculine اشربوا is not pronounced. It is only used in the orthography to mark the word as a verb.

If the penultimate vowel in the present tense of فَعَلَ is a *kasra*, as in جَلَسَ / يَجْلِسُ "to sit," the vowel beginning the imperative form is a *kasra*, as in the following:

$$جَلَسَ / يَـجْلِسُ$$

Singular:

Independent pronoun	Imperative form	Meaning
أَنْتَ	اِجْلِسْ	[you (M)] sit!
أَنْتِ	اِجْلِسي	[you (F)] sit!

Dual:

Independent pronoun	Imperative form	Meaning
أَنْتُما	اِجْلِسا	[you (M)] sit!
أَنْتُما	اِجْلِسا	[you (F)] sit!

Plural:

Independent pronoun	Imperative form	Meaning
أَنْتُمْ	اِجْلِسوا	[you (M)] sit!
أَنْتُنَّ	اِجْلِسْنَ	[you (F)] sit!

17.1.2 Middle vowel *hamza*

When فَعَلَ verbs have an initial *hamza*, as in أَكَلَ / يَأْكُلُ or أَخَذَ / يَأْخُذُ, the *hamza* drops, as in the following:

$$ أَكَلَ / يَأْكُلُ $$

Singular:

Independent pronoun	Imperative form	Meaning
أَنْتَ	كُلْ	[you (M)] eat!
أَنْتِ	كُلِي	[you (F)] eat!

Dual:

Independent pronoun	Imperative form	Meaning
أَنْتُمَا	كُلا	[you (M)] eat!
أَنْتُمَا	كُلا	[you (F)] eat!

Plural:

Independent pronoun	Imperative form	Meaning
أَنْتُم	كُلوا	[you (M)] eat!
أَنْتُنَّ	كُلْنَ	[you (F)] eat!

17.1.3 *Waaw*-beginning verbs

In *waaw*-beginning verbs as in وَصَفَ / يَصِفُ "to describe," the *hamza* that usually begins the imperative form does not appear. The vowel following the first consonant in the imperative form takes the middle vowel of the present tense of the verb for هُوَ.

An example of when the middle vowel is a *kasra*, as in وَصَفَ / يَصِفُ "to describe," is below:

وَصَفَ / يَصِفُ

Singular:

Independent pronoun	Imperative form	Meaning
أَنْتَ	صِفْ	[you (M)] describe!
أَنْتِ	صِفي	[you (F)] describe!

Dual:

Independent pronoun	Imperative form	Meaning
أَنْتُما	صِفا	[you (M)] describe!
أَنْتُما	صِفا	[you (F)] describe!

Plural:

Independent pronoun	Imperative form	Meaning
أَنْتُم	صِفوا	[you (M)] describe!
أَنْتُنَّ	صِفْنَ	[you (F)] describe!

An example of when the middle vowel is a *fat-Ha*, as in وَضَعَ / يَضَعُ "to put, to place," follows:

وَضَعَ / يَضَعُ

Singular:

Independent pronoun	Imperative form	Meaning
أَنْتَ	ضَعْ	[you (M)] put!
أَنْتِ	ضَعي	[you (F)] put!

Dual:

Independent pronoun	Imperative form	Meaning
أَنْتُما	ضَعا	[you (M)] put!
أَنْتُما	ضَعا	[you (F)] put!

Plural:

Independent pronoun	Imperative form	Meaning
أَنْتُم	ضَعوا	[you (M)] put!
أَنْتُنَّ	ضَعْنَ	[you (F)] put!

17.1.4 Hollow verbs

As with the *waaw*-beginning verbs, there is no initial *hamza* in the imperative of the فَعَلَ form of hollow verbs. The imperative of hollow verbs such as عادَ, زارَ, and نامَ results in the shortening of the long vowel of the present tense of the verb form for some pronouns.

The present tense of زارَ for أَنْتِ is تزورينَ, in other words, it has a long vowel in the suffix. The imperative of this form maintains the two long vowels, as in زوري. Below are examples of hollow verbs that contain the three long vowels in Arabic (*waaw, yaa'* and *'alif*) and their imperative forms:

زارَ / يَزورُ

Singular:

Independent pronoun	Imperative form	Meaning
أَنْتَ	زُرْ	[you (M)] visit!
أَنْتِ	زوري	[you (F)] visit!

Dual:

Independent pronoun	Imperative form	Meaning
أَنْتُما	زورا	[you (M)] visit!
أَنْتُما	زورا	[you (F)] visit!

Plural:

Independent pronoun	Imperative form	Meaning
أَنْتُم	زوروا	[you (M)] visit!
أَنْتُنَّ	زُرْنَ	[you (F)] visit!

سارَ / يَسيرُ

Singular:

Independent pronoun	Imperative form	Meaning
أَنْتَ	سِرْ	[you (M)] walk!
أَنْتِ	سيري	[you (F)] walk!

Dual:

Independent pronoun	Imperative form	Meaning
أَنْتُما	سيرا	[you (M)] walk!
أَنْتُما	سيرا	[you (F)] walk!

Plural:

Independent pronoun	Imperative form	Meaning
أَنْتُم	سيروا	[you (M)] walk!
أَنْتُنَّ	سِرْنَ	[you (F)] walk!

نامَ / يَنامُ

Singular:

Independent pronoun	Imperative form	Meaning
أَنْتَ	نَمْ	[you (M)] sleep!
أَنْتِ	نامي	[you (F)] sleep!

Dual:

Independent pronoun	Imperative form	Meaning
أَنْتُما	ناما	[you (M)] sleep!
أَنْتُما	ناما	[you (F)] sleep!

Plural:

Independent pronoun	Imperative form	Meaning
أَنْتُم	ناموا	[you (M)] sleep!
أَنْتُنَّ	نَمْنَ	[you (F)] sleep!

17.1.5 Defective verbs

The prosthetic *'alif* ا is followed by either a *kasra* if the indicative present tense is a *yaa'* as in بَنى / يَبْني or a *Dhamma* if the indicative present tense is a *waaw*:

The imperative form for the pronoun أَنْتَ must end with a *kasra* in verbs whose present tense ends with *yaa'*. The pronoun أَنْتِ in the imperative form must end with a *yaa'*. The dual pronoun أَنْتُمَا must maintain the *yaa'* followed by an *'alif* as the dual marker. The masculine plural pronoun أَنْتُمْ drops the *yaa'* and must end with a *waaw*, followed by an *'alif* in the orthography. Finally, the feminine plural pronoun أَنْتُنَّ must end with a *yaa'* followed by نَ. Examine the following table for the verb بَنَى / يَبْنِي "to build":

بَنَى / يَبْنِي

Singular:

Independent pronoun	Imperative form	Meaning
أَنْتَ	اِبْنِ	[you (M)] build!
أَنْتِ	اِبْنِي	[you (F)] build!

Dual:

Independent pronoun	Imperative form	Meaning
أَنْتُمَا	اِبْنِيا	[you (M)] build!
أَنْتُمَا	اِبْنِيا	[you (F)] build!

Plural:

Independent pronoun	Imperative form	Meaning
أَنْتُم	اِبْنُوا	[you (M)] build!
أَنْتُنَّ	اِبْنِينَ	[you (F)] build!

The imperative form of defective verbs whose present tense ends with a *waaw* as in عَلا / يَعْلو "to go up, to rise," must always begin with an *'alif* followed by a *Dhamma*.

The imperative form for the pronoun أَنْتَ must end with a *Dhamma*. The pronoun أَنْتِ in the imperative form ends with a *yaa'*. The dual pronoun أَنْتُما must maintain the *waaw*, followed by an *'alif* as the dual marker. The masculine plural pronoun أَنْتُمْ must end with a *waaw*, also followed by an *'alif* in the orthography to indicate that the word is a verb. Finally, the feminine plural pronoun أَنْتُنَّ must end with a *waaw* followed by نَ. Examine the following imperative forms of the verb دَعا / يَدْعو "to invite":

دَعا / يَدْعو

Singular:

Independent pronoun	Imperative form	Meaning
أَنْتَ	اُدْعُ	[you (M)] invite!
أَنْتِ	اِدْعي	[you (F)] invite!

Dual:

Independent pronoun	Imperative form	Meaning
أَنْتُما	اُدْعُوا	[you (M)] invite!
أَنْتُما	اُدْعُوا	[you (F)] invite!

Plural:

Independent pronoun	Imperative form	Meaning
أَنْتُمْ	اُدْعوا	[you (M)] invite!
أَنْتُنَّ	اُدْعونَ	[you (F)] invite!

17.1.6 Doubled verbs

Like *waaw*-beginning and hollow verbs, double verbs in Form I imperatives do not have a *prosthetic 'alif* .

The imperative form of doubled verbs always ends with a double consonant. For the pronoun أَنْتَ a *fat-Ha* follows the doubled consonants. For the pronoun أَنْتِ a *yaa'* follows the doubled consonants. For the dual pronoun أَنْتُمَا an *'alif* follows the doubled consonants. For the plural pronoun أَنْتُمْ a *waaw* must follow the doubled consonant, followed in the orthography by an *'alif*. The imperative form of defective verbs for the pronoun أَنْتُنَّ takes a different form, as in the table below for the verb رَدَّ / يَرُدُّ "to reply, to return, to respond":

$$رَدَّ / يَرُدُّ$$

Singular:

Independent pronoun	Imperative form	Meaning
أَنْتَ	رُدَّ	[you (M)] reply!
أَنْتِ	رُدِّي	[you (F)] reply!

Dual:

Independent pronoun	Imperative form	Meaning
أَنْتُمَا	رُدَّا	[you (M)] reply!
أَنْتُمَا	رُدَّا	[you (F)] reply!

Plural:

Independent pronoun	Imperative form	Meaning
أَنْتُمْ	رُدُّوا	[you (M)] reply!
أَنْتُنَّ	اُرْدُدْنَ	[you (F)] reply!

Note that in the imperative form for أَنْتُنَّ "you (F, Pl)," the geminated identical consonant of the doubled verb must be separated by a vowel.

17.2 FORM II–X IMPERATIVE VERBS الأَمْر - اِسْتَفْعَلَ - فَعَّلَ

Imperative verbs of these verb forms will be presented under two categories: The first category includes the following verb forms: فَعَّلَ (Form II), فاعَلَ (Form III), أَفْعَلَ (Form IV), اِنْفَعَلَ (Form VII), اِفْتَعَلَ (Form VIII) and اِسْتَفْعَلَ (Form X).

The imperative for the pronoun أَنتِ must end with a *yaa'*; the form for the dual pronoun أَنتُما must end with an *'alif*; verbs for the pronoun أَنتُم must end with a *waaw* followed by an *'alif* (in the orthography). Finally, verbs for the pronoun أَنـْتُـنَّ must end with نَ preceded by a *sukuun*. Examine the following verbs:

17.2.1 Form II verbs صيغة فَعَّلَ

دَرَّسَ / يُدَرِّسُ

Singular:

Independent pronoun	Imperative form	Meaning
أَنْتَ	دَرِّسْ	[you (M)] teach!
أَنْتِ	دَرِّسي	[you (F)] teach!

Dual:

Independent pronoun	Imperative form	Meaning
أَنْتُما	دَرِّسا	[you (M)] teach!
أَنْتُما	دَرِّسا	[you (F)] teach!

Plural:

Independent pronoun	Imperative form	Meaning
أَنْتُم	دَرِّسوا	[you (M)] teach!
أَنْتُنَّ	دَرِّسْنَ	[you (F)] teach!

17.2.2 Form III verbs صيغة فاعَلَ

سافَرَ / يُسافِرُ

Singular:

Independent pronoun	Imperative form	Meaning
أَنْتَ	سافِرْ	[you (M)] travel!
أَنْتِ	سافِري	[you (F)] travel!

Dual:

Independent pronoun	Imperative form	Meaning
أَنْتُما	سافِرا	[you (M)] travel!
أَنْتُما	سافِرا	[you (F)] travel!

Plural:

Independent pronoun	Imperative form	Meaning
أَنْتُم	سافِروا	[you (M)] travel!
أَنْتُنَّ	سافِرْنَ	[you (F)] travel!

17.2.3 Form IV verbs صيغة أَفْعَلَ

أَرْسَلَ / يُرْسِلُ

Singular:

Independent pronoun	Imperative form	Meaning
أَنْتَ	أَرْسِلْ	[you (M)] send!
أَنْتِ	أَرْسِلي	[you (F)] send!

Dual:

Independent pronoun	Imperative form	Meaning
أَنْتُما	أَرْسِلا	[you (M)] send!
أَنْتُما	أَرْسِلا	[you (F)] send!

Plural:

Independent pronoun	Imperative form	Meaning
أَنْتُم	أَرْسِلوا	[you (M)] send!
أَنْتُنَّ	أَرْسِلْنَ	[you (F)] send!

17.2.4 Form VII verbs صيغَة انْفَعَلَ

انْصَرَفَ / يَنْصَرِفُ

Singular:

Independent pronoun	Imperative form	Meaning
أَنْتَ	انْصَرِفْ	[you (M)] go away!
أَنْتِ	انْصَرِفي	[you (F)] go away!

Dual:

Independent pronoun	Imperative form	Meaning
أَنْتُما	انْصَرِفا	[you (M)] go away!
أَنْتُما	انْصَرِفا	[you (F)] go away!

Plural:

Independent pronoun	Imperative form	Meaning
أَنْتُم	اِنْصَرِفوا	[you (M)] go away!
أَنْتُنَّ	اِنْصَرِفْنَ	[you (F)] go away!

17.2.5 Form VIII verbs صيغَة اِفْتَعَلَ

اِجْتَمَعَ / يَجْتَمِعُ

Singular:

Independent pronoun	Imperative form	Meaning
أَنْتَ	اِجْتَمِعْ	[you (M)] meet!
أَنْتِ	اِجْتَمِعي	[you (F)] meet!

Dual:

Independent pronoun	Imperative form	Meaning
أَنْتُما	اِجْتَمِعا	[you (M)] meet!
أَنْتُما	اِجْتَمِعا	[you (F)] meet!

Plural:

Independent pronoun	Imperative form	Meaning
أَنْتُم	اِجْتَمِعوا	[you (M)] meet!
أَنْتُنَّ	اِجْتَمِعْنَ	[you (F)] meet!

17.2.6 Form X verbs صيغة اِسْتَفْعَلَ

اِسْتَقْبَلَ / يَسْتَقْبِلُ

Singular:

Independent pronoun	Imperative form	Meaning
أَنْتَ	اِسْتَخْدِمْ	[you (M)] use!
أَنْتِ	اِسْتَخْدِمي	[you (F)] use!

Dual:

Independent pronoun	Imperative form	Meaning
أَنْتُما	اِسْتَخْدِما	[you (M)] use!
أَنْتُما	اِسْتَخْدِما	[you (F)] use!

Plural:

Independent pronoun	Imperative form	Meaning
أَنْتُم	اِسْتَخْدِموا	[you (M)] use!
أَنْتُنَّ	اِسْتَخْدِمْنَ	[you (F)] use!

The second category includes تَفَعَّل (Form V) and تَفاعَل (Form VI) verb imperative forms. Examine the following verbs:

17.2.7 Form V verbs صيغة تَفَعَّل

تَكَلَّمَ / يَتَكَلَّمُ

Singular:

Independent pronoun	Imperative form	Meaning
أَنْتَ	تَكَلَّمْ	[you (M)] speak!
أَنْتِ	تَكَلَّمي	[you (F)] speak!

Dual:

Independent pronoun	Imperative form	Meaning
أَنْتُما	تَكَلَّما	[you (M)] speak!
أَنْتُما	تَكَلَّما	[you (F)] speak!

Plural:

Independent pronoun	Imperative form	Meaning
أَنْتُم	تَكَلَّموا	[you (M)] speak!
أَنْتُنَّ	تَكَلَّمْنَ	[you (F)] speak!

17.2.8 Form VI verbs صيغَة تَفاعَلَ

تَعاوَنَ / يَتَعاوَنُ

Singular:

Independent pronoun	Imperative form	Meaning
أَنْتَ	تَعاوَنْ	[you (M)] cooperate!
أَنْتِ	تَعاوَني	[you (F)] cooperate!

Dual:

Independent pronoun	Imperative form	Meaning
أَنْتُما	تَعاوَنا	[you (M)] cooperate!
أَنْتُما	تَعاوَنا	[you (F)] cooperate!

Plural:

Independent pronoun	Imperative form	Meaning
أَنْتُم	تَعاوَنوا	[you (M)] cooperate!
أَنْتُنَّ	تَعاوَنَّ	[you (F)] cooperate!

Note that if the verb ends with a ن as in تَعاوَنَّ, the ن is doubled and geminated, as in the following for the pronoun أَنْتُنَّ:

$$ أَنْتُنَّ تَعاوَنَّ $$

17.3 INDIRECT IMPERATIVE

As was mentioned at the beginning of this chapter, indirect imperatives convey suggestions to perform an act. Whereas the direct imperative applies only to the second person pronouns أَنْتِ and أَنْتَ and their plural and dual forms أَنْتُنَّ, أَنْتُم and أَنْتُما, the indirect imperative applies to all personal pronouns. This includes the first person plural pronouns أنا and نَحْنُ and the third person singular pronouns هُو and هِيَ in addition to their dual counterparts هُما (M) and هُما (F) and plural forms هُم and هُنَّ.

Indirect imperatives are formed by the use of لِ in front of the present tense form of the verb in the jussive. In other words, the verb must end with a *sukuun* or a long vowel (*'alif, waaw,* or *yaa'*). The only exceptions are the forms for أَنْتُنَّ and هُنَّ that we see in the following:

First person pronouns:

لِأَذْهَبْ I had better go

لِنَذْهَبْ let's go

Second person pronouns:

لِتَذْهَبْ you (M) had better go or you go

لِتَذْهَبي you (F) had better go or you go

لِتَذْهَبا you (M/F, D) had better go

لِتَذْهَبوا you (M, Pl) had better go

لِتَذْهَبْنَ you (F, Pl) had better go

Third person pronouns:

لِيَذْهَبْ	he had better go or let him go
لِتَذْهَبْ	she had better go or let her go
لِيَذْهَبا	they (M, D) had better go or let them go
لِتَذْهَبا	they (F, D) had better go or let them go
لِيَذْهَبوا	they (M, Pl) had better go or let them go
لِيَذْهَبْنَ	they (F, Pl) had better go or let them go

17.4 NEGATIVE IMPERATIVE اَلنَّهْي

The negative imperative is formed with لا followed by the jussive (see Chapter 15). Examine the following examples:

لا تَكْتُبْ!	Don't write (M, Sg)!
لا تَكْتُبي!	Don't write (F, Sg)!
لا تَكْتُبا!	Don't write (M/F, D)!
لا تَكْتُبوا!	Don't write (M, Pl)!

Note that if the ن is not preceded by a long vowel, it is not dropped as in the following:

لا تَكْتُبْنَ !	Don't write (F, Pl)!

17.5 WARNINGS التَّحذير

There is another way of expressing النَّهْي or warning التَّحذير, which is less frequently used in Modern Standard Arabic. The particle إيّا plus a pronoun in one of the second person suffixal forms functions as a warning when followed by the content of the warning. This can be provided by a dependent clause or a noun. It may be followed by أَنْ followed by the subjunctive verb form, as in the following examples:

إِيَّاكَ أَنْ تَلْعَبَ!   Be careful (M, Sg) not to play.

إِيَّاكِ أَنْ تَلْعَبِي!   Be careful (F, Sg) not to play.

إِيَّاكُمَا أَنْ تَلْعَبَا!   Be careful (M/F, D) not to play.

إِيَّاكُمْ أَنْ تَلْعَبُوا!   Be careful (M, Pl) not to play.

إِيَّاكُنَّ أَنْ تَلْعَبْنَ!   Be careful (F, Pl) not to play.

إِيَّا and the personal suffixal pronouns can be followed by مِنْ, which is followed by the subjunctive particle أَنْ and a subjunctive verb. Thus we can obtain the following as illustration:

إِيَّاكَ مِنْ أَنْ تَلْعَبَ!   Beware (M, Sg) of playing!

إِيَّاكُم مِنْ أَنْ تُهْمِلوا الواجِباتِ!   Never forget your (M, Pl) homework!

أَنْ plus the subjunctive verb form can be substituted with a *maSdar* preceded by a *waaw*. Thus إِيَّاكَ أَنْ تَلْعَبَ is equivalent in meaning to إِيَّاكَ واللَعبَ "take care not to play" or "be careful not to play."

إِيَّا plus the personal pronoun suffix can be followed by مِنْ in addition to *maSdar*, as in:

إِيَّاكَ مِنَ اللَعِبِ!   Beware (M, Sg) of playing!

Furthermore, إِيَّا plus the personal pronoun can be followed by a noun or a *maSdar* preceded by a *waaw* و, as in the following examples:

إِيَّاكُم والكَذِبَ!   Beware of lying!

إِيَّاكِ وَجَليسَ السُّوءِ!   Beware of bad companionship!

The *waaw* can be dropped only with *maSdar*s, as in the following:

إِيَّاكُم الفاحِشَةَ!   Beware of committing evil things!

إِيَّاكِ الكَذِبَ!   Beware of lying!

CHAPTER 18

Past continuous tense
الفِعْل الـماضي الـمُسْتَمِرّ

When كانَ was first introduced, its function was to transform equational sentences from the present to the past tense (see Chapter 10). كانَ has another function in Modern Standard Arabic. In the following discussion, كانَ is followed by an indicative verb in the present tense to express (1) a state in the past, (2) a past habitual action, (3) a past continuous event, or (4) the past perfect (also referred to as the pluperfect). We shall discuss each of these functions below:

18.1 A STATE IN THE PAST

There are certain verbs in Arabic that denote a quality or a condition but not an action. In English they are known as *stative verbs*. Such verbs include, for example, verbs of knowing and understanding, as in فَهِمَ "to understand," عَرَفَ "to know," or verbs of liking or loving, as in أَحَبَّ "to like, to love," رَغِبَ "to desire, to want," أَرادَ "to want, to wish," etc. When كانَ is followed by one of these verbs in the present tense, its use indicates a state or a condition in the past. This combination is equivalent to the English "used to." Examine the following examples:

كانَ يَعْرِفُ الـمُشْكِلَةَ.	He used to know the problem.
كانَ يَفْهَمُ الـمُشْكِلَةَ.	He used to understand the problem.
كُنْتُ أُحِبُّ الـمُوسيقى العَرَبِيَّةَ.	I used to like Arabic music.

18.2 PAST HABITUAL ACTION

Action verbs in the past tense express the occurrence of an event or action in the past. When كانَ is followed by the present tense of action verbs such as

أَكَلَ "to eat" or شَرِبَ "to drink," this usage expresses a past habitual action, in the sense that someone used to perform a certain action in the past as a habit. Examine the following:

كَانَتْ تَزورُهُ في الجامِعَة. She used to visit him at the university.

كَانَ يَلْعَبُ كُرَةَ القَدَم. He used to play soccer.

كُنْتُ أَشْرَبُ الحَليبَ. I used to drink milk.

18.3 PAST CONTINUOUS

كَانَ followed by a present tense verb can also convey the notion of an action that was progressing in the past. This notion is usually conveyed when another event or action intersects, as in the following examples.

كَانَ يَجْلِسُ في الـمَقْهى عِنْدَما شاهَدْتُهُ.
He was sitting in the café when I saw him.

كَانَت تَدْرُسُ هذا الصَّباحَ عِنْدَما زُرْتُها.
She was teaching this morning when I visited her.

ماذا كُنْتَ تَعمَلُ في الـمَكتَبَةِ عِنْدَما رَأَيْتُكَ؟
What were you doing in the library when I saw you?

It should be mentioned that it is more common to begin such sentences with adverbial clauses of time such as حينَما، عِنْدَما، لَـمّا, as in the following:

عِنْدَما شاهَدْتُهُ كانَ يَجْلِسُ في المَقْهى.
When I saw him, he was sitting in the café.

حينَما زُرْتُها هذا الصَّباح كانَتْ تُدَرِّسُ.
When I visited her this morning, she was teaching.

Furthermore, when the phrase كَانَ is followed by a present tense verb in the main clause, this clause can be immediately followed by a verb in the present tense, as in the following example:

كانَت تُراسِلُهُ مِنَ العِراق، تَتَحَدَّثُ عن الـمَشاكِلِ.
She used to correspond with him from Iraq, discussing problems.

The above sentence has undergone some truncation. In other words, كانَ in front of تَتَحَدَّثُ has not been repeated, perhaps for economy and style. Optionally, it can be repeated, of course, as in the following:

كانَت تُراسِلُهُ مِنَ العِراق وكانَت تَتَحَدَّثُ عَنِ الـمَشاكِل.

She used to correspond with him from Iraq and discuss the problems.

Similarly, the following sentence has undergone truncation as well.

كانَ يَجْتَمِعُ في الـمَقاهي مَعَ أَصْدِقائِه، يَلْعَبُ الوَرَقَ وَيَشْرَبُ الشايَ.

He used to meet in cafés with his friends, play cards and drink tea.

In other words, كانَ has been deleted in front of the present tense verbs يَلْعَبُ and يَشْرَبُ respectively.

18.3.1 Past continuous tense negation

الفِعْل الـماضي الـمُستَمِرّ - النَّفي

There are three ways of negating the past continuous in Arabic. The first two are to negate كانَ as any past tense verb, using either ما or لَمْ (see Chapter 11 on past tense; Chapter 15 on jussive). The third way is to negate the present tense verb following كانَ.

Recall that كانَ can simply be negated by placing ما immediately before it, as in the following example:

ما كانَ يَعْرِفُ الإِنْكليزِيَّةَ.   He used to not know English.

The preceding sentence in Arabic can be said about someone who is no longer with us. It can also have another reading. One can also infer from this sentence that while that person did not know English in the past, he does now, or he knew it at another stage in life. In other words, the above sentence implies the following meanings:

ما كانَ يَعْرِفُ الإِنْكليزِيَّةَ وَلَكِنَّهُ يَعْرِفُها الآنَ.

He used to not know English but he knows it now.

ما كانَ يَعْرِفُ الإِنْكليزِيَّة وَلَكِنَّهُ عَرَفَها فيما بَعْد.

He used to not know English but he learned it at a later stage.

The structure above can also be negated by the use of لَمْ placed in front of the present tense jussive of the verb كَانَ, as in the following:

لَمْ يَكُنْ يَعْرِفُ الإِنْكِليزِيَّةَ.

He used to not know English.

Such sentences can also be negated by the use of لا between the verb كَانَ and the present tense verb following it, as in the following example:

كَانَ لا يَعْرِفُ الإِنْكِليزِيَّةَ.

He used to not know English.

Or,

It used to be that he did not know English.

This form of negation can be found in Quranic Arabic as well as in Modern Standard. We will cite a couple of Quranic verses to illustrate this usage:

إِنَّهُ كَانَ لا يُؤْمِنُ.

He used to not believe.

كانوا لا يَتَناهَوْنَ عَنْ مُنْكَرٍ فَعَلوهُ.

They used to not cease from a bad act they were in the habit of doing.

CHAPTER 19

Past perfect tense
كان + قَد + الفِعْل الماضي

This tense is used to indicate two events that happened at different times in the past with one having happened prior to the other. Such events are generally organized in sequence by two clauses. Such a structure requires the particle قَد, one of whose functions is to indicate that an action had already been completed before another. قَد immediately precedes the past tense verb indicating the already completed action; it could also be preceded by كانَ or وَكانَ. Consider the following examples:

رَجَعَ أَخي مِنَ القاهِرة وكانَ قَدْ أَكْمَلَ دِراسَتَهُ الجامِعيَّة هُناكَ.

My brother returned from Cairo and he had completed his
   university study there.

ذَهَبَ الطالِبُ إلى مَكْتَبِ الأُستاذ فَوَجَدَهُ قَدْ غادَرَ.

The student went to the professor's office and found out that
   he had already left.

The times of events are indicated by time adverbial phrases such as قَبْلَ أَنْ، قَبْلَما "before" and بَعْدَ أَنْ، بَعْدَما "after." As these phrases organize the sequence of past events, verbs following them must be in the past tense.

The main clause containing كانَ must be followed by the particle قَد and the past tense of the verb expressing the action that happened first. The past tense verb following كانَ must be conjugated to indicate the person(s) involved in the events with respect to number and gender. The subordinate clause following قَبْلَ or قَبْلَما must have a verb in the past tense. Examine the following examples:

كانَ الطّالِبُ قَدْ أَكَلَ قَبْلَما ذَهَبَ إلى الصَّفِّ.

The student (M) had eaten before he went to class.

كانَتِ الطَّبِيبَةُ قَدْ وَصَلَت إلى الْـمُسْتَشْفى قَبْلَ أَنْ أُدْخِلَ الـمَريضُ.

The physician (F) had arrived at the hospital before the
  patient was admitted.

كانَ الـمُساعِدونَ قَدْ وَصَلوا قَبْلَما حَضَرَ الْمُديرُ.

The assistants (M, Pl) had arrived before the director came.

The positions of the two clauses are not rigid. In other words, the subordinate
clause can be placed at the beginning of the sentence. The above examples are
duplicated below to illustrate this flexibility:

قَبْلَما ذَهَبَ إلى الصَّفِّ كانَ الطّالِبُ قَدْ أَكَلَ.

Before he went to class, the student had [already] eaten.

قَبْلَ أَنْ أُدْخِلَ المَريضُ كانَتِ الطَّبِيبَةُ قَدْ وَصَلَت إلى المُسْتَشْفى.

Before the patient was admitted, the doctor had [already]
  arrived at the hospital.

قَبْلَما حَضَرَ المُديرُ كانَ الـمُساعِدونَ قَدْ وَصَلوا.

Before the director came, the assistants had [already] arrived.

The time adverb قَبْلَما can be replaced by عِنْدَما "when." Thus the sentences
above can be rendered in the following way to convey the same meaning:

كانَ الطّالِبُ قَدْ أَكَلَ عِنْدَما ذَهَبَ إلى الصَّفِّ.

The student (M) had [already] eaten when he went to class.

كانَتِ الطَّبِيبَةُ قَدْ وَصَلَت إلى المُسْتَشْفى عِنْدَما أُدْخِلَ الـمَريضُ.

The doctor (F) had [already] arrived at the hospital when
  the patient was admitted.

كانَ الـمُساعِدونَ قَدْ وَصَلوا عِنْدَما حَضَرَ الـمُديرُ.

The assistants had [already] arrived when the director arrived.

This structure can be used without necessarily requiring the adverbial particle عِنْدَما, as in the following more commonly used example:

إِسْتَقْبَلَ الرَّئِيسُ أَمِيرَ دَوْلَةِ الكُوَيْت. وكانَ الأَمِيرُ قَدْ وَصَلَ إلى دِمَشْق اللَّيْلَةَ الماضِيَةَ.

The president welcomed the *emir* of Kuwait, who had arrived in
   Damascus the previous night.

Moreover, instead of the phrase قَبْلَما and the past tense verb following it, *maSdar*s can be used to convey the same meaning, as in the following sentences:

كانَ الطّالِبُ قَدْ أَكَلَ قَبْلَ الذَّهابِ إلى الصَّفِّ.

The student (M) had [already] eaten before going to class.

كانَتِ الطَّبِيبَةُ قَدْ وَصَلَت إلى المُسْتَشْفى قَبْلَ إِدْخالِ المَرِيض.

The doctor (F) had already arrived before admitting the patient.

كانَ المُساعِدونَ قَدْ وَصَلوا قَبْلَ حُضُورِ المُدِير.

The assistants had [already] arrived before the director's arrival.

يا لَيْلى، كُنْتِ قَدْ وُلِدْتِ قَبْلَ اِنْتِقالِ العائِلَةِ إلى بَيْروت.

Laila, you had been born before the family moved to Beirut.

هَلْ كُنْتَ قَدْ أَكَلْتَ قَبْلَ الذَّهابِ إلى السّينَما؟

Had you eaten before you went to the movies?

CHAPTER 20

Conditionals اَلشَّرْط

Conditional sentences consist of two components: (1) the subordinate clause that contains the conditional particle, called in Arabic جُمْلَة الشَّرْط, and (2) the main clause that contains the consequence of the condition, known in traditional Arabic grammar as جُمْلَة الشَّرْط "the result clause." جَواب الشَّرْط clauses always begin with a conditional particle. Conditional sentences may express possible outcomes or unrealizable ones, depending on the particle used.

There are several conditional particles (أَدَوات الشَّرْط) in Arabic, listed below; each will be discussed separately: إذا، لَوْ، إِنْ، مَنْ، ما، مَهْما، أَيْنَما، مَتى، أَيُّ، حَيْثُما، كَيْفَما، أَيّانَ and أَنَّى. Of this list, أَيّانَ and أَنَّى are not commonly used in Modern Standard Arabic as they tend to be archaic; and, therefore, they will not be discussed in this work.

These particles can be divided into three categories:

1. Particles that can be followed by verbs in varying tenses. This includes إذا "if," لَوْ "were," "had been."
2. Particles that must be followed by jussive verbs فِعْل مَجزوم only (see Chapter 15 on Jussive). This includes the following: مَتى "when, whenever," مَنْ "who-ever," ما "whatever," مَهْما "whatever," أَيْنَ or أَيْنَما "wherever," حَيْثُما "wherever," كَيْفَما "however," and أَيُّ "whichever."
3. Different verb tenses besides the jussive form are permissible in the case of إِنْ "if."

20.1 PARTICLES WITH VARYING TENSES

20.1.1 إذا "if"

إذا "if" always begins the conditional clause; it must be followed by either a verb in the past tense or a verb negated by the jussive particle لَمْ. The use of

إذا conveys the idea of a possible condition and some degree of probability; it could be equivalent to either "if" or "when."

إذا سافَرْتُ إلى القاهِرَة زُرْتُ الأَهْرامَ.

If I travel to Cairo, I shall visit the pyramids.

The verb in the result clause can be in the past. Other verb tenses such as the future tense or imperative mood, for example, are also possible. The verb unit in this situation must be introduced by فَـ. Consider the following examples:

إذا سافَرْنا إلى القاهرة فَسَوْفَ نزورُ الأَهْرامَ.

If we travel to Cairo, we will visit the pyramids.

إذا دَرَسْنا كَثيراً فَسَنَنْجَحُ في الامْتِحانِ.

If we study hard, we will pass the exam.

The imperative verb form can also be used in the result clause; it must also begin with فَـ, as in the following example:

إذا أَرَدْتَ العَمَلَ فَقَدِّم طَلَباً غَداً.

If you want to work, submit an application tomorrow.

The result clause can contain an equational sentence whose head is a pronoun. The pronoun must have فَـ prefixed to it, as in the following:

إذا قالَ هذا فَهُوَ مُخْطِئٌ.

If he said this, he is wrong.

إذا حَدَثَ ذلِكَ فَهُوَ أَمْرٌ لَيْسَ باليَسيرِ.

If that happens, it will be a serious matter.

Clauses containing the conditional particle إذا can be switched around. This requires the *faa'* to be dropped at the beginning of سَوْفَ or the pronoun in equational sentences. Consider the following:

إذا دَرَسْتَ كَثيراً فَسَوْفَ تَنْجَحُ.   If you study hard, you will pass.

سَوْفَ تَنْجَحُ إذا دَرَسْتَ كَثيراً.   You will pass if you study hard.

Recall that by placing an element at the front of a sentence, more emphasis is put on that element.

20.1.2 لَوْ "were," "had...been"

لَوْ expresses conditions that are contrary to fact, or conditions that are not realizable. The use of لَوْ requires that the result clause begin with لَـ. Clauses containing the conditional لَوْ must always be sentence-initial. Certain conditions must apply on the use of لَوْ, however.

1. Both conditional and result clauses must have verbs in the past tense, as in the following examples:

   لَوْ زُرْتُ مِصْرَ، لَشاهَدْتُ الأَهرامَ.
   Had I visited Egypt, I would have seen the pyramids.

   لَوْ دَرَسَ لَنَجَحَ.
   Had he studied, he would have passed.

   The visit to Egypt has not been realized in the first sentence above. There-fore, the viewing of the pyramids did not happen. Similarly, in the second sentence, the person mentioned has not studied. Had he studied, he would have passed the examination.

2. The conditional clause may have a verb negated by لَمْ. The main clause must also begin with the negative particle ما linked to لَـ followed by a past tense verb, as in the following examples:

   لَوْ لَمْ أَكُنْ مَريضاً لَـما بَقيتُ في البَيتِ.
   Had I not been sick, I would not have stayed at home.

   لَوْ لَمْ يُسافِروا إلى لُبنان لَـما شاهَدوا بَعْلَبَك.
   Had they not traveled to Lebanon, they would not have seen
       Baalbek.

   Some changes have been noticed in Modern Standard Arabic in the rules introduced above. Some writing exhibits the dropping of لَـ when the negative particle ما is used, as in the following:

   لَوْ رافَقْتُكَ، ما قابَلَكَ.
   Had I accompanied you, he would not have received you.

لَوْ لَمْ أَكُنْ مَرِيضاً، ما بَقيتُ في البَيْتِ.

Had I not been sick, I would not have stayed at home.

لَوْ لَمْ تَنْجَحْ، طَرَدْتُكَ.

Had you not passed, I would have dismissed you.

3. لَوْ can be followed by أَنَّ, thus forming a conditional particle by combining the elements لَوْ and أَنَّ as a part of the conditional clause. Recall that أَنَّ must be followed by a sentence beginning with a noun, or a suffix pronoun (see Chapter 21 on 'Inna and its sisters). The result clause must begin with لَ followed by a complete sentence, as in the following:

لَوْ أَنَّ الطُّلّابَ دَرَسوا جَيِّداً لَحَصَلوا عَلى عَلاماتٍ عاليةٍ.

Had the students studied well, they would have obtained high grades.

لَوْ أَنَّها وَصَلَت أَمْس لاَتَّصَلَت بِنا.

Had she arrived yesterday, she would have contacted us.

4. لَوْ can be followed by the negative particle لا to form لَوْ لا "had it not been for." This construct can be followed by a nominative noun to form the conditional clause. The result clause must begin with لَ prefixed to the negative particle ما as in the following examples:

لَوْلا الـمـالُ لَما تَقَدَّمَتِ البِلادُ.

Had it not been for money, the country would not have progressed.

لَوْلا حُضُورُ الرَّئيسِ لَما اتَّفَقَتِ الأَطْرافُ.

Had it not been for the presence of the president, the parties would not have come to an agreement.

20.1.3 إنْ "if"

It is extremely important not to confuse the conditional particle إنْ with the particles أَنْ or إنَّ because of their homographic similarities, especially when they are not vocalized.

As a conditional particle, إنْ is used for a possible condition or a hypothetical one. Various verb tenses can be used in the result clause, as will be illustrated below. The conditional clause may use the past tense, as below, or the jussive form of the present tense, as follows in the next paragraph.

1. The clause containing إِنْ can have a past tense verb. In this case, the result clause can also have a verb in the past tense, as in the following example:

إِنْ سَافَرْتُ إِلى الـمَغْرِب زُرْتُ مَدينةَ فاس.

If I travel to Morocco, I will visit the City of Fez.

The use of إِنْ in the preceding sentence indicates that travel to Morocco is likely to happen, which makes it possible to visit Fez.

2. While the conditional clause containing إِنْ can have a past tense verb, the result clause can have a future tense verb with ف attached to the future particle:

إِنْ سَافَرْتُ إِلى الـمَغْرِب فَسَوْفَ أَزورُ فاس.

If I travel to Morocco, I will visit Fez.

Verbs in the main and/or subordinate clauses may be expressed in the past or future tenses in Arabic. They are usually expressed in the present and future tenses in English.

20.2 PARTICLES WITH THE JUSSIVE MOOD

إِنْ allows the use of the jussive form of the present tense. The result clause must also have a verb in the jussive. The meaning expresses a possible condition, as in the following examples:

إِنْ تَدْرُسْ تَنْجَحْ.

If you (M) study, you will pass.

إِنْ تَذهَبي مَعي تُشاهِدي أَخي.

If you (F) go with me, you will see my brother.

إِنْ يَدْرُسا يَنْجَحا.

If they (M, D) study, they will pass.

إِنْ تَذْهَبا إِلى السُّوق تُشاهِدا صَديقي.

If you (M/F, D) go to the *suq*, you will see my friend.

إِنْ يَعْمَلُوا كَثِيراً يَحْصُلُوا عَلَى فُلوس أَكْثَرَ.

If they (M, Pl) work a lot, they will get more money.

إِنْ تَذهَبْنَ إِلَى الأُرْدُن تُشاهِدْنَ البَتْراء.

If you (F, Pl) go to Jordan, you will see Petra.

إِنْ يَذهَبْنَ إِلَى الأُرْدُّن يُشاهِدْنَ البَتْراء.

If they (F, Pl) go to Jordan, they will see Petra.

Clauses containing the conditional إِنْ must always be sentence-initial. The conditional particle إِنْ can be dropped from the beginning of the conditional clause. In this case, the conditional clause begins with the imperative verb form (in the jussive); the result clause must also have a verb in the jussive, as in the examples below:

أُدْرُسْ تَنْجَحْ.   Study and you will succeed.

أُطْلُبِ الـمَالَ تَحْصُلْ عَلَيْهِ.   Seek wealth and you will get it.

20.2.1 مَنْ "whoever"

مَنْ has various functions in the language: as an interrogative particle, introduced in Chapter 6, and also as a relative pronoun (see Chapter 22). This section is concerned with مَنْ as a conditional particle, used for human nouns only.

The clause containing مَنْ "whoever" as a conditional particle requires the use of the jussive form of the verb. The result clause must also have a verb in the jussive, as in the following examples:

مَنْ يَجْتَهِدْ يَحْصُلْ عَلَى دَرَجاتٍ عالِيَةٍ.   Whoever studies hard gets high marks.

مَنْ يَصْبِرْ يَنَلْ.   Whoever demonstrates patience wins.

20.2.2 ما "whatever"

The clause containing the conditional particle ما "whatever" requires the use of the jussive form of the verb. It is used in reference to non-human nouns.

The result clause must also have a verb in the jussive, as in the following examples:

ما تَفْعَلْهُ يَعْرِفْهُ أَبوكَ.   Whatever you do, your father knows it.

ما تَطْلُبوهُ يُلَبَّ.   Whatever you (M, Pl) request will be provided.

The following observation should be made regarding the defective verb لَبَّى "to provide, to answer" in the second sentence above and similar other verbs. The insertion of a *fat-Ha* at the end of the verb breaks the consonant gemination, thus resulting in يُلَبَّ.

20.2.3 مَهْما "whatever"

مَهْما "whatever" requires the use of the jussive form. The result clause must also have a verb in the jussive, as in the following examples:

مَهْما يُؤْمَرْ يُنَفِّذْ.   Whatever he is ordered [to do], he performs.

مَهْما يَقُلْ يَقُلِ الصِّدْقَ.   Whatever he says, he says the truth.

20.2.4 أَيْنَما "wherever"

This particle consists of أَيْنَ plus ما. The clause containing أَيْنَما "wherever" requires the use of the verb in the jussive form. The result clause must also have a verb in the jussive, as in the following examples:

أَيْنَما يُسافِرْ تُسافِرْ.   Wherever he travels, she travels.

أَيْنَما تَذْهَبْ تَجِدِ الشَّجَرَ.   Wherever you go, you find trees.

The insertion of *kasra* at the end of تَجِد instead of the expected *sukuun* is to break the consonant cluster in this example.

20.2.5 مَتى "whenever"

مَتى "whenever" requires the use of the verb in the jussive form. The result clause must also have a verb in the jussive, as in the following examples:

مَتى تُحْضِرِ الإيصالَ تَحْصُلْ عَلى فُلوسِكَ.

Whenever you bring the receipt, you get your money.

مَتى يَأْمُرْ يَتَوَقَّعْ التَّنْفيذَ.

Whenever he issues an order, he expects execution [of the order].

The required use of the jussive form of the verb with several of the conditional particles mentioned above does not apply in two instances:

First, if the result clause is in the negative, the negative particle لَنْ must be preceded by فَ, as in the following:

مَهْما تُسافِرْ إلى الـمَغْرِب فَلَنْ تَجِدَ إلاَّ شَعْباً كَريماً.

lit. "No matter how many times you travel to Morocco,
   you will not find but a generous people."

Second, if the result clause is in the future tense, as in the following example:

مَهْما تُسافِرْ إلى الـمَغْرِب فَسَوْفَ تَجِدُ شَعْباً كَريماً.

No matter how many times you travel to Morocco, you will
   always find a generous people.

There are other cases where فَ is used at the beginning of the result clause. One such case is when the result clause is in the interrogative, as in the following example:

إذا حَضَرَ أَبوكَ فَهَلْ سَتَقولُ لَهُ؟

If your father comes, will you tell him?

The other case is when the particle قَدْ is used, followed by a present tense verb to indicate possibility or likelihood, as in the following example:

إذا حَضَرَ أَبوكَ فَقَدْ أُخْبِرُهُ.

If your father comes, it is possible that I will tell him.

20.2.6 أَيُّ "whoever, whichever"

This element was introduced in Chapter 6 as an interrogative particle in the sense of "which" or "who." It also has a conditional function in the sense of "whoever, whichever," used for both human as well as non-human nouns. The clause containing أَيُّ requires the use of the jussive verb form. The result clause must also have a verb in the jussive, as in the following examples:

أَيُّ إِنْسانٍ يَدْرُسْ يَنْجَحْ.
Whoever studies will succeed.

أَيُّ مَدينَةٍ تُسافِرْ إِلَيْها أُسافِرْ مَعَكَ!
Whichever city you travel to, I will go with you.

20.2.7 كَيْفَما "however"

This particle consists of كَيْفَ "how" and the particle ما. Verbs in the clause containing كَيْفَما and the main clause must be in the jussive, as in the following examples:

كَيْفَما يَأْمُرْ يُطَعْ.   However he demands, he is obeyed.

كَيْفَما تَفْعَلْ يُغْفَرْ لَها.   However she acts, she is forgiven.

20.2.8 حَيْثُما "wherever"

This particle comprises حَيْثُ, a place adverb in the sense of "where," in addition to ما. Verbs in both clauses must be in the jussive form, as in the following examples:

حَيْثُما يَرْحَلْ تَرْحَلْ مَعَهُ.   Wherever he relocates, she relocates with him.

حَيْثُما تُمْطِرْ يَنْبُتِ النَّباتُ.   Wherever it rains, plants grow.

CHAPTER 21

إِنَّ وَأَخَواتُها *'Inna* and its sisters

The following particles: لَيْتَ and كَأَنَّ، إِنَّ، أَنَّ، لَكِنَّ، أَنَّ، لِأَنَّ، لَعَلَّ generally conjoin sentences. إِنَّ and لَعَلَّ can also be used in non-conjoining functions in independent sentences. Each of these particles has a different meaning. However, all of these particles share the following characteristics:

1. They must be followed by a nominal sentence, that is to say, one that begins with a noun or a pronoun (see Chapter 9 on equational sentences). If the subject of this sentence is an explicitly expressed noun, its case must be in the accusative; the predicate of the equational sentence, however, must remain *marfuuᶜ*, nominative, as in the following examples:

   البَيْتُ جَميلٌ لَكِنَّ الشّارِعَ مُزْدَحِمٌ بِالسّيّاراتِ.
   The house is beautiful, but the street is overcrowded with cars.

   أُحِبُّ الجامِعَةَ لِأَنَّ الدِّراسَةَ مُـمْتِعَةٌ.
   I like the university because studying is interesting.

2. If the subject of the sentence following these particles is a pronoun, the suffixal form of that pronoun must be used, as in the following:

   سافَرَ صَديقي إلى بَيْروت لِأَنَّهُ يَدْرُسُ هُناكَ.
   My friend traveled to Beirut because he studies there.

   رَجَعَت إلى دِمَشْق لِأَنَّها تَعْمَلُ هُناكَ.
   She returned to Damascus because she works there.

We now turn to discussing each of these particles separately:

21.1 لَكِنَّ "BUT"

This particle contrasts two entities with respect to a particular characteristic. Examine the following two examples:

شيكاغو كَبِيرَةٌ لَكِنَّ شارْلوتسفيل صَغِيرَةٌ.

Chicago is large but Charlottesville is small.

البَيْتُ قَدِيمٌ لَكِنَّ السَّيّارَةَ جَدِيدَةٌ.

The house is old but the car is new.

لَكِنَّ can also contrast the same entity with respect to certain characteristics or actions of the same person, as in the following examples:

أَحْمَد غَنِيٌّ لَكِنَّهُ بَخِيلٌ.

Ahmad is rich but he is stingy.

لَيْلى ذَهَبَت إلى الـمَكْتَبَةِ لَكِنَّها ما دَرَسَت.

Leila went to the library but she did not study.

21.2 لِأَنَّ "BECAUSE"

This particle consists of the prepositions لِ "for, to" and أَنَّ. It is used to conjoin two sentences and indicates a reason for connecting them, as in the following examples:

حَلَب جَمِيلَةٌ لِأَنَّها قَدِيمَةٌ.

Aleppo is beautiful because it is old.

أَحْمَد سافَرَ إلى نيويورك لِأَنَّهُ طالِبٌ هُناكَ.

Ahmad traveled to New York because he is a student there.

تَذْهَبُ صَدِيقَتي إلى الـمَكْتَبَةِ لِأَنَّها تَعْمَلُ هُناكَ.

My friend (F) goes to the library because she works there.

Note that the verb following the noun or pronoun after لِأَنَّ may or may not agree in tense with the verb in the main clause, as in the following example:

ذَهَبَت صَدِيقَتي إلى الـمَكْتَبَةِ لِأَنَّها تَعْمَلُ هُناكَ.

My friend (F) went to the library because she works there.

In the preceding sentence, the verb in the main clause is in the past tense, whereas the verb in the subordinate clause is in the present. However, in the sentence. تَذْهَبُ صَدِيقَتِي إِلى الـمَكْتَبَةِ لِأَنَّها تَعْمَلُ هُناك the verb in the main clause is in the present tense, as is the verb in the subordinate clause. The use of tense depends on the meaning intended. It is important to note that لِأَنَّ provides answers to questions asking for reasons. Consider the two questions below and their answers:

لِماذا ما ذَهَبَ الطّالِبُ إِلى الجامِعَةِ؟

Why did the student not go to the university?

ما ذَهَبَ الطّالِبُ إِلى الجامِعةِ لِأَنَّهُ كانَ مَريضاً.

The student did not go to the university because he was sick.

لَماذا رَجَعَتْ مَرْيَم إِلى البَيْتِ؟

Why did Mariam return to the house?

رَجَعَت مَرْيَم إِلى البَيْتِ لِأَنَّها كانَت مَريضَةً.

Mariam returned to the house because she was sick.

21.3 إِنَّ "INDEED" AND "THAT"

This particle has two functions in Modern Standard Arabic:

1. It can begin a sentence to add emphasis to the proposition of the sentence, as in the following two sentences:

    إِنَّ الطَّقْسَ جَميلٌ اليَوْمَ!   Indeed, the weather is beautiful today.

    إِنَّ هذا الكِتابَ مُهِمٌّ!   Indeed, this book is important.

    إِنَّها تَدْرُسُ العَرَبِيَّةَ!   Indeed, she is studying Arabic.

The sentences are equivalent to:

الطَّقْسُ جَميلٌ اليومَ.   The weather is good today.

هذا الكِتابُ مُهِمٌّ.   This book is important.

هِيَ تَدْرُسُ العَرَبِيَّةَ.   She studies Arabic.

The sentences with إِنَّ, however, indicate more emphasis on the propositions in them.

2. It is also used to change direct into indirect, or reported, speech when the preceding verb is قال or any of its derived forms. Examine the following:

قَالَ الطَّالِبُ: «اللُّغَةُ العَرَبِيَّةُ جَمِيلَةٌ».

The student said: "Arabic is beautiful".

قَالَ الطَّالِبُ إِنَّ اللُّغَةَ العَرَبِيَّةَ جَمِيلَةٌ.

The student said that Arabic is beautiful.

دائِماً يُكَرِّرُ القَوْلَ إِنَّ العَرَبِيَّةَ سَهْلَةٌ.

He always repeats saying that Arabic is easy.

Note that in the sentence قَالَ الطَّالِبُ: «اللُّغَةُ العَرَبِيَّةُ جَمِيلَةٌ» the exact words of the student are enclosed between quotation marks. Those words are what is referred to as direct speech. In the sentence قَالَ الطَّالِبُ إِنَّ اللغةَ العربيةَ جميلةٌ however, the exact words by the student are not stated. What the student said is reported in indirect speech format. Another example will illustrate this point further:

قالَ الـمُديرُ: «سَأُسافِرُ إلى دِمَشْق».

The director said: "I will travel to Damascus."

قالَ الـمُديرُ إِنَّهُ سَيُسافِرُ إلى دِمَشْق.

The director said that he would travel to Damascus.

21.4 أَنَّ "THAT"

Like إِنَّ above this particle is also used to change direct into indirect or reported speech, as in the following examples:

ذَكَرَ الأُسْتاذُ: «اللُّغَةُ العَرَبِيَّةُ جَمِيلَةٌ».

The professor said: "Arabic is beautiful".

ذَكَرَ الأُسْتاذُ أَنَّ اللُّغَةَ العَرَبِيَّةَ جَمِيلَةٌ.

The professor stated that Arabic is beautiful.

Note that in the first sentence the exact words of the teacher are enclosed between quotation marks. Those words are what is referred to as direct speech. In the second sentence the exact words uttered by the professor are not stated and what the professor said is reported in indirect speech.

Examine the use of أَنَّ in the following examples:

أَخْبَرَنا المُديرُ أَنَّهُ سَوْفَ يُسافِرُ إلى لُبْنان في الصَّيْفِ.

The director informed us that he would travel to Lebanon
in the summer.

أَعْلَمَتْهُ الأُسْتاذَةُ أَنّها دَرَّسَت في جامِعَة كولُمْـبِيا.

The professor (F) informed him that she taught at Columbia
University.

The use of أَنَّ is restricted to verbs of "mention," "knowing," "hearing," etc.
It is not to be confused with أَنْ followed by the subjunctive (see Chapter 13
on the subjunctive).

The following list contains some of these verbs and their meanings. A more
comprehensive list appears in Appendix F.

Verbs that express knowing, understanding, doubting, believing, etc. include:

أَدْرَكَ / يُدْرِكُ	to realize
رَأَى / يَرَى	to see, to view, to think
عَرَفَ / يَعْرِفُ	to know, to be familiar with
عَلِمَ / يَعْلَمُ	to know
فَهِمَ / يَفْهَمُ	to understand
لاحَظَ / يُلاحِظُ	to observe
شَعَرَ / يَشْعُرُ	to feel, to sense
شَكَّ / يَشُكُّ	to doubt
ظَنَّ / يَظُنُّ	to think, to suspect
وَجَدَ / يَجِدُ	to find out, to discover
اِعْتَقَدَ / يَعْتَقِدُ	to believe
آمَنَ / يُؤْمِنُ	to believe

Verbs that express mentioning, hearing, reporting, etc. include:

أَخْبَرَ / يُخْبِرُ	to inform, to tell	زَعَمَ / يَزْعُمُ	to allege, to claim
أَعْلَمَ / يُعْلِمُ	to inform	سَأَلَ / يَسْأَلُ	to ask
ذَكَرَ / يَذْكُرُ	to mention	سَمِعَ / يَسْمَعُ	to hear

Verbs expressing anger, surprise, happiness, pride, etc. include:

أَسْعَدَ / يُسْعِدُ	to please, to make s.o. happy
أَفْرَحَ / يُفْرِحُ	to please, to make happy

Verbs expressing confirmation, certainty, etc. include:

أَكَّدَ / يُؤَكِّدُ	to confirm, ascertain, to assure
بَرْهَنَ / يُبَرْهِنُ	to prove

In addition, there are invariable phrases that require the use of أَنَّ. Below is a partial list:

رَغْمَ أَنَّ	despite, in spite of, although
عَلى الرَّغْم (مِن) أَنَّ	despite, although
بِالرَّغْم (مِنْ) أَنَّ	although, in spite of
لا شَكَّ أَنَّ	there is no doubt that
مِنَ الطَّبِيعِيِّ أَنَّ	it is natural that
مِنَ الواضِحِ أَنَّ	it is clear that

Note that many of these invariable phrases can function as connectors of statements within or between sentences, as in the following examples:

عَلى الرَّغْم مِنْ أَنَّهُ كانَ مَريضاً، اِسْتَمَرَّ الـمُديرُ في عَمَلِهِ.

Although he was sick, the director continued his work.

مِنَ الواضِح أَنَّ الطَّقْسَ يَتَغَيَّرُ دائِماً.

It is obvious that the weather always changes.

لا شَكَّ أَنَّ سِياسَةَ الرَّئيس كانَت خاطِئَةً.

Undoubtedly, the president's policy was faulty.

21.5 لَعَلَّ "PERHAPS"

This particle conveys the meaning of "perhaps", "maybe", "it is possible that." It should be strongly emphasized that this particle cannot stand alone, as can the English words "perhaps" and "maybe," in response to a question. As has been mentioned previously, لَعَلَّ is not necessarily used to conjoin sentences like the other particles in this group; like إِنَّ it can initiate discourse. لَعَلَّ must be followed immediately by a sentential structure that begins with a noun in the accusative case or by a suffixal pronoun attached to it, as in the following:

لَعَلَّ الطَّقْسَ يَتَحَسَّنُ غَداً.

The weather may improve tomorrow.

ما وَصَلَ صَديقي، لَعَلَّهُ مَريضٌ.

My friend did not arrive. Perhaps he is sick.

21.6 كَأَنَّ "AS IF, AS THOUGH"

This particle has the meaning of "as if" or "as though." Like the other members in this set, كَأَنَّ must be followed by a nominal sentence. If followed by a pronoun, the suffixal pronoun form must be attached. When followed by a regular noun, the noun must be in the accusative. Examine the following:

يَلْعَبُ الأَوْلادُ في الشّارِع كَأَنَّ الثَّلْجَ ما هَطَلَ.

The kids play in the street as if snow had not fallen.

يَمْشي كَأَنَّهُ مَريضٌ.

He walks as though he were sick.

يَتَصَرَّفُ هذا الرَّجُلُ كَأَنَّهُ مِلْيونيرٌ.

This man behaves as if he were a millionaire.

كَأَنَّ does not always have to be preceded by a verb as in the preceding examples. Its position can be at the beginning of a sentence to express a simile or a description of condition or a state, as in the following:

كَأَنَّ اَلعَروسَ قَمَرٌ!

The bride is beautiful (*lit.* "The bride has the beautiful looks of a moon!")

كَأَنَّ اَلبَيْتَ قَصْرٌ!

The house has the appearance of a palace!

21.7 لَيْتَ "IF ONLY"

لَيْتَ expresses a wish that is not realizable. It has the meaning of "if only," or "if it were." Syntactically, it must be followed by a nominal (equational) sentence, with either a suffix pronoun or an accusative noun, as in the following:

لَيْتَني كُنْتُ غَنِيّاً.

I wish I were rich!

لَيْتَ الحَرْبَ ما وَقَعَت.

If only the war had not happened.

Note that after the particles إنَّ، أَنَّ، لَكِنَّ، لأَنَّ، لَعَلَّ and the rest of this group, the suffixal pronoun for أنا "I" is ي or ني. Either form is acceptable. Examine the two pairs of examples below:

ما ذَهَبْتُ إلى الجامِعَةِ لأَني كُنْتُ مَريضاً.

I did not go to the university because I was sick.

ما ذَهَبْتُ إلى الجامِعَةِ لأَنَّني كُنْتُ مَريضاً.

I did not go to the university because I was sick.

رَجَعْتُ إلى البَيْتِ لَكِنّي ما أَكَلْتُ.

I returned to the house, but I did not eat.

رَجَعْتُ إلى البَيْتِ لَكِنَّني ما أَكَلْتُ.

I returned to the house, but I did not eat.

Similarly, if followed by the pronoun نَحْنُ "we," the suffixal form نا or ا is acceptable, as in the following:

نَشْعُرُ بالتَّعَب لِأَنّا عَمِلْنا كَثيراً اليَوْمَ.

We feel tired because we worked a lot today.

نَشْعُرُ بالتَّعَب لِأَنَّنا عَمِلْنا كَثيراً اليَوْمَ.

We feel tired because we worked a lot today.

CHAPTER 22

Relative pronouns الاِسْم الـمَوْصول

22.1 SINGULAR RELATIVE PRONOUNS
الاِسْم الـمَوْصول الـمُفْرَد

The relative pronouns (M) اَلَّذي, (F) اَلَّتي "who / whom, which," and their dual
and plural forms, presented below, are used to conjoin two sentences. Hence
the name الاِسْم الـمَوْصول, in which الـمَوْصول is derived from the verb وَصَلَ,
one of whose meanings is "to connect, to tie together." In order for these elements to function grammatically, there must be two sentences, the first of which
must have a definite noun referred to as the antecedent. This noun can be a
subject of a sentence or a direct object of a transitive verb, or it can be preceded
by a preposition. The second sentence must also contain a noun that relates
or refers to the antecedent. The two sentences are then conjoined to form one
sentence by using the relative pronoun اَلَّذي or اَلَّتي depending on the gender
of the antecedent, thus forming two clauses: a main clause and a dependent
clause. The dependent clause is called a relative clause. In effect, the dependent
clause becomes a sentential adjective that modifies the definite noun in the
main clause, i.e. the antecedent. اَلَّذي، اَلَّتي are invariable in form. Arab grammarians call the structure beginning with the relative pronoun صِلَة الـمَوْصول.

الذي is used to introduce clauses modifying masculine nouns. اَلَّتي, on
the other hand, is used to introduce feminine nouns in the singular, and is also
used with non-human plural nouns.

22.1.1 اَلَّذي and اَلَّتي replacing subject nouns

اَلَّذي replaces masculine singular nouns only. اَلَّتي replaces feminine singular
nouns. Examine the following:

سافَرَ الرَّجُلُ.   The man departed.

دَرَّسَ الرَّجُلُ في الجامِعَة.   The man taught at the university.

The second sentence provides extra information about الرَّجُلُ in the first sentence (the antecedent). In other words, this sentence functions like an adjective in the form of a sentence, rather than a single-word adjective. Since الرَّجُلُ in these two sentences refers to the same entity, the second occurrence of الرَّجُلُ is replaced, for style and more idiomatic Arabic, by the relative pronoun الَّذي, which must follow the antecedent immediately, thus resulting in:

سافَرَ الرَّجُلُ اَلَّذي دَرَّسَ في الجامِعَةِ.

The man who taught at the university departed.

If the antecedent is a feminine noun, اَلَّتي must be used, as in the following pair of sentences:

سافَرَتِ الـمَرْأَةُ.   The woman departed.

دَرَّسَتِ الـمَرْأَةُ في الجامِعَةِ.   The woman taught at the university.

Instead of repeating الـمَرْأَةُ in the second sentence, this noun is replaced by the relative pronoun الَّتي, thus resulting in:

سافَرَتِ الـمَرْأَةُ اَلَّتي دَرَّسَت في الجامِعَةِ.

The woman who taught at the university departed.

Note that الَّذي or الَّتي can be followed by a verb. This verb can vary in tense. The use of the appropriate tense depends on the meaning intended to be conveyed. They can also be followed by a nominal sentence, as in the following:

شاهَدْتُ الطّالِبَ الذي أَخوهُ وَزيرٌ.

I saw the student whose brother is a minister.

شاهَدْنا البِـنْتَ التي أُمُّها مُمَرِّضَةٌ.

We saw the girl whose mother is a nurse.

عَرَفْنا الطالِبَةَ التي يُدَرِّسُ أَبوها في الجامِعَةِ.

We knew the student whose father teaches at the university.

قابَلوا الصَّديقَ الذي كانَ زائِراً مِن العِراقِ.

They met the friend who was visiting from Iraq.

22.1.2 اَلَّذِي and اَلَّتِي replacing object nouns

We shall now examine examples in which the noun in the second sentence is a direct object of a transitive verb:

سَافَرَ الرَّجُلُ.   The man departed.

شَاهَدْتُ الرَّجُلَ فِي الجَامِعَةِ.   I saw the man at the university.

In the second sentence above, الرَّجُلَ is a direct object of the verb شَاهَدْتُ. The two sentences can be conjoined by اَلَّذِي. However, الرَّجُلَ in the second sentence must be replaced by a suffixal form of the pronoun هُوَ, namely هُ. This pronoun must attach to the verb, as in the example below:

سَافَرَ الرَّجُلُ الَّذِي شَاهَدْتُهُ فِي الجَامِعَةِ.

The man whom I saw at the university departed."

Similarly, a feminine noun is replaced by a suffix form of the pronoun هِيَ in the example below:

سَافَرَتِ الـمَرْأَةُ.

The woman departed.

شَاهَدْتُ الـمَرْأَةَ فِي الجَامِعَةِ.

I saw the woman at the university.

must have for objects. — the ها or ه are the objects)

سَافَرَتِ الـمَرْأَةُ الَّتِي شَاهَدْتُها فِي الجَامِعَةِ.

The woman whom I saw at the university departed.

22.1.3 اَلَّذِي and اَلَّتِي replacing nouns governed by prepositions

Some verbs are said to be transitive in Arabic by the use of prepositions in order for syntax to be grammatical. Examples of such verbs include بَحَثَ عَن "to look for," حَصَلَ عَلَى "to get, obtain," رَجَعَ مِن / إِلَى "to return from / to," etc. When اَلَّذِي or اَلَّتِي is used to begin a sentence with such verbs, the suffixal form of the pronoun in the second sentence refers to the antecedent, called الضَّمِير العَائِد in Arabic. This pronoun must be attached to the preposition, as in the following examples:

قَرَأْتُ الكِتابَ.   I read the book.

حَصَلْتُ عَلَى الكِتابِ في واشِنْطُن.   I got the book in Washington.

Thus the two sentences can be conjoined by اَلَّذي as follows:

قَرَأْتُ الكِتابَ اَلَّذي حَصَلْتُ عَلَيْهِ في واشِنْطُن.

I read the book that I obtained in Washington.

The suffixal pronoun ـهُ replacing the masculine noun الكِتاب must be attached to the preposition عَلى. Recall that in the orthography, the *'alif maqSuura* changes to a regular *yaa'* when a suffix is attached to it. As was mentioned in Chapter 5, ـهُ changes to ـهِ when preceded by a *kasra* or a *yaa'*. Thus instead of عَلَيْهُ we obtain عَلَيْهِ.

In the following two sentences, اَلَّتي replaces the feminine noun اَلوَرَقَةُ in the second sentence. The suffixal pronoun replacing this feminine noun is ها, which must be attached to the preposition عَن. Examine the following:

هذِهِ هِيَ الوَرَقَةُ.   This is the paper.

بَحَثْتُ عَن الوَرَقَةِ في البَيْتِ.   I looked for the paper in the house.

هذِهِ هِيَ الوَرَقَةُ اَلَّتي بَحَثْتُ عَنها في البَيْتِ.   This is the paper that I looked for in the house.

If in the second sentence the فاعِل is the same as the antecedent, the use of a suffixal pronoun is not called for, as in the following example:

قَرَأْتُ الكِتابَ.   I read the book.

يَتَكَوَّنُ الكِتابُ مِنْ أَرْبَعَةِ فُصولٍ.   The book consists of four chapters.

قَرَأْتُ الكِتابَ اَلَّذي يَتَكَوَّنُ مِنْ أَرْبَعَةِ فُصولٍ.   I read the book that consists of four chapters.

22.1.4 اَلَّتي replacing non-human plural nouns

As was stated in Chapter 4, non-human plural nouns are treated as feminine singular in Arabic. Therefore اَلَّتي must be used to replace non-human plural nouns such as كُتُبٌ، جامعاتٌ، سَيّاراتٌ, and كُتُبٌ. In the following examples الَّتِي replaces subject nouns:

رَجَعَتِ السَّياراتُ.   The cars returned.

سافَرَتِ السَّياراتُ إلى بَغْداد.   The cars traveled to Baghdad.

رَجَعَتِ السَّياراتُ التي سافَرَتْ إلى بَغْداد.   The cars that traveled to Baghdad returned.

When الَّتِي is used to replace non-human nouns functioning as objects of transitive verbs, these nouns are replaced by the suffixal form of the pronoun هِيَ, i.e., ها. This suffix pronoun must attach to the verb, as in the following:

قَرَأَ صَديقي الكُتُبَ.   My friend (M) read the books.

هَمِنْجواي كَتَبَ الكُتُبَ.   Hemingway wrote the books.

قَرَأَ صَديقي الكُتُبَ التي كَتَبَها هَمِنْجواي.   My friend read the books which Hemingway wrote.

Likewise, when a noun is preceded by a preposition, the suffix pronoun must attach to the preposition, as in the following:

زُرْنا الجامعاتِ.   We visited the universities.

أُخْتي دَرَسَت في الجامعاتِ.   My sister studied in universities.

زُرْنا الجامعاتِ التي دَرَسَت أُخْتي فيها.   We visited the universities in which my sister studied.

22.1.5 Relative pronouns without antecedents

The relative pronouns الَّذي and الَّتِي are also used in situations where no antecedent is present. This is equivalent to the English structure "he who," "she who," or "the one who." Such usage can occur as:

1. Subjects of sentences, as in the following examples:

اَلَّذي يَدْرُسُ كَثيراً يَحْصُلُ عَلى جائِزَةٍ.
He who studies hard will win a prize.

اَلَّتي وَصَلَت أَمْس تَعْمَلُ في الجامِعَة.

The one (F) who arrived yesterday works at the university.

2.   Objects of verbs, as in the following examples:

قابَلْنا الَّذي وَصَلَ أَمْس.

[handwritten: قابلنا الذي وصل أمس]

We met the one who arrived yesterday.

شاهَدْنا الَّتي حاضَرَت عَن العِراق.

We saw the one (F) who lectured about Iraq.

3.   Governed by a preposition, as in the following examples:

[handwritten: حاضَرَ = to lecture]

هَل اِسْتَمَعْتَ إلى الَّذي حاضَرَ أَمْس؟

Did you listen to the one who lectured yesterday?

بَحَثْتُ عَن الَّتي وَصَلَت مِن اليَمَن.

I looked for the one (F) who arrived from Yemen.

A final note about the verb tenses used in الاِسْم الـمَوْصول is in order. The preceding examples mostly have past tense verbs. However, the use of other tenses is possible. Sentences containing verbs in the present or future tenses can be conjoined by الَّذي or الَّتي, as in the following example:

[handwritten: Can you put future right after التي ?]

الأُسْتاذَةُ الَّتي تُدَرِّسُ في الجامِعَة سَوْفَ تُسافِرُ إلى القاهِرَة.

The professor (F) who teaches at the university will travel to Cairo.

Note that in the preceding sentence, الَّتي is followed by a verb in the present whereas the main clause contains the future tense.

22.2 DUAL RELATIVE PRONOUNS   الاِسْم الـمَوْصول الـمُثَنَّى

Dual masculine nominative	Dual masculine accusative/genitive	Dual feminine nominative	Dual feminine accusative/genitive
اللذان	اللذَيْن	اَللتان	اللتَيْن

[handwritten: Yuck!]

22.2.1 اَللذان and اَللتان replacing subject nouns

اَللذان is the dual form of اَلَّذي. It is used when referring to a dual, masculine noun in the nominative case, as in the following example:

وَصَلَ الصَّديقان أَمْسِ.   The two friends (M) arrived yesterday.

كَتَبَ الصَّديقان الكِتابَ.   The two friends (M) wrote the book.

الصَّديقان in the second sentence is replaced by اَللَذان, resulting in the following:

وَصَلَ الصَّديقان اَللذان كَتَبا الكِتابَ أَمْسِ.
The two friends (M) who wrote the book arrived yesterday.

Note that the verb following اَللَذان must also be in the dual. اللتان replaces feminine, dual and nominative nouns, similarly to the preceding discussion, as in the following example:

وَصَلَتِ الصَّديقَتان أَمْسِ.   The friends (F, D) arrived yesterday.

الصَّديقَتان كَتَبَتا الكِتابَ.   The friends (F, D) wrote the book.

وَصَلَتِ أَمْسِ الصَّديقَتان اَللتان كَتَبَتا اَلكِتابَ.   The friends (F, D) who wrote the book arrived yesterday.

22.2.2 اَللذَيْن and اَللتَيْن replacing direct object nouns and objects of prepositions

اَللتان and اَللذان assume a different form, namely اَللذَيْن and اَللتَيْـن, when they are in the accusative or genitive cases. Thus, when their antecedents are in the accusative (or genitive), as we shall see below, اَللذَيْن and اَللتَيْن must be used, as in the following two sets of examples:

داوَى الطَّبيبُ الـمَريضَيْنِ.
The doctor treated the two patients (M).

شاهَدْنا الـمَريضَيْنِ في العِيادَةِ.
We saw the two patients (M) in the clinic.

داوَى الطَّبِيبُ الـمَريضَيْنِ اَللذَيْنِ شاهَدْناهُما في العِيادَةِ.

The doctor treated the two patients (M) whom we saw in the clinic.

[handwritten: defective focus 6]

Note that in the sentences above, the antecedent الـمَريضَيْنِ "the two patients (M)," is in the accusative case because it is a direct object of the verb داوَى "to treat." Consequently, الـمَريضَيْنِ in the second sentence is replaced by the relative pronoun اَللذَيْنِ. The dual noun in the second sentence is replaced by the suffixal dual pronoun هُما. This suffixal form must obligatorily attach to the verb شاهَدْنا.

داوَى الطَّبِيبُ الـمَريضَتَيْنِ.

The doctor treated the two patients (F).

شاهَدْنا الـمَريضَتَيْنِ في العِيادَةِ.

We saw the two patients (F) in the clinic.

داوَى الطَّبِيبُ الـمَريضَتَيْنِ اَللتَيْنِ شاهَدْناهُما في العِيادَةِ.

The doctor treated the two patients (F) whom we saw in the clinic.

[handwritten right margin: داوى الطبيب المريضتين اللتين / شاهدناهما في العيادة / (clinic)]

On the other hand, الـمَريضَتَيْنِ in the second sentence above is replaced by اللتَيْنِ. The dual noun in the second sentence is replaced by the suffixal dual pronoun هُما. This suffixal form must obligatorily attach to the verb شاهَدْنا.

With verbs requiring the use of prepositions such as حَصَلَ عَلى "to obtain, acquire," the suffixal form of the pronoun replacing the noun in the second sentence must attach to the preposition, as in the following examples:

قَرَأْتُ الكِتابَيْنِ.

I read the two books.

حَصَلْتُ عَلى الكِتابَيْنِ في واشِنْطُنَ.

I got the two books in Washington.

[handwritten right margin: قرأتُ الكتابين اللتين / حصلتُ عليهما في واشنطن]

قَرَأْتُ الكِتابَيْنِ اللذَيْنِ حَصَلْتُ عَلَيْهِما في واشِنْطُنَ.

I read the two books that I got in Washington.

[handwritten: هما actually cuz 3akei]

Note that the suffixal pronoun هُما replaces the noun الكِتابَيْنِ in the second sentence, and that it must attach to the preposition عَلى. Note also the phonological change of ـهُما to ـهِما. Recall that this change must take place when the suffixal pronoun is preceded by a *yaa'* ي or a *kasra*.

اَللَتِين replaces a feminine dual antecedent and the suffixal pronoun replacing this noun is ها, which must attach to the preposition used, as in the following:

قَرَأْتُ الجَريدَتَيْن. I read the two newspapers.

حَصَلْتُ عَلى الجَريدَتَيْن في واشِنْطُن. I got the two newspapers in Washington.

قَرَأْتُ الجَريدَتَيْن اَللَتَيْن حَصَلْتُ عَلَيْهِما في واشِنْطُن. I read the two newspapers that I got in Washington.

[handwritten: Aye?]
[handwritten: قَرَأْتُ الجَريدَتَيْن اللَتَين / حصلتُ على]

22.3 PLURAL RELATIVE PRONOUNS الاِسْم الـمَوْصول الجَمْع

Plural masculine nominative accusative/genitive	Plural feminine nominative accusative/genitive
اَلَّذينَ	اَللواتي

[handwritten: Is the لل vs. لـ to distinguish the dual from the plural easier?]

اَلَّذينَ is invariable in form and is used only with human plural masculine nouns. اللواتي, also invariable, is only used in reference to human plural feminine nouns. We shall discuss these elements in the following sections in some detail:

22.3.1 اَلَّذينَ

اَلَّذينَ is used as the head of relative clauses to replace masculine plural nouns. Its form is invariable, as we shall see below.

[handwritten: thank god]

22.3.1.1 اَلَّذينَ *replacing subject nouns*

[handwritten: حَضَر المُعَلِّمون / الذين يُدَرِّس / العربية]

حَضَرَ الـمُعَلِّمونَ أَمْس. The teachers came yesterday.

يُدَرِّسُ الـمُعَلِّمونَ العَرَبِيَّة. The teachers teach Arabic.

حَضَرَ الـمُعَلِّمونَ اَلَّذينَ يُدَرِّسونَ العَرَبِيَّةَ أَمْس. The teachers who teach Arabic came yesterday.

[handwritten: shouldn't you put أمس]

22.3.1.2 اَلَّذين *replacing direct object nouns and nouns governed by prepositions*

(handwritten: قَابَلَ = to meet)

شَاهَدْنا الـمُعَلِّمينَ.

We saw the teachers.

قَابَلَ الأَصْدِقاءُ الـمُعَلِّمينَ في الـمَدْرَسَةِ.

The friends met the teachers at school.

شَاهَدْنا الـمُعَلِّمينَ اَلَّذينَ قابَلَهُم الأَصْدِقاءُ في الـمَدْرَسَةِ.

We saw the teachers whom the friends met at school.

(handwritten: شاهدنا المعلمين الزين قابلهم الأصدقاء في المدرسة.)

Note that الـمُعَلِّمينَ "the teachers" in the second sentence is a direct object of قَابَلَ. It is replaced by the plural pronoun هُم, which must attach to the verb.

In conjoining two sentences, the plural masculine noun governed by a preposition in the second sentence must be replaced by a suffix form of the pronoun. This suffix pronoun must attach to the preposition, as in the following:

شَاهَدْنا الـمُعَلِّمينَ.

We saw the teachers.

(handwritten: شاهدنا المعلمين بحثنا عنهم في المدرسة.)

بَحَثْنا عَن الـمُعَلِّمينَ في الـمَدْرَسَةِ.

We looked for the teachers at school.

شَاهَدْنا الـمُعَلِّمينَ اَلَّذينَ بَحَثْنا عَنهُم في الـمَدْرَسَةِ.

We saw the teachers whom we looked for at school.

22.3.2 اَللَّواتي / اللاّئي / اللوائي / اللاّتي

اَللَّواتي, on the other hand, is used to head a relative clause functioning as a sentential adjective in reference to *feminine plural nouns*. It has another form that one is likely to encounter in writing, namely اللاّئي. Like اَلَّذين, the feminine form اللواتي is invariable.

(handwritten: human ones, not non-human pl.)

22.3.2.1 اللواتي *replacing subject nouns*

حَضَرَتِ النِّساءُ أَمْس.
The women came yesterday.

تَعْمَلُ النِّساءُ في الجامِعَة.
The women work at the university.

حَضَرَتِ النِّساءُ اللواتي يَعْمَلْنَ في الجامِعَةِ أمْس.
The women who work at the university came yesterday.

The time adverb أَمْس has more mobility as it can be placed closer to the verb it modifies, as in the following:

حَضَرَت أَمْس النِّساءُ اللواتي يَعْمَلْنَ في الجامِعَة.
The women who work at the university came yesterday.

The preceding sentence conveys nuance in meaning by emphasizing time due to the fronting of the adverb أَمْس closer to the verb.

22.3.2.2 اللواتي *replacing direct object nouns and nouns governed by prepositions*

شاهَدْنا النِّساءَ.
We saw the women.

قابَلَ الأَصْدِقاءُ النِّساءَ في الجامِعَة.
The friends met the women at the university.

شاهَدْنا النِّساءَ اللواتي قابَلَهُنَّ الأَصْدِقاءُ في الجامِعَة.
We saw the women whom the friends met at the university.

When the noun in the second sentence is governed by a preposition, this noun must be replaced by the plural noun هُنَّ. The suffixal pronoun form must be attached to the preposition, as in the following example:

شاهَدْنا النِّساءَ.

We saw the women.

بَحَثْنا عَن النِّساءِ في الجامِعَةِ.

We looked for the women at the university.

شاهَدْنا النِّساءَ اللواتي بَحَثْنا عَنْهُنَّ في الجامِعَةِ.

We saw the women whom we looked for at the university.

22.4 RELATIVE CLAUSES WITH INDEFINITE ANTECEDENTS جُمْلَةُ الصِّفَة

It has been mentioned that the relative pronouns الَّذي، الَّتي and their dual and plural variants are used to conjoin two sentences in which the second sentence contains a noun related to the noun in the first. It has also been emphasized that these relative pronouns are only used when the antecedent in the first sentence is definite. In cases when the antecedent is indefinite, the relative pronouns are not used. Instead, a verbal sentence must be used to modify the antecedent, essentially functioning as a sentential adjective, hence the Arabic name جُمْلَة الصِّفَة for such structures. The tense of verbs in such sentences may vary depending on the time the interlocutor intends to convey: past, present or future tense. Verbs in جملة الصِّفَة must agree with the indefinite antecedent in number and gender, however. Recall that non-human plural nouns are always treated as feminine singular and the verb used in جُمْلة الصِّفَة following such nouns must be in the singular. Examine the following examples:

وَصَلَ طالِبٌ زارَ القاهِرَة.

A student (M, Sg) who visited Cairo arrived.

غادَرَتِ البِلادَ مُوَظَّفَةٌ تَعْمَلُ في الشَّرِكَةِ.

An employee (F, Sg) who works in the company left the country.

زارَنا صَديقانِ يُحِبّانِ مَدينَتَنا كَثيراً.

Two friends (M) who love our city very much visited us.

قابَلوا طالِبَتَيْنِ دَرَسَتا في لُبْنان.

They met two students (F) [who] studied in Lebanon.

هَلْ تَعْرِفُونَ مُدَرِّسِينَ يُتْقِنُونَ العَرَبِيَّةَ؟

Do you know teachers (M, Pl) who master Arabic?

عَيَّنَ الـمُسْتَشْفَى طَبِيبَاتٍ دَرَسْنَ في مِصر.

The hospital employed physicians (F, Pl) who studied in Egypt.

حَصَلَت مَكْتَبَةُ الجامِعَةِ عَلَى مَجَلَّاتٍ تَصْدُرُ في مِصر.

The university library acquired journals [which are] published in Egypt.

شاهَدْنا أَنْهاراً كَثيرَةً تَجْري في أمريكا.

We saw many rivers [which run] in America.

If the noun modified is a subject of a verb, the subject pronoun is expressed in the verb of جُملة الصِّفة, as in the following:

زارَتْنا طالِبَةٌ دَرَست العَرَبِيَّةَ.

A student who studied Arabic visited us.

أَجْرى العَمَلِيَّةَ طَبيبانِ تَخَصَّصا في القَلْبِ.

Two doctors who specialized in the heart performed the surgery.

وَصَلَ مُهَنْدِسونَ عَمِلوا في الشَّرِكَةِ الجَديدَةِ.

[Some] engineers who worked in the new company arrived.

On the other hand, if the noun modified is an object of a verb or object of a preposition, a suffixal pronoun, i.e. الضَّمير العائد, must be attached to the verb of جُملة الصِّفة, as in the following examples:

أَكَلوا أَكْلاً طَبَخَهُ سامي.

They ate food which Sami cooked.

وَجَدتُ رِسالةً بَحَثْتُ عَنها كَثيراً.

I found a letter for which I searched a lot.

نُحِبُّ أَغانِيَ غَنَّتها فَيْروز.

We like songs which Fayrouz sang.

اِشْتَرَتِ الشَّرِكَةُ سَيَّاراتٍ صَنَعَتها اليابان.

The company brought cars which Japan made.

اِسْتَمْتَعْتُ بِكِتابَيْنِ كَتَبَهُما نَجيب مَحفوظ.

I enjoyed two books [which] Najeeb Mahfouz wrote.

22.5 RELATIVE CLAUSES WITHOUT ANTECEDENTS
الاِسْمُ الـمَوْصول مَرْجِعُهُ غائِب

22.5.1 مَنْ and ما as relative pronouns

If the antecedent is not explicitly mentioned, the relative pronouns cannot be used. Instead of الَّذي and الَّتي there are two other elements that function as relative pronouns: مَنْ "who" (for human nouns, masculine or feminine) and ما "what" (for non-human nouns):

22.5.1.1 مَنْ

Examine the following examples:

وَصَلَ أَمْسِ.	He arrived yesterday.
كَتَبَ الكِتابَ الجَديدَ.	He wrote the new book.
وَصَلَ مَنْ كَتَبَ الكِتابَ الجَديدَ.	The one who wrote the new book arrived.

Note that وَصَلَ أَمْسِ amounts to a complete sentence by itself in which there is no mention of the person who arrived, presumably a masculine entity, i.e. هُوَ "he." On the other hand, كَتَبَ الكِتابَ الجَديدَ "He wrote the new book," is also a sentence, the subject of which, while not explicitly expressed, is deduced to be human, i.e. the pronoun هُوَ. In both sentences, the referent is the same. In other words, the subject of both sentences refers to the same human entity. Thus, these two sentences are conjoined by مَن, as in وَصَلَ مَنْ كَتَبَ الكِتابَ الجَديدَ. We should mention that the above sentence is equivalent to the following, which contains the relative pronoun الذي discussed earlier:

وَصَلَ الذي كَتَبَ الكِتابَ الجَديدَ.
He who wrote the new book arrived.

Note that if the antecedent is known and explicitly expressed, the relative pronoun الَّذي must be used, as in the following:

وَصَلَ الكاتِبُ الذي كَتَبَ الكِتابَ الجَديدَ.
The writer who wrote the new book arrived.

22.5.1.2 ما

If, on the other hand, the subject of the second sentence is non-human, ما is used, as in the following:

نَعْرِفُ.   We know.

حَدَثَ أَمْسِ.   It happened yesterday.

نَعْرِفُ ما حَدَثَ أَمْسِ.   We know what happened yesterday.

The preceding sentence is equivalent in meaning to the following:

نَعْرِفُ الذي حَدَثَ أَمْسِ.   We know what happened yesterday.

Note that if the antecedent is stated, the referent and the relative pronoun الَّذي must appear, as in:

نَعْرِفُ الشَّيءَ الذي حَدَثَ أَمْسِ.   We know the thing that happened yesterday.

If the second sentence contains a transitive verb such as طَبَخَ "to cook" and قابَلَ "to meet," for example, the verb in the second sentence must have a suffixal form of a pronoun attached to it, expressing the direct object of the verb. Examine the following examples:

أُحِبُّ ما طَبَخَهُ صَديقي.   I like what my friend cooked.

حَضَرَ مَنْ قابَلْتُهُ في القاهِرَة.   The one I met in Cairo arrived.

In أُحِبُّ ما طَبَخَهُ صَديقي we observe that ما is in a direct object position. In this situation, the verb following ما, namely طَبَخَ "to cook," must have a suffixal form of the pronoun هُوَ attached to it. It is also possible to delete the pronoun, so the preceding sentence would be equivalent to the following:

أُحِبُّ ما طَبَخَ صَديقي.   I like what my friend cooked.

Similarly, in the sentence حَضَرَ مَنْ قابَلْتُهُ في القاهِرَة "The one I met in Cairo arrived," the verb قابَلَ has the suffixal form of هُوَ, namely ـهُ as a direct object to this verb.

If the verb requires a preposition when the antecedent is not explicitly stated, the suffix pronoun must attach to this preposition, as in the following:

قَرَأْنا ما حَصَلَ عَلَيْهِ الأُسْتاذُ.   We read what the teacher obtained.

شاهَدْنا مَنْ بَحَثْنا عَنْهُ.   We saw who we looked for.

قَرَأْنا ما حَصَلَ عَلَيهِ الأُسْتاذُ

CHAPTER 23

Agentive nouns اِسْمُ الفاعِلِ

اِسْمُ الفاعِلِ agentive nouns, often referred to as active participles, are derived from verbs to denote the performer of the action as expressed in the verb. In the same way that the English word "teacher" indicates "the person who teaches," the Arabic كاتِبٌ "writer," derived from the verb كَتَبَ "to write," signifies "the person who performs the act of writing." Hence the name اِسْم الفاعِل in Arabic, "noun representing the performer." These derivations function primarily as regular nouns in the language. Secondarily, they can function as adjectives. The derivation of اسم الفاعِل and its functions are shown below.

23.1 FORM I VERBS فَعَلَ

اسْم الفاعِل are derived from فَعَلَ verbs (Form I) according to the فاعِلٌ (faaʿilun) pattern. Thus, from دَرَسَ we obtain دارِسٌ "he who studies, i.e., a student, or a researcher (M)." The feminine form of this agentive noun is دارِسَةٌ "a researcher, a student (F)." From the verb شَرِبَ "to drink," we obtain شارِبٌ, "he who drinks, a drinker (M)," and its feminine counterpart شارِبَةٌ "a drinker (F)." The plural of such nouns will be discussed in Chapter 28.

23.1.1 Hollow verbs اِسْم فاعِل

To derive اسم فاعِل from verbs like زارَ "to visit," or نامَ "to sleep," the فاعِل pattern is used with a minor variation. The expected middle consonant in the case of hollow verbs is always a *hamza*, written on a *yaa'* seat minus the two dots of the *yaa'*. Accordingly, from زارَ "to visit," we obtain زائِرٌ "a visitor"; from نامَ "to sleep," we obtain نائِمٌ "he who sleeps, a sleeper."

The following examples illustrate agentive nouns functioning as a performer of action, an object of a transitive verb, and, finally, when preceded by a preposition.

هَلْ وَصَلَ الفائِزُ؟	Did the winner (M) arrive?
شاهَدَ الطّالِبُ السّائِحَ.	The student saw the tourist (M).
ذَهَبَ إلى الـمَطْعَمِ مَعَ الجائِعَةِ.	He went to the restaurant with the hungry one (F).

23.1.2 Defective verbs اِسم فاعِل

The derivation of agentive nouns from defective verbs (a subcategory of فَعَلَ verbs (Form I)) follows the aforementioned فاعِلٌ pattern. For example, from the verb دَعا "to invite," we derive the agentive noun داعي "inviter (M)," and from the verb حَمَى "to protect," we derive the agentive noun حامي "protector (M)." When such nouns are indefinite and masculine, they end with an *-in* sound (*tanwiin*), represented in the orthography by two *kasras*, and we thus obtain داعٍ "he who invites, an inviter (M)"; حامٍ "a protector (M)."

However, when such nouns are made definite by the use of the definite article الـ, the *tanwiin* changes to a *yaa'*. For example, داعٍ and حامٍ become الدّاعي "the inviter (M)," and الحامي "the protector (M)," respectively. Similarly, when a suffix pronoun is attached to such nouns, the *tanwiin* changes to a *yaa'* as in, for example, داعيهِ "his inviter," and حاميها "her protector."

The *yaa'* is also realized in these masculine nouns when they are put in the accusative, or in the *IDhaafa*-construct, as in the following examples:

قابَلْتُ داعِياً إلى حَفْلَةٍ.	I met an inviter (M) to a party.
قابَلْتُ الدّاعِيَ إلى حَفْلَةٍ.	I met the inviter to the party.
قابَلْتُ داعِيَ الحَفْلَةِ.	I met the party's inviter (M).

In addition, the *yaa'* is also realized when such nouns are put in the feminine. Thus داعٍ becomes داعِيَةٌ "an inviter (F)" and حامٍ becomes حامِيَةٌ "a protector (F)." The masculine اِسْمُ الفاعِلِ in the preceding sentences is rendered into the feminine as follows:

قابَلْتُ داعِيَةً إلى حَفْلَةٍ.	I met an inviter (F) to a party.
قابَلْتُ الدّاعِيَةَ إلى حَفْلَةٍ.	I met the inviter (F) to a party.
قابَلْتُ داعِيَةَ الحَفْلَةِ.	I met the party's inviter (F).

23.1.3 Doubled verbs اِسم فاعِل

Agentive nouns derived from doubled verbs according to the فاعِلٌ pattern maintain the geminate consonants. For example, from the verb مَرَّ "to pass through," we derive مارٌّ "one who passes by/through (M)," and from شَكَّ "to doubt," we derive شاكٌّ "a doubter (M)." The feminine counterparts of these nouns are مارَّةٌ "one who passes through (F)," and شاكَّةٌ "a doubter (F)." The following are examples of how such nouns are used:

الـمارُّ أَمامَ البَيْتِ سَأَلَ عَن العُنْوان.

The passer-by (M) in front of the house inquired about the address.

الشّاكَّةُ في هذِهِ الـمَعلوماتِ لَجَأَت إلى الـمَكْتَبَة.

The doubter (F) of this information resorted to the library.

Agentive nouns from *waaw*-beginning verbs, *yaa'*-initial verbs and verbs beginning with a *hamza* follow the same pattern. Thus, from وَجَدَ "to find," we obtain واجِدٌ "finder," from يَئِسَ "to despair," we derive يائِسٌ "despairer," and from أَكَلَ "to eat," we obtain آكِلٌ "eater." Note the change of the *hamza* into a longer *hamza،*, labeled *madda* ه in Arabic.

23.2 FORM II–X VERBS فَعَّلَ - اِسْتَفْعَلَ

Now we turn to examine how اسْم فاعِل is derived from فَعَّلَ (Form II) through اسْتَفْعَلَ (Form X). A general statement can be made about deriving agentive nouns from these verb forms. اِسْمُ الفاعِل in these verb patterns always begins with a *miim* followed by a *Dhamma*, namely مُـ. The penultimate vowel in اسم فاعِل in this group of verbs is always a *kasra*. Thus, from the verb دَرَّسَ "to teach," we obtain مُدَرِّسٌ "a teacher (M)"; from سافَرَ "to travel," we obtain مُسافِرٌ "a traveler (M)"; from أَرْسَلَ "to send," we obtain مُرْسِلٌ "a sender (M)." And so on with the other verb forms.

The feminine form of agentive nouns in the derived verb forms is made by suffixing the *taa' marbuuTa*, as in مُدَرِّسَةٌ "a teacher (F)," مُسافِرَةٌ "a traveler (F)", مُرْسِلَةٌ "a sender (F)," etc.

The plural formation of such agentive nouns is regular. (See Chapter 28 on plural nouns.)

The table below illustrates the derivation of agentive nouns of verb forms
II through X:

Roman verb form	فَعَلَ verb form	Agentive noun pattern	Example verb	Agentive noun	Meaning
II	فَعَّلَ	مُفَعِّلٌ	دَرَّسَ	مُدَرِّسٌ	teacher
			سَمَّى	مُسَمِّي / مُسَمٍّ	namer
III	فاعَلَ	مُفاعِلٌ	ساعَدَ	مُساعِدٌ	helper
			نادى	مُنادٍ / مُنادي	caller
IV	أَفْعَلَ	مُفْعِلٌ	أَرْسَلَ	مُرْسِلٌ	sender
			أَدارَ	مُديرٌ	director
			أَعْطى	مُعْطي / مُعْطٍ	giver
			أَعَدَّ	مُعِدٌّ	preparer
V	تَفَعَّلَ	مُتَفَعِّلٌ	تَكَلَّمَ	مُتَكَلِّمٌ	speaker
			تَبَنَّى	مُتَبَنِّي / مُتَبَنٍ	adopter
VI	تَفاعَلَ	مُتَفاعِلٌ	تَشارَكَ	مُتَشارِكٌ	participant
			تَداوى	مُتَداوي / مُتَداوٍ	patient
VII	اِنْفَعَلَ	مُنْفَعِلٌ	اِنْسَحَبَ	مُنْسَحِبٌ	quitter
			اِنْحاز	مُنْحازٌ	s.o./s.th. aligned with
			اِنْدَعَى	مُنْدَعٍ	invitee
			اِنْضَمَّ	مُنْضَمٌّ	s.o./s.th. joining
VIII	اِفْتَعَلَ	مُفْتَعِلٌ	اِحْتَفَلَ	مُحْتَفِلٌ	celebrant
			اِخْتارَ	مُخْتارٌ	chosen
			اِحْتَلَّ	مُحْتَلٌّ	occupier
			ادَّعى	مُدَّعي / مُدَّعٍ	claimant
			اِعْتَدى	مُعْتَدي / مُعْتَدٍ	aggressor
IX	اِفْعَلَّ	مُفْعَلٌّ	اِحْمَرَّ	مُحْمَرٌّ	he who turns red

Roman verb form	فَعَلَ verb form	Agentive noun pattern	Example verb	Agentive noun	Meaning
X	اِسْتَفْعَلَ	مُسْتَفْعِلٌ	اِسْتَعْمَلَ	مُسْتَعْمِلٌ	user
			اِسْتَطاعَ	مُسْتَطيعٌ	he who is able
			اِسْتَقَلَّ	مُسْتَقِلٌّ	independent
			اِسْتَدْعى	مُسْتَدْعِي/ مُسْتَدْعٍ	plaintiff
Quadriliteral			تَرْجَمَ	مُتَرْجِمٌ	translator

23.2.1 Hollow verbs in فَعَّلَ - اِسْتَفْعَلَ (Forms II–X) اِسْم فاعِل

Hollow verbs can be augmented to derive the following forms: أَفْعَلَ (Form IV), اِنْفَعَلَ (Form VII), اِفْتَعَلَ (Form VIII) and اِسْتَفْعَلَ (Form X). Note that due to the presence of the long 'alif in hollow verbs, the penultimate vowel also presents some variation: it is either an 'alif as in forms VII and VIII, or a yaa', as in forms IV and X. The following table illustrates the way agentive nouns are derived in this group of verbs:

Roman verb form	فَعَلَ verb form	Agentive noun pattern	Example verb	Agentive noun	Meaning
IV	أَفْعَلَ	مُفْعِلٌ	أَدارَ	مُديرٌ	director
VII	اِنْفَعَلَ	مُنْفَعِلٌ	اِنْحازَ	مُنْحازٌ	s.o./s.th. aligned with
VIII	اِفْتَعَلَ	مُفْتَعِلٌ	اِعْتادَ	مُعْتادٌ	s.o. who is used to
X	اِسْتَفْعَلَ	مُسْتَفْعِلٌ	اِسْتَعادَ	مُسْتَعيدٌ	retriever

23.2.2 Doubled verbs in فَعَّلَ - اِسْتَفْعَلَ (Forms II–X) اِسْم فاعِل

Like hollow verbs, doubled verbs can be augmented to forms أَفْعَلَ (Form IV), اِنْفَعَلَ (Form VII), اِفْتَعَلَ (Form VIII) and اِسْتَفْعَلَ (Form X). Agentive nouns from these patterns are derived in similar ways to the agentive noun derivation mentioned earlier. Examine the table below:

Roman verb form	فَعَلَ verb form	Agentive noun pattern	Example verb	Agentive noun	Meaning
IV	أَفْعَلَ	مُفْعِلٌ	أَعَدَّ	مُعِدٌّ	preparer
VII	اِنْفَعَلَ	مُنْفَعِلٌ	اِنْضَمَّ	مُنْضَمٌّ	s.o. who joins
VIII	اِفْتَعَلَ	مُفْتَعِلٌ	اِحْتَلَّ	مُحْتَلٌّ	occupier
X	اِسْتَفْعَلَ	مُسْتَفْعِلٌ	اِسْتَعَدَّ	مُسْتَعِدٌّ	one who is ready

23.3 FUNCTIONS OF AGENTIVE NOUNS

Agentive nouns can function as regular nouns and as adjectives modifying other nouns. As nouns they may be the subjects of sentences, direct objects of transitive verbs, or governed by prepositions. They may also be a part of an *IDhaafa*-construct. As adjectives, agentive nouns must agree with the noun they modify in gender, number, case and determination.

23.3.1 Agentive nouns functioning as nouns

As nouns, agentive nouns could be rendered into English as nouns that end with "-er" or "-or", or "-ant" such as "teacher," "professor," or "applicant."

23.3.1.1 As subjects

Examine the agentive nouns as subjects in the following sentences:

العامِلُ ذَهَبَ إلى الـمَصْنَعِ.

The worker went to the factory.

الكاتِبَةُ الـمَشهورَةُ نَشَرَت كِتاباً جَديداً.

The famous writer (F) published a new book.

Note that العامِلُ "the worker" in the first sentence and الكاتِبَةُ "the writer (F)" in the second sentence are subjects of the sentences.

23.3.1.2 As objects

اِسْمُ الفاعِل nouns can also be direct objects of transitive verbs, as in the following examples:

قابَلَ أَبِي السّاكِنَ الجَديدَ أَمْسِ.

My father met the new resident yesterday.

هَلْ عَرَفْتَ الخارِجَ مِنَ البَيْتِ؟

Did you know the person who exited from the house?

23.3.1.3 Preceded by prepositions

Additionally, اِسْمُ الفاعِل can be governed by a preposition. If the noun is singular, it must end with a *kasra*, as in the following:

الكِتابُ مَعَ الطّالِبَةِ.

The book is with the student (F).

It is worth noting how the agentive noun الطّالِبُ with its feminine counterpart الطّالِبَةُ has come to mean "a student." The verb طَلَبَ originally meant "to seek, request." A "student," therefore, is the person who seeks, in this case knowledge and learning in a school or university setting. In other situations, it simply means "a seeker," as in the following example:

اِسْتَقْبَلوا طالِبَ العَوْنِ.

They received the help-seeker.

23.3.1.4 In an IDhaafa-construct

As a noun, اِسْمُ الفاعِل can also be part of an *IDhaafa*-construct, as in the following:

سافَرَ مُدَرِّسُ الجامِعَةِ إلى لُبْنان.

The university professor traveled to Lebanon.

تَكَلَّمْتُ مَعَ مُسْتَقْبِلِ الزّائِرِ.

I talked with the "welcomer" of the visitor.

23.3.2 Agentive nouns functioning as adjectives

Adjectives cannot stand independently in sentences when they are functioning in their primary role as adjectives: they must always be used with nouns as a way of adding more information about them. Note that when agentive nouns function as adjectives, the English translation tends to be the "-ing" form of the verb. Examine the following:

وَصَلَ الأُسْتاذُ الزّائِرُ أَمْس.   The visiting professor arrived yesterday.

شاهَدْتُ الـمَرْأَةَ الـمُسافِرَةَ أَمْس.   I saw the traveling woman yesterday.

In the first sentence, وَصَلَ الأُسْتاذُ الزّائِرُ أَمس, the word الزّائِرُ "visiting" has the form of اِسْم فاعِل. Since it follows the noun الأُسْتاذُ "the professor, teacher," it must therefore be an adjective. Note that it agrees with the noun in determination (definite/indefinite), gender (masculine), case (nominative), and number (singular).

Similarly, in the second sentence, شاهَدْتُ المَرْأَةَ المُسافِرَةَ أَمْس, the word الـمُسافِرَةَ as اسم فاعِل modifies the noun الـمَرْأَةَ and agrees with this noun in determination, case, gender and number.

اِسْمُ الفاعِل is primarily used as a noun. Its function as adjective is secondary.

23.3.3 Agentive nouns functioning as transitive verbs

Agentive nouns derived from transitive verbs sometimes maintain the behavior of these verbs by causing the nouns that follow them to be in a direct object position, and consequently in the accusative case. In the following two sentences, the agentive noun in the first sentence functions as the first noun in *IDhaafa*, causing the noun following it to be in the genitive case. In the second, the agentive noun functions as a transitive verb, causing the noun that follows it to be in the accusative case:

زائِرُ الجامِعَةِ وَصَلَ مِنَ العِراق أَمْس.
The university visitor arrived from Iraq yesterday.

هَلْ قابَلْتَ الرَّجُلَ الزّائِرَ صَديقَهُ؟
Did you meet the man [who is] visiting his friend?

More examples of agentive nouns that demonstrate the function of transitive verbs are provided below:

مَحمود قارِئٌ دَرْسَهُ.   Mahmoud is reading his lesson.

هذا الـمُوَظَّفُ مُهْمِلٌ واجِبَهُ.   This employee is ignoring his duties.

كانَتِ الزَّوْجَةُ أَمسِ طابِخَةً الأَكْلَ.   The wife was cooking the food yesterday.

هَلْ عَرَفْتُم أَنَّهُ دارِسٌ الطِّبَّ؟   Did you know that he is studying medicine?

CHAPTER 24

Passive participles اِسْمُ الـمَفْعُول

اِسْمُ الـمَفْعُول, the passive participle, is a derivation of verbs used to convey that an action has happened or is happening to someone or something else. For example, the English word "written" denotes that something was penned down, put on paper; in other words, it has undergone the action of writing. The passive participle can function as an adjective or a noun. It also appears in a number of idiomatic expressions that are followed by dependent clauses.

24.1 DERIVATION OF PASSIVE PARTICIPLES اِسْمُ الـمَفْعُول

24.1.1 فَعَلَ (Form I)

Passive participles from فَعَلَ verb forms are derived according to the مَفْعولٌ (*mafʿuul*) pattern. Thus, from the verb شَرِبَ "to drink," we obtain مَشْروبٌ "that which is/was drunk," i.e., "a drink;" and from the verb كَتَبَ "to write," we obtain مَكتوبٌ "that which is/was written," i.e., "a letter."

24.1.1.1 Hollow verbs

Passive participles can be derived from hollow verbs according to the *mafʿuul* pattern. Thus, from زارَ / يَزورُ "to visit," we obtain مَزورٌ "that which is visited."

From سارَ / يَسيرُ "to walk, traverse," we obtain مَسيرٌ "that which was traversed."

Verbs that have *'alif* in their present tense, such as خافَ / يَخافُ "to be afraid," form their passive participle with a *waaw*, as in مَخوفٌ in some cases. This pertains to the formation of their *maSdar*. The *maSdar* of this verb is خَوْفٌ "fear." This explains why there is a *waaw* in مَخوفٌ "that which is feared." On the other hand, نالَ / يَنالُ "to obtain, to win," has its passive participle as مَنيلٌ or مَنالٌ. The *maSdar* of this verb is نَيْلٌ "winning," which explains why the passive participle has a *yaa'*, not a *waaw*.

Such passive participle forms are derivable in theory, according to the rules advanced above. However, passive participles such as مَخُوف and/or مَنيل are not commonly used in the language. As a proper noun, however, مَنَال appears as a woman's name.

24.1.1.2 Defective verbs

The *maf ͨuul* pattern for defective verbs manifests the *waaw* or the *yaa'* of the verb's present tense. Thus for passive participles we obtain مَدْعُوٌّ "a guest," from دَعا "to invite," and مَرْمِيٌّ "thrown," from رَمى "to throw, cast." The presence of the *waaw* in مَدْعُوٌّ reflects the *waaw* in يَدْعو, which is the present tense of دَعا. Similarly, the presence of the *yaa'* in مَرْمِيٌّ reflects the *yaa'* in the present tense of يَرْمي.

24.1.1.3 Doubled verbs

Doubled verbs are easy to fit into the *maf ͨuul* pattern by separating the doubled consonants with a *waaw*. Thus from عَدَّ "to count, to consider," we obtain مَعْدودٌ "that which is/was counted." From حَسَّ "to feel, to touch," we obtain مَحْسوسٌ "tangible, material," and, finally, from شَكَّ we obtain مَشْكوكٌ "doubted, suspected."

24.1.2 فَعَّلَ - اِسْتَفْعَلَ (Forms II–X)

Passive participles from فَعَّلَ verbs (Form II) through اِسْتَفْعَلَ verbs (Form X) are derived by a simple process. This involves the positioning of the prefix *mu-* مُ at the beginning of the verb. The penultimate vowel is always a *fat-Ha*. In verbs beginning with a *hamza*, the *hamza* is dropped. Examine the following:

Verb form	Passive participle form	Example verb	Passive participle	Meaning
فَعَّلَ	مُفَعَّلٌ	دَرَّسَ	مُدَرَّسٌ	s.th. taught
		سَمَّى	مُسَمَّى	s.o./s.th. named
فاعَلَ	مُفاعَلٌ	ساعَدَ	مُساعَدٌ	s.o. helped
أفعَلَ	مُفْعَلٌ	أرْسَلَ	مُرْسَلٌ	s.th. sent
		أدارَ	مُدارٌ	s.th./s.o. managed
		أعْطى	مُعْطىً	s.th. given
		أعَدَّ	مُعَدٌّ	s.th./s.o. prepared
تَفَعَّلَ	مُتَفَعَّلٌ	تَكَلَّمَ	مُتَكَلَّمٌ	s.th. spoken
		تَبَنَّى	مُتَبَنَّىً	s.th./s.o. adopted
تَفاعَلَ	مُتَفاعَلٌ	تَشارَكَ	مُتَشارَكٌ	s.th. shared
		تَداوى	مُتَداوىً	s.o. treated
انْفَعَلَ	مُنْفَعَلٌ	انْصَرَفَ	مُنْصَرَفٌ	s.th. withdrawn
		انْحازَ	مُنْحازٌ	s.o. aligned
		انْقَضى	مُنْقَضىً	s.th. spent
		انْضَمَّ	مُنْضَمٌّ	s.o. who joined
افْتَعَلَ	مُفْتَعَلٌ	احْتَفَلَ	مُحْتَفَلٌ	s.o./s.th. celebrated
		اخْتارَ	مُخْتارٌ	s.th./s.o. chosen
		احْتَلَّ	مُحْتَلٌّ	s.o./s.th. occupied
افْعَلَّ	مُفْعَلٌّ	احْمَرَّ	مُحْمَرٌّ	s.th. made red
اسْتَفْعَلَ	مُسْتَفْعَلٌ	اسْتَقْبَلَ	مُسْتَقْبَلٌ	s.th. expected (future)
		اسْتَطاعَ	مُسْتَطاعٌ	s.th. capacitated
		اسْتَقَلَّ	مُسْتَقَلٌّ	—
		اسْتَدْعى	مُسْتَدْعىً	s.o. called
Quadriliteral		تَرْجَمَ	مُتَرْجَمٌ	s.th. translated

24.1.2.1 Augmented hollow verbs passive participles

Hollow verbs can be augmented to derive the following forms: أَفْعَلَ (Form IV), اِنْفَعَلَ (Form VII), اِفْتَعَلَ (Form VIII) and اِسْتَفْعَلَ (Form X). Passive participle forms can be derived from verbs in these forms by prefixing *mu* مُ while maintaining the penultimate *'alif*.

The following table illustrates how agentive nouns are derived in this group of verbs:

Verb form	Passive participle	Example verb	Passive participle	Meaning
أَفْعَلَ	مُفْعَلٌ	أَدَارَ	مُدَارٌ	managed
اِنْفَعَلَ	مُنْفَعَلٌ	اِنْقَادَ	مُنْقَادٌ	led
اِفْتَعَلَ	مُفْتَعَلٌ	اِعْتَادَ	مُعْتَادٌ	s.o./s.th. used to
اِسْتَفْعَلَ	مُسْتَفْعَلٌ	اِسْتَعَادَ	مُسْتَعَادٌ	retrieved

24.1.2.2 Augmented defective verbs passive participles

Derivations of passive participles of الأَفْعال الـمُضَعَّفَة الآخِر, augmented defective verbs of فَعَّلَ (Form II) through اِسْتَفْعَلَ (Form X), follow the same rules of derivation mentioned above. The passive participle form begins with مُ *mu-*. Due to the absence of a consonant at the end of the verb, however, the passive participle ends up with *tanwiin*, or two *fat-Ha*s, in the orthography. For example, from سَمَّى / يُسَمِّي "to name," we obtain مُسَمًّى "that which is named"; from نادى / يُنادي "to call," we obtain مُنادىً "he who is called"; from اِشْتَرَى / يَشْتَرِي "to buy," we obtain مُشْتَرىً "that which is bought"; from اِسْتَـثْنى / يَسْتَـثْني "to exclude, to except," we obtain مُسْتَثْنىً "that which is excluded."

When the definite article الـ is prefixed to such derivations, the *tanwiin* is dropped. In this case, such words are pronounced with an *'alif* sound at their end. Thus, مُسَمًّى becomes الـمُسَمَّى and مُنادىً becomes الـمُنادى and so on.

Additionally, the *tanwiin* is dropped when such derivations are put in the feminine. In the orthography, the *'alif maqSuura* in this case changes to a regular *'alif*. For example, the feminine of مُسَمًّى is مُسَمَّاةٌ and the feminine of مُسْتَثْنىً is مُسْتَثْناةٌ and so on. The following sentences illustrate the use of the above passive participles:

قَابَلْتُ الرَّجُلَ الـمُسَمّى أَحْمَد.

I met the man (who is) called Ahmad.

حَضَرَتِ الأُسْتاذَةُ الـمُسْتَثْناةُ مِنَ الوَظيفَةِ.

The professor (who is) excluded from the job came.

24.1.2.3 Augmented doubled verbs passive participles

The passive participles of الأَفعالُ الـمُضَعَّفَة الآخِر "the doubled verbs" of forms II through X are derived by placing the prefix مـُ mu- at the beginning of the verb. Here, the penultimate vowel is always a *fat-Ha*. Thus from اِحْتَلَّ / يَحْتَلُّ "to occupy," we obtain مُحْتَلّ "occupied"; from اِمْتَدَّ / يَمْتَدُّ "to extend," we derive مُمْتَدّ "extended." Examine the following sentence:

ناقَشَ الرَّئيسُ مُشكِلَةَ الأَرْض الـمُحْتَلَّةِ.

The president debated the issue of the occupied territory.

حُدودُ أمريكا مُمْتَدَّةٌ مِنْ كَندا إلى المَكْسيك.

The boundaries of the USA are extended from Canada to Mexico.

24.2 FUNCTIONS OF PASSIVE PARTICIPLES

24.2.1 Passive participles as adjectives

Passive participles are used primarily as adjectives, as illustrated in the examples below:

قَرَأْتُ الكِتابَ الـمَكْتوبَ باللُّغَة الإِنْكليزِيَّةِ.

I read the book [which is] written in English.

قابَلَتِ الأُسْتاذَةَ الـمَعْروفَةَ في الجامِعَةِ.

She met the professor (F) [who is] known at the university.

Note that الـمَكْتوبَ الكِتابَ قَرَأْتُ "that which is written," in the sentence الـمَكْتوبَ الكِتابَ قَرَأْتُ باللُّغَة الإِنْكليزِيَّةِ, is derived from the verb كَتَبَ "to write." Also, note that its position after the noun indicates its function as an adjective modifying the noun الكِتابَ "the book." Additionally, note the agreement between الكِتابَ and

الـمَكْتُوبَ in determination (definite/indefinite), gender (masculine), number (singular), and, finally, case (accusative), because of the fact that الكِتابَ is a direct object of the verb قَرَأْتُ.

In the sentence قابَلتِ الأُستاذَةَ الـمَعروفَةَ في الجامِعَةِ the passive participle الـمَعروفَة is derived from the verb عَرَفَ according to the مَفْعول (*maf'uul*) pattern. In this sentence, الـمَعروفَة is used to modify الأُسْتاذَةَ. Furthermore, it agrees with this noun in gender, case determination, and number.

The following are more examples of passive participles that illustrate their functions as adjectives:

وَصَلَ اليَوْمَ الرَّجُلُ الـمَدْعُوُّ إلى الحَفْلَةِ.
The man [who was] invited to the party arrived today.

أُحِبُّ البِناءَ الـمَبْنِيَّ مِنَ الحَجَرِ.
I like the building [which is] built of stone.

سَلَّمْتُ عَلى الأُسْتاذَةِ الـمَدْعُوَّةِ إلى العَشاءِ.
I greeted the teacher (F) [who is] invited to dinner.

24.2.2 Passive participles as nouns

Some passive participles have attained the status of nouns. For example, مَكْتوبٌ is used to mean "a letter, an epistle"; مَشْروبٌ is used to mean "a drink"; مُسْتَخْدَمٌ and مُوَظَّفٌ are both used to mean "employee." It should be emphasized that not all passive participle derivations can be used as nouns. The following examples illustrate passive participles that do function as nouns:

قابَلَتِ الـمُوَظَّفَ في مَكْتَبِهِ أمْسِ.
She met the employee in his office yesterday.

وَصَلَ الـمَكْتوبُ أمْسِ.
The letter arrived yesterday.

الـمَشْروبُ الوَطَنِيُّ في هذِهِ البِلادِ هُوَ الشّايُ.
The national drink in this country is tea.

وَصَلَ الـمُسْتَخْدَمُ في الشَّرِكَةِ أمْسِ.
The employee in the company arrived yesterday.

زادَ عَدَدُ الـمُنْضَمّينَ إلى الحِزْبِ.

The number of the party members increased.

حَضَرَ مَنْدوبٌ مُخْتارٌ مِنَ الشَّركَةِ الجَديدَةِ.

A delegate chosen by the new company came.

24.3 PASSIVE PARTICIPLE PHRASES

There are common phrases in Arabic that include a small set of passive participles. Such phrases have become idiomatic expressions in the language and are invariable in form. They are followed by dependent clauses.

24.3.1 Passive participle phrases used with أَنَّ

Passive participle phrases can be used with *'anna* أَنَّ to express statements of fact. Recall that *'anna* أَنَّ must be followed by a nominal sentence beginning with a noun in the accusative case, or a suffix pronoun (see Chapter 21.)

مِنَ الـمَشْهورِ أَنَّ	it is commonly known that
مِنَ الـمَعْروفِ أَنَّ	it is known that
مِنَ الـمَعْلومِ أَنَّ	it is known that
مِنَ الـمَفْهومِ أَنَّ	it is understood that

24.3.2 Passive participle phrases used with أَنْ

Passive participle phrases in idiomatic phrases expressing hope, permission, fear, surprise and the like must be followed by أَنْ. Recall that أَنْ must be followed by a present tense verb in the subjunctive.

مِنَ المَأْمُولِ أَنْ	it is hoped that
مِنَ الـمُتَّفَقِ عَلَيْهِ أَنْ	it is agreed that
مِنَ الـمُتَوَقَّع أَنْ	it is expected that
مِنَ الـمُحْتَمَلِ أَنْ	it is probable that
مِنَ الـمُسْتَحْسَنِ أَنْ	it is preferred that
مِنَ الـمَسْموح (بِهِ) أَنْ	it is permitted that
مِنَ الـمَطْلوبِ أَنْ	it is required that
مِنَ الـمُعْتادِ أَنْ	it is customary that
مِنَ الـمَفْروضِ أَنْ	it is supposed that
مِنَ الـمُفَضَّلِ أَنْ	it is preferred that
مِنَ الـمَقْبولِ أَنْ	it is accepted that
مِنَ الـمُقَرَّرِ أَنْ	it is decided that

CHAPTER 25

Verbal nouns الـمَصادِر: *maSdars*

A *maSdar* or "verbal noun," as the English translation indicates, is a noun that names the activity of a verb. *MaSdars* are roughly equivalent to gerunds in English grammar. These are nouns that end with "-ing" such as "swimming," "eating," or nouns that end with other morphological elements, derived from verbs such as "arrival," from the verb "to arrive," or "application," from the verb "to apply." A single verb may have two or more *maSdars* in Arabic, sometimes with nuanced differences in meaning.

The *maSdar* in Arabic behaves as a regular noun but also retains some properties of its original verb. As a noun, it can take the definite article, be singular, dual or plural, be masculine or feminine, and function in sentences like any noun by taking cases according to its role in the sentence.

We present below, as an example, the *maSdar* زِيارَةٌ "a visit" (from the verb زارَ "to visit"), to illustrate its various functions:

1. The subject of equational sentences:

الزِّيارَةُ كانَت قَصيرَةً.
The visit was short.

In addition to the use of the definite article الـ "the," nouns can be made definite by the use of suffixal pronouns (possessive), or by the use of *ID-haafa*, as in the following examples:

زيارَتُها كانَت مُمْتِعَةً.
Her visit was enjoyable.

زيارَةُ مِصر أَعْجَبَت أَبي.
The visit to Egypt pleased my father. (*lit.* "The Egypt visit")

2. The predicate of a sentence:

هذِهِ زِيارَةٌ قَصيرَةٌ.

This is a brief visit.

3. The فاعِل of a verbal sentence:

دامَتِ الزِّيارَةُ يَوْماً واحِداً.

The visit lasted one day.

4. The direct object of a transitive verb:

أَحَبَّ أَصْدِقائي الزِّيارَةَ كَثيراً.

My friends liked the visit very much.

5. Preceded by a preposition:

كانَ سَليم في زِيارَةٍ طَويلَةٍ.

Saleem was on a long visit.

25.1 DERIVATION OF *MASDARS*

25.1.1 فَعَلَ (Form I) *maSdar*s

It is not possible to provide predictable rules about the derivation of verbal nouns from فَعَلَ (Form I) verbs. Therefore, learners are encouraged to memorize the verbal nouns derived from فَعَلَ verbs. A list of commonly used فَعَلَ verbs and their verbal nouns is provided below. *MaSdar*s that end with *taa' marbuuTa* are grammatically feminine; otherwise, they are masculine.

1. فِعالَةٌ

Verb	MaSdar	Meaning
دَرَسَ	دِراسَةٌ	studying
قَرَأَ	قِراءَةٌ	reading
كَتَبَ	كِتابَةٌ	writing

2. فُعولٌ

Verb	MaSdar	Meaning
جَلَسَ	جُلوسٌ	sitting
حَصَلَ	حُصولٌ	obtaining
حَضَرَ	حُضورٌ	attending
رَجَعَ	رُجوعٌ	returning
قَبِلَ	قُبولٌ / قَبولٌ	accepting
نَهَضَ	نُهوضٌ	rising
وَجَبَ	وُجوبٌ	obliging
وَجَدَ	وُجودٌ	existing
وَصَلَ	وُصولٌ	arriving
وَقَعَ	وُقوعٌ	happening

3. فَعْلٌ

Verb	MaSdar	Meaning
أَخَذَ	أَخْذٌ	taking
أَكَلَ	أَكْلٌ	eating
بَحَثَ	بَحْثٌ	searching
تَرَكَ	تَرْكٌ	leaving
فَهِمَ	فَهْمٌ	understanding
نَشَرَ	نَشْرٌ	publishing
نَقَلَ	نَقْلٌ	transporting
وَصَفَ	وَصْفٌ	describing
وَعَدَ	وَعْدٌ	promising

4. فُعْلٌ

Verb	MaSdar	Meaning
شَرِبَ	شُرْبٌ	drinking
شَكَرَ	شُكْرٌ	thanking

5. فَعَالٌ

Verb	MaSdar	Meaning
ذَهَبَ	ذَهابٌ	going
سَمَحَ	سَماحٌ	permitting
سَمِعَ	سَماعٌ	hearing

6. فَعِيلٌ

Verb	MaSdar	Meaning
غَسَلَ	غَسِيلٌ	washing
رَحَلَ	رَحِيلٌ	relocating

7. مَفْعِلَةٌ

Verb	MaSdar	Meaning
عَرَفَ	مَعْرِفَةٌ	knowing
قَدِرَ	مَقْدِرَةٌ	ability

Needless to say, there are other commonly used *maSdar*s that do not fall under the above patterns, such as:

Verb	MaSdar	*Meaning*
سَأَلَ	سُؤَالٌ	question
عَمِلَ	عَمَلٌ	working
فَعَلَ	فِعْلٌ	acting

25.1.1.1 Hollow verb maSdars

It is also difficult to generalize about the derivation of *maSdar*s from hollow verbs. For example, learners should memorize that the *maSdar* of زَارَ "to visit" is زِيَارَةٌ "visit, visiting," the *maSdar* of نَامَ "to sleep" is نَوْمٌ "sleep," and so on. Here is a list of some common hollow verbs and their *maSdar*s:

Verb	MaSdar	*Meaning*
بَاعَ	بَيْعٌ	selling
جَاعَ	جوعٌ	hunger
خافَ	خَوْفٌ	fear
سارَ	سَيْرٌ	walking
صام	صِيامٌ / صَوْمٌ	fasting
طارَ	طَيَرانٌ	flying
عادَ	عَوْدَةٌ	returning
فازَ	فَوْزٌ	winning
قالَ	قَوْلٌ	saying
قامَ	قِيامٌ	rising
مات	مَوْتٌ	dying

25.1.1.2 Doubled verb maSdars

Doubled verbs such as مَرَّ "to pass, go through" do not follow a set pattern for the derivation of verbal nouns. Here is a list of common doubled verbs and their *maSdar*s:

Verb	MaSdar	*Meaning*
حَسَّ	حَسٌّ / حِسٌّ	feeling
حَلَّ	حَلٌّ	solving
شَكَّ	شَكٌّ	doubting
عَدَّ	عَدٌّ	counting
فَرَّ	فَرٌّ / فَرارٌ	escaping
مَرَّ	مُرورٌ / مَرٌّ	passing

Some of the doubled verbs have two *maSdar*s, with little, if any, difference in meaning. For example, حَسَّ بِـ "to feel," has the *maSdar*s حَسٌّ and حِسٌّ "feeling," which have practically the same meaning. As can be seen from this example, the *maSdar*s of these doubled verbs resemble their past tense form, with *tanwiin* terminating the verb. Thus we get فَرَّ "to escape, to flee" and its *maSdar* فَرٌّ and the more commonly used فَرارٌ "the act of escaping;" from مَرَّ "to pass," we obtain مَرٌّ and the more common مُرورٌ "passing through, transit, traffic."

25.1.1.3 Defective verb maSdars

Defective verbs الأَفعال الـمُعْتَلَّة الآخِر can be divided into two groups with respect to the derivation of their verbal nouns. The first group consists of verbs that end with a *yaa'* in the present tense verb form for the pronoun هُوَ as in رَمَى / يَرمي "to throw." Examine the following list of verbs and their *maSdar*s below:

Verb	MaSdar	*Meaning*
بَنى	بِناءٌ	building
رَمى	رَمْيٌ	throwing
شَوى	شَوْيٌ	grilling
قَلى	قَلْيٌ	frying
مَشى	مَشْيٌ	walking
هَدى	هَدْيٌ	guiding

The second group includes verbs that end with a *waaw* in the present tense for the pronoun هُوَ, as in رَجا / يَرْجو "to request." Examine the following list of verbs and their *maSdar*s below:

Verb	MaSdar	*Meaning*
دَعا	دُعاءٌ	praying
دَعا	دَعْوَةٌ	inviting
رَجا	رَجاءٌ	requesting
عَلا	عُلُوٌّ	rising
سَما	سُمُوٌّ	transcending

Some defective verbs do not fit the above patterns. For example, from the verb رَأى / يَرى we obtain two *maSdar*s with different meanings: رُؤْيَةٌ "visibility" or "outlook" and رَأْيٌ "opinion." From the verb لَقِيَ / يَلْقى "to find, encounter," we obtain لِقاءٌ، لُقْيَةٌ and لُقْيا, all meaning "a meeting, an encounter." Of these three *maSdar*s, لِقاءٌ is more common in usage.

There are other verbs whose verbal nouns do not fit any of the above patterns; they are learned individually and incrementally.

25.1.2 اِسْتَفْعَلَ - فَعَّلَ (Forms II–X) *maSdars*

Beginning with فَعَّلَ through اِسْتَفْعَلَ verbs (Form II through Form X), the formation of verbal nouns is regulated by set, and largely predictable, rules. It is quite possible for two verbal nouns derived from the same verb to exist, however, one generated from the set rule and another not generated from the rule, with more currency in actual usage. Such preferences will be indicated in the separate verb patterns.

25.1.2.1 فَعَّلَ (Form II) maSdars

MaSdars from فَعَّلَ verbs are derived according to the pattern تَفْعِيلٌ. Below we mention a few illustrative verbs and their maSdars:

فَعَّلَ	تَفْعِيلٌ	Meaning
دَرَّسَ	تَـدْريسٌ	teaching
حَسَّنَ	تَحْسينٌ	improving
صَوَّرَ	تَصْويرٌ	depicting

While it is possible to derive تَحْديثٌ as a verbal noun from حَدَّثَ "to tell, to inform," the maSdar حَديثٌ "talk, discussion," is more commonly used. In theory, one can obtain تَحْديثٌ according to the verbal noun pattern for this verb category; however, in practice this form is rarely used in the sense of "talk, discussion." تَحْديثٌ has a separate meaning altogether. It relates to a secondary meaning of حَدَّثَ which is "renew, renovate." Hence تَحْديثٌ as maSdar has the meaning of "renovating, modernizing."

MaSdars from defective فَعَّلَ verbs (Form II) ending with 'alif maqSuura are derived according to the تَفْعِلَةٌ tafʿilatun pattern, as in the following examples:

فَعَّلَ	تَفْعِيلٌ	Meaning
سَمَّى	تَسْمِيَةٌ	naming
قَوَّى	تَقْوِيَةٌ	strengthening
عَزَّى	تَعْزِيَةٌ	consoling

25.1.2.2 فَاعَلَ *(Form III)* maSdars

There are two verbal nouns from فَاعَلَ verbs: مُفَاعَلَةٌ and فِعالٌ. The use of مُفَاعَلَةٌ is more prevalent. A few verbs use another form of *maSdar* entirely.

Knowing which فَاعَلَ (Form III) *maSdar* to use requires study. For example, from قَاتَلَ "to fight," we obtain مُقَاتَلَةٌ and قِتالٌ, which mean "fighting" in both instances but قِتالٌ is more commonly used. In addition, قِتالٌ collocates with the word سَاحَةٌ "domain, area," as in the term سَاحة قِتال "battlefield." Similarly, from كَافَحَ "to struggle, to oppose, to fight," we obtain the two *maSdar*s مُكَافَحَة and كِفَاح with the same meaning. Yet مُكَافَحَة المُخَدِّرات "fighting [against] drugs" and مُكَافَحَة الإرْهاب "fighting terrorism" are appropriate collocations, whereas كِفَاح المُخَدِّرات and كِفَاح الإرْهاب are not.

25.1.2.2.1 The مُفَاعَلَةٌ form

فَاعَلَ	مُفَاعَلَةٌ	*Meaning*
سَاعَدَ	مُسَاعَدَةٌ	helping
كَاتَبَ	مُكَاتَبَةٌ	corresponding
شَاهَدَ	مُشَاهَدَةٌ	viewing
نَادَى	مُنَاداةٌ	calling

25.1.2.2.2 The فِعال form

فَاعَلَ	فِعالٌ	*Meaning*
قَاتَلَ	قِتالٌ	fighting
كَافَحَ	كِفَاحٌ	struggling
نَاضَلَ	نِضالٌ	striving

One could theoretically obtain the *maSdar* مُسَافَرَةٌ "traveling" from the verb سَافَرَ "to travel," and مُحَارَبَةٌ "fighting" from حَارَبَ. These words exist in older writings in specialized contexts. However, in Modern Standard Arabic the nouns سَفَرٌ "travel" and حَرْبٌ "war" are used instead.

25.1.2.3 أَفْعَلَ *(Form IV)* maSdars

*MaSdar*s from أَفْعَلَ verbs are derived according to the pattern إِفْعَالٌ. We present a few examples in a table format:

أَفْعَلَ	إِفْعَالٌ	*Meaning*
أَرْسَلَ	إِرْسَالٌ	sending
أَعْلَنَ	إِعلانٌ	advertising
أَخْبَرَ	إِخْبَارٌ	informing

25.1.2.3.1 Hollow verb أَفْعَلَ (Form IV) *maSdars*

*MaSdar*s from the أَفْعَلَ hollow verb form follow the pattern إِفْعَالٌ but end with a *taa' marbuuTa*, as in the table below:

أَدارَ	إِدَارَةٌ	managing
أَفادَ	إِفَادَةٌ	benefiting
أَعادَ	إِعَادَةٌ	repetition

25.1.2.3.2 Defective verb أَفْعَلَ (Form IV) *maSdars*

*MaSdar*s from defective verb forms follow the pattern إِفْعَالٌ; they must end with a *hamza*, as in the following examples:

أَعْطى	إِعْطَاءٌ	giving
أَفْنى	إِفْنَاءٌ	annihilation
أَبْقى	إِبْقَاءٌ	retention

25.1.2.3.3 Doubled verb أَفْعَلَ (Form IV) *maSdars*

Finally, *maSdars* from doubled verb forms follow the pattern إِفْعالٌ; however, the two identical consonants in the verb must be separated by an *'alif*, as in the table below:

أَعَدَّ	إِعْدادٌ	preparing
أَمَدَّ	إِمْدادٌ	supplying
أَقَرَّ	إِقْرارٌ	approving

25.1.2.4 تَفَعَّلَ *(Form V)* maSdars

The تَفَعَّلُ pattern is employed to derive *maSdars* in this category, as in the table below:

تَفَعَّلَ	تَفَعُّلٌ	*Meaning*
تَعَلَّمَ	تَعَلُّمٌ	learning
تَحَسَّنَ	تَحَسُّنٌ	improving
تَقَدَّمَ	تَقَدُّمٌ	progressing

25.1.2.4.1 Defective verb تَفَعَّلَ (Form V) *maSdars*

In this category, *maSdars* from defective verb forms follow the pattern تَفَعُّلٍ; however, such *maSdars* end with the final consonant having two *kasra*s, as in the table below:

تَبَنَّى	تَبَنٍّ	adopting
تَخَطَّى	تَخَطٍّ	overstepping
تَعَدَّى	تَعَدٍّ	transgressing

Such verbal nouns lose their *tanwiin* (nunation) and end with a *yaa'* when they are definite, either by the attachment of the definite article الـ, through the formation of an *IDhaafa*-construct or when a suffix pronoun is attached to them, as in the following examples, respectively: التَّبَنِّي "the adoption," تَبَنِّي هذِهِ الأفكار "adopting such ideas," تَبَنِّيها هذا الطِّفل "her adoption of this child."

25.1.2.5 تَفاعَلَ (Form VI) maSdars

MaSdars from تَفاعَلَ verbs are derived according to the تَفاعُل pattern, as in the table below:

تَفاعَلَ	تَفاعُلٌ	Meaning
تَخاصَمَ	تَخاصُمٌ	conflicting
تَكاتَبَ	تَكاتُبٌ	corresponding
تَناوَلَ	تَناوُلٌ	handling, receiving

25.1.2.5.1 Defective verb تَفاعَلَ (Form VI) *maSdars*

MaSdars from تَفاعَلَ defective verbs are derived according to the تَفاعُل pattern. However, such verbal nouns end with two *kasra*s on the final consonant, as in the table below:

تَفادى	تَفادٍ	avoiding
تَنادى	تَنادٍ	calling each other
تَعادى	تَعادٍ	antagonizing

The *tanwiin* reverts to *yaa'* when such nouns are put in the definite either by the attachment of the definite article الـ, through the formation of an *IDhaafa*-construct, or when a suffix pronoun is attached to them, as in the following examples: التَّفادي "the avoiding [of]," تَفادي الخَطَرِ "avoiding of danger," تَفاديها "her avoiding," etc.

25.1.2.6 اِنْفَعَلَ *(Form VII)* maSdars

The اِنْفِعَالٌ pattern is employed to derive *maSdar*s in this verb category, as in the table below:

اِنْفَعَلَ	اِنْفِعَالٌ	*Meaning*
اِنْسَحَبَ	اِنْسِحَابٌ	withdrawing
اِنْصَرَفَ	اِنْصِرَافٌ	leaving

In the writing system, the initial *'alif* is followed by a *kasra*.

25.1.2.6.1 Doubled augmented verb اِنْفَعَلَ (Form VII) *maSdars*

*MaSdar*s of the double augmented verb form اِنْفَعَلَ pattern maintain the geminated consonant, separated by an *'alif*, as in the following:

اِنْحَلَّ	اِنْحِلالٌ	dissolution
اِنْسَدَّ	اِنْسِدادٌ	blocking
اِنْجَرَّ	اِنْجِرارٌ	drifting, floating withdrawal
اِنْضَمَّ	اِنْضِمامٌ	joining

25.1.2.6.2 Defective augmented verb اِنْفَعَلَ (Form VII) *maSdars*

*MaSdar*s of defective verb forms end with *hamza* preceded by an *'alif*, as in the following examples:

اِنْقَضَى	اِنْقِضَاءٌ	expiring
اِنْعَدَى	اِنْعِدَاءٌ	being inflicted
اِنْحَنَى	اِنْحِنَاءٌ	bending

25.1.2.6.3 Hollow augmented verb اِنْفَعَلَ (Form VII) *maSdar*s

*MaSdar*s of hollow verb forms have a *yaa'* after the first radical, as in the following:

اِنْحَازَ	اِنْحِيَازٌ	aligning with
اِنْقَادَ	اِنْقِيَادٌ	obeying, following

25.1.2.7 اِفْتَعَلَ *(Form VIII)* maSdars

Verbal nouns from اِفْتَعَلَ verbs are derived according to the اِفْتِعَالٌ pattern, as illustrated in the table below:

اِفْتَعَلَ	اِفْتِعَالٌ	*Meaning*
اِسْتَمَعَ	اِسْتِمَاعٌ	listening
اِحْتَفَلَ	اِحْتِفَالٌ	celebrating
اِجْتَمَعَ	اِجْتِمَاعٌ	meeting

Assimilation in this verb category also takes place when the inserted *taa'* in اِفْتَعَلَ is contiguous with a voiced consonant such as *zayn*. The verb زَادَ "to become more, to increase" in the اِفْتَعَلَ pattern results in اِزْتَادَ. The *taa'* changes to a *daal*, as in اِزْدَادَ "s.th. increased," as a result of its adjacency to the two voiced sounds: the preceding *zayn*, on the one hand, and the following *'alif* on the other. The verbal noun, therefore, is اِزْدِياد "increase, increment."

From the verb صَدَمَ "to hit, collide," we obtain اِصْتَدَمَ, according to the اِفْتَعَلَ pattern. The *maSdar* is اِصْطِدام "collision." Through assimilation, the *taa'* in the verb changes to its emphatic counterpart *Taa'* because of the following *daal*.

25.1.2.7.1 Hollow verb اِفْتَعَلَ (Form VIII) *maSdar*s

*MaSdar*s of hollow verbs in this form have a *yaa'* after the first radical, as in the following:

اِخْتَارَ	اِخْتِيَارٌ	choosing
اِعْتَادَ	اِعْتِيَادٌ	getting used to
اِحْتَاجَ	اِحْتِيَاجٌ	needing

25.1.2.7.2 Doubled verb اِفْتَعَلَ (Form VIII) *maSdars*

On the other hand, verbal nouns of geminated doubled verbs in this form maintain the geminated consonants separated by an *'alif*, as in the following examples:

اِحْتَلَّ	اِحْتِلالٌ	occupying
اِرْتَدَّ	اِرْتِدادٌ	regressing
اِعْتَدَّ	اِعْتِدادٌ	showing pride

25.1.2.7.3 Waaw-beginning verb اِفْتَعَلَ (Form VIII) *maSdars*

In tri-consonantal verbs beginning with a *waaw*, such as وَصَلَ "to arrive," the *waaw* changes to a *taa'* through the process of assimilation. Thus, instead of اوْتَصَلَ, a form that does not exist in the vocabulary, we obtain اتَّصَلَ "to contact, communicate with." Therefore, the verbal noun becomes اتِّصالٌ "communication, contact." Similarly, instead of اوْتَحَدَ (augmented from the root وَحَدَ according to the اِفْتَعَلَ pattern), we obtain اتَّحَدَ "to unite with." Its *maSdar* is اتِّحادٌ "union, unification," and so on.

25.1.2.8 اِفْعَلَّ *(Form IX) maSdars*

The اِفْعِلالٌ pattern is used to derive verbal nouns from this category, as in the table below:

اِفْعَلَّ	اِفْعِلالٌ	*Meaning*
اِحْمَرَّ	اِحْمِرارٌ	turning red
اِسْوَدَّ	اِسْوِدادٌ	turning black

Note that the doubled identical consonants at the end of this verb category are separated by the *'alif*, which forms an integral part of the verbal noun pattern for this category.

25.1.2.9 اِسْتَفْعَلَ *(Form X)* maSdars

The اِسْتِفْعَال pattern is employed to derive *maSdars* from this category, as in the table below:

اِسْتَفْعَلَ	اِسْتِفْعَالٌ	Meaning
اِسْتَقْبَلَ	اِسْتِقْبَالٌ	receiving
اِسْتَعْمَلَ	اِسْتِعْمَالٌ	using

25.1.2.9.1 Hollow verb اِسْتَفْعَلَ (Form X) *maSdars*

In deriving *maSdars* from augmented hollow verbs, verbal nouns maintain the *'alif* and must end with *taa' marbuuTa*, as in the following examples:

اِسْتَطَاعَ	اِسْتِطَاعَةٌ	capacity
اِسْتَفَادَ	اِسْتِفَادَةٌ	benefiting
اِسْتَقَامَ	اِسْتِقَامَةٌ	becoming straight

25.1.2.9.2 Doubled verb اِسْتَفْعَلَ (Form X) *maSdars*

Verbs ending in double consonants in this pattern maintain the doubled identical consonants separated by the *'alif*, as in the following:

اِسْتَقَلَّ	اِسْتِقْلَالٌ	independence
اِسْتَمَرَّ	اِسْتِمْرَارٌ	continuation
اِسْتَرَدَّ	اِسْتِرْدَادٌ	retrieving

25.1.2.9.3 Defective verb اِسْتَفْعَلَ (Form X) *maSdars*

MaSdars of defective verbs in this category follow the pattern اِسْتِفْعَالٌ; however they must end with a *hamza*, as in the following:

اِسْتَثْنى	اِسْتِثْناءٌ	excepting
اِسْتَقْوى	اِسْتِقْواءٌ	becoming strong
اِسْتَعْدى	اِسْتِعْداءٌ	inciting against

25.1.3 Quadriliteral verb *maSdar*s

The derivation of *maSdar*s from الأَفْعال الرُّباعِيَّة "quadriliteral verbs" (four-consonant verbs), such as تَرْجَمَ "to translate," سَيْطَرَ "to control," هَنْدَسَ "to engineer," and طَمْأَنَ "to reassure, to calm s.o. down" are obtained according to the pattern فَعْلَلَةٌ, as in the following table:

فَعْلَلَ	فَعْلَلَةٌ	*Meaning*
تَـرْجَمَ	تَرْجَمَةٌ	translating
هَنْدَسَ	هَنْدَسَةٌ	engineering
سَيْطَرَ	سَيْطَرَةٌ	control, domination
بَلْبَلَ	بَلْبَلَةٌ	confusion

A common form of الأَفْعال الرُّباعية are the duplicative verbs. These are verbs in which the initial syllable is duplicated to form quadriliteral verbs such as وَسْوَسَ "to instill evil," زَلْزَلَ "to shake," خَشْخَشَ "to rustle, to rattle," بَلْبَلَ "to confound, confuse," عَشْعَشَ "to nest," قَلْقَلَ "to disturb."

25.1.3.1 Quadriliteral *maSdar*s from duplicative verbs

فَعْلَلَ	فَعْلَلَةٌ	*Meaning*
زَلْزَلَ	زَلْزَلَةٌ	earth quaking
بَلْبَلَ	بَلْبَلَةٌ	confounding
وَشْوَشَ	وَشْوَشَةٌ	whispering
عَشْعَشَ	عَشْعَشَةٌ	nesting

The quadriliteral pattern فَعْلَلَ is also used in Modern Standard Arabic to coin verbs from borrowed nouns such as names of countries, or of imported modern equipment, as illustrated in the table below:

Noun	Quad. verb	Meaning
تَلِفون	تَلْفَنَ	to telephone
تَلِفِزيون	تَلْفَزَ	to televise
أَمْريكا	أَمْرَكَ	to Americanize
السَّعوديَّة	سَعْوَدَ	to Saudize

*MaSdar*s from the preceding quadriliteral verbs are derived according to the فَعْلَلَة pattern. Thus, we obtain تَلْفَنَةٌ "telephoning," تَلْفَزَةٌ "televising," أَمْرَكَةٌ "Americanizing, Americanization," and سَعْوَدَةٌ "Saudizing."

25.1.4 Color word *maSdars*

Some of the basic color words have two *maSdar*s, derived according to the patterns افعِلال and فُعْلَةٌ. This applies to three colors, namely, أَحْمَر "red," أَصْفَر "yellow," and أَخْضَر "green." Thus we obtain احْمِرارٌ and حُمْرَةٌ, both meaning "redness;" اصْفِرارٌ and صُفْرَةٌ "yellowness;" and اخْضِرارٌ and خُضْرَةٌ "greenness, verdancy." There is no difference in meaning between these *maSdar*s. From أَسْوَد "black," we obtain اسْوِدادٌ and سَوادٌ, both meaning "blackness;" but from أَبْيَض "white," we obtain only بَياضٌ "whiteness;" from أَزْرَق "blue," we obtain only زُرْقَةٌ "blueness;" and, finally, from أَشْقَر "blond," we only have شَقارٌ "blondness."

25.1.5 *Miim*-beginning *maSdars* الـمَصْدَر الـميمي

The *maSdar miimi*, as the name indicates, is a verbal noun that always has a *miim* at its beginning. The *maSdar miimi* is always *singular* and *masculine*. It is derived from regular tri-consonantal verbs only, according to the pattern مَفْعَل *mafʿal(un)*. Thus, from the verb طَلَبَ "to request," we derive مَطْلَبٌ "a request." This *maSdar* has the same meaning as the regularly derived *maSdar* طَلَبٌ "a request." And from the verb أَكَلَ "to eat," the *maSdar miimi* مَأْكَلٌ "eating" can be derived, which has the same meaning as the regular *maSdar* أَكْلٌ.

25.1.5.1 Miim-beginning maSdars from waaw-beginning verbs

The *maSdar miimi* from tri-consonantal verbs beginning with *waaw* is derived according to the pattern مَفْعِلٌ (*mafᶜil(un)*). Thus, from the verb وَصَلَ "to arrive," we can derive مَوْصِلٌ, which has the same meaning as the regular *maSdar* وُصولٌ "arrival." And from the verb وَعَدَ "to promise," we can derive مَوْعِدٌ "time appointment," which is used commonly, roughly with the same meaning as the regular *maSdar* وَعْدٌ "a promise."

25.1.6 Abstract nouns of quality الـمَصْدَر الصِّناعِي

Abstract nouns in general often end with the *nisba* adjective doubled *yaa'* followed by the feminine *taa' marbuuTa*. MaSdars expresssing abstract nouns follow this pattern. This form of *maSdar* can be derived from other *maSdars*. For example, from the *maSdar* تَعاوُنٌ "cooperation," we derive by way of adding the *nisba* adjective and the feminine *taa' marbuuTa* تَعاوُنِيَّة "a cooperative." This form of *maSdar* is known as a *maSdar Sinaaci*, a derived *maSdar*.

In addition, this *maSdar* is derived from other forms of speech such as nouns, adjectives, pronouns or interrogative particles. For example, from the noun إِنْسانٌ "human being, *homo sapiens*" we derive إِنْسانِيَّة "humanity." From the adjective حُرٌّ "free," we derive حُرِّيَّة "freedom." From the pronoun هُوَ "he," we derive هُوِيَّة "identity." Finally, from the interrogative word كَيْفَ "how," we derive كَيْفِيَّة "quality."

25.2 BEHAVIOR OF *MASDARS*

MaSdars in Arabic behave as regular nouns. They can take the definite article, have a suffix pronoun, change number into dual and plural, form *IDhaafa*-constructs, and be modified by adjectives. Some *maSdars* can also behave like a verb in retaining the preposition of the original verb or taking a direct object if they are derived originally from transitive verbs. *maSdars* can also substitute for dependent clauses with أَنْ plus a verb in the subjunctive.

25.2.1 Definite and indefinite *maSdar*s

*MaSdar*s are almost always in the definite except in two situations:

1. When they are used as cognate objects, discussed in some detail in the following section.
2. When they are modified by a delimiting adjective such as كَبِيرٌ "big," طَويلٌ 'long, tall," قَصيرٌ "short," قَريبٌ "near, realizable," etc. Consider the following examples:

زارَنا زِيارَةً طَويلَةً.   He paid us a long visit.

أَكَلْنا أَكْلاً كَثيراً.   We ate a lot.

25.3 COGNATE OBJECTS الـمَفْعول الـمُطْلَق

*MaSdar*s can also be used as cognate objects, also known as the cognate accusative form. Cognate objects in Arabic are *maSdar*s derived from related verbs, sharing the same consonants. Both the verb and the *maSdar* must be used concomitantly followed by adjectives denoting intensity, length, degree, etc. The use of a *maSdar* plus an adjective amounts to an adverbial function. Note the following about cognate objects:

1. They can be derived from transitive or intransitive verbs.
2. They tend to be in the accusative case. They are often modified by adjectives indicating quality or quantity, related to duration or intensity.
3. They tend to be indefinite. Consider the following examples:

نامَت البِنْتُ نَوْماً عَميقاً.   The girl slept deeply.

مَشَيْنا مَشْياً طَويلاً.   We walked a lot.

4. They can be preceded by the comparative form of adjectives, thus resulting in *IDhaafa*. In this case, the *maSdar* is in the genitive case. Examine the following examples:

قابَلَني أَجْمَلَ مُقابَلَةٍ.   He met me graciously.

شَكَرَتِ الأُسْتاذَةُ الطّالِباتِ أَجْزَلَ شُكْرٍ.   The teacher (F) thanked the students (F) profusely.

5. When *maSdar*s are preceded by one of the quantifiers such as بَعْض "some of," or كُلّ "all of" (see Chapter 31), this combination also forms an *IDhaafa*-construct. The *maSdar* in this case is both definite and genitive, as in the following examples:

تُحِبُّهُ كُلَّ الحُبِّ.   She loves him a lot.

ساعَدَها بَعْضَ الـمُساعَدَة.   He helped her some.

6. Cognate objects can be the first noun in an *IDhaafa*-construct. In this case, it cannot have الـ. In such situations, the *maSdar* must be accusative but without *tanwiin*, as in the following examples:

ساعَدَهُ مُساعَدَةَ الأَخِ لأَخيهِ.   He helped him like a brother.

أَحَبَّها حُبَّ الأَبِ لابْنَتِه.   He loved her as a father loves his daughter.

25.4 *MASDARS* WITH DIRECT OBJECTS

*MaSdar*s derived from transitive verbs generally maintain the behavior of these verbs in taking direct objects. The nouns immediately following the *maSdar*s in this case are in the genitive case because they function as the second nouns of *IDhaafa*-constructs. The following nouns in the three sentences below are direct objects of the *maSdar*s نَيْل "obtaining, awarding," زيارة "visit, visiting," and لقاء "meeting," respectively. Examine the following sentences:

تَكَلَّمْنا عَنْهُ كَثيراً مُنْذُ نَيْلِ الطّالِبِ الجائِزَةَ.

We have talked about the student a lot since his obtaining the prize.

أَثْناءَ زيارَةِ صَديقي البِلادَ تَوَقَّفَ كَثيراً في الـمُدُنِ الأَثَرِيَّةِ.

During my friend's visit in the country, he stopped a lot in ancient cities.

خِلالَ لِقاءِ الرَّئيسِ الطُّلّابَ تَحَدَّثَ عَن هُموم الجامِعَة.

During his meeting (with) the students, the president discussed the concerns of the university.

326 FUNDAMENTALS OF ARABIC GRAMMAR

We should also note that *maSdar*s can be made definite, like the ones in the preceding sentences, by having suffix pronouns, as in the following example:

شَجَّعَت الأُمُّ دِراسَتَهُ تاريخَ مِصر.

[His] mother encouraged his study of the history of Egypt.

25.5 *MASDARS* WITH PREPOSITIONS

Prepositions that are used with intransitive verbs are maintained with *maSdar*s derived from such verbs, as in the following:

أُحِبُّ أَنْ أُسافِرَ إلى القاهِرَة.

I like to travel to Cairo.

أُحِبُّ السَّفَرَ إلى القاهِرَة.

I like traveling to Cairo.

أُريدُ أَنْ أَحْصُلَ عَلى هذا الكِتابِ.

I want to acquire this book.

أُريدُ الحُصولَ عَلى هذا الكِتابِ.

I want to acquire this book.

يَجِبُ أَنْ تَتَكَلَّمي عَنْ هذا الـمَوْضوعِ.

You (F) must discuss this topic.

يَجِبُ الكَلامُ عَنْ هذا الـمَوْضوعِ.

You must discuss this topic.

25.6 *MASDARS* SUBSTITUTING FOR

أَنْ + الفِعْل المُضارِع المَنصوب / أَنْ المَصْدَرِيَّة

*MaSdar*s can be used to replace the construct 'an and the subjunctive verb form to provide stylistic variation in the language. Examine the *maSdar* in the second sentence below, which substitutes for 'an and the subjunctive verb:

أُحِبُّ أَنْ أَدْرُسَ كَثيراً.

I like to study a lot.

أُحِبُّ الدِّراسَةَ كَثيراً.

I like studying a lot.

The choice of using the *maSdar* instead of أَنْ plus the subjunctive verb is interchangeable; this is done for stylistic variation. In Chapter 3, lists of verbs are provided as well as invariable expressions that require the use of أَنْ. These verbs and expressions can be followed by *maSdar*s.

The *maSdar* replacing أَنْ plus the subjunctive verb must be in the nominative after phrases such as مِنَ الواجِبِ أَنْ "it is incumbent that," مِنَ الضَّروري أَنْ

"it is necessary that," etc. In this case, the *maSdar* functions as a subject of the sentence. Consider the examples below:

يَجِبُ عَلَيْهِ أَنْ يَعُودَ.

He must return.

يَجِبُ عَلَيْهِ العَوْدَةُ.

It is incumbent upon him to return.

سَهُلَ عَلى الطّالِبِ أَنْ يَزورَ عائِلَتَهُ.

It was easy for the student to visit his family.

سَهُلَ عَلى الطّالِبِ زيارَةُ عائِلَتِهِ.

It was easy for the student to visit his family.

مِنَ الواجِبِ أَنْ يُسافِرَ أَخي إلى الكُوَيْت.

It is necessary that my brother travel to Kuwait.

مِنَ الواجِبِ سَفَرُ أَخي إلى الكُوَيْت.

It is necessary for my brother to travel to Kuwait.

25.7 OBJECTS OF PURPOSE الـمَفْعول لأَجْلِه

Another function that *maSdars* perform in Arabic is to express reasons for actions performed. If the *maSdar* is derived from a transitive verb, it must be followed by the preposition لِ "for the purpose of," plus a noun. The preposition لِ becomes لَ if followed by a pronoun.

MaSdars in this construct are indefinite accusative, ending with *tanwiin*, as in the following:

لِـماذا أَقاموا الحَفْلَةَ؟

Why did they hold a party?

أَقاموا الحَفْلَةَ تَكْريماً لِلزّائِرِ الجَديدِ.

They held the party in honor of the new visitor.

لِـماذا تَظاهَرَ العُمّالُ؟

Why did the workers demonstrate?

تَظاهَرَ العُمّالُ طَلَباً لِفُلوسٍ أَكْثَرَ.

The workers demonstrated to demand more money.

لِـماذا سافَرَ الطّالِبُ إلى بَيْروت؟

Why did the student travel to Beirut?

سافَرَ الطّالِبُ إلى بَيْروت طَلَباً لِلعِلْمِ.

The student traveled to Beirut in pursuit of learning.

On the other hand, if the verb from which the *maSdar* is derived is intransitive, the *maSdar* must be followed by the preposition that is most often associated with the intransitive verb. For example, the verbs اِسْتَفْسَرَ "to inquire" and بَحَثَ "to search" are generally followed by the preposition عَنْ "about," as in the following:

لِـماذا هاتَفوا بَيْتَ العائِلَة؟

Why did they telephone the family's house?

هاتَفوا بَيْتَ العائِلَة اِسْتِفساراً عَنْهُ.

They called the family's house to inquire about him.

لِـماذا نُشِرَت إعلاناتٌ كَثيرَةٌ؟

Why were many advertisements published?

نُشِرَت إعْلاناتٌ كَثيرَةٌ بَحْثاً عَنْهُم.

Many advertisements were published in search of them.

Additionally, *maSdar*s in this construct can be made definite by the use of الـ or by the second definite term of *IDhaafa* preceded by the preposition لِ "for, for the purpose of," thus rendering the *maSdar* to be in the genitive, as in the following:

لِـماذا اِجتَمَعوا؟

Why did they meet?

اِجْتَمَعوا لِلحَديثِ في الأَمْرِ الهامِّ.

They met to discuss the important issue.

لِــماذا سافَرَ الوَزيرُ؟

Why did the minister travel?

سافَرَ الوزيرُ لِــمُقابَلَةِ الرَّئيسِ.

The minister traveled to meet the president.

The *maSdar*s حَديث and مُقابَلة in the preceding sentences have the preposition
لِـ attached to them.

25.8 NEGATION OF *MASDARS* WITH عَدَم

عَدَم precedes *maSdar*s, thus forming *IDhaafa*-constructs, to express the inverse
meaning of the *maSdar* following it. Its case can vary depending on its function in the sentence. However, the noun following عَدَم must always be in the
genitive, as in the following examples:

عَدَمُ النَّوْمِ يُسَبِّبُ المَرَضَ.

Lack of sleep causes illness.

ما رَأْيُكُم في عَدَمِ الصِّدْقِ؟

What do you think of lack of truthfulness?

يُعاني دائماً مِن عَدَمِ الاسْتِعِدادِ للامْتِحانِ.

He always suffers from a lack of preparation for the examinations.

لا يُحِبُّ عَدَمَ الصِّدْقِ.

He does not like falsehoods.

CHAPTER 26

Diminutive nouns اِسْمُ التَّصْغير

In Arabic, a diminutive is a form that a noun takes to convey a distinct characteristic of smallness. The diminutive of a noun can be used for a number of reasons. One such reason is simply to provide a more accurate representation of the entity described. For example, to describe a mountain lacking the scale of a big mountain, the diminutive noun جُبَيْلٌ "a little mountain" is used instead of جَبَلٌ "a mountain."

Diminutive nouns are also used to express endearment, as in يا بُنَيَّ "O, my dear [little] son!", يا بُنَيَّتي "O, my dear [little] daughter!", or يا أُخَيَّتي "O, my dear [little] sister!" In addition, diminutive nouns may be used to express contempt, as in عُوَيْلِمٌ "a little scholar," to describe someone pretending to be عالِـمٌ "a scholar," but who has not attained, in reality, the stature of a recognized scholar, or شُوَيْعِرٌ "an insignificant poet," instead of شاعِرٌ "a [recognized] poet."

The most commonly used pattern to form diminutive nouns is فُعَيْلٌ. As a general rule, the first consonant in this pattern is followed by a *Dhamma*, the second by a *fat-Ha*, then by a *yaa'* not followed by a vowel and the last consonant of the noun. Thus, from كَلْبٌ "a dog," we obtain the nouns كُلَيْبٌ "a little dog, a puppy," and from قَصْرٌ "a palace," قُصَيْرٌ "a small palace."

Feminine nouns are derived according to the pattern فُعَيْل plus the feminine marker, the *taa' marbuuTa*, i.e. فُعَيْلَةٌ. Thus we obtain دُوَيْلَةٌ "a small state," from دَوْلَةٌ "a body politic," قُفَيْفَةٌ "a little basket," from the noun قُفَّةٌ "a basket," and شُجَيْرَةٌ "a little tree," from شَجَرَةٌ "a tree."

Other diminutive feminine nouns may end with an *'alif maqSuura*, as in سُلَيْمى, Sulayma, a woman's name, from the name سَلْمى Salma, or they may end with a regular *'alif* followed by a *hamza*, as in حُمَيْراء, from حَمْراء, also a woman's name but now archaic.

Diminutive noun forms are used in names of people, both masculine and feminine (some such names are historical; others are outmoded), and in the names of ancient, as well as extant, Arab tribes, cities, and other localities, as in the following examples:

Names of men:

الجُنَيْد	a tenth-century sufi in Baghdad	صُهَيْب	Suhaib
حُسَيْن	Hussein	شُعَيْب	Shuᶜaib
الحُطَيْئَة	a famous early Islamic-era poet	عُبَيْد	ᶜubaid
حُنَيْن	Hunain	عُبَيْدالله	ᶜubaidallah
دُرَيْد	Duraid, a pre-Islamic poet	أبو عُبَيْدَة	Abu ᶜubaidah
زُهَيْر	Zuhair	عُمَيْر	ᶜumair
سُلَيْمان	Sulaiman	كُمَيْت	Kumait
سُهَيْل	Suhail		

Names of women:

أُمَيْمَة	'Umaima	سُكَيْنَة	Sukaina
بُثَيْنَة	Buthaina	سُلَيْمى	Sulaima
حُمَيْراء	Humairaa'	سُمَيَّة	Sumaiyya
رُقَيَّة	Ruqaiyya	سُهَيْلَة	Suhaila
رُوَيْدَة	Ruwaida	عُلَيَّة	ᶜUlaiyya
زُبَيْدَة	Zubaida	هُوَيْدَة	Huwaida

Names of Arab tribes:

جُهَيْنَة	Juhaina	قُرَيْش	Quraish
الحُوَيْطات	al-HuwaiTaat	بَني كُلَيْب	Bani Kulaib
بَني سُلَيْم	Bani Sulaim	هُذَيْل	Hudhail
العُبَيْدات	al-ᶜubaidat		

Names of places:

الأُبَيِّض	a city in Western Sudan
بُرَيْدَة	a city in Najd, Central Arabia
عُنَيْزَة	a twin city to بُرَيْدَة in Najd, Central Arabia
بِنْت جُبَيْل	a town in Southern Lebanon
بَني سُوَيْف	a city in Egypt
جُبَيْل	a town near Beirut, historically known as Byblos
الجُبَيْل	an oil center in Eastern Arabia
الحُدَيْبِيَة	a *wadi* near Mecca
الحُدَيْدَة	a seaport city on the Red Sea in Yemen
الحُسَيْمَة	a city on the Mediterranean in Morocco
الحُمَيْمَة	a historical place in southern Jordan; also a settlement in E. Syria
حُنَيْن	a *wadi* between Mecca and al-Ta'if in Arabia
الحُوَيْجَة	a town in north east Iraq in the Kerkuk area
دُجَيْل	a river in Iraq; also a town north of Baghdad
الرُمَيْثَة	a town in Iraq known in the 1920 revolt
الرُمَيْلَة	a village in Lebanon, also an oil center in Iraq
الزُّبَيْر	a town in southern Iraq
السُّلَيْمانِيَّة	a city in the Kurdish region in north east Iraq
السُّوَيْداء	a city in southern Syria
السُّوَيْس	a city in Egypt; also the Suez Canal
الصُّوَيْرَة	a city on the Atlantic coast in Morocco; also in Iraq to the south of Baghdad
الفُجَيْرَة	one of the United Arab Emirates
القُنَيْطِرَة	a city in the Golan Heights in Syria; also in West Morocco
الكُوَيْت	Kuwait

Diminutive nouns of quadriliteral (four-consonant) nouns in Arabic can also be formed according to فُعَيْعِل, as in دُرَيْهِم "a little coin," from دِرْهَم "a monetary unit, Gk. drachma." The diminutive form دُرَيْهِم is often used in the plural, i.e. دُرَيْهِمات, to express the notion of a small amount of money, as in the following example:

اِشْتَرَى أَرْضَ بَيْتِهِ بِدُرَيْهِماتٍ قَلِيلَةٍ.

He bought the land of his house for little money.

Another pattern used to generate diminutives from quadriliteral nouns is فُعَيْعِيل, which produces قُنَيْدِيل "a little lamp," from قِنْديل "a lamp." Some of these quadriliteral and cinqueliteral [i.e. five-consonant] nouns were borrowed into Arabic from Greek, Latin, and Persian.

Diminutives can be formed from certain adverbs of time and/or place according to the فُعَيْل pattern. Thus, we obtain قُبَيْلَ "a little before" from قَبْلَ "before" and بُعَيْدَ "a little after" from بَعْدَ "after," for both time and place. Examine the use of these diminutives in the following sentences:

سافَروا قُبَيْلَ الظُّهْرِ.

They traveled a little before noon.

وَصَلوا قُبَيْلَ الفَجْرِ.

They arrived a little before dawn.

مَشَيْنا حَتّى بُعَيْدَ مَرّاكِش.

We walked until a little [distance] after Marrakesh.

وَقَفوا في الطَّريقِ بُعَيْدَ الـمَدينَةِ.

They stopped on their way a little [distance] after Medina.

Verbs, pronouns, attributes of God, days of the week, interrogative words, and conditional words cannot be formed in the diminutive.

CHAPTER 27

Comparative adjectives أَسْماءُ التَّفْضيل

27.1 THE FUNCTION OF ADJECTIVES

The primary use of adjectives in languages is to modify nouns, in order to add more information about them. In Arabic, modifying adjectives are placed after nouns and exhibit total agreement in form. In other words, they agree with the nouns they modify in gender (masculine or feminine), number (singular, dual or plural), case (nominative, accusative or genitive), and, finally, in determination (definite or indefinite). The following examples illustrate these points:

وَصَلَتِ الطَّالِبَةُ الجَديدَةُ.	The new student (F) arrived.
شاهَدَ الطَّالِبُ الـمُعَلِّمَ الفِرَنسيَّ.	The student (M) saw the French teacher (M).
حَصَلَ عَلى كِتابٍ جَديدٍ.	He obtained a new book.

The adjective الجَديدَةُ in the first sentence modifies الطَّالِبَةُ and agrees with this noun in definiteness, gender, number and case. Similarly, الفِرَنسيَّ (or الفِرَنْسيّ) in the second sentence agrees with الـمُعَلِّمَ in these four aspects: definiteness, gender, number and case. In the last sentence, there is also complete agreement in case, gender, number and determination between the noun كِتابٍ and its modifier جَديدٍ.

In addition to modifying nouns and adding information about them, adjectives can also be used as predicates of equational sentences. Adjectives functioning as predicates agree with the subject nouns in gender, case and number *only* but must always be indefinite, as in the following examples:

الطَّالِبَةُ جَديدَةٌ.	The student (F) is new.
الـمُدَرِّسُ مَشهورٌ.	The instructor (M) is famous.

Note that جَدِيدَةٌ as predicate in the first sentence agrees with the subject اَلطَّالِبَةُ in number, gender and case. It is indefinite because it is no longer used as an adjective to modify اَلطَّالِبَةُ. It is used as predicate of the sentence. In other words, this indefinite adjective is used not to modify اَلطَّالِبَةُ but to complete the sentence. مَشْهُورٌ in the second sentence functions in the same way as جَدِيدَةٌ in the first.

27.2 COMPARATIVE ADJECTIVES

Adjectives can not only modify nouns (see Chapter 4 on adjectives) but can be used to compare two nouns with respect to some shared feature or features. When we compare two cities with respect to size, for example, the form of the adjective used assumes a different shape from the regular degree. This use of adjectives is referred to as the comparative degree. Examine the following sentences:

القاهِرة كَبِيرَةٌ.   Cairo is big.

القاهِرة أَكْبَرُ مِن دِمَشْق.   Cairo is bigger than Damascus.

Note that in the first sentence, the feminine adjective كَبِيرَةٌ functions as a predicate of the subject القاهِرة. In the second sentence, we obtain another form of the adjective, related phonetically and semantically to كَبِيرٌ. It is used in the comparison of القاهِرَة "Cairo" and دَمَشْق "Damascus" with respect to their sizes. The comparative form of adjectives is characterized by the following:

1. They are always derived according to the أَفْعَل pattern. The derived adjective form must always be followed by the preposition مِن when comparing two entities. Thus, the comparative adjective of جَمِيلٌ "beautiful" is أَجْمَلُ مِن "more beautiful than," and so on.

2. In adjectives that have identical consonants such as عَزِيزٌ "dear," جَدِيدٌ "new," and لَذِيذٌ "delicious," the comparative degree of such adjectives is derived according to the أَفْعَل pattern by geminating the duplicated consonants. In other words, one consonant is doubled in pronunciation. Only one consonant is used in the orthography, marked by the use of a *shadda*. Thus, we obtain أَعَزُّ "dearer," أَجَدُّ "newer," and أَلَذُّ "more delicious." Examine the following sentences:

صَديقي أَعَزُّ مِن أَخي.

My friend is dearer [to me] than my brother.

هذا القَميصُ أَجَدُّ مِن ذلِكَ القَميص.

This shirt is newer than that one.

الكَبابُ أَلَذُّ مِن الهامْبِرغَر.

Shish kebab is more delicious than hamburger.

3. Adjectives derived from defective verbs always end with a *tanwiin*. For example عال "tall," دان "near," سام "sublime, noble," etc. are derived from the defective verbs عَلَا "to ascend, go up," دَنا "to become nearer, closer," and سَما "to become higher, more sublime," respectively. The comparative forms of such adjectives always end with an *'alif maqSuura* in the writing system, as in أَسْمَى مِن "taller than," أَدْنَى مِن "nearer than," and أَعْلَى مِن "nobler than." Consider the following examples:

جَبَلُ الشَّيْخ أَعْلى مِن جِبالِ عَجلون.

Mount Hermon is taller than the Ajloun mountains.

حَلَب أَدْنى إلى أَنْطاكِية مِن دِمَشْق.

Aleppo is closer to Antioch than Damascus.

الحُرِّيَةُ أَسمى مِن العُبوديَّةِ.

Freedom is more noble than slavery.

Because of the final *'alif maqSuura* in these adjectives, the case is not marked; in other words, the adjectives maintain their form regardless of the case used.

4. The comparative degree adjective form is invariable, regardless of the gender or number of the noun or nouns used in the comparison. However, أَفْعَل form adjectives change case depending on their function in the sentence. In other words, the أَفْعَل form of adjectives can be nominative, accusative or genitive. Examine the following examples, and note the case markers of the comparative adjectives in them:

دِمَشْق أَقْدَمُ مِن القاهِرَة.   Damascus is older than Cairo.

أَصْبَحَت القاهِرَة أَكبَرَ مِنْ دِمَشْق.   Cairo became bigger than Damascus.

It is important to note that no matter how many nouns the subject may include, the comparative form is always invariable, as in the following example:

دِمَشْق وَبَغداد وبَيْروت أَقْدَمُ مِن الرِّياض.

Damascus, Baghdad and Beirut are older than Riyadh.

27.3 COMPARATIVE OF COLOR WORDS

Comparing two or more things in terms of their color requires the use of the color's *maSdar* preceded by one of two adjectives in the أَفْعَل pattern: أَكْثَرُ from كَثِيرٌ "many," and أَشَدُّ from شَدِيدٌ "strong," or أَقَلُّ from قَلِيلٌ "a little." The case of these adjectives is either nominative with one *Dhamma*, or accusative with one *fat-Ha*, depending on the antecedent noun. The case of the color *maSdar* must always be accusative and indefinite (see Chapter 25, section 25.1.4 for *maSdar*s of colors; Chapter 4, section 4.1.2 for color adjectives). The following examples are illustrative:

هذِهِ الشَّجَرَةُ أَكْثَرُ خُضْرَةً مِنْ تِلْكَ الشَّجَرَةِ.

This tree is greener than that one.

or

هذِهِ الشَّجَرَةُ أَكْثَرُ اِخْضِراراً مِنْ تِلْكَ الشَّجَرَةِ.

This tree is greener than that one.

السَّماءُ اليَوْمَ أَكْثَرُ زُرْقَةً مِنْ أَمْسِ.

The sky today is bluer than yesterday.

هذا اللَوْنُ أَشَدُّ حُمْرَةً مِنْ ذلِكَ اللَوْنِ.

This color is more red than that color.

اِشْتَرَيْتُ وَرَقاً أَكْثَرَ بَياضاً من هذا الوَرَقِ.

I bought paper whiter than this.

كانَ الرَّبِيعُ السَّنَةَ الماضِيَةَ أَقَلَّ اِخْضِراراً مِنْ هذِهِ السَّنَةِ.

Spring last year was less green than this year.

When a color adjective has two *maSdar*s there is no difference in meaning between the two.

27.4 SUPERLATIVE ADJECTIVES

In addition to modifying nouns and providing a basis for comparison between two nouns that share some feature(s), adjectives can also be used to compare an entity with more than two others, with respect to some shared feature or features and to identify which entity has the most of this feature. Adjectives used to provide this comparison are in the superlative, and their forms are derived according to the أَفْعَل pattern. This function can be accomplished in two ways:

1. أَفْعَل forms can be followed by a singular noun which is always both indefinite and genitive, thus forming an *IDhaafa*-construct. Like comparative adjectives, أَفْعَل form adjectives are always invariable but the case of the adjective forms can vary, depending on their function in the sentence. These adjectives can be in the nominative, accusative, or genitive cases. Examine the following examples:

دِمَشْق أَقْدَمُ مَدينةٍ.

Damascus is the oldest city [in the world].

زُرْنا أَقْدَمَ مَدينةٍ.

We visited the most ancient city [in the world].

سافَروا إلى أَقْدَم مَدينَةٍ.

They traveled to the most ancient city [in the world].

Note that the adjective in the first sentence is in the nominative case, as it is the predicate in the equational sentence دَمَشْق أَقْدَمُ مَدينةٍ. The same adjective in the sentence زُرْنا أَقْدَمَ مَدينة is in the accusative because it is the direct object of the verb زُرْنا. And, finally, أَقْدَم in the last example is in the genitive because it is preceded by a preposition.

2. أَفْعَل can be followed by a plural noun. This noun is always definite and also genitive, thus forming an *IDhaafa*-construct. The preceding examples in (1) above are duplicated below, using the plural form of مَدينةٌ:

دِمَشْق أَقْدَمُ الـمُدُنِ.

Damascus is the oldest city. (*lit.* "the oldest of cities")
[in the world]

زُرْنا أَقْدَمَ الـمُدُنِ.

We visited the oldest city. (*lit.* "the oldest of cities")
　[in the world]

سافَروا إلى أَقْدَم الـمُدُنِ.

They traveled to the oldest city. (*lit.* "the oldest of cities")
　[in the world]

In addition to the أَفْعَلُ comparative pattern, there is a small set of adjectives in Arabic that follows a different rule, namely using فُعْلى, a feminine adjective form, to generate the superlative form of the adjective. These feminine forms are invariable in case, number, and gender, as illustrated in the table below:

Adjective form	أَفْعَلُ *pattern*	فُعْلى *pattern*	*Meaning*
كَبيرٌ	أَكْبَرُ	كُبْرَى	older
صَغيرٌ	أَصْغَرُ	صُغْرَى	younger
وَسَطٌ	أَوْسَطُ	وُسْطى	middle
عَظيمٌ	أَعْظَمُ	عُظْمى	greater

The following two sentences have the same meaning:

مَرْيَم أَكْبَرُ البَناتِ.　Maryam is the oldest of the girls.

مَرْيَم كُبْرَى البَناتِ.　Maryam is the oldest of the girls.

The meaning of these two sentences can also be conveyed by placing أَكْبَر or كُبْرَى after the noun. Adjectives in this case must be in the definite, as in the examples below:

مَرْيَم البِنْتُ الأَكْبَرُ.　Maryam is the oldest girl.

مَرْيَم البِنْتُ الكُبْرى.　Maryam is the oldest girl.

Adjectives in the كُبْرَى form are used with feminine nouns and always remain invariable in any case, as in the following examples:

مَرْيَم وَهِنْد وَلَيْلى كُبْرَى البَنات.

Miryam, Hind and Leila are the eldest daughters.

رَأَيْتُ كُبْرَى البَنات.

I saw the eldest daughter.

سافَرْتُ مَعَ كُبْرَى البَنات.

I traveled with the eldest daughter.

With masculine nouns, the comparative أَفْعَل form is used, as in the following example:

رَأَيْتُ أَكْبَرَ الرِّجالِ.   I saw the oldest man.

Some adjectives in the فُعْلى pattern have come to collocate with certain nouns, especially names of countries or regions, to make a proper noun. Examine the following:

آسيا الصُّغْرى	Asia Minor, Turkey
آسيا الوُسْطى	Central Asia
بَريطانيا العُظْمى	Great Britain
الدُّوَلُ العُظْمى or الدُّوَلُ الكُبْرى	The Superpowers

Finally, the word أَوَّل "first" has the feminine form أُولى. Examine the following sentences:

جورج واشِنْطُن هُوَ الرَّئيسُ الأَوَّلُ.

George Washington is the first president.

مَرْيَم هِيَ أُولى البَنات.

Maryam is the first of the daughters.

مَرْيَم هِيَ البِنْتُ الأُولى.

Maryam is the first daughter. (i.e. the eldest daughter)

27.5 SUPERLATIVE ADJECTIVES OF COLOR

In comparing three items in terms of color, the appropriate comparative form
أَكْثَرُ or أَشَدُّ or أَقَلُّ is used in addition to the *maSdar* of the color word. The
item that is more distinguished in color is listed as well as the other two com-
pared items. This applies to the primary color words like أَسْوَدُ "black," أَحْمَرُ
"red," etc. Consider the following example:

شَعْرُ لَيْلَى أَكْثَرُ سَواداً مِنْ شَعْرِ هُدى ومِنْ شَعْرِ سَلْمى.

Laila's hair is more black than Huda and Salma's hair.

Secondary colors like بُنِّيّ "brown," زَهْرِيّ "pink," etc. follow a different structure, as in the following:

ثَوْبُ فاطِمَة زَهْرِيٌّ أَكْثَرُ مِنْ ثَوْبِ سامِية ومِنْ ثَوْبِ عالِيَة.

Fatima's dress is more pink than Samia and Alia's dresses.

CHAPTER 28

Plural nouns الجُمُوع

There are two types of plural nouns in Arabic: (1) regular and (2) irregular. The former is known in Arabic as الجَمْع المُذَكَّر السّالِم, translated as "sound or regular plural." The latter is known by the Arabic name جَمْع التَّكسير "broken plurals." In the following sections, we shall discuss regular plurals of masculine and feminine nouns, followed by irregular plurals and other plurals of various nouns.

28.1 REGULAR MASCULINE PLURALS الجَمْع الـمُذَكَّر السّالِم

Singular masculine human nouns are changed into their plurals by attaching the suffix ونَ -uuna to the end of those nouns. These noun categories follow a regular pattern in their pluralization. It should be noted that ونَ -uuna as a plural marker of nouns is used to mark the nominative case only. ونَ -uuna changes to ينَ -iina when nouns are in either the accusative or the genitive case, as in the following examples in which مُسْتَقْبِلونَ is the plural of مُسْتَقْبِلٌ:

وَصَلَ الـمُسْتَقْبِلونَ.
The greeters/welcomers arrived. (nominative)

شاهَدْنا الـمُسْتَقْبِلينَ.
We saw the greeters/welcomers. (accusative)

جاءوا مَعَ الـمُسْتَقْبِلينَ.
They came with the greeters/welcomers. (genitive)

Nouns that follow this pattern are especially those active or passive participles derived from فَعَّلَ verb forms (Form II) through اسْتَفْعَلَ (Form X) that represent human entities. Examples are provided in the table below.

Verb	Active participle singular	Plural	Meaning
دَرَّسَ	مُدَرِّسٌ	مُدَرِّسونَ	teachers
عَلَّمَ	مُعَلِّمٌ	مُعَلِّمونَ	teachers
ساعَدَ	مُساعِدٌ	مُساعِدونَ	assistants
شاهَدَ	مُشاهِدٌ	مُشاهِدونَ	spectators
أَخْبَرَ	مُخْبِرٌ	مُخْبِرونَ	informers
أَرْسَلَ	مُرْسِلٌ	مُرْسِلونَ	dispatchers
تَحَدَّثَ	مُتَحَدِّثٌ	مُتَحَدِّثونَ	interlocutors
تَكَلَّمَ	مُتَكَلِّمٌ	مُتَكَلِّمونَ	speakers
تَعاوَنَ	مُتَعاوِنٌ	مُتَعاوِنونَ	helpers
تَفاوَضَ	مُتَفاوِضٌ	مُتَفاوِضونَ	negotiators
اِنْسَحَبَ	مُنْسَحِبٌ	مُنْسَحِبونَ	quitters
اِنْصَرَفَ	مُنْصَرِفٌ	مُنْصَرِفونَ	leavers
اِحْتَفَلَ	مُحْتَفِلٌ	مُحْتَفِلونَ	celebrants
اِسْتَمَعَ	مُسْتَمِعٌ	مُسْتَمِعونَ	listeners
اِسْوَدَّ	مُسْوَدٌّ	مُسْوَدّونَ	s.o. turning s.th. black
اِحْمَرَّ	مُحْمَرٌّ	مُحْمَرّونَ	s.o. turning s.th. red
اِسْتَخْدَمَ	مُسْتَخْدِمٌ	مُسْتَخْدِمونَ	employers
اِسْتَقْبَلَ	مُسْتَقْبِلٌ	مُسْتَقْبِلونَ	greeters/welcomers

28.1.1 فَعَلَ (Form I) active participle plurals

Active participles derived from فَعَلَ verbs (Form I) present a different, yet interesting, way of forming plurals. In general, active participles derived from tri-consonantal verbs according to the pattern فاعِلٌ can be made plural by the use of the suffix ونَ -uuna. Yet some of the active participles derived from this form exhibit different plurals in the language. For example, from the verb كَتَبَ "to write," we obtain the active participle كاتِبٌ "writer," the plural of which is كُتَّابٌ "writers." However, the forms كاتِبونَ and كَتَبَةٌ, both meaning "writers," also exist in the language. What is the difference, then, between كُتَّابٌ on the one hand, and كاتِبونَ and كَتَبَةٌ on the other? كُتَّابٌ tends to be used in the sense of "[creative, or professional] writers." Thus, if one were to make a list of novelists, essayists, short story writers, journalists, etc. one would use the plural كُتَّابٌ. On the other hand, كاتِبونَ and كَتَبَةٌ are used to mean just "writers," without the specific and specialized meaning of كُتَّابٌ. For example, كاتِبو الطَّلَبات and كَتَبَةُ الطَّلَبات "application writers," convey a special group of writers.

Another example is the active participle طالِبٌ derived from the verb طَلَبَ "to request, seek, order." The plural forms طُلَّابٌ and طَلَبَةٌ are used to mean "students." We should note that طُلَّابٌ is more current than طَلَبَةٌ. The regular plural form طالِبونَ is used, however, to denote "seekers" or "those who place demands in pursuit of a goal," as in طالِبو الحَقِّ "seekers of rights," and so on.

28.1.1.1 Hollow verbs الأَفْعالُ الجَوْفاءُ

There is a tendency for active participles from hollow verbs to follow the regular pattern of pluralization. Recall that active participles derived from hollow verbs substitute a *hamza* for the missing middle consonant (see Chapter 23 on active participles). For example, the active participle of عادَ "to return" is عائِدٌ "a returner." The plural follows the regular pattern of having ونَ *-uuna* suffixed to the singular form, as in عائِدونَ.

Not all active participles from hollow verbs follow the pattern of sound plurals, however. For example, the plural of زائِرٌ "a visitor" could end with *-uuna*, as in زائِرونَ "visitors." The irregular زُوَّارٌ is also an attested, commonly used plural form. The question then arises as to which one to adopt, since both are accepted and have the same meaning. The answer is quite simple: both are seen in writing; however, زُوَّار has more currency as far as we can ascertain. The use of زائِرونَ may represent a tendency by language speakers toward regularization of forms—such tendencies are present in many languages.

28.1.1.2 Defective verbs الأَفْعال الـمُعْتَـلَّة الآخِر

Recall that the active participle from the verb دَعا "to invite" is داعٍ "inviter," and from مَشى "to walk," we derive ماشٍ "a walker" (see Chapter 23 on active participles). These active participles tend to have two plural forms, one regular and the other irregular. Thus, from داع we obtain داعونَ and دُعاةٌ and from ماشٍ we derive ماشونَ and مُشاةٌ. Both plurals are used, although they convey different nuances of meaning. داعونَ, for example, as in داعونَ إلى حَفْلَةٍ, is used in the sense of mundane "inviters, hosts," whereas دُعاةٌ has a loftier meaning, as in دُعاةُ العَدْلِ "advocates of justice," or preachers; ماشونَ denotes "walkers," whereas مُشاةٌ connotes "pedestrians," and also infantry in the army.

Note that the plural of such words results in the dropping of the *yaa'*. This is because of the impossibility of combining two different vowels in Arabic. Thus, the plural forms of الدّاعي and الـماشي are الدّاعونَ and الـماشونَ respectively.

28.1.1.3 Doubled verbs الأَفْعالُ الـمُضَعَّفَةُ

Masculine plurals of active participles derived from this verb category are made regular by suffixing ونَ -*uuna* in the nominative case and ينَ -*iina* in the accusative and genitive cases. Recall that the doubled, geminated consonant at the end of Form I doubled verbs produces a final consonant in the active participle which is also doubled and geminated. In the writing system, this is indicated by writing the consonant in question with a *shadda*. Active participles from the verbs عَدَّ "to count" and شَكَّ "to doubt" are عادٌّ "one who counts" and شاكٌّ "a doubter," respectively, and are rendered plural in the nominative as عادّونَ "those who count, counters" and شاكّونَ "doubters," and as عادّينَ and شاكّينَ in the accusative and genitive, respectively.

28.1.1.4 Regular masculine plural nouns in IDhaafa

The *nuun* at the end of these plural nouns, regardless of their case, is dropped when they are used as a part of an *IDhaafa*-construct, as in the following examples:

وَصَلَ مُعَلِّمو الـمَدرَسَةِ.
The schoolteachers arrived.

شاهَدْنا مُعَلِّمي الـمَدْرَسَةِ.
We saw the schoolteachers.

سافَرَتْ مَعَ مُعَلِّمي الـمَدرَسَةِ.
She traveled with the schoolteachers.

If suffix pronouns are attached to plural nouns ending with a *nuun*, the *nuun* is dropped before attaching the suffix pronouns, as in the following examples:

وَصَلَ مُعَلِّمونا.   Our teachers arrived.

شاهَدْنا مُعَلِّميكُم.   We saw your (M, Pl) teachers.

سافَرَت مَعَ مُعَلِّميها.   She traveled with her teachers.

28.2 REGULAR FEMININE PLURALS الجَمْع المُؤَنَّث السّالِم

Thus far, we have been examining regular masculine plural nouns, with an occasional reference to feminine nouns. We now turn to examining the formation of regular plural feminine nouns. Feminine nouns show more regularity than their masculine counterparts in plural formation. Feminine sound plurals are formed by suffixing to the feminine singular noun *-aatun* اتٌ in the nominative, and *-aatin* اتٍ in the accusative and genitive.

One way to pluralize feminine nouns is by dropping the *taa' marbuuTa* of singular feminine nouns and replacing it with اتٌ. Another way of pluralizing is to replace the *fat-Ha* preceding the *taa' marbuuTa* with an *'alif* (essentially elongating it) and then changing the *taa' marbuuTa* to a regular "open" *taa'*. Thus, مُعَلِّمَةٌ "a teacher (F)," becomes مُعَلِّماتٌ "teachers (F)," and طالِبَةٌ "a student (F)," becomes طالِباتٌ "students (F)."

Consider the following examples:

شاهَدْنا مُعَلِّماتٍ.   We saw teachers (F).

جاءَ مَعَ مُعَلِّماتٍ.   He came with teachers (F).

شاهَدْنا الـمُعَلِّماتِ.   We saw the teachers (F).

جاءَ مَعَ الـمُعَلِّماتِ.   He came with the teachers (F).

The preceding feminine plural nouns all indicate human nouns. Non-human feminine singular nouns form their plurals in this regular way as well. For example, the plural of طاوِلةٌ "a table" is طاوِلاتٌ "tables," and the plural of جامِعةٌ "a university" is جامِعاتٌ "universities," and so on.

A word of caution, however, is in order. It does not follow that every noun ending with a feminine marker is made plural by suffixing اتٌ *-aatun*. For example, the plurals of مَدْرَسَةٌ "a school" and جَرِيدَةٌ "a newspaper" are مَدارِسُ "schools" and جَرائِدُ "newspapers." Such irregular forms are learned through exposure to the language and frequent usage.

28.3 IRREGULAR (BROKEN) PLURALS جُمُوعُ التَّكْسِيرِ

جُمُوعُ التَّكْسِيرِ "broken plurals" are formed in four ways:

1. By internal vowel change in the singular form. For example, كِتابٌ "a book" becomes كُتُبٌ "books" in the plural.
2. By doubling a consonant in the singular noun, in addition to internal vowel change. For example, the plural of طالِبٌ "a student" is طُلّابٌ "students." طَلَبَةٌ also exists but may be used less frequently.
3. By using a prefix, usually a *hamza* plus a *fat-Ha* أ, in addition to the internal vowel change. For example, وَلَدٌ "a boy, offspring" becomes أَوْلادٌ "boys, children" and بابٌ "a door" becomes أَبْوابٌ "doors."
4. By adding the prefix *hamza* and a suffix, also a *hamza*, in addition to internal vowel change. For example, the plural of صَديقٌ "a friend" is أَصْدِقاءُ "friends" and قَريبٌ "a relative" is أَقْرِباءُ "relatives."

It is not possible to establish one master rule about the formation of broken plurals. Learners eventually become acquainted with these plural forms through practice and exposure to the language, written or spoken. We provide below the most commonly used broken plural patterns. Singular nouns are provided with their irregular plurals in parentheses, along with their meanings:

أَفْعالٌ

(أَبْناءٌ) اِبْنٌ	sons	(أَعْدادٌ) عَدَدٌ	numbers
(أَسْماءٌ) اِسْمٌ	names, nouns	(أَعْمالٌ) عَمَلٌ	works, deeds
(أَبْوابٌ) بابٌ	doors	(أَفلامٌ) فِلْمٌ	films
(أَخْبارٌ) خَبَرٌ	news items	(أَقلامٌ) قَلَمٌ	pens, pencils
(أَشْياءٌ) شَيْءٌ	things, affairs	(أَوْلادٌ) وَلَدٌ	sons, offspring

فُعَّالٌ *Is this for all اسم الفاعل in Form 1?*

زائِرٌ (زُوّارٌ) visitors (note also its
regular plural زائِرونَ)

طالِبٌ (طُلّابٌ) students

عامِلٌ (عُمّالٌ) laborers, workers

كاتِبٌ (كُتّابٌ) writers

فِعالٌ

بَلَدٌ (بِلادٌ) countries

جَمَلٌ (جِمالٌ) camels

رَجُلٌ (رِجالٌ) men

فِعَلٌ

قِصَّةٌ (قِصَصٌ) stories

حِكْمَةٌ (حِكَمٌ) wise sayings

عِبْرَةٌ (عِبَرٌ) lessons, examples, rules
to be followed

فُعَلٌ

تُحْفَةٌ (تُحَفٌ) articles of
curiosity

جُمْلَةٌ (جُمَلٌ) sentences

قُبْلَةٌ (قُبَلٌ) kisses

فُعُلٌ

كِتابٌ (كُتُبٌ) books

قَسٌّ (قُسُسٌ) clergymen

مَدينةٌ (مُدُنٌ) cities

فُعُولٌ

دَرْسٌ (دُروسٌ) lessons

جَيْشٌ (جُيوشٌ) armies

طَبْلٌ (طُبولٌ) drums

In the plurals of singular nouns that end with a doubled geminated consonant, these are separated by a *waaw*. Examine the following:

حَدٌّ (حُدودٌ) borders

خَدٌّ (خُدودٌ) sides of the face, cheeks

رَدٌّ (رُدودٌ) responses, answers

رَفٌّ (رُفوفٌ) shelves

دَفٌّ (دُفوفٌ) musical instruments, tambourines

سَدٌّ (سُدودٌ) dams

شَرٌّ (شُرورٌ) evil acts, acts of mischief

صَفٌّ (صُفوفٌ)   classrooms, classes

قَدٌّ (قُدودٌ)   [human] figures, shapes

كَفٌّ (كُفوفٌ)   palms of the hand

نَصٌّ (نُصوصٌ)   texts

*فُعَلاءُ

أَميرٌ (أُمَراءُ)   princes

رَئيسٌ (رُؤَساءُ)   chiefs, presidents

حَليفٌ (حُلَفاءُ)   allies, supporters

خَليفَةٌ (خُلَفاءُ)   caliphs, leaders

زَعيمٌ (زُعَماءُ)   leaders, chieftains

زَميلٌ (زُملاءُ)   companions

وَزيرٌ (وُزَراءُ)   cabinet members

وَكيلٌ (وُكَلاءُ)   agents

*أَفْعِلاءُ

صَديقٌ (أَصْدِقاءُ)   friends

قَريبٌ (أَقْرِباءُ)   relatives (note also its other irregular plural أَقارِب)

* فَواعِلُ

تَوْأَمٌ (تَوائِمُ)   twins

دافِعٌ (دَوافِعُ)   impetuses, reasons

شارِعٌ (شَوارِعُ)   streets

عامِلٌ (عَوامِلُ)   factors

فاصِلَةٌ (فَواصِلُ)   separators, commas

فاكِهَةٌ (فَواكِهُ)   fruits

قافِلَةٌ (قَوافِلُ)   caravans

*مَفاعيلُ

مَرْجوحَةٌ (مَراجيحُ)   swings

مِصْباحٌ (مَصابيحُ)   lamps, lanterns

مِفْتاحٌ (مَفاتيحُ)   kcys

مَفْهومٌ (مَفاهيمُ)   viewpoints, concepts

مِنْديلٌ (مَناديلُ)   handkerchiefs

مَنْشورٌ (مَناشيرُ)   leaflets, pamphlets

*فَعائِلُ

جَريدَةٌ (جَرائِدُ)	newspapers
حَقيقَةٌ (حَقائِقُ)	truths, facts
رِسالَةٌ (رَسائِلُ)	letters, messages
طَبيعَةٌ (طَبائِعُ)	characteristics, natures
فائِدَةٌ (فَوائِدُ)	benefits, advantages

قَصيدَةٌ (قَصائِدُ)	poems
مائِدَةٌ (مَوائِدُ)	festival meals
نَتيجَةٌ (نَتائِجُ)	results
وَسيلَةٌ (وَسائِلُ)	methods, ways

*فَواعيلُ

قارورَةٌ (قَواريرُ)	long-necked bottles
زاروبٌ (زَواريبُ)	alleyways
صاروخٌ (صَواريخُ)	rockets

فَعالِلُ

سُلَّمٌ (سَلالِمُ)	ladders, staircases
طَلْسَمٌ (طَلاسِمُ)	cryptic characters
حُنْجَرَةٌ (حَناجِرُ)	throats

*فَعاليلُ

صُنْدوقٌ (صَناديقُ)	boxes
قِنْديلٌ (قَناديلُ)	lamps
ماسورَةٌ (مَواسيرُ)	pipes

*أَفاعيلُ

أُسْطورَةٌ (أَساطيرُ)	myths
قَوْلٌ (أَقاويلُ)	told stories
كَذِبٌ (أَكاذيبُ)	lies, falsehoods
أُسْطولٌ (أَساطيلُ)	fleets

Note that we have marked some of these patterns with asterisks for good reason. Such plural nouns end only with one *Dhamma* in the nominative case and cannot have a *tanwiin*. In the genitive and accusative they take one *fat-Ha*. This will be explained in more detail in Chapter 29.

Finally, we should cite at least one example where the plural noun does not resemble its singular. The plural of مَرْأَةٌ and اِمْرَأَةٌ, both meaning "a woman," is نِساءٌ "women." This phenomenon of lacking phonetic similarity between related words such as in مَرْأَةٌ / اِمْرَأَةٌ and نِساءٌ is called *suppletion*. This phenomenon occurs in many languages. For example, there is no phonetic similarity between the English verb "go" and its past tense "went," or between the cardinal number "one" and its ordinal form "first." It should be mentioned that نِساءٌ as a plural form of اِمْرَأَةٌ is genetically related to the nouns إِنْسَانٌ "*homo sapiens*," إِنْسٌ "humankind," آنِسَةٌ "young, unmarried lady, miss," and نَاسٌ "people, human beings."

28.4 PLACE NOUN PLURALS اِسْمُ الـمَكان وجَمْعُهُ

Plural nouns are also regularly formed in the case of place nouns, i.e. nouns derived from tri-consonantal verbs to denote places. There are two patterns that can be used to generate singular place nouns in Arabic, namely مَفْعَلٌ with a penultimate *fat-Ha* and, in a limited number of nouns, مَفْعِلٌ with a penultimate *kasra*. In some other nouns we also encounter the feminine counterparts of those patterns, namely مَفْعَلَةٌ and مَفْعِلَةٌ. Thus, from كَتَبَ "to write," we obtain مَكْتَبٌ "office, bureau," according to the مَفْعَلٌ pattern, and we obtain مَدْرَسَة "a school" from دَرَسَ "to study," according to the مَفْعَلَةٌ pattern. The following place nouns can be put in the plural according to the مَفَاعِلُ pattern. Note that these plural nouns end with only one *Dhamma*; they never end with a *tanwiin*.

Also note that مَكْتَبَةٌ "a library, a bookstore" is a place noun derived from the verb كَتَبَ "to write," according to the feminine place noun pattern مَفْعَلَةٌ. Its plural, however, follows the regular pattern of suffixing ات -*aatun*, as in مَكْتَبَاتٌ "libraries, bookstores." On the other hand, مَكْتَبٌ "office, desk" is also a place noun derived from the verb كَتَبَ; yet its plural follows the مَفَاعِلُ pattern, thus obtaining مَكَاتِبُ. This is indeed an interesting phenomenon in the language. The addition of the *taa' marbuuTa* to مَكْتَبٌ generates مَكْتَبَةٌ. Perhaps this is a way to distinguish the two place nouns, derived from the same root, from each other and indicate their different meanings. It is also interesting to note that historically, the place where books were stored or housed was referred to as دار الكُتُب "house of books." مَكْتَب was used to denote what is now referred to in Modern Standard Arabic as مَدْرَسَة "school."

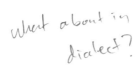

what about in dialect?

Plural مَفَاعِلُ / مَفْعَلٌ*

مَتْحَفٌ (مَتَاحِفُ)	museums	مَصْنَعٌ (مَصَانِعُ)	factories
مُخْبَزٌ (مَخَابِزُ)	bakeries	مَطْبَخٌ (مَطَابِخُ)	kitchens
مُخْرَجٌ (مَخَارِجُ)	exits	مَطْعَمٌ (مَطَاعِمُ)	restaurants
مَدْخَلٌ (مَدَاخِلُ)	entrances	مَعْمَلٌ (مَعَامِلُ)	workshops, factories
مَسْرَحٌ (مَسَارِحُ)	theaters	مَكْتَبٌ (مَكَاتِبُ)	offices
مَسْكَنٌ (مَسَاكِنُ)	residences, domiciles	مَلْعَبٌ (مَلَاعِبُ)	playgrounds, stadiums
		مَنْهَجٌ (مَنَاهِجُ)	curriculums

Plural مَفَاعِلُ / مَفْعِلٌ*

مَنْصِبٌ (مَنَاصِبُ)	positions, statures
مَجْلِسٌ (مَجَالِسُ)	places of sitting, councils, seats
(مَعْرِضٌ (مَعَارِضُ)	exhibition

Plural مَفَاعِلُ / مَفْعَلَةٌ* ⟶ some just have *taa marboota* form 40 heard

مَدْخَنَةٌ (مَدَاخِنُ)	chimneys, smokestacks
مَدْرَسَةٌ (مَدَارِسُ)	schools
مَحْكَمَةٌ (مَحَاكِمُ)	courthouses
مَغْسَلَةٌ (مَغَاسِلُ)	washing-places, sinks
مَقْبَرَةٌ (مَقَابِرُ)	cemeteries
مَطْبَعَةٌ (مَطَابِعُ)	printing press
مَطْحَنَةٌ (مَطَاحِنُ)	flour mills
مَعْصَرَةٌ (مَعَاصِرُ)	oil presses

28.5 INSTRUMENT NOUN PLURALS اِسْمُ الآلَةِ وجَمْعُهُ

The previous section treated nouns that denote places derived from tri-consonantal verbs. Plurals of such nouns tend to follow rules. This section will introduce another type of noun in Arabic, nouns that denote instruments, which are also derived from tri-consonantal verbs. Plurals of these nouns also follow regular patterns.

There are three patterns used to generate singular instrument nouns in Arabic: (1) مِفْعَلَةٌ, (2) مِفْعَلٌ, and (3) مِفْعالٌ. Note that مِفْعَلَةٌ has a feminine ending. Thus, from فَتَحَ "to open" we derive مِفْتاحٌ "a key, an instrument that opens," according to the مِفْعالٌ pattern. From بَرَدَ "to file (metal)" we obtain مِبْرَدٌ "a file," according to مِفْعَلٌ. And, finally, from كَنَسَ "to sweep" we obtain مِكْنَسَةٌ "a broom," according to مِفْعَلَةٌ.

Instrument nouns derived according to مِفْعالٌ are made plural according to the مَفاعيلُ pattern. For example, the plural of مِفْتاحٌ "a key" is مَفاتيحُ. Note that this plural form does not end with a *tanwiin* (see Chapter 29 on indeclinable nouns). On the other hand, plural nouns derived according to مِفْعَلٌ and مِفْعَلَةٌ patterns are made plural according to one pattern, namely مَفاعِلُ. Thus the plural of مِبْرَدٌ "a file" is مَبارِدُ "files"; the plural of مِكْنَسَةٌ "a broom" is مَكانِسُ "brooms." Plural nouns according to the مَفاعِلُ pattern do not end with a *tanwiin* (see Chapter 29 on indeclinable nouns).

The following are lists of tri-consonantal verbs, instrument nouns, their plural forms, and their meanings:

مِفْعالٌ / *مَفاعيلُ pattern

Verb	مِفْعال *pattern*	Plural	Meaning
حَرَثَ	مِحْراثٌ	مَحاريثُ	plow
زَرَبَ	مِزْرابٌ	مَزاريبُ	spout
زَمَرَ	مِزْمارٌ	مَزاميرُ	woodwind instrument
فَتَحَ	مِفْتاحٌ	مَفاتيحُ	key
قاسَ	مِقياسٌ	مَقاييسُ	measure
قَلَعَ	مِقْلاعٌ	مَقاليعُ	slingshot

مَفَاعِيلُ* / مِفْعَال pattern (*cont'd*)

Verb	مِفْعَال *pattern*	Plural	Meaning
نَشَرَ	مِنْشَارٌ	مَنَاشِيرُ	saw
نَطَدَ	مِنْطَادٌ	مَنَاطِيدُ	hot-air balloon
نَظَرَ	مِنْظَارٌ	مَنَاظِيرُ	binoculars
نَفَخَ	مِنْفَاخٌ	مَنَافِيخُ	bellows
نَقَرَ	مِنْقَارٌ	مَنَاقِيرُ	pick-ax
هَمَزَ	مِهْمَازٌ	مَهَامِيزُ	spur
وَزَنَ	مِيزَانٌ	مَوَازِينُ	scales

مَفَاعِلُ* / مِفْعَل pattern

Verb	مِفْعَل *pattern*	Plural	Meaning
بَرَدَ	مِبْرَدٌ	مَبَارِدُ	file
بَضَعَ	مِبْضَعٌ	مَبَاضِعُ	scalpel
ثَقَبَ	مِثْقَبٌ	مَثَاقِبُ	drill
جَهَرَ	مِجْهَرٌ	مَجَاهِرُ	microscope
خَرَزَ	مِخْرَزٌ	مَخَارِزُ	punch
سَبَرَ	مِسْبَرٌ	مَسَابِرُ	explorer
شَرَطَ	مِشْرَطٌ	مَشَارِطُ	scalpel
عَجَنَ	مِعْجَنٌ	مَعَاجِنُ	kneading trough
غَزَلَ	مِغْزَلٌ	مَغَازِلُ	spindle
قَادَ	مِقْوَدٌ	مَقَاوِدُ	steering wheel
قَرَضَ	مِقْرَضٌ	مَقَارِضُ	scissors

مِفْعَلَةٌ / *مَفَاعِلُ pattern

Verb	مِفْعَلَةٌ pattern	Plural	Meaning
حَفِظَ	مِحْفَظَةٌ	مَحَافِظُ	briefcase
خَرَطَ	مِخْرَطَةٌ	مَخَارِطُ	lathe
رَوَّحَ	مِرْوَحَةٌ	مَرَاوِحُ	fan
سَرَجَ	مِسْرَجَةٌ	مَسَارِجُ	oil lamp
سَطَرَ	مِسْطَرَةٌ	مَسَاطِرُ	ruler
صَادَ	مِصْيَدَةٌ	مَصَائِدُ	trap
طَوَى	مِطْوَاةٌ	مَطَاوٍ	knife
عَجَنَ	مِعْجَنَةٌ	مَعَاجِنُ	kneading trough
قَلَى	مِقْلَاةٌ	مَقَالٍ	frying pan
كَحَلَ	مِكْحَلَةٌ	مَكَاحِلُ	kohl pouch
كَنَسَ	مِكْنَسَةٌ	مَكَانِسُ	broom
نَشَفَ	مِنْشَفَةٌ	مَنَاشِفُ	towel
نَفَضَ	مِنْفَضَةٌ	مَنَافِضُ	ash tray
كَوَى	مِكْوَاةٌ	مَكَاوٍ	clothes iron

Note that instrument nouns derived from defective verbs in the preceding list assume a different plural form in that they end with a *tanwiin*, as in (مَكَاوٍ) مِكْوَاةٌ "a clothes iron."

Plurals of instrument nouns derived from doubled verbs assume the form of regular feminine plural nouns, as in the following examples:

Verb	Instrument noun	Plural	Meaning
قَصَّ	مِقَصٌّ	مِقَصَّاتٌ	scissors
سَلَّ	مِسَلَّةٌ	مِسَلَّاتٌ	large needle
شَدَّ	مِشَدٌّ	مِشَدَّاتٌ	fastener

In recent years, the Arabic language academies (in Amman, Baghdad, Cairo and Damascus) have sanctioned words derived according to the فَعَّال pattern, the more commonly used feminine pattern فَعَّالَة and their plural forms according to فَعَّالات as means of deriving instrument nouns. Examples in these patterns are provided below:

Verb	فَعَّال *pattern*	Plural	Meaning
خَرَطَ	خَرَّاطٌ	خَرَّاطاتٌ	turner
خَلَطَ	خَلَّاطٌ	خَلَّاطاتٌ	mixer
قَلَبَ	قَلَّابٌ	قَلَّاباتٌ	tipcart

فَعَّالَة pattern

Verb	فَعَّالَة *pattern*	Plural	Meaning
ثَلَجَ	ثَلَّاجَةٌ	ثَلَّاجاتٌ	refrigerator
خَرَطَ	خَرَّاطَةٌ	خَرَّاطاتٌ	lather, turner
خَرَمَ	خَرَّامَةٌ	خَرَّاماتٌ	punch
خَلَطَ	خَلَّاطَةٌ	خَلَّاطاتٌ	mixer
سارَ	سَيَّارَةٌ	سَيَّاراتٌ	car
شَوى	شَوَّايَةٌ	شَوَّاياتٌ	grill
طارَ	طَيَّارَةٌ	طَيَّاراتٌ	airplane
كَسَرَ	كَسَّارَةٌ	كَسَّاراتٌ	grinder, cracker
نَشَفَ	نَشَّافَةٌ	نَشَّافاتٌ	blotter

We should note that while طَيَّارَةٌ "airplane" is derived according to this pattern and is commonly used in daily speech, the form طائِرَةٌ has been sanctioned as a loftier lexical item used in more formal situations, as in formal writing. On the other hand, common usage has popularized the use of مُنْخُلٌ "a sieve," instead of the expected مِنْخَلٌ.

In addition, common usage has created doublets in the language. Examples include خَلَّاطٌ and خَلَّاطَةٌ "a mixer," خَرَّاطٌ and خَرَّاطَةٌ "a turner," مِقْرَضٌ and مِقْراضٌ "scissors," and مِسْبارٌ and مِسْبَرٌ "explorer."

28.6 THE FIVE NOUNS AND THEIR PLURALS
اَلأَسْمَاءُ الخَمْسَةُ

The following five singular nouns, known by the Arabic name الأَسْمَاءُ الخَمْسَة "the five nouns," are marked by a *waaw* in the nominative case, an *'alif* in the accusative, and a *yaa'* in the genitive. Some grammarians include a sixth noun which is, in essence, rarely used; therefore, we will restrict the discussion here to the following five only.

Nominative	Accusative	Genitive	Meaning
أَبُو	أَبا	أَبي	father
أَخُو	أَخا	أَخي	brother
حَمُو	حَما	حَمي	father-in-law
فو	فا	في	mouth
ذو	ذا	ذي	owner of

The long vowels for the three different cases are assumed only under two conditions:

1. When these nouns are in the *IDhaafa*-construct, as in the examples below:

وَصَلَ أَبُو الطّالِبِ أَمْسِ. The student's father arrived yesterday.

شاهَدْنا أَخا العَرِيس. We saw the bridegroom's brother.

هَلْ تَكَلَّمَ مَعَ حَمِيكِ؟ Did he speak to your (F) father-in-law?

2. When they have a suffix pronoun attached to them, which is, in fact, a form of *IDhaafa*, as in the following examples:

يا مَرْيَم، أَيْنَ أَبوكِ؟ Maryam, where is your father?

هَلِ السَّيّارَةُ مَعْ أَخِيكَ؟ Is the car with your (M) brother?

Two things should be mentioned about these five nouns. First, there exist in the language four "counter-nouns" to the five nouns above. There is no counterpart to ذو "owner of." Instead of the long vowels, these counter nouns end with *Dhamma* in the nominative case, with a *fat-Ha* in the accusative and with a *kasra* in the genitive when the definite article اَل is prefixed to them. Thus, for example, for اَلأَبُ "the father," اَلأَبَ and اَلأَبِ are realized. When these nouns are indefinite, the case markers are duplicated, thus resulting in a *tanwiin* written on a dummy *'alif* in the accusative only, as in the table below:

Nominative	Accusative	Genitive	Meaning
أَبٌ	أَبًا	أَبٍ	father
أَخٌ	أَخًا	أَخٍ	brother
حَمٌ	حَمًا	حَمٍ	in-law
فَمٌ	فَمًا	فَمٍ	mouth

Second, فو "mouth" is obsolete and is rarely used except in frozen phrases. فَمٌ is more frequently used instead. حَمو "father-in-law" is seen only in highly literary styles. The following sentences illustrate how these nouns are used:

سافَرَ الأَبُ قَبْلَ ساعَةٍ.	The father left an hour ago.
هَلْ سَتُقابِلُ الأَخَ؟	Will you meet the brother?
الأَلَمُ في الفَمِ ولَيْسَ في الرَّأْسِ.	The pain is in the mouth, not in the head.

The plurals of these five nouns are irregular, as shown below:

أَبٌ (آباءٌ)	fathers
أَخٌ (إِخْوَةٌ)، (إِخْوانٌ)	brothers
حَمٌ (أَحْماءٌ)	in-laws
فو (أَفْواهٌ)	mouths
ذو (ذَوو)	owners of

The plural of فَمٌ "mouth" is أَفْمامٌ "mouths," a noun that is not commonly used. أَفْواهٌ enjoys more currency and is used in frozen structures as in the following:

خُذوا الحِكْمَةَ مِن أَفْواهِ المَجانين!

Seek wisdom from the mouths of fools.

Additionally, ذو "owner of, holder of" has a feminine counterpart, namely ذات, as in the example below:

تِلْكَ الـمَرْأَةُ ذاتُ الشَّعْرِ الأَسْوَدِ تَعْمَلُ طَبيبَةً.

That woman with black hair works as a physician.

Finally, ذات has the plural ذَوات, as in phrases such as النِّساءُ ذَواتُ الـمالِ الكَثير "women of abundant means, who have lots of money." ذَوات also connotes those who are well-placed in society, as in أَبْناءُ الذَّواتِ "children of the upper crust [in society]."

28.7 UNIT NOUN PLURALS اِسْم الوَحْدَةِ وَجَمْعُه

A reference to one instance of collective or mass nouns can be expressed by making the collective noun into a feminine singular by suffixing a *taa' marbuuTa*, the feminine marker. For example, we obtain خَشَبَةٌ "one piece of wood" from the mass noun خَشَبٌ "wood," and وَرَقَةٌ "one piece of paper" from وَرَقٌ "paper."

Unit nouns can be made plural to indicate a number of distinct individuals of collective nouns. This is accomplished by the addition of the regular feminine plural marker ـاتٌ, as in, for example:

سَبْعُ دَجاجاتٍ   seven chickens

عَشْرُ وَرَقاتٍ   ten sheets of paper

Often a noun expressing a "unit" or "measure" is used with instances of collective nouns. For example, لَحْمَةٌ "a piece of meat" is more appropriately expressed by the use of قِطْعَةٌ مِنْ "a piece of," as in قِطْعَةٌ مِنَ اللَحْم "a piece of meat." Other words are used to express the unit noun, as in the following:

حَبَّةٌ a piece of grain, seed, as in حَبَّةٌ مِنَ القَمْحِ or حَبَّةُ قَمْحٍ a grain
of wheat

حَفْنَةٌ a handful, a scoop, as in حَفْنَةٌ مِنَ التُّرابِ or حَفْنَةُ تُرابٍ a scoop
of dirt / earth

ذَرَّةٌ a tiny amount, as in ذَرَّةٌ مِنَ الشَّكِّ or ذَرَّةُ شَكٍّ an iota of doubt

كِسْرَةٌ a piece, as in كِسْرَةٌ مِنَ الخُبْزِ or كِسْرَةُ خُبْزٍ a morsel of bread

Other measure nouns such as فِنْجانٌ "a cup of," كَأْسٌ "a glass of," or مِلْعَقَةٌ
"a spoon of" are often used with mass or collective nouns, as in the
following:

فِنْجانٌ مِنَ القَهْوَةِ or فِنْجانُ قَهْوَةٍ   a cup of coffee

كَأْسٌ مِنَ السماءِ or كَأْسُ ماءٍ   a glass of water

مِلْعَقَةٌ مِنَ الدَّواءِ or مِلْعَقَةُ دَواءٍ   a spoonful of medicine

28.8 PLURAL NOUNS OF SINGLE OCCURRENCE
اِسْمُ الـمَرَّة وجَمْعُهُ

This noun form expresses a single occurrence of a generic action. It is often
formed by the addition of the feminine marker such as a *taa' marbuuTa* to
the *maSdar*, the verbal noun. To form this single-occurrence noun, the verbal
noun of فَعَلَ verbs (Form I) is constructed according to the فَعْل pattern. Thus,
the *maSdar* from the verb أَكَلَ "to eat" is أَكْلٌ "eating, act of eating," and one
instance of eating is أَكْلَةٌ. From the verb ضَرَبَ "to hit" we obtain the *maSdar*
ضَرْبٌ "act of hitting, hitting." The noun of a single occurrence is ضَرْبَةٌ
"one hit."

Hollow verbs form this single occurrence noun in the same manner.
From قامَ / يَقومُ "to stand up, to rise" we obtain قَوْمَةٌ "uprising," and from
صاحَ / يَصيحُ "to shout" we obtain صَيْحَةٌ "one shout, one crying out."

Single-occurrence nouns are formed from defective verbs in the same
manner. From غَزا / يَغْزو "to invade, to raid," for example, we obtain غَزْوَةٌ
"one invasion, one raid" and from رَمى / يَرْمي "to throw" we obtain رَمْيَةٌ "one
throw."

Nouns of a single occurrence can be formed in the dual and/or plural, as in the following examples:

Singular	Dual	Plural	Meaning
ضَرْبَةٌ	ضَرْبَتَانِ	ضَرْبَاتٌ	hit
صَيْحَةٌ	صَيْحَتَانِ	صَيْحَاتٌ	cry
غَزْوَةٌ	غَزْوَتَانِ	غَزْوَاتٌ	raid

*MaSdar*s of فَعَّلَ (Form II) through اِسْتَفْعَلَ (Form X) verbs are used to form this type of noun in a similar fashion. While some nouns of single occurrence can be formed according to these rules, it should be emphasized that not many of them are actually used in the singular. Their plurals, however, are common. Examine the following:

Verb form	Verbal noun	Noun of occurrence	Plural form	Meaning
عَلَّمَ	تَعْلِيمٌ	تَعْلِيمَةٌ	تَعْلِيمَاتٌ	instructions
سَاعَدَ	مُسَاعَدَةٌ	مُسَاعَدَةٌ	مُسَاعَدَاتٌ	aids
أَرْسَلَ	إِرْسَالٌ	إِرْسَالَةٌ	إِرْسَالَاتٌ	dispatches
تَقَلَّبَ	تَقَلُّبٌ	تَقَلُّبَةٌ	تَقَلُّبَاتٌ	changes
تَنَاوَلَ	تَنَاوُلٌ	تَنَاوُلَةٌ	تَنَاوُلَاتٌ	dealings
اِنْدَهَشَ	اِنْدِهَاشٌ	اِنْدِهَاشَةٌ	اِنْدِهَاشَاتٌ	surprises
اِلْتَفَتَ	اِلْتِفَاتٌ	اِلْتِفَاتَةٌ	اِلْتِفَاتَاتٌ	side looks
اِسْتَنْشَقَ	اِسْتِنْشَاقٌ	اِسْتِنْشَاقَةٌ	اِسْتِنْشَاقَاتٌ	breathings
تَرْجَمَ	تَرْجَمَةٌ	تَرْجَمَةٌ	تَرْجَمَاتٌ	translations

Note that if the *maSdar* ends with a *taa' marbuuTa*, the word مَرَّةٌ "one time, one occurrence" or مَرَّةً وَاحِدَةً "one occurrence" is used. Thus, instead of using the *maSdar*, such verbs are used with the word مَرَّةً, as in the following:

عَلَّمَهُ الدَّرْسَ مَرَّةً وَاحِدَةً.   He taught him the lesson once.

28.9 PROFESSION NOUN PLURALS اِسْمُ الـمِهْـنَةِ وجَمْعُهُ

Nouns that indicate performers of a trade or a profession are usually formed from tri-consonantal verbs according to the فَعّالٌ pattern. Thus, from طَبَخَ "to cook" we obtain طَبّاخٌ "a cook," and from صَبَغَ "to paint, to dye" we obtain صَبّاغٌ "painter, dyer," etc. Additionally, profession nouns are derived from regular nouns. From the noun سَمَكٌ "fish" we obtain سَمّاكٌ "fisherman," i.e. the person connected to fish, be he the seller or catcher of fish. The following are some common nouns of profession derived from nouns:

حَدّادٌ blacksmith, from حَديدٌ iron

عَطّارٌ perfume maker, from عِطْرٌ perfume

لَـحّامٌ butcher, meat seller, from لَـحْمٌ meat

The following are common nouns of profession derived from verbs:

خَبّازٌ bread maker, from خَبَزَ to make bread, or to sell it

رَسّامٌ drawer, draftsman from رَسَمَ to draw, draft

The plural of such nouns is regular by the suffixing of ونَ -uuna in the nominative, and ينَ -iina in the accusative and genitive. These and other nouns denoting profession or trade are commonly used in Arab family names, parallel to the English family names Painter, Cooper, Thatcher, and so on. Below are a few sentences that illustrate how profession nouns are used in the plural:

يَصْنَعُ العَطّارونَ العُطورَ مِنَ الزُّهورِ.
Perfume makers make perfumes from flowers.

البِلادُ بحاجَةٍ إلى خَبّازينَ ولَـحّامينَ.
The country is in need of bakers and butchers.

We should also add that other forms of profession nouns exist in the language beyond the preceding patterns. There are, for example, nouns derived according to اِسْمُ الفاعِلِ, the active participle, as in مُصَوِّرٌ "photographer," and the like.

28.10 NOUNS OF INTENSITY AND THEIR PLURALS
اِسْمُ الـمُبالَغَةِ

We mentioned in a previous section that active participles derived from tri-consonantal verbs according to the فاعِل pattern are used primarily as nouns and secondarily as adjectives. Some of these active participles generate, according to the فَعّالٌ pattern, nouns indicating intensity. Thus from كاذبٌ "a liar," which is derived from كَذَبَ / يَكْذِبُ "to tell lies," we obtain كَذّابٌ "habitual liar, one who is known for his [repeated] lies," and from ناظِمٌ "a lyric writer," we obtain نَظّامٌ "a prolific lyric writer."

The pattern فَعولٌ also conveys intensity or excess, as in أَكولٌ "a gluttonous eater," or كَذوبٌ "a habitual liar." Furthermore, nouns derived according to the مِفْعال pattern also convey this sense of a person performing actions in height-ened degrees. Thus we realize مِقْدام "a man with a high level of courage," مِفْضال "a man who performs generous deeds," مِزْواج "one who marries frequently," and so on.

Forms that indicate intensity may end with a *taa' marbuuTa*. Thus, from عالِمٌ "a savant, a learned person" (derived from عَلِمَ "to know"), we derive عَلّامَةٌ "a very learned person." Other nouns in this pattern include رَحّالَةٌ "an avid traveler," نَسّابَةٌ "a famous genealogist," فَهّامَةٌ "extremely capable of understand-ing," etc. Despite the fact that these nouns end with a *taa' marbuuTa*, they are masculine in their syntactic behavior. The plurals of such nouns are made regular by suffixing ونَ -*uuna*, as in the following:

اِبْنُ بَطوطَة رَحّالَةٌ عَرَبِيٌّ مَشْهورٌ.
Ibn Batuúta is a famous Arab traveler.

قَرَأْنا عَن رَحّالينَ عَرَب مَشْهورينَ.
We read about famous Arab travelers.

28.11 PLURAL NOUNS AND ADJECTIVES
أَسْماءُ الجَمْعِ والصِّفات

It was mentioned earlier that adjectives in Arabic assume the same form as the nouns they modify in four aspects: (1) gender, (2) number, (3) case, and (4) determination (definite/indefinite). Thus, the adjective modifying a regular definite plural noun in the nominative case must also be nominative and definite, as in the following examples:

وَصَلَ الـمُدرِّسونَ الـمَشهورونَ.

The famous professors (M, Pl) arrived.

قابَلَ الـمُديرُ الـمُدَرِّسينَ الـمَشهورينَ.

The principal met with the famous teachers.

Certain adjectives do not assume the regular plural marker ونَ in the nominative or ينَ in the accusative and genitive when used with masculine plural human nouns. Examine the following list of adjectives in the singular and plural:

Plural	Singular	Meaning
كِبارٌ	كَبيرٌ	big, important
صِغارٌ	صَغيرٌ	young, small
عِظامٌ/ عُظَماءُ	عَظيمٌ	great
جُدُدٌ	جَديدٌ	new
طِوالٌ	طَويلٌ	tall
قِصارٌ	قَصيرٌ	short
أَقوِياءُ	قَويٌّ	powerful
أَذكِياءُ	ذَكِيٌّ	intelligent
أَوْفِياءُ	وَفيٌّ	faithful, loyal
أَعِزّاءُ	عَزيزٌ	dear

To illustrate how they modify regular plural nouns, examine the following sentences:

حَضَرَ الـمُعَلَّمونَ الجُدُدُ. The new teachers arrived.

سَوْفَ نُشاهِدُ الـمُسافِرينَ الصِّغارَ. We shall see the young passengers.

حَضَرَ الـمُوظَّفونَ الكِبارُ. The top-ranking employees arrived.

نَتَكَلَّمُ عَن الكُتّابِ العِظامِ. We talk about the famous writers.

The above adjectives, however, assume the regular feminine ending when used
with regular feminine plural human nouns, as in the following:

حَضَرَتِ الـمُعَلِّماتُ الجَديداتُ.   The new teachers (F, Pl) arrived.

سَوْفَ نُشاهِدُ البَناتِ الصَّغيراتِ.   We shall see the young girls.

نَتَكَلَّمُ عَنِ الكاتِباتِ العَظيماتِ.   We talk about the famous
writers (F, Pl).

Adjectives for non-human plural nouns must be in the feminine singular, as in
the examples below:

حَضَرَتِ السَّيّاراتُ الجَديدَةُ.   The new cars arrived.

قَرَأَ الكُتُبَ الجَديدَةَ.   He read the new books.

زاروا الـمُدُنَ الكَبيرَةَ.   They visited the big cities.

One encounters examples where plural (instead of singular) adjectives are used
with non-human nouns, such as:

أَقاموا في هذِهِ البِلادِ سَنَواتٍ طِوالاً.   They resided in this country for
many years.

Nisba adjectives modifying regular masculine or feminine human nouns show
agreement with such nouns. For example, the *nisba* adjective derived from أَمريكا
is أَمريكِيٌّ. This adjective has regular endings in the plural, as in the examples
below:

حَضَرَ الـمُدَرِّسونَ الأَمْريكيّونَ.   The American teachers (M) came.

حَضَرَتِ الـمُدَرِّساتُ الأَمْريكيّاتُ.   The American teachers (F) came.

If this same adjective modifies a non-human plural noun, however, the adjective form must be in the feminine singular, as in the following example:

حَضَرَتِ السّيّاراتُ الأَمْريكِيَّةُ.   The American cars arrived.

However, the *nisba* adjectives from عَرَبٌ "Arabs," يَهودٌ "Jews," and أَجانِبُ "for-eigners," are عَرَبِيٌّ "Arab," يَهودِيٌّ "Jewish," and أَجْنَبِيٌّ "foreigner," as illustrated in the following sentences, first in the singular and then in the plural:

سافَرَ الـمُدَرِّسُ العَرَبِيُّ.	The Arab teacher left.
شاهَدْنا الـمُديرَ الأَجْنَبِيَّ.	We saw the foreign director.
دَرَّسَ الأُسْتاذُ اليَهودِيُّ الكِتابَ الـمُقَدَّسَ.	The Jewish teacher taught the Holy Book.
سافَرَ الـمُدَرِّسونَ العَرَبُ.	The Arab teachers left.
شاهَدْنا الـمُدَراءَ الأَجانِبَ.	We saw the foreign directors.
شارَكَ الرِّجالُ اليَهودُ في الحَرْبِ.	Jewish men participated in the war.

These singular adjectives can also function as nouns, as in the following sentences:

يُواجِهُ العَرَبِيُّ مَشاكِلَ كَثيرَةً.	The Arab faces many problems.
يُقيمُ أَجْنَبِيٌّ في هذِهِ البِنايَةِ.	A foreigner resides in this building.
يَدْرُسُ اليَهودِيُّ العَرَبِيَّةَ.	The Jewish man is studying Arabic.

As nouns or adjectives, they do not take the masculine regular plural suffix ونَ -*uuna*, as shown in the following sentences:

يُقيمُ العَرَبُ في البِلادِ العَرَبِيَّةِ.	Arabs reside in the Arab countries.
يُقيمُ أَجانِبُ كَثيرونَ في هذِهِ الـمَدينَةِ.	Many foreigners reside in this city.
يَسْكُنُ اليَهودُ في هذِهِ البِلادِ.	Jews live in these countries.

28.12 COLLECTIVE/MASS NOUNS اِسْمُ الجِنْس / النَّوْع

Nouns representing entities that form a class of their own, such as chickens, oranges, or a mass such as bread or wood, are a class of nouns called اِسْمُ النَّوْع or اِسْمُ الجِنْس in Arabic. Here is a list illustrating this noun group:

خَشَبٌ wood	لَحْمٌ meat	خُبْزٌ bread
دَجاجٌ chickens	بُرْتُقالٌ oranges	وَرَقٌ paper

Such nouns are always masculine and singular in their syntactic behavior, as illustrated in the following examples:

الخَشَبُ مُسْتَعْمَلٌ في البِناءِ.   Wood is used in construction.

أُحِبَّ الدَّجاجَ الـمَشْويَّ.   I like grilled chicken.

البُرْتُقالُ مُفيدٌ لِلصِّحَّةِ.   Oranges are beneficial to health.

Also some of these nouns relate to unit nouns (see above). From بُرْتُقالٌ "oranges" we obtain بُرْتُقالَةٌ "one orange," and from وَرَقٌ "paper" we have وَرَقَةٌ "a sheet of paper."

CHAPTER 29

Indeclinable nouns/diptotes
الـمَمْنوع مِنَ الصَّرْف

Nouns exhibit different endings according to their function in sentences. The majority of nouns have three cases (see Chapter 2 on nouns). Singular definite common nouns take three case endings: a *Dhamma* in the nominative case, a *fat-Ha* in the accusative, and a *kasra* in the genitive. The case marker is doubled in indefinite singular nouns in the orthography; in pronunciation such nouns are pronounced with an *-n* sound, called a *tanwiin* in Arabic terminology.

Dual nouns exhibit two endings for these three cases: the nominative is marked by انِ and the accusative and genitive by يْنِ. Similarly, regular masculine plural nouns exhibit two endings for the three cases: ـونَ- in the nominative, and ـينَ- in the accusative and genitive. Regular feminine plural nouns exhibit two endings: ـاتٌ- in the nominative and ـاتٍ- in the accusative and genitive.

Some nouns and adjectives are marked at their end with only one *Dhamma* in the orthography in the nominative case. In the accusative and genitive, they end with only one *fat-Ha*. A *tanwiin*, in other words, is not applied in the pronunciation of such words, nor is it applied in their writing. Such nouns are said to be *indeclinable nouns* or *diptotes*. Arab grammarians use الـمَمْنوعُ مِنَ الصَّرْف for such nouns and adjectives. These nouns include most commonly the following, among others: (1) plural nouns of a certain pattern as presented below, (2) proper compound nouns, (3) comparative adjectives and color adjectives, both masculine and feminine, and (4) proper nouns of foreign origin as well as indigenous ones. The following examples illustrate the three cases of مَدارِسُ "schools" in the indefinite:

في الـمَدينةِ مَدارِسُ كَثيرَةٌ.	There are many schools in the city.
زُرْنا مَدارِسَ كَثيرَةً.	We visited many schools.
دَرَسوا في مَدارِسَ كَثيرَةٍ.	They studied in many schools.

Indeclinable nouns or adjectives exhibit a regular form when they are definite, however. Recall that nouns can be made definite either by:

1. prefixing the definite article ال;
2. attaching a possessive suffix; or
3. using them in an *IDhaafa*-construct.

Examine the following sentences in which مَدارِسُ is definite:

الـمَدارِسُ في هذهِ الـمَدينَةِ كَثيرَةٌ.	Schools in this city are numerous.
شاهَدْنا الـمَدارِسَ الكَثيرَةَ.	We saw the numerous schools.
دَرَسوا في الـمَدارِسِ الكَثيرَةِ.	They studied in the numerous schools.
دَرَسوا في مَدارِسِ الـحُكومَةِ.	They studied in the public schools.

Indeclinable nouns of the following patterns were listed in Chapter 28. We cite just a few examples in each category to refresh the reader's memory:

29.1 INDECLINABLE PLURAL NOUNS

فُعَلاءُ

رُؤَساءُ chiefs, presidents, خُلَفاءُ allies, supporters, زُمَلاءُ colleagues, companions, وُزَراءُ cabinet members, عُلَماءُ learned men

أَفْعِلاءُ

أَصْدِقاءُ friends, أَقْرِباءُ relatives

فواعِلُ

شَوارِعُ streets, فَواكِهُ fruits, عَوامِلُ factors, reasons

فَواعيلُ

قَواريرُ bottles, جَواريرُ drawers in an office cabinet

مَفاعيلُ

مَفاتيحُ keys, مَصابيحُ lamps, مَناديلُ handkerchiefs, مَفاهيمُ viewpoints, concepts

فَعائِلُ

جَرائِدُ newspapers, رَسائِلُ letters, messages, فَوائِدُ benefits, قَصائِدُ poems, وَسائِلُ methods, ways, means, نَتائِجُ results

فَعالِلُ

حَناجِرُ throats, سَلالِمُ ladders, قَناطِرُ bridges, arches

فَعاليلُ

صَناديقُ boxes, قَناديلُ lanterns

أَفاعيلُ

أَحاسيسُ feelings, أَساطيرُ myths, أَقاويلُ [unsubstantiated] sayings

29.2 INDECLINABLE ADJECTIVES

1. The comparative adjective forms of the pattern أَفْعَلُ, as in أَكْبَرُ "bigger," أَجْمَلُ "more beautiful," etc. In addition, many basic color terms in Arabic are according to this pattern, as in أَحْمَرُ "red," أَزْرَقُ "blue," and so on. Such adjectives do not take a *tanwiin* in pronunciation, nor do they take two *Dhammas* in orthography.

2. The feminine form of the أَفْعَلُ pattern is obtained according to the فَعْلاءُ pattern. These adjectives generally apply to producing feminine color terms and feminine adjectives that are often used in names of women. As examples of feminine color terms we cite حَمْراءُ "red," زَرْقاءُ "blue," etc. Regular adjectives or names of women include: حَسْناءُ "a pretty young woman," عَلْياءُ "a lofty woman," شَمّاءُ "a sublime woman," etc.

3. Feminine adjectives of the فُعْلى pattern, as in كُبْرَى "bigger/older (F)," صُغْرى "younger," عُظْمى "greater," and وُسْطى "more in the middle." These adjectives are invariable as they do not take case endings.

4. Plurals of some adjectives and/or nouns derived from adjectives according to the أَفاعِل pattern, as in the following: أَعاظِمُ "most notable," derived from عَظيمٌ "great;" أَكابِرُ "most dignified," derived from كَبيرٌ "big, important;" أَقارِبُ "close ones, i.e. relatives," derived from قَريبٌ "near [one], relative;" and أَجانِبُ "foreigners," derived from أَجْنَبِيٌّ "a foreigner."

29.3 INDECLINABLE PROPER NOUNS

Proper nouns shared with other Semitic languages such as إبْراهيم "Abraham," داوود "David," إسْحق "Isaac," and سُلَيْمان "Solomon," are indeclinable, as well as proper nouns ending with ان-, such as عُثْمان / عَدْنان and عَمّان "capital of Jordan." In addition, the following proper nouns are treated like other indeclinable nouns: عُمَر "a man's name," سُعاد "a woman's name," مِصر "Egypt."

29.4 INDECLINABLE COMPOUND PROPER NOUNS

Compound proper nouns such as حَضْرَمَوْت "region in South Yemen;" بَيْتَ لَحْم "Bethlehem, Palestine;" بَعْلَبَك "The Roman city of Baalbek, Lebanon."

CHAPTER 30

Numbers العَدَد

The grammar of numbers in Arabic is believed by some to be daunting. Many speakers of Arabic educated in the language commit errors in using the forms of numbers, both in speaking and in writing. Still, knowledge of some basic rules of the grammar of numbers is essential to learners of Arabic. In the following sections, we will introduce rules that will gradually guide the learner through these seemingly complex aspects of the language. The focus of the discussion here will be cardinal numbers—those numbers that are used to count objects or entities as in, for example, "three books" or "five women." Ordinal numbers, i.e. numbers that indicate the order of objects or entities, such as "the fourth house," will also be addressed in this chapter.

30.1 "ONE" واحِد AND "TWO" اِثْنان

The numbers "one" and "two" behave as adjectives in Arabic. In other words, واحِد "one" and اِثْنان "two" must follow counted nouns in sentences and agree with them in gender and case. The number is referred to as عَدَدٌ "number," and the counted noun is اِسْم مَعْدودٌ "counted noun." Examine the examples related to واحِد below:

وَصَلَ طالِبٌ واحِدٌ.	One student (M) arrived.
وَصَلَت طالِبةٌ واحِدَةٌ.	One student (F) arrived.
شاهَدَ الأُسْتاذُ طالِباً واحِداً.	The teacher saw one student (M).
رَجَعَ أَحْمَد مَعَ طالِبةٍ واحِدَةٍ.	Ahmad returned with one student (F).

Note that in the first sentence واحِدٌ agrees with the preceding noun in gender (masculine) and also in case (nominative). Similarly, in the second sentence, واحِدَةٌ agrees with the feminine noun preceding it in both gender (feminine) and case (nominative).

In the third sentence, the noun طالباً is masculine and accusative due to its function as object of the verb شاهَدَ. This explains why واحداً is also both masculine and accusative. On the other hand, the feminine noun طالبَة in the fourth sentence is preceded by the preposition مَعَ, which explains why it is in the genitive. Therefore, the number واحِد in this sentence must be both feminine and in the genitive case.

The behavior of اثْنان (M) and اثْنَتان (F) exactly mirrors the behavior of واحد in Arabic grammar, as explained above. اثْنان (M) becomes اثْنَيْـن in the accusative or genitive; and اثْنَتان (F) becomes اثْنَتيْـن in the accusative or genitive. These forms are similar to the way dual nouns are derived from their singular counterparts. اثْنان (M) and اثْنَتان (F) must follow counted nouns and agree with them in gender and case. Examine the following examples and note the agreement of اثْنان or اثْنَتان (nominative) and their variants اثْنَيْـن or اثْنَتيْـن (accusative or genitive) with the nouns that precede them:

رَجَعَ طالبانِ اثْنانِ.	Two students (M) returned.
شاهَدْنا طالِبَيْـنِ اثْنَيْـنِ.	We saw two students (M).
رَجَعوا مَعَ طالِبَيْـنِ اثْنَيْـنِ.	They returned with two students (M).
رَجَعَت طالِبَتانِ اثْنَتانِ.	Two students (F) returned.
شاهَدْتُّ طالِبَتَيْـنِ اثْنَتَيْـنِ.	I saw two students (F).
رَجَعوا مَعَ طالِبَتَيْـنِ اثْنَتَيْـنِ.	They returned with two students (F).

واحِد or اثْنان are used after nouns to emphasize and clarify the number of entities expressed in sentences. Their use can be redundant as the singular and dual forms of nouns already indicate number. However, the use of اثْنان after the noun can help in avoiding confusion in differentiating between the dual and plural forms of nouns like بَلَد "country," as in بَلَدانِ اثْنان "two countries" and بُلْدان "many countries." The use of واحِد "one" helps in discerning one distinct thing as opposed to a simple indefinite noun, as in كِتابٌ واحِدٌ "one book," for example, versus كِتابٌ "a book."

30.2 "THREE" TO "TEN" ثَلاثَةٌ إِلَى عَشَرَة

The numbers ثَلاثَةٌ "three," أَرْبَعَةٌ "four," خَمْسَةٌ "five," سِتَّةٌ "six," سَبْعَةٌ "seven," ثَمانِيَةٌ "eight," تِسْعَةٌ "nine," and عَشَرَةٌ "ten" precede and can also follow the counted nouns. The numbers themselves are subject to certain rules that we shall discuss below. The counted nouns following the numbers ثَلاثَةٌ "three" through عَشَرَة "ten" are also subject to certain grammatical requirements. We will first present the conditions put on the counted noun (الاسْمُ الـمَعْدود) that occurs after the numbers ثَلاثَةٌ "three" through عَشَرَة "ten." It is important to note that there is a slight phonological change in the word عَشَرَة "ten." When it is used before masculine nouns, it is pronounced عَشَرَة; before feminine nouns, it becomes عَشْرُ.

30.2.1 The counted noun from "three" to "ten" for indefinite nouns

1. The counted noun (الاسْمُ الـمَعْدود) must always be in the plural.
2. It must always be in the genitive case as it is in the IDhaafa-construct.
3. The counted noun must always be indefinite, thus ending with a *tanwiin* "nunation."

The following examples illustrate the preceding grammatical requirements of the counted noun:

سافَرَ ثَلاثَةُ طُلّابٍ.	Three students (M) traveled.
شاهَدْنا عَشَرَ طالِباتٍ.	We saw ten students (F).
ذَهَبَ مَعَ خَمْسَةِ رِجالٍ.	He went with five men.

Now, we turn to examine the conditions put on the numbers from ثَلاثَةٌ "three" through عَشَرَة "ten."

1. ثَلاثَةٌ "three" through عَشَرَة "ten" vary in terms of case depending on their function in the sentence. In other words, ثَلاثَةٌ "three" through عَشَرَة "ten" may be in the nominative (subject of a sentence), in the accusative (direct object of a transitive verb), or in the genitive (preceded by a preposition).

2. The numbers ثَلاثَة "three" through عَشْرَة "ten" vary in gender from the counted noun following them. If the singular form of the counted noun is masculine, the numbers ثَلاثَة "three" through عَشْرَة "ten" must be feminine. If the singular form of the counted noun is feminine, ثَلاثَة "three" through عَشْرَة "ten" must be masculine. This is often referred to as *gender polarity*. In brief, the number is opposite in gender from the gender of the singular form of the counted noun.

Examine the following sentences:

سافَرَ ثَلاثَةُ طُلّابٍ.   Three students (M) traveled.

Or, in the accusative (object of a verb), for example:

شاهَدْتُ ثَلاثَةَ طُلّابٍ.   I saw three students (M).

Or, in the genitive (preceded by a preposition), as in the following:

سافَرَ الأُسْتاذُ مَعَ ثَلاثَةِ طُلّابٍ.   The professor traveled with three students (M).

Note that ثَلاثَة "three" through عَشْرَة "ten" maintain the feminine marker when the singular form of the noun following these numbers is masculine. On the other hand, these numbers drop the feminine marker, the *taa' marbuuTa*, when they are followed by feminine nouns, as in the following:

وَصَلَ ثَلاثُ طالِباتٍ.   Three students (F) arrived.

شاهَدَ الأُسْتاذُ خَمْسَ سَيّاراتٍ.   The professor saw five cars (F).

وَصَلَ صَديقي مَعَ سَبْعِ أُستاذاتٍ.   My friend arrived with seven professors (F).

ثَمانِيَة "eight," when followed by a masculine noun, behaves in a regular fashion, as in the following:

رَجَعَ ثَمانِيَةُ طُلّابٍ.   Eight students (M) returned.

ثَمَانِيَةٌ exhibits a slightly different ending when followed by a feminine noun. It becomes ثَمَانِي in the nominative and genitive, as in the following examples:

ثَمَانِي طَالِبَاتٍ رَجَعْنَ أَمْسِ.	Eight students (F) returned yesterday.
الأُسْتَاذُ مَعَ ثَمَانِي طَالِبَاتٍ.	The professor is with eight students (F).

However, it becomes ثَمَانِيَ in the accusative, as in the following example:

شَاهَدَ ثَمَانِيَ طَالِبَاتٍ.	He saw eight students (F).

Arabic has a word specifically used when counting from three to nine (or ten, as some grammarians state), namely بِضْع "several, some." Like the numbers three to ten, بِضْع must be followed by a plural noun in the genitive case and it differs in gender from the noun following it. For example, بِضْع remains in the masculine when it is followed by feminine, plural nouns, as in the following:

هَؤُلَاءِ بِضْعُ طَالِبَاتٍ.	These are several students (F).
بِضْعُ طَبِيبَاتٍ يَعْمَلْنَ فِي هَذَا الْمُسْتَشْفَى.	Several physicians (F) work in this hospital.

When بِضْع is followed by a masculine or a non-human plural noun, its gender changes into the feminine, as in the following:

هَؤُلَاءِ بِضْعَةُ طُلَّابٍ.	These are several students (M).
هَذِهِ بِضْعَةُ كُتُبٍ.	These are several books.
قَرَأَ الْمُتَدَرِّبُونَ بِضْعَةَ مَقَالَاتٍ.	The trainees read several articles.

Additionally, بِضْع changes case, depending on its function in the sentence as the examples below illustrate:

دَرَّسَ الأُسْتَاذُ بِضْعَةَ طُلَّابٍ أَمْرِيكِيِّينَ.	The teacher taught several American students (M).
تَقَابَلْنَا مَعَ بِضْعِ طَالِبَاتٍ زَائِرَاتٍ.	We met with several visiting students (F).

30.3 CARDINAL NUMBERS AS ADJECTIVES FOR DEFINITE NOUNS

Thus far, we have presented examples where the numbers three to ten precede the counted noun and show disagreement in gender between the number word and the singular form of the counted noun. As has been stated earlier in this chapter, three to ten can also follow the counted noun. As in the previous examples, the number word must be opposite in gender to the singular form of the counted noun, as in the following examples:

عادَت الـمُوَظَّفاتُ الخَمْسُ.   The five employees (F, Pl) returned.

عادَ الـمُوَظَّفونَ الخَمْسَةُ.   The five employees (M, Pl) returned.

Recall that non-human plural nouns are always treated as feminine singular, regardless of the gender of those nouns in the singular. For example, كِتاب in the singular is masculine whereas its plural form كُتُب is treated as feminine singular. وَثيقَةٌ, the feminine singular noun, and its plural form وَثائِق are both treated in the same way with respect to gender. Examine the following examples:

قَرَأنا الوَثائِقَ الأَرْبَعَ.   We read the four documents.

اِشْتَرَيْنا ثَلاثَةَ كُتُب.   We bought three books.

شاهَدْنا خَمْسَةَ عَصافيرَ.   We saw five birds.

Cardinal numbers from three to ten function as adjectives when placed after the counted nouns. The rule of opposites in gender must apply. The number and the nouns they modify must be identical in case. Examine the following pairs of sentences in the nominative, accusative and genitive, respectively:

رَجَعَ الطُّلّابُ الخَمْسَةُ.   The five (F) students (M) returned.

رَجَعَتِ الطّالِباتُ الخَمْسُ.   The five (M) students (F) returned.

شاهَدْنا الـمُعَلِّمينَ الثَّلاثَةَ.   We saw the three teachers.

شاهَدْنا الـمُعَلِّماتِ الثَّلاثَ.   We saw the three teachers (F).

سافَرَتِ الطَّبِيبَةُ مَعَ الوُزَراءِ الخَمْسَةِ. The doctor (F) traveled with the
five (F) cabinet members (M).

سافَرَ الطَّبِيبُ مَعَ الوَزِيراتِ الأَرْبَعِ. The doctor (M) traveled with
the four cabinet members (F).

30.4 "ELEVEN" AND "TWELVE" أَحَدَ عَشَرَ وَاثْنا عَشَرَ

The number أَحَدَ عَشَرَ "eleven" is used before masculine nouns. Its variant
إِحْدَى عَشْرَةَ is used before feminine nouns. These numbers are invariable with
respect to case. Both of their components always end with a *fat-Ha*. The counted
nouns (الاسْمُ الـمَعْدُود) following these numbers are always (1) singular, (2) indefinite, and (3) accusative, as in the following examples:

وَصَلَ أَحَدَ عَشَرَ طالباً. Eleven students (M) arrived.

وَصَلَت إِحْدى عَشْرَةَ طالبَةً. Eleven students (F) arrived.

Similarly, the number اثْنا عَشَرَ "twelve" is used with masculine nouns.
Its feminine counterpart اثْنَتا عَشْرَةَ is used with feminine nouns. These forms
اثْنَتا عَشْرة and اثْنا عَشَرَ are used in the nominative case. Examine the following:

وَصَلَ اثْنا عَشَرَ طالباً. Twelve students (M) arrived.

وَصَلَتِ اثْنَتا عَشْرَةَ طالبَةً. Twelve students (F) arrived.

in اثْنَتَيْ عَشْرَةَ and اثْنَيْ عَشَرَ assume the forms اثْنَتا عَشْرَةَ and اثْنا عَشَرَ
the accusative and genitive (just like dual noun endings), as in the following
examples:

شاهَدتُّ اثْنَيْ عَشَرَ طالباً. I saw twelve students (M).

شاهَدتُّ اثْنَتَيْ عَشْرَةَ طالبَةً. I saw twelve students (F).

رَجَعَ الأُسْتاذُ مَعَ اثْنَيْ عَشَرَ طالباً. The professor (M) returned with
twelve students (M).

رَجَعَتِ الأُستاذَةُ مَعَ اثْنَتَيْ عَشْرَةَ طالبَةً. The professor (F) returned with
twelve students (F).

30.5 "THIRTEEN" TO "NINETEEN"

ثَلاثَ عَشْرَةَ / ثَلاثَةَ عَشَرَ - تِسْعَ عَشْرَةَ / تِسْعَةَ عَشَرَ

The numbers تِسْعَ عَشْرَةَ / ثَلاثَةَ عَشَرَ "thirteen" through ثَلاثَ عَشْرَةَ
"nineteen," like أَحَدَ عَشَرَ "eleven" and اثْنا عَشَرَ "twelve," must be followed
by singular, indefinite, and accusative nouns. Additionally, these numbers
are always invariable with respect to their endings, which is always a *fat-Ha*
on both parts. However, the first element of these numbers is always in the
gender opposite to that of the counted noun. If the gender of the singular form
of the counted noun is masculine, the first component of "thirteen through
nineteen" is feminine, and vice versa. This condition is similar to what was
mentioned previously about the numbers ثَلاثَة "three" through عَشْرَة "ten," i.e.,
the gender polarity discussed earlier. However, the second term of the number,
namely عَشَر "ten," has the same gender as the counted noun. Examine the
following:

وَصَلَ ثَلاثَةَ عَشَرَ طالِباً.	Thirteen students (M) arrived.
شاهَدْنا تِسْعَ عَشْرَةَ سَيَّارَةً.	We saw nineteen cars.
وَصَلَتْ مَعَ خَمْسَ عَشْرَةَ طالِبَةً.	She arrived with fifteen students (F).

With definite nouns, gender polarity applies; both terms of the numbers are in
the accusative. The nouns in the preceding examples are changed into the
definite plural to illustrate the use of numbers with definite nouns:

وَصَلَ الطُّلّابُ الثَّلاثَةَ عَشَرَ.	The thirteen students arrived.
شاهَدْنا السَّيّاراتِ التِّسْعَ عَشْرَةَ.	We saw the nineteen cars.
وَصَلَتْ مَعَ الطالِباتِ الخَمْسَ عَشْرَةَ.	She arrived with the fifteen students.

30.6 THE TENS ("TWENTY," "THIRTY," ETC.) أَلْفاظُ الْعُقودِ

The number "twenty" is formed from the word عَشْرَة "ten" by omitting the *taa'*
marbuuTa ة and attaching the regular masculine plural nominative suffix ـونَ.
Note that the vowel following the first consonant changes from a *fat-Ha* in عَشْرَة
to a *kasra* in عِشْرون.

"Thirty" through "ninety" are formed by dropping the *taa' marbuuTa* ة at the end of the cardinal numbers "three" through "nine" and attaching ‍ـونَ, thus resulting in the following numbers:

ثَلاثونَ	thirty	سَبْعونَ	seventy
أَرْبَعونَ	forty	ثَمانونَ	eighty
خَمْسونَ	fifty	تِسْعونَ	ninety
سِتّونَ	sixty		

عِشْرونَ "twenty" through تِسْعونَ "ninety" are invariable with respect to the gender of the nouns following them. However, they change with respect to case. Note that the counted noun following these numbers must be singular and accusative. Examine the following:

سافَرَ ثَلاثونَ مُعلِّماً.   Thirty teachers (M) traveled.

سافَرَت ثَلاثونَ مُعَلِّمَةً.   Thirty teachers (F) traveled.

The regular masculine plural suffix ‍ـونَ changes to ‍ـينَ in the accusative and in the genitive case. This is similar to the behavior of regular plural nouns. Examine the following:

شاهَدْنا خَمْسينَ طالِباً.   We saw fifty students (M)."

رَجَعَ الـمُعَلِّمونَ مَعَ خَمْسينَ طالِبةً.   The teachers (M) returned
with fifty students (F).

30.7 "TWENTY-ONE" TO "NINETY-NINE"
واحِدٌ وعِشْرونَ إلى «تِسْعٌ وَتِسْعونَ»

"Twenty-one" through "twenty-nine" are formed by conjoining the cardinal number واحِد "one" through تِسْعَة "nine" with the word عِشْرونَ, using the conjunctive particle وَ, as in the following masculine forms:

واحِدٌ وعِشْرونَ   twenty-one

اِثْنانِ وعِشْرونَ   twenty-two

ثلاثَةٌ وعِشْرونَ   twenty-three

etc.

The same rule applies to the other tens, as in the following illustrative examples:

خَمْسَةٌ وسَبْعونَ   seventy-five

تِسْعَةٌ وتِسْعونَ   ninety-nine

and so on.

Recall that the number واحِد "one" and its feminine form واحِدَةٌ or إِحْدَى, and اِثْنانِ "two" and its feminine form اِثْنَتانِ in the nominative or اِثْنَتَيْنِ in the accusative or genitive, agree with the counted noun in gender. Examine the following examples:

سافَرَ واحِدٌ وعِشْرونَ مُديراً.   Twenty-one directors (M) traveled.

سافَرَتْ إِحْدَى وعِشْرونَ مُديرَةً.   Twenty-one directors (F) traveled.

سافَرَ إِثْنانِ وعِشْرونَ مُديراً.   Twenty-one directors (M) traveled.

سافَرَتْ اِثْنَتانِ وعِشْرونَ مُديرَةً.   Twenty-one directors (F) traveled.

On the other hand, the cardinal numbers ثَلاثَة "three" through تِسْعَة "nine" must be the opposite in gender from the counted nouns. This gender polarity requires that the counted noun be in the gender opposite to that of the number. Examine the following examples:

سافَرَ تِسْعَةٌ وخَمْسونَ طالِباً.   Fifty-nine students (M) traveled.

سافَرَتْ تِسْعٌ وخَمْسونَ طالِبَةً.   Fifty-nine students (F) traveled.

Numbers ending with the nominative marker -uuna ونَ change this form to -iina ينَ in the genitive or accusative case, as in the following examples:

شاهَدَ الأُستاذُ تِسْعَةً وَخَمْسِينَ طالِباً.

The professor (M) saw fifty-nine students (M).

شاهَدَ الأُستاذُ تِسْعاً وَخَمْسِينَ طالِبَةً.

The professor (M) saw fifty-nine students (F).

وَصَلَ الأُستاذُ مَعَ تِسْعَةٍ وَخَمْسِينَ طالِباً.

The professor arrived with fifty-nine students (M).

وَصَلَ الأُستاذُ مَعَ خَمْسَةٍ وَتِسْعِينَ طالِبَةً.

The professor (M) arrived with fifty-nine students (F).

30.8 HUNDRED(S) مِئَة / مِئاتٌ

مِئَة "hundred," pronounced as *mi'at-un* as the orthographic components indicate, is also written less commonly with an *'alif* as مائَة. Regardless of which spelling one adopts, مِئَة is invariable with respect to the gender of the noun following it. The case marker of مِئَة changes, however, depending on its function in the sentence. In other words, it can be in the nominative, accusative or genitive case. The counted noun following مِئَة must be singular, indefinite and genitive, thus forming an *IDhaafa*-construct, as in the following examples:

وَصَلَ مِئَةُ طالِبٍ.

A hundred students (M) arrived.

دَرَّسَ الـمُـعَلِّمُ مِئَةَ طالِبَةٍ.

The teacher (M) taught a hundred students (F).

سافَرَ الـمُـعَلِّمُ مَعَ مِئَةِ طالِبٍ.

The teacher (M) traveled with a hundred students (M).

30.8.1 "Two hundred" مِئَتانِ

مِئَة takes on a dual form by attaching the nominative masculine dual suffix ـانِ-. The addition of the dual suffix results in the writing of the *taa' marbuuTa* as a regular *taa'*, resulting in مِئَتانِ. This nominative form has accusative and genitive counterparts, as in مِئَتَيْنِ. The counted noun following مِئَتَيْنِ is always singular, indefinite, and genitive, thus forming an *IDhaafa*-construct, just like مِئَة above. If مِئَتَانِ is the head noun in the *IDhaafa*-construct, its final *nuun* must be dropped, as in all dual and plural nouns ending with *nuun*, when forming a part of *IDhaafa*. Examine the following examples:

وَصَلَ مِئَتا طالِبٍ.   Two hundred students (M) arrived.

قَرَأْنا مِئَتَيْ مَقالةٍ.   We read two hundred articles.

يَسْكُنُ الطُّلابُ في مِئَتَيْ بَيْتٍ.   The students live in two hundred houses.

"Three hundred" through "nine hundred" are expressed by the intended cardinal number, which is always in the masculine, followed by the noun مِئَة in the singular and genitive. This formation amounts to an *IDhaafa*-construct in which the second noun is indefinite, genitive and singular. This structure is represented in two ways in the orthography (as we see in the list below); both orthographic representations are equally acceptable. The dropping of the *'alif*, however, is more common:

ثَلاثُمِئَةٍ or ثَلاثُمائَةٍ	three hundred
أَرْبَعُمِئَةٍ or أَرْبَعُمائَةٍ	four hundred
خَمْسُمِئَةٍ or خَمْسُمائَةٍ	five hundred
سِتُّمِئَةٍ or سِتُّمائَةٍ	six hundred
سَبْعُمِئَةٍ or سَبْعُمائَةٍ	seven hundred
ثَمانِمِئَةٍ or ثَمانِمائَةٍ	eight hundred
تِسْعُمِئَةٍ or تِسْعُمائَةٍ	nine hundred

Recall that the first term of *IDhaafa* varies in case depending on its function. When the second term in this *IDhaafa*-construct, namely مِئَة, is followed by another noun in an expanded *IDhaafa*-construct, مِئَة loses its *tanwiin*. Examine the following examples:

وَصَلَ خَمْسُمِئَةِ طالِبٍ.

Five hundred students (M) arrived.

عَلَّمَتِ الأُسْتاذَةُ سَبْعَمِائَةِ طالِبَةٍ.

The teacher (F) taught seven hundred students (F).

ذَهَبَتِ الـمُديرَةُ مَعَ ثَلاثِمِئَةِ طالِبٍ.

The director (F) went with three hundred students (M).

30.9 THOUSAND(S) أَلْفٌ / آلافٌ

أَلْفٌ "one thousand" always assumes the masculine form. However, its case can vary depending on its function in the sentence. The counted noun following أَلْفٌ "thousand" must be singular, genitive and indefinite. In other words, أَلْفٌ forms an *IDhaafa*-construct. Examine the following examples:

وَصَلَ أَلْفُ طالِبٍ.	A thousand students (M) arrived.
وَصَلَت أَلْفُ طالِبَةٍ.	A thousand students (F) arrived.
عَلَّمَتِ الأُسْتاذَةُ أَلْفَ طالِبٍ.	The teacher (F) taught a thousand students.
يَسْكُنُ الطُّلّابُ في أَلْفِ غُرْفَةٍ.	The students live in a thousand rooms.

30.9.1 "Two thousand" أَلْفان

أَلْفٌ "one thousand" has a dual form generated by attaching the nominative masculine dual suffix ان, as in أَلْفان; and by attaching the accusative and genitive form يْن, as in أَلْفَيْن. The counted noun following the dual form أَلْفان or أَلْفَيْن is always singular, indefinite and genitive. أَلْفان or أَلْفَيْن thus form an *IDhaafa*-construct, causing the *nuun* to drop, as in the following:

وَصَلَ أَلْفا طالِبٍ.	Two thousand students (M) arrived.
وَصَلَت أَلْفا طالِبَةٍ.	Two thousand students (F) arrived.
عَلَّمَتِ الأُسْتاذَةُ أَلْفَيْ طالِبٍ.	The teacher (F) taught two thousand students.
يَسْكُنُ الطُّلّابُ في أَلْفَيْ غُرْفَةٍ.	The students live in two thousand rooms.

30.9.2 Thousands and dates أُلُوفٌ or آلَافٌ

"Three thousand" through "ten thousand" are expressed by the intended cardinal number, which is always in the feminine, followed by the noun آلَاف in the plural. This formation amounts to an *IDhaafa*-construct in which the second noun is plural, indefinite, and genitive, as in the following:

ثَلاثَةُ آلَافٍ	three thousand	سَبْعَةُ آلَافٍ	seven thousand
أَرْبَعَةُ آلَافٍ	four thousand	ثَمانِيَةُ آلَافٍ	eight thousand
خَمْسَةُ آلَافٍ	five thousand	تِسْعَةُ آلَافٍ	nine thousand
سِتَّةُ آلَافٍ	six thousand	عَشْرَةُ آلَافٍ	ten thousand

The first term of *IDhaafa* varies in case depending on its function. When the second term in this *IDhaafa*-construct, namely آلَاف, is followed by another noun in an expanded *IDhaafa*-construct, the word آلَاف loses its *tanwiin*. Examine the following examples:

وَصَلَ ثَلاثَةُ آلَافِ طالِبٍ.

Three thousand students (M) arrived.

عَلَّمَت الأُسْتاذَةُ سَبْعَةَ آلَافِ طالِبَةٍ.

The teacher (F) taught seven thousand students (F).

تَسْكُنُ العائِلاتُ في خَمْسَةِ آلَافِ بَيْتٍ.

The families live in five thousand houses.

The word أَلْفٌ is very handy in reading dates in formal spoken or written Arabic. Thus, reading a date begins with the mention of the word for year as the first item of the *IDhaafa*-construct, followed by the word أَلْفٌ "thousand" in the genitive case (or its dual for the present calendar), then the hundreds of years, then any other number of years. For example, the year 1967 is read as follows:

في سَنَةِ أَلْفٍ وتِسْعِمائَةٍ وسَبْعٍ وسِتّينَ

in the year one thousand, nine hundred and sixty-seven

Note that the word سَبْع in the preceding date is in the masculine, opposite in gender to the feminine word سَنَة "year."

The phrase في سَنَة "in the year of" in the preceding example can be replaced by another equivalent phrase to mean the same thing, namely في عام "in the year of." Because عام "year" is masculine, سَبْع in the preceding date must be used in the feminine. The above date can be read in the following way:

$$في عام أَلْفٍ وتِسْعِمِئَةٍ وسَبَعَةٍ وسِتِّينَ$$

in the year one thousand, nine hundred and sixty-seven

We should mention that أُلُوفٌ is another plural form for أَلْفٌ. This plural form is restricted in use: it is not used with cardinal numbers as آلافٌ is. In addition, it is generally followed by the preposition مِن "from," as in أُلُوفٌ مِن الطُّلَّابِ "thousands of students," to express a large unspecified number of entities.

30.10 MILLION(S) مِلْيُونٌ / مَلايين

The word مِلْيُونٌ "million," borrowed from a western European language, has as its plural form مَلايينُ "millions." This plural form is always masculine. However, the plural form varies in case, as in the following examples:

تَظاهَرَ مَلايينُ الأَشْخاصِ.	Millions of people demonstrated.
شاهَدْنا مَلايينَ الأَشْخاصِ.	We saw millions of people.
اِسْتَمَعْنا إلى مَلايينِ الأَشْخاصِ.	We listened to millions of people.

مِلْيُون is used as a first noun in the *IDhaafa*-construct, thus making the noun that follows it genitive, singular, and indefinite, as in the following:

$$تَظاهَرَ مِلْيُونُ عامِلٍ في شَوارِعِ القاهِرَة.$$

A million workers demonstrated in the streets of Cairo.

Like, أَلْفٌ "three million" through "ten million" are expressed by the intended cardinal number, which is always in the feminine, followed by the noun مَلايين in the plural. This formation amounts to an *IDhaafa*-construct. Examine the

ثَلاثَةُ مَلايين	three million	سَبْعَةُ مَلايين	seven million
أَرْبَعَةُ مَلايين	four million	ثَمانِيَةُ مَلايين	eight million
خَمْسَةُ مَلايين	five million	تِسْعَةُ مَلايين	nine million
سِتَّةُ مَلايين	six million	عَشَرَةُ مَلايين	ten million

The numbers ثَلاثَةُ "three" through عَشَرَةُ "ten" before مَلايين "millions" are always in the feminine. In other words, since the singular for مَلايين is the masculine مَلْيون or مَلْيون "million," the gender polarity rule applies. The counted noun after such numbers is always in the singular and genitive, forming a part of *IDhaafa*, as in the following:

في مَكْتَبَةِ الجامِعَةِ ثَلاثَةُ مَلايينِ كِتابٍ.

There are three million books in the university library.

في الـمَكْتَبَةِ ثَلاثَةُ مَلايينِ وَثيقَةٍ.

There are three million documents in the library.

Instead of *IDhaafa*, the use of مِنْ plus the noun can express the same meaning. The above sentences can be expressed by the following:

في مَكْتَبَةِ الجامِعَةِ ثَلاثَةُ مَلايينَ مِنَ الكُتُبِ.

There are three million books in the university library.

في المَكْتَبَةِ ثَلاثَةُ مَلايينَ مِنَ الوَثائِقِ.

There are three million documents in the library.

The number مِلْيار "billion" has been introduced in Arabic, a borrowing from French. Occasionally, one hears the English بِلْيون "billion" as a synonym, from individuals trained in the English-speaking world and in the United Nations' New York Headquarters.

30.11 ORDINAL NUMBERS "FIRST" TO "TENTH" AS ADJECTIVES

(اَلأَعْدادُ التَّرتيبِيَّةُ لِلأَعْدادِ مِنْ واحِدٍ إلى عَشَرَة)

أَوَّل is the ordinal number of واحِد in the masculine. The feminine form is أُولى. Note that the ordinal number for واحِد "one" is phonetically dissimilar to the consonants that comprise أَوَّل. This is not surprising in comparison with several languages. The cardinal numbers are different from the ordinals in many western European languages, including English, French, Spanish, and Italian, among many others. Consider, for example, the English "one" and "first," and "two" and "second." Ordinal numbers function as adjectives. They follow the nouns they modify and agree with them in gender, case, and determination (definite/indefinite). Examine the following sentences:

جورج واشِنْطُن هُوَ الرَّئِيسُ الأَوَّلُ.	George Washington is the first president.
جورج واشِنْطُن كانَ الرَّئِيسَ الأَوَّلَ.	George Washington was the first president.
هذِه الجامِعَةُ هِيَ الجامِعَةُ الأُولى.	This university is the first university.
قَرَأْتُ الكِتابَ الأَوَّلَ.	I read the first book.
قَرَأْتُ الجَرِيدَةَ الأُولى.	I read the first newspaper.

الأُولى is invariable with respect to its case. Moreover, الأُولى is not used to tell time in the same way as the other ordinal numbers (الثّاني والثّالِث، والرّابِع) are used. For example, in time-telling in formal spoken or written Arabic, السّاعةُ الثّانِية "two o'clock," السّاعةُ الثّالِثَة "three o'clock," etc. are used. However, for "one o'clock," only السّاعةُ الواحِدة is used.

Ordinal numbers for اثنان "two" to عَشَرَة "ten" are derived according to the pattern فاعِل. For instance from ثَلاثَة "three" we obtain ثالِث; from سَبعَة "seven" we obtain سابِع and so on. The numbers اثنان "two" and سِتّة "six" present interesting phonetic forms. From اثنان we obtain ثانٍ. However, when ثانٍ is made definite or feminine, a *yaa'* is retrieved, thus we obtain الثّاني (M) and الثّانِية (F), respectively.

On the other hand, the number سِتّة should yield ساتِت according to the فاعِل pattern, a word that is not used in the language. Because of phonetic processes, or the original root of this number in the language, we obtain سادِس instead. A table illustrating cardinal and ordinal numbers is provided at the end of this section.

The ordinal numbers generated by the فاعِل pattern are used as adjectives, with all the conditions required of noun–adjective phrases. The examples below are illustrative:

توماس جَفَرْسون هُوَ الرَّئيسُ الثّالِثُ. — Thomas Jefferson is the third president.

شاهَدْنا الفِلْمَ الخامِسَ. — We saw the fifth movie.

السَّيِّدَةُ سوزان هِيَ الأُسْتاذَةُ الرّابِعَةُ. — Susan is the fourth professor.

تَكَلَّمَ الطُلّابُ مَعَ الأُسْتاذَةِ السّادِسَةِ. — The students spoke with the sixth teacher.

In addition, ordinal numbers are used in reading dates in formal spoken or written Arabic. For example, in reading the date "sixth of April," for example, the following is used:

$$\text{في السادِسِ مِنْ شَهْرِ نيسان (أبريل) عام أَلْفٍ وتِسْعِمائةٍ وتِسْعين.}$$

Or

$$\text{في اليَوْمِ السّادِس مِنْ شَهْرِ نيسان (أبريل) عام أَلْفٍ وتِسْعِمئةٍ وتِسْعين.}$$

30.12 ORDINAL NUMBERS AS ADVERBS

The ordinal numbers generated by فاعِل can also be used as adverbs. In this case, the ordinal number forms must be in the accusative and written with a *tanwiin*. Recall that adverbs are used to modify verbs, as in the following examples:

قَرَأْتُ الكِتابَ أَوَّلاً. — I read the book first.

These adverbial forms of the ordinal numbers, i.e. أَوَّلاً / ثانياً / ثالثاً, can be used to enumerate a list of actions performed. Examine the following discourse:

كَيْفَ تَعْمَلُ القَهْوةَ العَرَبِيَّةَ؟
How do you make Arabic coffee?

أَوَّلاً، نَضَعُ الماءَ في الإِبْريقِ، وثانياً، نُضيفُ السُّكَّرَ، وثالثاً نُضيفُ القَهْوَةَ ثُمَّ نَغْلي الماءَ والسُّكَّرَ والقَهْوَةَ.

First, we put water in the coffee pot, second, we add some sugar, third, we add some coffee, and then we boil the water, sugar and coffee.

30.13 LISTS OF CARDINAL AND ORDINAL NUMBERS

30.13.1 Cardinal and ordinal numbers from 1 to 10

Cardinal	Ordinal masculine	Ordinal feminine	Meaning
واحِدٌ	أَوَّل	أُولى	first
اثْنان	ثانٍ	ثانِيَةٌ	second
ثَلاثَةٌ	ثالِثٌ	ثالِثَةٌ	third
أَرْبَعَةٌ	رابِعٌ	رابِعَةٌ	fourth
خَمْسَةٌ	خامِسٌ	خامِسَةٌ	fifth
سِتَّةٌ	سادِسٌ	سادِسَةٌ	sixth
سَبْعَةٌ	سابِعٌ	سابِعَةٌ	seventh
ثَمانِيَةٌ	ثامِنٌ	ثامِنَةٌ	eighth
تِسْعَةٌ	تاسِعٌ	تاسِعَةٌ	ninth
عَشَرَةٌ	عاشِرٌ	عاشِرَةٌ	tenth

The following two tables illustrate examples of the cardinal and ordinal numbers with the same counted masculine and feminine nouns:

30.13.2 Cardinal numbers with counted nouns

Cardinal number	Counted noun masculine	Counted noun feminine	Meaning
واحِدٌ	كِتابٌ واحِدٌ	سَيّارَةٌ واحِدَةٌ	one car
اثْنان	كِتابان اثْنان	سَيّارتان اثْنَتان	two cars
ثَلاثَةٌ	ثَلاثَةُ كُتُب	ثَلاثُ سَيّارات	three cars
أَرْبَعَةٌ	أَرْبَعَةُ كُتُب	أَرْبَعُ طالِباتٍ	four students (F)
خَمْسَةٌ	خَمْسَةُ مُعَلِّمِينَ	خَمْسُ جامِعاتٍ	five universities
سِتَّةٌ	سِتَّةُ مُدَرِّسِينَ	سِتُّ مُدَرِّساتٍ	six teachers (F)
سَبْعَةٌ	سَبْعَةُ طُلّابٍ	سَبْعُ جَرائِدَ	seven newspapers
ثَمانِيَةٌ	ثَمانِيَةُ مُدَراءَ	ثَماني مُديراتٍ	eight directors (F)
تِسْعَةٌ	تِسْعَةُ أَساتِذَةٍ	تِسْعُ أُسْتاذاتٍ	nine professors (F)
عَشَرَةٌ	عَشَرَةُ مُوَظَّفِينَ	عَشْرُ مُوَظَّفاتٍ	ten employees (F)

30.13.3 Ordinal numbers with counted nouns

Ordinal	Counted noun masculine	Counted noun feminine	Meaning
الأَوَّل	الكِتَابُ الأَوَّلُ	السَّيَّارَةُ الأُولى	the first car
الثَّاني	الكِتَابُ الثَّاني	السَّيَّارَةُ الثَّانِيَةُ	the second car
الثَّالِثُ	الكِتَابُ الثَّالِثُ	السَّيَّارَةُ الثَّالِثَةُ	the third car
الرَّابِعُ	الكِتَابُ الرَّابِعُ	السَّيَّارَةُ الرَّابِعَةُ	the fourth car
الخَامِسُ	الأُسْتَاذُ الخَامِسُ	الأُسْتَاذَةُ الخَامِسَةُ	the fifth teacher (F)
السَّادِسُ	الـمُدِيرُ السَّادِسُ	الـمُدِيرَةُ السَّادِسَةُ	the sixth director (F)
السَّابِعُ	الرَّئِيسُ السَّابِعُ	الجَامِعَةُ السَّابِعَةُ	the seventh university
الثَّامِنُ	الـمُدَرِّسُ الثَّامِنُ	الـمُدَرِّسَةُ الثَّامِنَةُ	the eighth teacher (F)
التَّاسِعُ	البَيْتُ التَّاسِعُ	الـمَدِينَةُ التَّاسِعَةُ	the ninth city
العَاشِرُ	الطَّالِبُ العَاشِرُ	الطَّالِبَةُ العَاشِرَةُ	the tenth student (F)

30.14 FRACTIONS الكُسور

With the exception of نِصْف "half," fractions are formed according to the فُعْلٌ pattern for the numbers three to ten. Thus, from ثَلاثَةٌ "three" we obtain ثُلُثٌ "one third," from أَرْبَعَةٌ "four," رُبْعٌ "one quarter," and so on. سِتَّةٌ "six" presents an interesting case. According to the فُعْلٌ pattern we obtain سُتٌّ, which is not a true word in the language. As a result of some phonetic processes, mainly voicing and forward assimilation, the real word for one sixth is سُدْسٌ.

These fractions are treated as nouns in Arabic. They can be definite or indefinite, can be changed into the dual and plural, they can change their case endings according to their functions in sentences, etc. Thus, we obtain نِصْفان "two halves," أَنْصَاف "halves," سُدْسان "two sixths," أَسْدَاسٌ "sixths," etc. As nouns, these fractions can be counted by the use of the cardinal numbers, forming an *IDhaafa*-construct. Thus, we obtain, for example, ثَلاثَةُ أَرْباع "three quarters," أَرْبَعَةُ أَعْشار "four tenths," etc. It is interesting to note that the plurals of two fractions in particular, namely أَخْماسٌ "fifths" and أَسْداسٌ "sixths" combine to form the commonly used saying ضَرَبَ أَخْماساً في أَسْداس "to be at one's wits' end," to express a state when a person racks his or her brain to find a solution to a dilemma encountered. We should note that the tense of the verb ضَرَبَ "to multiply," can be heard in the present tense.

Fractions are frequently used in statistical literature, in pricing items, and also in time telling. The fractions نِصْف "half," ثُلْث "third," and رُبْع "quarter" are frequently used in these cases.

In pricing items, the question word بِكَم "how much" is followed by the item to be purchased, or the weight unit used, as in the following:

بِكَم هذا القَميصُ؟	How much is this shirt?
هذا القَميصُ بِعَشْرَةِ دَنانيرَ ورُبْعٍ.	This shirt is (for) ten dinars and a quarter.
بِكَم كيلو التُّفاح؟	How much are the apples (by kilogram)?
الكيلو بِدينارٍ ونِصْفٍ.	A dinar and a half for the kilo.

In asking the time, the question word كَم "how much?, how many?," is used followed by the word for hour or time, as in the following:

كَم السّاعَةُ؟	What time is it?
السّاعَةُ الآنَ الواحِدَةُ والثُّلْث.	It is now one o'clock and twenty. (*lit.* "one o'clock and a third")
كَم الوَقْتُ الآنَ؟	What is the time now?
السّاعَةُ الآنَ الخامِسَةُ إلّا رُبْعاً.	It is quarter to five now. (*lit.* "five except/ minus a quarter")

Furthermore, these fractions also become verbs according to the فَعَّلَ (Form II) pattern. We obtain خَمَّسَ "to increase fivefold," سَبَّعَ "to increase sevenfold," etc. From such verbs, اِسْم فاعِل "active participle," اِسْم مَفْعُول "passive participle," and مَصْدَر "verbal nouns" can be derived. For example, from خَمَّسَ "to increase fivefold" we can derive مُخَمِّسٌ "one who increases something fivefold," مُخَمَّسٌ "something that is turned into five parts," and تَخْميسٌ "the act of increasing something fivefold."

CHAPTER 31

Quantifiers
كُلّ، بَعْض، جَميع، مُعْظَم، كِلا، كِلْتا، عِدَّةٌ

Quantifiers are words that express how much of an entity or group is under discussion, for example, كُلّ "all," بَعْض "some," جَميع "all," مُعْظَم "most," عِدَّةٌ مِن "a number of." Quantifiers function mainly as nouns in Arabic and are used as determiners of other nouns in *IDhaafa*-constructs. Quantifiers can add emphasis to a statement. For discussion of emphasis see Chapter 38. Each of these quantifiers is discussed in some detail below.

31.1 كُلّ

31.1.1 كُلّ plus indefinite singular nouns: "each and every"

كُلّ can be followed by indefinite, singular nouns, forming an *IDhaafa*-construct. In this case, كُلّ means "each and every." كُلّ case varies depending on its function in the sentence, as the following examples illustrate:

وَصَلَ كُلُّ طالِبٍ.	Each and every student (M) arrived.
وَصَلَت كُلُّ طالِبَةٍ.	Each and every student (F) arrived.
شاهَدَ الأُسْتاذُ كُلَّ طالِبٍ.	The teacher (M) saw each and every student (M).
سافَرَ الأُسْتاذُ مَعَ كُلِّ طالِبٍ.	The teacher (M) traveled with each and every student.

31.1.2 كُلّ plus definite singular nouns: "the whole of"

In addition, كُلّ can be followed by a definite singular noun to mean "the whole of, all of." This applies only to nouns that are divisible and broken into parts.

The noun following كُلّ must be in the genitive case, forming an *IDhaafa*-construct. Examine the examples below:

هذا هُوَ كُلُّ الكِتابِ.	This is the whole book.
هذِهِ هِيَ كُلُّ المَقالَةِ.	This is the whole essay.
قَرَأْتُ كُلَّ الكِتابِ.	I read the whole book.
هذا السُّؤالُ في كُلِّ الكِتابِ.	This question is in the whole book.

Note that nouns like كِتابٌ and خُبْزٌ, unlike nouns like طالِبٌ and أُستاذٌ, can be divided into portions or parts. In other words, the following asterisked sentences, while technically grammatically correct, are semantically odd:

**شاهَدَ كُلَّ الطّالِبِ.	He saw the whole student.
**وَصَلَ مَعَ كُلِّ الأُستاذِ.	He arrived with the whole teacher.

31.1.3 كُلّ plus definite plural nouns: "all of"

كُلّ can also be followed by definite plural nouns to mean "all of," forming an *IDhaafa*-construct. The case marker of كُلّ varies depending on its function in the sentence, as the following sentences illustrate:

وَصَلَ كُلُّ الطُّلّابِ.	All the students arrived.
هؤُلاءِ كُلُّ الطُّلّابِ.	These are all the students.
شاهَدْنا كُلَّ الطُّلّابِ.	We saw all the students.
وَصَلَ سامي مَعَ كُلِّ الطُّلّابِ.	Sami arrived with all the students.

31.2 بَعْض "SOME OF"

Like كُلّ, the noun بَعْض "some" can form an *IDhaafa*-construct. Its case can also vary, depending on its function in the sentence. Examine the following examples:

هذا بَعْضُ الأَكْلِ. This is some of the food.

أَكَلْتُ بَعْضَ الأَكْلِ. I ate some of the food.

البَطاطا في بَعْضِ الأَكْلِ. There are potatoes in some of the food.

بَعْض can be followed by plural nouns, forming an *IDhaafa*-construct, as in the following:

هؤُلاءِ بَعْضُ الطُّلّابِ. These are some of the students.

شاهَدَ المُديرُ بَعْضَ الطُّلّابِ. The director (M) saw some of the students.

وَصَلَ المُديرُ مَعَ بَعْضِ الطُّلّابِ. The director (M) arrived with some of the students.

31.3 جَميع "ALL OF"

جَميع "all of" must be followed by a plural noun. This quantifier functions as the first term of an *IDhaafa*-construct. Its case also varies depending on its function in the sentence, as in the examples below:

هؤُلاءِ جَميعُ الطُّلّابِ. These are all of the students.

شاهَدَ الأُسْتاذُ جَميعَ الطُّلّابِ. The professor (M) saw all the students.

وَصَلَ المُديرُ مَعَ جَميعِ الطُّلّابِ. The director (M) arrived with all the students.

31.4 مُعْظَم "MOST OF"

مُعْظَم "most of" can be followed by a divisible noun, such as كِتابٌ or أَكْلٌ. Like the preceding quantifiers, it forms *IDhaafa*-constructs; its case can vary, depending on its function in the sentence, as in the following examples:

هذا مُعْظَمُ الأَكْلِ. This is most of the food.

أَكَلوا مُعْظَمَ الأَكْلِ. They ate most of the food.

البَطاطا في مُعْظَمِ الأَكْلِ. Potatoes are in most foods.

As مُعْظَم has the meaning of "most of," this logically implies a larger group of entities and, therefore, can be followed by plural nouns, as in the following examples:

هَؤُلاءِ مُعْظَمُ الطُّلابِ.	These are most of the students.
شاهَدْنا مُعظَمَ الطُّلابِ.	We saw most of the students.
سافَروا مَعَ مُعْظَمِ الطُّلابِ.	They traveled with most of the students.

31.5 كِلا "BOTH"

كِلا is used with dual masculine nouns. It remains invariable when it precedes nouns and forms an *IDhaafa*-construct, as in the following examples:

وَصَلَ كِلا الـمُوَظَّفَيْنِ.	The two employees [both] arrived.
شاهَدْنا كِلا الفِلـمَيْنِ.	We saw [both of] the two films.

كِلا can also follow the noun. In this case, it adds affirmation or emphasis. It also agrees with the noun preceding it in case. The dual suffix pronoun هُما must attach to كِلا. Examine the following:

وَصَلَ الـمُوَظَّفانِ كِلاهُما.	Both of the two employees arrived.
شاهَدْنا الفِلْمَيْنِ كِلَيْهِما.	We saw both of the two films.
هَلْ هذا النَّصُّ في الكِتابَيْنِ كِلَيْهِما؟	Is this text in both of the two books?

31.6 كِلْتا "BOTH"

كِلْتا is used with dual feminine nouns, and behaves in the same way as كِلا. When it precedes the noun, كِلْتا remains invariable and forms an *IDhaafa*-construct, as in the following:

وَصَلَتْ كِلْتا البِنْتَيْنِ.	Both girls arrived.
شاهَدْنا كِلْتا السَّيّارَتَيْنِ.	We saw both cars.

When كِلْتا follows the noun, it must agree with the feminine noun in case. Examine the following:

وَصَلَتِ البِنْتانِ كِلْتاهُما.   Both girls arrived.

شاهَدْنا السَّيّارَتَيْـنِ كِلْتَيْهِما.   We saw both cars.

هذِهِ الأَخْبارُ في الجَريدَتَـيْنِ كِلْتَيْهِما.   This news is in both papers.

31.7 عِدَّةٌ "MANY, A NUMBER OF"

عِدَّةٌ is used with plural indefinite nouns, both masculine and feminine. It functions as the first noun in an *IDhaafa*-construct. Its case can vary depending on its function in the sentence. Examine the following examples:

حَضَرَ الاجْتِماعَ عِدَّةُ مُوَظَّفينَ.
A number of employees attended the meeting.

قابَلَ صَديقي عِدَّةَ زُوّارٍ.
My friend met many visitors.

تَكَلَّمْنا مَعَ عِدَّةِ مُوَظَّفاتٍ.
We talked with many employees (F, Pl).

31.8 THE QUANTIFIERS AS ADJECTIVES

The quantifiers introduced in this chapter can be used as adjectives, i.e., they follow nouns to add emphasis. However, two conditions must be met: (1) The quantifiers must be followed by suffixal pronouns identical in number and gender to the nouns they modify; and (2) the quantifiers must agree with the preceding nouns in case, as in the examples below:

قَرَأْنا الكِتابَ كُلَّهُ.   We read the book, all of it.

شاهَدْنا الأَفْلامَ كُلَّها.   We saw the movies, all of them.

رَجَعَ الطُّلّابُ جَميعُهُم.   All of the students (M) returned.

تَقابَلَتِ الأُستاذَةُ مَعَ الطّالِباتِ جَميعِهِنَّ.   The professor (F) met with all of the students (F).

This construction is known as *apposition* (see Chapter 37). The preceding sentences, in which جَمِيع and كُلّ are used as adjectives, are equivalent in meaning to the following sentences, where جَمِيع and كُلّ form a part of the *IDhaafa*-construct:

قَرَأْنا كُلَّ الكِتابِ.	We read the whole book.
شاهَدْنا كُلَّ الأَفلامِ.	We saw all of the films.
رَجَعَ جَمِيعُ الطُّلابِ.	All of the students returned.
تَقابَلَتِ الأُستاذَةُ مَعَ جَمِيعِ الطّالِباتِ.	The professor (F) met with all of the students (F), all of them.

The difference between these structures is only a stylistic variation.

CHAPTER 32

Haal clauses الحَال
(accusative of circumstance)

الحَال, a "circumstantial clause," provides information about the circumstance or condition of the action expressed in the main verb of the sentence. This structure answers the question of "how" the event took place. There are often two events happening simultaneously, the main event expressed in the main clause, and another, subordinate clause, that describes the circumstance under which this action takes or took place. حَال clauses can be expressed in the following five ways:

32.1 A NOMINAL SENTENCE AS A SUBORDINATE CLAUSE

A nominal sentence must be conjoined to the main clause by a *waaw* referred to as *Haal-waaw*, وَاو الحَال. This *Haal*-sentence must have as its head an independent pronoun that refers to the subject of the verb in the main clause. The tense of the verb in the main clause can vary. The verb in the subordinate clause is usually in the present tense, as in the following sentences in the singular:

وَصَلتِ الطَّالِبَةُ وَهِيَ تَحْمِلُ الكُتُبَ.

The student (F) arrived [while she was] carrying the books.

تَرَكَ صَديقي البَيْتَ وَهُوَ يَضْحَكُ.

My friend (M) left the house [while he was] laughing.

تَمْشي صَديقَتي في الشَّارِعِ وهِيَ دائِماً تُدَنْدِنُ.

My friend (F) walks down the street constantly humming.

The following sentences replicate the preceding in the dual:

وَصَلَتِ الطّالِبَتانِ وَهُما تَحْمِلانِ الكُتُبَ.

The students (F, D) arrived carrying the books.

تَرَكَ صَديقايَ البَيْتَ وَهُما يَضْحَكانِ.

My friends (M, D) left the house laughing.

تَمْشي صَديقتايَ في الشّارِع وَهُما دائِماً تُدَنْدِنانِ.

My friends (F, D) walk down the street constantly humming.

The following are in the plural:

وَصَلَتِ الطّالِباتُ وَهُنَّ يَحْمِلْنَ الكُتُبَ.

The students (F, Pl) arrived carrying books.

تَرَكَ أَصْدِقائي البَيْتَ وُهُم يَضْحَكونَ.

My friends (M, Pl) left the house laughing.

تَمْشي صَديقاتي في الشّارِع وهُنَّ دائِماً يُدَنْدِنَّ.

My friends (F, Pl) walk down the street constantly humming.

32.2 VERBAL SENTENCES WITHOUT واو الحال

This structure amounts to two verbal sentences conjoined without the presence of واو الحال and without the presence of the independent pronoun in reference to the subject of the main sentence. The verb in the subordinate sentence, however, must always be in the present tense.

The three preceding sentences in 32.1 above are replicated below with the necessary changes to illustrate this structure:

وَصَلَتِ الطّالِبَةُ تَحْمِلُ الكُتُبَ.

The student (F) arrived carrying the books.

تَرَكَ صَديقي البَيْتَ يَضْحَكُ.

My friend left the house laughing.

تَمْشي صَديقتي في الشّارِع دائِماً تُدَنْدِنُ.

My friend (F) walks down the street constantly humming.

The preceding sentences in the dual and plural are replicated below indicating the verbal sentence *Haal* clause without the *Haal waaw*:

وَصَلَتِ الطّالِبَتانِ تَحْمِلانِ الكُتُبَ.

The students (F, D) arrived carrying the books.

تَرَكَ صَديقايَ البَيْتَ يَضْحَكانِ.

My friends (M, D) left the house laughing.

تَمْشي صَديقتايَ في الشّارِعِ دائِماً تُدَنْدِنانِ.

My friends (F, D) walk down the street constantly humming.

وَصَلَتِ الطّالِباتُ يَحْمِلْنَ الكُتُبَ.

The students (F, Pl) arrived carrying books.

تَرَكَ أَصْدِقائي البَيْتَ يَضْحَكونَ.

My friends (M, Pl) left the house laughing.

تَمْشي صَديقاتي في الشّارِعِ دائِماً يُدَنْدِنَّ.

My friends (F, Pl) walk down the street constantly humming.

32.3 EQUATIONAL SENTENCES

The حال clause could also be expressed by the use of an equational sentence. The main and subordinate clauses must be conjoined by واو الحال. In addition, the subject of the subordinate equational sentence must begin with an independent pronoun referring to the subject in the main clause. Examples below will include sentences in the singular, dual, and plural in the masculine and feminine:

عادَ المُسافِرُ وهُوَ سَعيدٌ.	The traveler (M, Sg) returned happily.
عادَتِ المُسافِرَةُ وهِيَ سَعيدَةٌ.	The traveler (M, F) returned happily.
رَجَعَ الرَّجُلانِ وهُما غاضِبانِ.	The men (M, D) returned angrily.
سافَرَتِ المَرْأَتانِ وهُما سَعيدَتانِ.	The women (F, D) traveled happily.
رَجَعَ الرِّجالُ وهُمْ غاضِبونَ.	The men (Pl) returned angrily.
سافَرَتِ النِّساءُ وهُنَّ سَعيداتٌ.	The women (Pl) traveled happily.

32.4 USE OF ACTIVE PARTICIPLES اِسْم فاعِل PASSIVE PARTICIPLES اِسْم مَفْعول OR NOUNS

Active participles, passive participles, or regular nouns can also be used to express الحَال, in other words, the circumstance in which the action in the main clause was performed. These elements must always be accusative and indefinite. They must also agree with the subject of the main verb in number and gender. Consider the following examples in the singular, dual, and plural:

جاءَ إلى الـمُسْتَشْفى مَجْروحاً.

He came to the hospital wounded.

عَرَفْتُهُ أُسْتاذاً.

I knew him as a teacher.

رَجَعَتْ أُخْتي ضاحِكَةً.

My sister returned laughing.

حَضَرَتِ الطّالِبَتانِ ضاحِكَتَيْنِ.

The students (F, D) returned laughing.

غادَرَ الـمُوَظَّفانِ الـمَكْتَبَ سَعيدَيْنِ.

The employees (M, D) left the office happy.

جاءوا إلى الـمَكْتَبِ مُسْتَفْسِرينَ عَنِ الحادِثِ.

They (M, Pl) came to the office inquiring about the accident.

تَخَرَّجَتِ الـمُمَرِّضاتُ مِنَ الجامِعَةِ سَعيدات.

The nurses (F, Pl) graduated from the university happily.

32.5 USE OF PREPOSITIONAL PHRASES شِبْهُ جُمْلَة

The use of a prepositional phrase, called شِبْهُ جُمْلَة in traditional Arabic grammar, can also be used to provide information regarding the manner in which a certain event has happened as expressed by the verb in the main clause. Examine the following examples:

أَقْبَلَ عَلَيْنا في لَهْفَةٍ.

He approached us anxiously.

تَكَلَّمَ الوَلَدُ إلى أُمِّهِ في أَدَبٍ.

The boy spoke to his mother politely.

تَحَدَّثَ عَنْ هذا الـمَوْضوع عَنْ مَعرِفَةٍ.

He discussed this topic knowledgeably.

قابَلَ الأوْلادُ أفْرادَ الأُسْرَةِ بِشَوْقٍ كَبيرٍ.

The children (M, Pl) met the members of the family with immense eagerness.

32.6 NEGATION OF *HAAL* CLAUSE نَفْي الحال

Present tense verbs in *Haal* clauses are negated by the use of the negative particle لا placed immediately before the verb in the subordinate clause, as in the following examples:

وَصَلتِ الطّالِبَةُ وهِيَ لا تَـحْمِلُ الكُتُبَ.

The student (F) arrived [while she was] not carrying books.

تَرَكَ صَديقي البَيْتَ وهُوَ لا يَضْحَكُ.

My friend left the house [while he was] not laughing.

If the *Haal* clause is an equational sentence, the negative form of the verb كانَ is used. This is done in two ways, either (1) by the use of the negative particle ما with the past tense of كانَ or (2) لَمْ with the present tense of كانَ in the jussive. Examine the following two pairs of sentences in which the first sentence is in the affirmative, the second in the negative:

رَجَعَتِ البِنْتُ وهِيَ غاضِبَةٌ.

The girl returned angrily (*lit.* "and she was angry").

رَجَعَتِ البِنْتُ وما كانَت غاضِبَةً.

The girl came back (while she was) not angry.

رَجَعَ الـمُعَلِّمونَ وهُمْ غاضِبونَ.

The teachers returned angrily (*lit.* "and they are / were angry").

رَجَعَ الـمُعَلِّمونَ وَلَمْ يكونوا غاضِبينَ.

The teachers returned (while they were) not angry.

32.7 *HAAL* CLAUSES IN THE PAST TENSE

The examples of *Haal* clauses in verbal sentences from 32.2 had verbs in the present tense. *Haal* clauses can also have verbs in the past tense. However, the use of the particle قَد followed by a past tense verb is obligatory in this case (see Chapter 19 on past perfect tense). Examine the following examples:

جاءَ الأُسْتاذُ إلى الجامِعَةِ وَقَد اجْتَمَعَ مَعَ الرَّئيسِ.

The professor came to the university having met with the president.

عادَ الأَصْدِقاءُ مِنَ الحَفلَةِ وَقَدْ أَكلوا وَشَرِبوا كَثيراً.

The friends returned from the party having eaten and drunk a lot.

CHAPTER 33

Tamyiiz التَّمييز
(accusative of specification)

Tamyiiz, "accusative of specification," is a construct using the indefinite and accusative form of a noun to add specification to a sentence by narrowing its terms. This structure is used in declarative sentences, or in reported statements introduced by verbs such as قالَ إنَّ "he said that," ذَكَرَ أَنَّ "he mentioned that," تَقَرَّرَ أَنَّ "it was affirmed that," and so on.

33.1 COMPARISONS USING *TAMYIIZ*

Tamyiiz may be used to compare two or more entities in one or more respect(s), as in the following example:

القاهِرَة أَكْثَرُ مِن دِمَشْق سُكّاناً.

Cairo is more than Damascus population-wise.

The use of سُكّاناً singles out the specific, shared feature that is used as the point of comparison between Cairo and Damascus.

Recall that comparative adjectives اِسْم التَّفْضيل can also be used to make comparisons between two or more entities (see Chapter 27):

سُكّانُ القاهِرَة أَكْثَرُ مِنْ سُكّانِ دِمَشْق.

The population of Cairo is larger than the population of Damascus.

A *tamyiiz* construct may have a comparative form of an adjective expressing quantity or quality, followed by a noun that is always accusative and indefinite. Consider the examples below:

دِمَشْق أَعْرَقُ مِنْ الرِّياض تاريخاً.

Damascus is more deep-rooted in history than Riyadh.

سوزان أَقْدَرُ مِنْ لَيْلى طَبْخاً.

Suzanne is more capable in cooking than Laila.

الرُّزُ أَغْلى مِنَ البُرْغُل سِعْراً.

Rice is more expensive than bulgur price-wise.

لُبْنان أَجْمَلُ مِنَ الكُوَيْت طَقْساً.

Lebanon is more clement than Kuwait with respect to weather.

السَّعوديّة أَكْثَرُ مِنَ اليَمَن نَفْطاً.

Saudi Arabia is richer than Yemen with respect to oil.

العائلَةُ العَرَبيَّةُ أَكْثَرُ مِنَ العائلَةِ الأمريكيّة أَطفالاً.

The Arab family is larger than the American family with respect to
children.

33.2 NUMERALS 11 TO 99 AND *TAMYIIZ*

The numerals 11 to 99 are followed by accusative nouns (see Chapter 30 on
numbers), which are considered part of the *tamyiiz* structure in Arabic. The
counted noun must be indefinite and singular, as in the following examples:

سافَرَ أَحَدَ عَشَرَ طالِباً.	Eleven students (M) traveled.
قابَلْنا خَمسينَ طالِبَةً.	We interviewed fifty students (F).
رَجَعَت ثَمانيَ عَشَرَةَ مُوَظَّفَةً.	Eighteen employees (F) returned.
قَرَأوا تِسْعَةً وتِسْعينَ كِتاباً.	They read ninety-nine books.

33.3 WEIGHTS, MEASURES, AND *TAMYIIZ*

Materials that are explicitly conveyed in units of weight or measure may be
expressed in a *tamyiiz* construct in the accusative, following the unit of weight
or measure. Terms expressing weight include رَطْلٌ "pound" and the newly-
introduced كيلوغرام "kilogram," طَنٌّ "a thousand kilograms," the classical قِنْطارٌ
"a varying weight, *kantar*." Terms that express measure include ذِراعٌ "cubit, length
measure," or newly-introduced foreign word مِتْرٌ "meter," كيلو مِتر "kilometer,"
ميل "a mile," يارْدة "a yard," هِكتار "a hectare," and the Egypt-specific فَدّان "a
land measure." These nouns form the *tamyiiz* construct, as in the following:

اِشْتَرَيْتُ مِتْرَيْن قُطْناً.   I bought two meters of cotton.

باعَنا ثَلاثَةَ أَرْطالٍ تَمْراً.   He sold us three pounds of dates.

يَمْلِكُ هِكْتاراً أَرْضاً.   He owns a hectare of land.

Thus the nouns following the measure or weigh words قُطْناً "cotton," تَمْراً "dates," and أَرْضاً "land" in the preceding sentences must always be indefinite and accusative. They specify the substances of the measure and weight unit nouns that precede them.

Weights and measures can also be expressed by an *IDhaafa*-construct (see Chapter 8 on *IDhaafa*). The preceding examples can be expressed by the use of an *IDhaafa* structure as follows:

اِشْتَرَيْتُ مِتْرَيْ قُطْنٍ.   I bought two meters of cotton.

باعَنا ثَلاثَةَ أَرْطالٍ تَمْرٍ.   He sold us three pounds of dates.

يَمْلِكُ هِكْتارَ أَرْضٍ.   He owns a hectare of land.

The weights and measures in the preceding examples can be expressed by the use of the preposition مِن followed by the noun expressing the materials, as follows:

اِشْتَرَيْتُ مِتْرَيْنِ مِنَ القُطْنِ.   I bought two meters of cotton.

باعَنا ثَلاثَةَ أَرْطالٍ مِنَ التَّمْرِ.   He sold us three *pounds* of dates.

يَمْلِكُ هِكْتاراً مِنَ الأَرْضِ.   He owns a hectare of land.

This last pattern is more common in Modern Standard Arabic.

33.4 كَمْ "HOW MUCH," "HOW MANY" AND *TAMYIIZ*

Nouns following the interrogative word كَمْ are always in the singular, indefinite, accusative. These nouns are considered to be a *tamyiiz* construct. Examine the following:

كَم كِتاباً قَرَأْتَ؟   How many books did you read?

كَم بَيْتاً بَنَتِ الشَّرِكَةُ؟   How many houses did the company build?

CHAPTER 34

Exception الاِسْتِثْناء

Several particles are used to express exception in Arabic, the notion that some entity is singled out as a non-participant in the performance of an event or as its only participant. These include: سِوى / عَدا إلّا "except," غَيْرُ "other than," ما خَلا and ما عَدا / and حاشا – all meaning "except," or "except for." ما خَلا and حاشا appear more in classical texts; they are not as frequently used in Modern Standard Arabic. عَدا has another equivalent preceded by the negative particle ما to express the same meaning. ما خَلا on the other hand is invariable and always preceded by the negative particle ما. However, حاشا is never preceded by the negative particle ما. Each of these particles will be presented separately in the following sections:

34.1 إلّا

This particle is used in affirmative sentences to indicate that someone or some entity is not a participant in an event performed by several others. The noun following إلّا in this case must be in the accusative and indefinite (marked by *tanwiin*), as in the following:

سافَرَ الطُّلّابُ إلّا طالِباً. The students traveled except one.

تَكَلَّمَتِ الـمُعَلِّماتُ إلّا مُعَلِّمَةً. All the teachers spoke except one.

The accusative noun following إلّا can be definite by virtue of its being a part of a definite *IDhaafa*-construct, as in the following:

حَضَرَ الـمُدَرِّسونَ إلّا مُدَرِّسَ العَرَبِيَّةِ.
All the instructors came except the Arabic instructor.

إلّا can be used before nouns in sentences negated by one of the negative particles لا / ما / لَم / لَن / لَيْس. The case of the noun following إلّا can be accusative or nominative, as in the following:

لَمْ يُسافِرِ الـمُعَلِّمونَ إلّا مُعَلِّماً واحِداً.

The teachers did not travel except for one.

لَمْ يُسافِرِ الـمُعَلِّمونَ إلّا مُعَلِّمٌ واحِدٌ.

The teachers did not travel except for one.

In sentences where the فاعِل is not explicitly stated, the case of the noun following إلّا depends on the verb used. If the verb is intransitive, the noun following it must be in the nominative, as in the following:

لَمْ يَفُزْ إلّا طالِبانِ.

None succeeded except two students.

لَمْ يَضْحَكْ إلّا مُدَرِّسونَ ثَلاثَةٌ.

No one laughed except (for) three instructors.

On the other hand, if the verb whose فاعِل is not explicitly stated is transitive, the noun following إلّا is treated as a direct object marked for the accusative case, as in the following:

ما شاهَدوا إلّا فِلْماً واحِداً.

lit. "They did not see but one film." or "They only saw one film."

لَمْ يَقْرَأْ إلّا كِتابَيْنِ.

lit. "He did not read but two books." or "He only read two books."

34.2 ما عَدا

The noun following ما عَدا must be in the accusative. Examine the following sentences:

شاهَدَتِ الـمُعَلِّمَةُ كُلَّ الطُّلّابِ ما عَدا طالِباً واحِداً.

The teacher (F) saw all the students except (for) one student.

زُرْنا الـمَدارِسَ ما عَدا «مَدرَسَةَ غَرْناطة».

We visited the schools except Granada School.

حَضَرَ الطُّلّابُ ما عَدا طالِباً واحِداً.

All the students (M, Pl) came but one.

وَصَلَت كُلُّ الـمُدَرِّساتِ ما عَدا مُدَرِّسَةً واحِدَةً.

All the teachers (F, Pl) came but one.

34.3 عَدا

A variation of ما عَدا is عَدا without the negative particle ما. The noun following this particle can be either in the accusative, as in the following example:

شاهَدَتِ الـمُعَلِّمَةُ الطُّلّابَ عَدا طالِباً واحِداً.

The teacher saw the students except (for) one.

Or it can be in the genitive, as in the following:

شاهَدَتِ الـمُعَلِّمَةُ الطُّلّابَ عَدا طالِبٍ واحِدٍ.

The teacher saw the students except (for) one.

34.4 غَيْرُ

This particle can be used in affirmative or negated sentences. It functions as the first term of the *IDhaafa*-construct; the noun following غَير is in the genitive. غَير is in the accusative in affirmative sentences, as in the following example:

سافَرَ كُلُّ الطُّلّابِ غَيْرَ واحِدٍ.

All the students traveled except (for) one.

حَضَرَ الطُّلابُ غَيْرَ خالِد.

The students all came except Khaled.

Following transitive verbs, غَيْرُ is marked for the accusative case, as in the following:

ما شاهَدَتِ الأُسْتاذَةُ غَيْرَ طالِبٍ واحِدٍ.

The teacher (F) did not see (anyone) except (for) one student.

ما زاروا غَيْرَ مَدينَةٍ واحِدَةٍ.

lit. "They did not visit but one city." or "They only visited one city."

Following prepositions, غَير ends with *kasra*, the genitive marker, as in the following:

مَرّوا بِغَيْرِ مَدينَةٍ.

They passed through more than one city.

Following a negated intransitive verb غَير is in the nominative, as in the following:

ما سافَرَ غَيرُ طالِبٍ واحِدٍ.

No one traveled except (for) one student.

34.5 سِوى

This invariable particle must be followed by a noun in the genitive, thus forming an *IDhaafa*-construct. The noun following this particle can be indefinite or definite, as in the following examples:

سافَرَ كُلُّ الطلّابِ سِوى طالِبٍ واحِدٍ.

All the students traveled except (for) one.

سافَرَ كُلُّ الطُّلّابِ سوى الطّالِبِ الجَديدِ.

All the students traveled except the new one.

زاروا الجامِعاتِ سِوى جامِعَةِ خَلَب.

They visited (all) the universities except Aleppo University.

In addition, سِوى can have a suffixal pronoun attached to it. This pronoun is usually a referent to someone previously mentioned in the discourse:

ما سافَرَ أَحَدٌ سِواها.

None traveled except for her.

لَمْ نُقابِلْ سِواهُ.

We did not meet anyone except him.

In the sentence above, the pronoun refers to a female who has been previously mentioned by discourse participants; in the second the pronoun refers to a person previously introduced.

34.6 ما خَلا

This particle, infrequently used, is invariable; its behavior is similar to that of ما عَدا introduced above. In other words, the noun following ما خَلا must be in the accusative, as in the following:

شاهَدَتِ الـمُعَلِّمَةُ كُلَّ الطُّلّابِ ما خَلا طالِباً واحِداً.

The teacher saw all the students except (for) one.

زُرْنا الـمَدارِسَ ما خَلا «مَدْرَسَةَ غَرْناطَة».

We visited (all) the schools except Granada School.

34.7 خَلا

A variation of ما خَلا is خَلا without the negative particle ما. The noun following this particle can be either in the accusative, as in the following example:

شاهَدَتِ الـمُعَلِّمَةُ الطُّلّابَ خَلا طالِباً واحِداً.

The teacher saw (all) the students except (for) one.

Or it can be in the genitive, as in the following:

شاهَدَتِ الـمُعَلِّمَةُ الطُّلّابَ خَلا طالِبٍ واحِدٍ.

The teacher saw (all) the students except (for) one.

34.8 حاشا

This particle is invariable; it cannot be preceded by the negative particle ما. The noun following حاشا can be either in the accusative, as in the following:

حَضَرَ الـمُديرونَ حاشا مُديراً.

The directors came except for one.

Or it can be in the genitive, as in:

حَضَرَ الـمُديرونَ حاشا مُدير.

The directors came except for one.

The particles that are not preceded by the negative particle ما, namely عَدا / حاشا and خَلا, exhibit identical behavior in that they are followed by either accusative or genitive nouns.

34.9 باسْتِثْناء

The notion of exception can be expressed by the use of the invariable prepositional phrase باسْتِثْناء, which consists of the preposition بِ and the *maSdar* اسْتِثْناء. It may be used with affirmative or negated sentences. This phrase could be the first noun in the *IDhaafa*-construct, as in the following example:

حَضَرَ كُلُّ الطلّابِ باسْتِثْناءِ طالِب واحِدٍ.
All the students came except (for) one student.

ما سافَرَتِ الـمُعَلِّماتُ باستِثْناءِ مُعَلِّمَةٍ واحِدَةٍ.
The teachers (F) did not travel except (for) one.

دَخَلَت كُلَّ الصُّفوفِ باسْتِثْناءِ صَفٍّ واحِدٍ.
She entered all the classrooms except (for) one.

CHAPTER 35

Vocative الـمُنادى

The vocative structure is the means of calling for an addressee's attention. The most commonly used vocative particles, حُروف النِّداء in Arabic, are the following: يا followed by أَيُّها and أَيَّتُها. There are less commonly used particles that include أَيا and أَيُّ. Each of these particles is restricted in usage. In addition, each has an impact on the case and determination (definite/indefinite) of nouns following it. Each particle is presented separately.

35.1 يا

يا is commonly used to address a specific person or specific persons directly. Masculine or feminine nouns can follow this particle. يا can be followed by:

1. A proper noun, such as أَحْمَد، مَرْيَم, as in يا أَحْمَد or يا مَرْيَم
2. A common indefinite noun or title of a person familiar to the interlocutor. The noun in this instance must be in the nominative case without the *tanwiin* "nunation," as in the following examples:

يا أُسْتاذُ	O, professor
يا طالبُ	O, student
يا سَيِّدَةُ	O, madam
يا آنِسَةُ	O, miss

3. An *IDhaafa*-construct. The noun following يا, in this case, i.e. the first noun of the *IDhaafa*, must be in the accusative without the *tanwiin*, as in the following examples:

يا أُسْتاذَ الأَدَبِ العَرَبِيِّ...	O, professor of Arabic literature
يا مَلِكَ البِلادِ...	O, your majesty

يا أَخا العَرَب...   O, dear friend

يا مُعَلِّمَ الصَّفِّ...   O, teacher

يا طالِبَ الجامِعَةِ...   O, university student

يا أَميرَ الـمُؤْمنينَ...   O, the commander of the faithful

Dual nouns in the accusative can follow this particle. In the *IDhaafa*-construct the *nuun* in dual or plural nouns must be dropped, as in the following:

يا مُهَنْدِسَيْ الشَّرِكَةِ...   O, you (D) engineers (M)

يا طالِبَتَيْ الصَّفِّ...   O, you (D) students (F)

يا أُسْتاذَتَيْ الجامِعَةِ...   O, you (D) university professors (F)

Similarly, plural nouns can also follow this particle. Regular masculine plural nouns in the *IDhaafa*-construct lose their *nuun*, as in the following:

يا مُعَلِّمي الجامِعَةِ...   O, you (Pl) university professors (M)

يا مُديري الشَّرِكَةِ...   O, you (Pl) company directors (M)

يا طالِباتِ الصَّفِّ...   O, you (Pl) students (F)

يا مُهَنْدِساتِ الشَّرِكَةِ...   O, you (Pl) engineers (F)

4. A common indefinite noun. The noun in this instance must be indefinite, accusative with the *tanwiin*. This construction is used when the addressee is not known or familiar to the speaker, as in the following examples:

يا رَجُلاً لا تَرْمِ الوَرَقَ في الشّارِعِ!   Sir, don't throw paper in the street!

يا طالِباً، اُدْرُسْ تَنْجَحْ!   O, student (M), if you study, you will be successful!

يا سَيِّدةً، اِرْجَعي إلى الوَراءِ مِنْ فَضْلِك!   Madam, please go back!

5. A derived adjective, whether اِسْمُ الفاعِل "active participle," or اِسْمُ الـمَفْعولِ "passive participle," or a regular adjective, as in the following:

يا ظالِماً، اِتَّقِ اللهَ!   O, you oppressor, fear God!

يا كَسولاً حانَ وَقْتُ العَمَلِ!   O, you lazy one, time to work!

يا مَظلوماً، الفَرَجُ آتٍ!   O, you oppressed, relief is near/coming!

يا مُحْسِناً لا تَبْخَلْ عَلى الفُقَراءِ!   O, you charitable one, don't be tight-fisted with the poor!

It is possible to drop the vocative particle يا in addressing a person or persons familiar to the caller. The structure is an *IDhaafa*-construct with the first noun in the accusative, as in the following examples:

صَديقَ العُمْرِ!   O, my lifelong friend!

طُلّابَ الصَّفِّ!   Students!

زَيْنَ الشَّبابِ!   You, the handsomest of men!

However, the deletion of يا is not possible with اللہ "God," as in the following:

يا اللهِ!   O, God!

The use of يا as a vocative particle denotes a stylistic variation known in Arabic grammar as اِسْتِغاثَة "invocation for help." The use of يا in this case is obligatory and must be followed by لِ in specifying the problem, as in:

يا لَلْحُرّاسِ لِلنّارِ!   O, guards, fire!

يا لَلنّاسِ لِلْمُصابِ!   O, people, the injured one!

Moreover, يا expresses exclamation when a person witnesses an awe-inspiring phenomenon or event. يا can be followed, in this case, by لَ or لِ attached to a definite noun, as in the following, expressing exclamation about an awe-inspiring event or person:

يا لِلْحُسْنِ! or يا لَلْحُسْنِ!   What a beauty!

يا لِلْغُروبِ! or يا لَلْغُروبِ!   What a sunset!

The preceding exclamation can be expressed without لَ or لِ, thus making the nouns accusative, as in the following:

يا حُسْناً! What a beauty!

يا غُروباً! What a sunset!

The phrase يا إلهي "Oh, my God!" is not so much a call to God for help as it is an expression of wonderment and surprise as a result of observing some event or phenomenon. Whereas the phrase يا إلهي uses the vocative particle يا this particle is dropped in the use of اللّهُمَّ, as in:

اللّهُمَّ، أَعْطِنا الصَّبْرَ! God, give us patience!

اللّهُمَّ، مِنْكَ العَفْوُ والـمَغْفِرَةُ! God, we seek forgiveness from You!

35.2 نُدْبَة "LAMENTATION"

Another form of the vocative is what Arab grammarians refer to as نُدْبَة "lamentation," which is often used to express sadness, impatience, or a feeling of impending or manifest disaster, or one that has happened. Two particles are used in *nudba*, namely يا or وا. However, the use of يا is less common than وا, which is often followed by the name of a person or a place in the nominative to whom a disaster has befallen, as in the following:

وا مُحَمَّدُ! O, Muhammad!

وا فاطِمَةُ! O, Fatima!

The noun following وا often has the suffixal pronoun for third person masculine singular appended to it, namely ه, by which someone bemoans the fate of a person or thing dear to his/her heart. Consider the following:

وا لَيْلاه! O, my Laila!

وا قُدْساه! O, what befell Jerusalem!

The *nudba* particle can be followed by the *IDhaafa*-construct, in which the first noun must be in the accusative, as in the following:

وا مُصلِحَ الوَطَنِ!   O, reformer of the land!

وا ناشِرَ العِلمِ!   O, promulgator of knowledge!

35.3 أَيُّها

أَيُّها is used in public speeches with masculine nouns, or with a mixed group of males and females. In modern Arab societies, this particle is often used to introduce radio or television programs, or speakers in a public speech setting. Nouns following this particle must have the definite article الـ and must be in the nominative. Nouns following singular, dual, or plural nouns can follow أَيُّها. Consider the following examples:

أَيُّها الأَخُ الكَريمُ!   My dear friend!

أَيُّها الأَخَوانِ الكَريمانَ!   My dear friends (M, D)!

أَيُّها الإِخوَةُ المُواطِنون!   My countrymen (M, Pl)!

أَيُّها الأَساتِذَةُ الكِرامُ!   Distinguished professors (M, Pl)!

أَيُّها السَّيِّداتُ والآنِساتُ والسّادَةُ الكِرامُ!   Esteemed ladies and gentlemen (F/M, Pl)!

35.4 أَيَّتُها

أَيَّتُها is used with feminine nouns to address an all-female group. The noun following أَيَّتُها must be in the nominative, as in the following:

أَيَّتُها السَّيِّداتُ الكَريماتُ!   Gracious ladies (F)!

أَيَّتُها المُعَلِّماتُ الفاضِلاتُ!   Highly esteemed teachers (F)!

أَيَّتُها الخِرِّيجاتُ النَّجيباتُ!   Distinguished graduates (F)!

35.5 يا أَيُّها / يا أَيَّتُها

In Quranic Arabic يا and أَيُّها are combined in one vocative particle يا أَيُّها, as in:

يا أَيُّها الَّذينَ آمَنوا...   O, believers...

يا أَيُّها النّاس...   O, people...

أَيَّتُها and يا are also combined to address feminine nouns, as in:

يا أَيَّتُها النَّفْسُ المُطْمَئِنَّة   O, [thou] soul in complete satisfaction...

يا أَيُّها and يا أَيَّتُها are heard in Modern Standard Arabic, especially in formal speeches.

35.6 أَي

The vocative particle أَيْ is used less frequently in Modern Standard Arabic. This particle is likely to be encountered in elevated styles of written Arabic, usually followed by a definite diminutive or proper noun, typically a son or a daughter. Its usage expresses emotional closeness to the addressee, as in the following:

أَيْ بُنَيَّ!   O, my [little] son!

أَيْ بُنَيَّتي!   O, my [little] daughter!

أَيْ أَحَمَد!   O, Ahmad!

The word بُنَيّ is the diminutive form of اِبْن "son." On the other hand, بُنَيَّتي has the diminutive form بُنَيَّة derived from بِنْتٌ "daughter, girl," plus the possessive suffix ي "my."

CHAPTER 36

Exclamation التَّعَجُّب

Several forms are used to express exclamation, wonderment, a sense of awe or disgust.

36.1 ما PLUS COMPARATIVE ADJECTIVES

One method is by the use of the particle ما followed by a comparative form of an adjective expressing a state. The comparative adjective must always be in the accusative case, ending with one *fat-Ha*. Following ما plus the comparative adjective form, a noun in the accusative case must be used. Consider the following examples:

ما أَجْمَلَ السَّماءَ!	How beautiful the sky is!
ما أَلَذَّ الطَّعامَ !	How delicious this food is!
ما أَفْظَعَ هذِهِ الحَرْبَ!	How horrible this war is!

With basic color words such as أَحْمَرُ "red," أَزْرَقُ "blue," and others formed from اِفْعَلَّ verbs (Form IX), the preceding paradigm does not apply. Instead, the accusative comparative forms of adjectives which express the intensity of color such as أَشَدَّ (from شَديدٌ "strong, intense") and أَغْمَقَ (from غامِق "deep in color") are used (see Chapter 4 on color adjectives). This adjective form is followed by the *maSdar* for colors in the accusative. The noun following the *maSdar* is in the genitive, essentially forming the second noun of the *IDhaafa*-construct. Examine the following examples:

ما أَشَدَّ حُمْرَةَ الأَزْهارِ!	How deep the redness of flowers is!
ما أَغْمَقَ خُضْرَةَ الشَّجَرِ!	How deep the verdancy of trees is!

Similarly, the expression مَا أَشَدَّ "how intense," or others expressing degrees of intensity such as مَا أَكْثَرَ "how much," or مَا أَقَلَّ "how less, few," for example, are used with *maSdar*s derived from intransitive verbs, such as غَضَبٌ "anger," from غَضِبَ "to be angry," and نَوْمٌ "sleep," from نَامَ "to sleep." This also applies to *maSdar*s such as حُبٌّ derived from the transitive verb أَحَبَّ "to love, to like." Examine the following:

مَا أَشَدَّ غَضَبَهَا!	How deep her anger is!
مَا أَسْرَعَ نَوْمَهُ!	How fast he goes to sleep!
مَا أَعْمَقَ حُبَّ الأُمِّ!	How deep is a mother's love!
مَا أَكْثَرَ إِيمَانَهُ!	How deep his belief is!

A nominal relative clause can follow the exclamatory مَا plus the comparative adjective form. Such a clause may begin with أَنْ followed by a verb in the subjunctive, as in the following:

مَا أَصْعَبَ أَنْ يَتَأَقْلَمَ الإِنْسَانُ فِي بِيئَةٍ جَدِيدَةٍ!
How difficult for people to adapt to a new environment!

مَا أَرْوَعَ أَنْ يُحِبَّ الأَخُ أَخَاهُ!
How wonderful for people to love one another!

أَنْ plus the subjunctive verb can be replaced by a *maSdar* derived from the verb following أَنْ producing an *IDhaafa*-construct. The previous two examples can be expressed as follows:

مَا أَصْعَبَ تَأَقْلُمَ الإِنْسَانِ فِي بِيئَةٍ جَدِيدَةٍ!
How difficult for people to adapt to a new environment!

مَا أَرْوَعَ حُبَّ الأَخِ لأَخِيهِ!
How wonderful for people to love one another!

36.2 مَا ... مَا PLUS VERBAL PHRASES

Another type of exclamatory clause begins with the exclamatory مَا plus a comparative adjective, followed by مَا and a verb in the present tense indicative, as in the following:

ما أَشَدَّ ما يُقاسي مِن آلام!	How intense are his pains!
ما أَسْرَعَ ما يَفورُ غَضَبُهُ!	How fast his anger boils!

Again, accusative *maSdar*s of the verbs following the second ما in the preceding sentences can replace ما plus the indicative verb to convey the same meaning, as in the following:

ما أَشَدَّ مُقاساتُهُ مِن آلام!	How intense are his pains!
ما أَسْرَعَ فَوْرَةَ غَضَبِهِ!	How fast his anger boils!

36.3 أَفْعِلْ بِـ

Another less frequently used way of expressing exclamation in Modern Standard Arabic is by constructing verbs from adjectives according to the أَفْعِل بِـ pattern. Such verbal patterns must adhere to the following conditions: the verb from which the adjective is derived must be tri-consonantal in the active voice, not preceded by a negative particle. Additionally, these adjectives must express characteristics that allow comparison. Thus, the adjective كَريم "noble, generous," is based on كرم "to be generous, noble." The exclamatory form according to أَفْعِلْ بِـ is, therefore, أَكْرِم بِـ. From حَسَنٌ "to be good," the form أَحْسِنْ بِـ is derived. In discourses, one hears the following:

أَكْرِمْ بِزَيْد مِنْ رَجُلٍ!	What a noble man, Zayd!
أَحْسِنْ بِهِ مِنْ صَديقٍ!	What a good friend he is!

36.4 يا لَ / لِ

Exclamation can also be expressed by the use of the vocative particle يا followed by a noun in the genitive case that must begin with the preposition لِ or لَ. Examine the following examples:

يا لِجَمالِ هذِهِ الـمَرْأَةِ!	How beautiful this woman is!
يا لَجَمالِ هذِهِ الـمَرْأَةِ!	How beautiful this woman is!
يا لِغَرابَةِ هذا السُّؤالِ!	How strange this question is!
يا لَغَرابَةِ هذا السُّؤالِ !	How strange this question is!

The preceding exclamatory phrases form an *IDhaafa*-construct. The exclamatory يا, however, can be followed by a single noun with the preposition لِـ or كَـ prefixed to it. Examine the following:

يا لِلعَجَبِ!	How strange this is!
يا لَلْعَجَبِ!	How strange this is!
يا لِلزَّمَنِ!	*lit.* "Woe to time!" [Times have changed!]
يا لَلزَّمَنِ!	*lit.* "Woe to time!" [Times have changed!]

يا can be followed by كَـ with a pronoun suffix attached to it, as in the following:

يا لَهُ مِنْ رَجُلٍ!	What a man!
يا لَها مِنْ سَيِّدَةٍ فاضِلَةٍ!	What a gracious lady!

Finally, the following commonly used phrases are considered a part of exclamation:

سُبْحانَ اللهِ!	Praise the Lord!
ما شاءَ اللهُ!	Amazing!
يا إلهي!	O my God!
يا سَلامُ!	Good heavens!
اللهُ أَكْبَرُ!	What a wonderful thing!

36.5 كَمْ

كَمْ "how much, how many," was introduced in Chapter 6 as an interrogative particle and mentioned as a particle used in *tamyiiz* (see Chapter 33 on *tamyiiz*). It can also be used to express exclamation, as in the following examples:

كَمْ هُوَ غَبِيٌّ!	How stupid he is!
كَمْ هِيَ جَميلَةٌ!	How beautiful she is!
كَمْ هذا الطَّقْسُ رائِعٌ!	How wonderful this weather is!

36.6 نِعْمَ AND بِئْسَ

There are two fossilized lexical items not considered part of exclamation, the subject of study in this chapter. These two items are used to extoll someone's or something's virtue, or to disparage or derogate someone or something: one positive نِعْمَ "how good," and the other negative بِئْسَ "how awful." These can be followed by nouns in the nominative or clauses beginning with ما, as in the following examples:

نِعْمَ الرَّجُلُ!	What a good man he is!
نِعْمَ ما أُلاقي مِن كَرَمٍ في هذِهِ البِلادِ!	How wonderful, what I encounter of generosity in this country!
بِئْسَتْ تِلْكَ الأَوْضاعُ!	How awful these situations are!
بِئْسَ ما قالَهُ مِنْ هُراءٍ!	How awful, what nonsense he said!

CHAPTER 37

Apposition البَدَل

The literal meaning of بَدَل is substitution. The accepted term among grammarians is "apposition," or "appositional noun," or "noun in apposition." Some traditional grammarians of Arabic have called this grammatical structure "explanation," "clarification," or "repetition."

Structurally, this amounts to juxtaposing a noun or noun phrase to another noun to reinforce the former and to provide more complete information, or to remove possible ambiguities. Generally, there is agreement between these two nouns in case, number, gender, and determination (definiteness/indefiniteness). Nouns of apposition, or substitution, are of four kinds:

37.1 SUBSTITUTION OF A NOUN FOR THE WHOLE

Examine the following examples:

كَلَّمَني أَحْمَد أخوكَ.   Ahmad, your brother, talked to me.

قَرَأْنا عَن عُمَرَ، الخَليفَةِ العادِلِ.   We read about Omar, the just Caliph.

In these sentences, أخوكَ "your brother" can totally substitute for the noun أَحْمَد and the phrase الخَليفَة العادل "the Just Caliph" can substitute for عُمَر "Omar." They are in agreement with these nouns in case, in addition to number, gender, and determination.

Repetition of nouns or noun phrases for further descriptive purposes is often encountered, as in the following examples:

مَشَيْنا في الشَّوارِعِ، الشَّوارِعِ الـمُزْدَحِمَةِ بالـمُصْطافينَ.

We walked in the streets, the streets full of tourists.

تَسَلَّقْنا الجِبالَ العالِيَةَ، وأيَّ جِبال!

We climbed the high mountains, what mountains!

37.2 SUBSTITUTION OF A PART FOR THE WHOLE

In this case, the noun in apposition must have attached to it a suffix pronoun that agrees in number and gender with the antecedent noun, as in the following:

قَرَأْتُ الكتابَ نِصْفَهُ.   I read the book, one-half of it.

شَرِبْتُ الكَأْسَ ثُلْثَها.   I drank the glass, one-third of it.

37.3 COMPREHENSIVE SUBSTITUTION

The noun in apposition agrees with the substituted noun in case, and it must also attach to a suffix pronoun agreeing in number and gender with the substituted noun. Examine the following example:

أَعْجَبَني الـمُديرُ صَبْرُهُ.   The director pleased me, his patience.

37.4 CORRECTING ONESELF

Finally, a noun is said to be in apposition to another noun when a speaker corrects himself or herself by mentioning a noun unlike the one which he or she uttered erroneously. Thus, if one intends to state that one read a book, but slipped up and mentioned another object of reading, one repeats the intended noun. Examine the following example:

قَرَأْتُ رِسالَةً، كِتاباً.   I read a letter, a book.

Thus كِتاباً "a book" in the preceding example is in apposition to رِسالَةً "a letter." Note that these words share the same case marker and determination.

CHAPTER 38

Emphasis التَّوْكيد

The quantifiers كُلّ and جَميع "all of," بَعْض and مُعْظَم "most of," were presented in Chapter 31. Their use in sentences can indicate emphasis of nouns. Additionally, the use of إِنَّ "indeed" at the beginning of equational sentences (see Chapter 21) was indicated to add emphasis to propositions expressed in sentences. In what follows, two more elements that indicate emphasis of nouns will be presented, namely نَفْس and عَيْن, both with the meaning of "same [himself/herself]."

38.1 عَيْن / نَفْس

نَفْس and عَيْن must follow the nouns intended for emphasis. However, the use of these two elements in positions before nouns is becoming increasingly widespread in Modern Literary Arabic. When they follow nouns, نَفْس or عَيْن function as adjectives (see Chapter 4 on adjectives). However, نَفْس and عَيْن are invariable with respect to gender. When either نَفْس or عَيْن follow a noun, the masculine, singular suffix pronoun هُ (or ﻪ when preceded by a *kasra* or a *yaa'*) or the feminine, singular pronoun ها must attach to نَفْس or عَيْن, as in the following examples:

وَصَلَ الـمُديرُ عَيْنُهُ.   The director (M, Sg) himself arrived.

وَصَلَت الـمُديرَةُ عَيْنُها.   The director (F, Sg) herself arrived.

عَيْن and نَفْس assume the same case of the noun preceding them. Consider the following:

قابَلْنا الـمُديرَ نَفْسَهُ.   We met the director (M, Sg) himself.

قابَلْنا الـمُديرَةَ نَفْسَها.   We met the director (F, Sg) herself.

38.1.1 عَيْن / نَفْس in the dual

When نَفْس or عَيْن follows a noun in the dual, two options are available: Either the singular forms of these words are used, or their dual forms نَفْسان and عَيْنان, respectively. The dual forms are invariable with respect to gender; however, they must agree in case with the preceding noun. Examine the following examples, in which the first pair is in the singular, the second in the dual:

سافَرَ الـمُديرانِ نَفْسُهُما.	The two directors (M) themselves left.
سافَرَتِ الـمُديرَتانِ نَفْسُهُما.	The two directors (F) themselves left.
سافَرَ الـمُديرانِ نَفْساهُما.	The two directors (M) themselves left.
سافَرَتِ الـمُديرَتانِ نَفْساهُما.	The two directors (F) themselves left.

Recall that the *nuun* of نَفْسان is dropped when the dual suffix هُما is attached, essentially forming an *IDhaafa*-construct.

The noun emphasized in the following two sentences, i.e., الـمُديرَتَيْنِ, is in the accusative case. In the first sentence عَيْن is in the singular; in the second it is in the dual.

قابَلْنا الـمُديرَتَيْنِ عَيْنَهُما.	We met the two directors (F) themselves.
قابَلْنا الـمُديرَتَيْنِ عَيْنَيْهِما.	We met the two directors (F) themselves.

38.1.2 عَيْن / نَفْس in the plural

The plural of نَفْس or عَيْن is formed according to the pattern أَفْعُل generating أَنْفُس or أَعْيُن. The appropriate masculine plural suffix pronoun هُمْ, or the feminine plural suffix pronoun هُنَّ must attach to أَنْفُس or أَعْيُن. أَنْفُس or أَعْيُن are invariable with respect to gender; however, they must agree in case with the noun preceding them, as in the following examples:

وَصَلَتِ الـمُعَلِّماتُ أَنْفُسُهُنَّ.
The teachers (F, Pl) themselves arrived.

قابَلْنا الـمُعَلِّماتِ أَنْفُسَهُنَّ.
We met the teachers (F, Pl) themselves.

تَكَاتَبوا مَعَ الـمُديرينَ أَنْفُسِهِمْ.

They corresponded with the directors (M, Pl) themselves.

Recall that the accusative marker of feminine plural nouns ending with ات is always a *kasra*, not a *fat-Ha*.

With non-human plurals such as مُدُنٌ "cities" or كُتُبٌ "books," for example, only the singular form نَفْس or عَيْن can be used. The suffix pronoun attached to these words must be the feminine singular form ها, used in reference to non-human plural nouns, as in the following examples:

زارَتِ الصَّديقَةُ الـمُدُنَ نَفْسَها.

The friend (F) visited the same cities. (*lit.* "the cities themselves")

قَرَأَ الطُّلابُ الكُتُبَ نَفْسَها.

The students read the same books. (*lit.* "the books themselves")

38.2 ذات "SELF"

In Modern Standard Arabic, the word ذات "self" is often used for emphasis. Thus, one frequently encounters sentences like the following:

سَنُقابِلُ الـمُدَيرَ ذاتَهُ.

We shall meet the director himself.

كُلَّ أُسْبوع نَجْتَمِعُ مَعَ الـوَزيرَة ذاتِها.

Every week, we meet with the minister herself.

38.3 EMPHASIS BY PRONOUN REPETITION

Emphasis can also be indicated by the repetition of an independent pronoun in reference to a suffixal pronoun mentioned in the sentence. This suffixal pronoun functions as antecedent to the independent pronoun used. Examine the following sentences:

قابَلْنا الـمُديرَ وتَكَلَّمْنا مَعَهُ هُوَ.

We met the director and we spoke with him.

مَرَرْتُ بِكَ أَنْتَ.

I passed you.

رُجوعُها هِيَ مِنَ الـمَـنْفَى كانَ نَصْراً كَبيراً للحِزْب.

Her return from exile was a big victory for the [political] party.

The independent pronouns هُوَ "he," أَنْتَ "you (M)," and هِيَ "she" in the preceding sentences add emphasis to the referents that preceded them in these sentences.

Appendix A: hollow verbs

WAAW HOLLOW VERBS

باحَ / يَبوحُ	to reveal a secret
باسَ / يَبوسُ	to kiss
بالَ / يَبولُ	to urinate
تابَ / يَتوبُ	to repent
تاقَ / يَتوقُ	to long, to yearn
ثابَ / يَثوبُ	to return, to come back to s.th.
ثارَ / يَثورُ	to rebel, to revolt
جابَ / يَجوبُ	to travel extensively
جادَ / يَجودُ	to become good, to grant generously
جارَ / يَجورُ	to wrong, to deviate
جازَ / يَجوزُ	to become possible
جاعَ / يَجوعُ	to get hungry
جالَ / يَجولُ	to wander around, to roam
حازَ / يَحوزُ	to obtain, to acquire
حالَ / يَحولُ	to prevent, to be in the way of s.th.
حامَ / يَحومُ	to rotate around, to navigate around
خاضَ / يَخوضُ	to wade through, to discuss, to wage
خانَ / يَخونُ	to betray
داخَ / يَدوخُ	to become dizzy
دارَ / يَدورُ	to rotate, to evolve
داسَ / يَدوسُ	to tread, to step
دامَ / يَدومُ	to last

ذادَ / يَذودُ	to defend
ذاقَ / يَذوقُ	to taste
راجَ / يَروجُ	to be spread, to circulate, to sell well
راحَ / يَروحُ	to go away
رادَ / يَرودُ	to walk about, to move about
رازَ / يَروزُ	to weigh, to assess
راقَ / يَروقُ	to be clear (liquid), to give s.o. pleasure
زالَ / يَزولُ	to cease, to go away
ساحَ / يَسوحُ	to travel
ساخَ / يَسوخُ	to be or become slippery, soft
سادَ / يَسودُ	to prevail, to be or become master
ساسَ / يَسوسُ	to govern, to rule, to dominate
ساغَ / يَسوغُ	to be easy to swallow
ساقَ / يَسوقُ	to drive
سامَ / يَسومُ	to offer for sale
صاغَ / يَصوغُ	to form, to shape
صالَ / يَصولُ	to assault
صامَ / يَصومُ	to fast
صانَ / يَصونُ	to protect
طافَ / يَطوفُ	to walk around
عادَ / يَعودُ	to return
عامَ / يَعومُ	to swim, to float
غاصَ / يَغوصُ	to plunge deep into
فاتَ / يَفوتُ	to pass away
فاحَ / يَفوحُ	to diffuse an aroma
فارَ / يَفورُ	to boil over
فازَ / يَفوزُ	to succeed, to win
فاقَ / يَفوقُ	to exceed
قادَ / يَقودُ	to lead
قالَ / يَقولُ	to say

قامَ / يَقومُ	to stand up
كانَ / يَكونُ	to be
لاحَ / يَلوحُ	to appear, to emerge, to loom
لاذَ / يَلوذُ	to take refuge in, to seek shelter
لاكَ / يَلوكُ	to chew, to talk constantly about s.th.
لامَ / يَلومُ	to blame
ماتَ / يَموتُ	to die
نابَ / يَنوبُ	to represent s.o., to replace
هانَ / يَهونُ	to become easy, simple

YAA' HOLLOW VERBS

باتَ / يَبيتُ	to spend a night
باضَ / يَبيضُ	to lay eggs
باعَ / يَبيعُ	to sell
تاهَ / يَتيهُ	to lose one's way, to get lost
جاءَ / يَجيءُ	to come, to arrive
حاكَ / يَحيكُ	to weave, to knit, to plot
حانَ / يَحينُ	to arrive, to come (of time)
خابَ / يَخيبُ	to fail, to be disappointed
خاطَ / يَخيطُ	to sew, to tailor
ذاعَ / يَذيعُ	to spread (like news)
زاحَ / يَزيحُ	to remove
زادَ / يَزيدُ	to increase, to surpass
سالَ / يَسيلُ	to flow
شابَ / يَشيبُ	to become gray (of hair)
شاخَ / يَشيخُ	to become old
شاعَ / يَشيعُ	to spread (of news)
شالَ / يَشيلُ	to carry
صارَ / يَصيرُ	to become
صاحَ / يَصيحُ	to shout

ضاعَ / يَضيعُ	to become lost, to get lost
ضافَ / يَضيفُ	to visit, to be a guest
ضاقَ / يَضيقُ	to become tight, to become narrow
طابَ / يَطيبُ	to heal, to become healthy
طارَ / يَطيرُ	to fly
طاشَ / يَطيشُ	to be inconstant, to be fickle
عابَ / يَعيبُ	to blame, to fault
عاثَ / يَعيثُ	to create a disaster, to create havoc
عاشَ / يَعيشُ	to live, to dwell, to survive
غابَ / يَغيبُ	to be absent
قاسَ / يَقيسُ	to measure
كالَ / يَكيلُ	to weigh
مالَ / يَميلُ	to be inclined, to tend toward
هاجَ / يَهيجُ	to be stirred up, to be or get excited

'ALIF HOLLOW VERBS

حارَ / يَحارُ	to be in a quandary, to be confused
خافَ / يَخافُ	to be afraid
خال / يَخالُ	to imagine, to fancy, to think
عافَ / يَعافُ	to loathe, to have an aversion to
غارَ / يَغارُ	to be jealous
كادَ / يَكادُ	to be just on the point of
نالَ / يَنالُ	to obtain, to acquire
هابَ / يَهابُ	to fear, to dread
طالَ / يَطالُ	to extend to

Appendix B: defective verbs

DEFECTIVE VERBS ENDING WITH LONG *'ALIF*

بَدا / يَبْدو	to appear
تَلا / يَتْلو	to follow, to recite
حَلا / يَحْلو	to become sweet
حَشا / يَحْشو	to stuff
خَلا / يَخْلو	to be empty
دَعا / يَدْعو	to invite, to call
دَنا / يَدْنو	to become close/nearer, to approach
رَتا / يَرْتو	to darn, to mend
رَجا / يَرْجو	to request
رَسا / يَرْسو	to anchor
رَشا / يَرْشو	to bribe s.o.
سَما / يَسْمو	to become sublime, elevated
شَكا / يَشْكو	to complain
عَدا / يَعْدو	to run
عَلا / يَعْلو	to rise, go up
غَزا / يَغْزو	to invade
مَحا / يَمْحو	to erase, to obliterate

Appendix C: doubled verbs

DOUBLED VERBS: MIDDLE *DHAMMA*

بَلَّ / يَبُلُّ	to wet
جَرَّ / يَجُرُّ	to pull, to drag, to draw
حَلَّ / يَحُلُّ	to solve
دَلَّ / يَدُلُّ	to guide
رَدَّ / يَرُدُّ	to reply, respond
سَبَّ / يَسُبُّ	to curse, to insult, to call s.o. names
سَدَّ / يَسُدُّ	to plug, to close, to dam
سَرَّ / يَسُرُّ	to please
شَدَّ / يَشُدُّ	to make firm, to tighten
شَكَّ / يَشُكُّ	to pierce, to doubt
صَبَّ / يَصُبُّ	to pour
ضَرَّ / يَضُرُّ	to harm, to injure
ضَمَّ / يَضُمُّ	to bring together, to join, to embrace
ظَنَّ / يَظُنُّ	to doubt
عَدَّ / يَعُدُّ	to count, to enumerate
قَصَّ / يَقُصُّ	to cut, to shear, to narrate, to tell
لَفَّ / يَلُفُّ	to wrap, to go around s.th.
مَدَّ / يَمُدُّ	to extend, to stretch
مَرَّ / يَمُرُّ	to pass through
مَصَّ / يَمُصُّ	to suck, to absorb

نَصَّ / يَنُصُّ	to stipulate
هَبَّ / يَهُبُّ	to get in motion, to start
هَزَّ / يَهُزُّ	to shake

DOUBLED VERBS: MIDDLE *KASRA*

تَمَّ / يَتِمُّ	to come to completion, to end
جَدَّ / يَجِدُّ	to be new
جَسَّ / يَجِسُّ	to examine by touch
جَفَّ / يَجِفُّ	to become dry
حَلَّ / يَحِلُّ	to settle down, to dismount
رَنَّ / يَرِنُّ	to ring
شَدَّ / يَشِدُّ	to tighten, to make firm
شَذَّ / يَشِذُّ	to deviate, to be an exception
طَنَّ / يَطِنُّ	to buzz, to drone
قَلَّ / يَقِلُّ	to become less, few

DOUBLED VERBS: MIDDLE *FAT-HA*

ظَلَّ / يَظَلُّ	to remain
وَدَّ / يَوَدُّ	to want, to desire
مَلَّ / يَمَلُّ	to become bored

Appendix D: فاعَلَ verbs (Form III)

بارَكَ / يُبارِكُ	to bless
تابَعَ / يُتابِعُ	to pursue
حادَثَ / يُحادِثُ	to converse with
حارَبَ / يُحارِبُ	to fight
حاضَرَ / يُحاضِرُ	to lecture
حافَظَ عَلى / يُحافِظُ عَلى	to protect, to defend, to keep
حاوَلَ / يُحاوِلُ	to try, to attempt
راجَعَ / يُراجِعُ	to review
راسَلَ / يُراسِلُ	to correspond with
ساعَدَ / يُساعِدُ	to assist, to help, to aid
سافَرَ إِلى / يُسافِرُ إِلى	to travel
سامَحَ / يُسامِحُ	to forgive
سانَدَ / يُسانِدُ	to support, to buttress
ساهَمَ / يُساهِمُ	to share in s.th., to partake
ساوَمَ / يُساوِمُ	to bargain
شارَكَ في / يُشارِكُ في	to participate
شاهَدَ / يُشاهِدُ	to view, to see
صادَقَ / يُصادِقُ	to befriend
صافَحَ / يُصافِحُ	to shake hands
طالَبَ / يُطالِبُ	to demand

عالَجَ / يُعالِجُ	to treat medically, to discuss a topic
عاوَنَ / يُعاوِنُ	to aid, to assist, to help
غادَرَ / يُغادِرُ	to depart
فاوَضَ / يُفاوِضُ	to negotiate
قابَلَ / يُقابِلُ	to encounter, to meet
قارَنَ / يُقارِنُ	to compare
قاسَمَ / يُقاسِمُ	to share
قاطَعَ / يُقاطِعُ	to boycott
قاوَمَ / يُقاوِمُ	to resist, to oppose
كاتَبَ / يُكاتِبُ	to correspond with
لاحَظَ / يُلاحِظُ	to observe, to notice
مارَسَ / يُمارِسُ	to practice
نافَسَ / يُنافِسُ	to compete with
ناقَشَ / يُناقِشُ	to debate, to discuss
ناوَلَ / يُناوِلُ	to hand s.th. over
هاجَرَ / يُهاجِرُ	to immigrate

Appendix E: أَفْعَلَ verbs (Form IV)

أَبْرَزَ / يُبْرِزُ	to highlight, to make prominent
أَجْلَسَ / يُجْلِسُ	to seat
أَحْضَرَ / يُحْضِرُ	to bring
أَخْبَرَ / يُخْبِرُ	to inform
أَخْرَجَ / يُخْرِجُ	to expel, to bring out
أَدْخَلَ / يُدْخِلُ	to let in, to insert
أَرْبَكَ / يُرْبِكُ	to confuse, to confound
أَرْسَلَ / يُرْسِلُ	to send, to dispatch
أَسْرَعَ / يُسْرِعُ	to hurry, to speed up
أَعْجَبَ / يُعْجِبُ	to please
أَعْلَمَ / يُعْلِمُ	to inform
أَعْلَنَ / يُعْلِنُ	to announce, to advertise
أَقْبَلَ / يُقْبِلُ	to approach
أَقْدَمَ / يُقْدِمُ	to embark upon
أَكْرَمَ / يُكْرِمُ	to honor, to treat generously
أَكْمَلَ / يُكْمِلُ	to complete, to finish
أَنْتَجَ / يُنْتِجُ	to produce, to put out

Appendix F: verbs requiring the use of 'anna أَنَّ

VERBS OF "KNOWING," "UNDERSTANDING," "DOUBTING," ETC.

أَدْرَكَ / يُدْرِكُ	to realize
اِتَّضَحَ / يَتَّضِحُ	to become obvious, to become clear
اِسْتَنْتَجَ / يَسْتَنْتِجُ	to conclude
أَظْهَرَ / يُظْهِرُ	to reveal, to show
اِعْتَبَرَ / يَعْتَبِرُ	to consider, to count
اِفْتَرَضَ / يَفْتَرِضُ	to suppose
اِقْتَنَعَ / يَقْتَنِعُ	to become convinced
بَدا / يَبْدو	to appear, to seem
بَيَّنَ / يُبَيِّنُ	to reveal, to show
تَبَيَّنَ / يَتَبَيَّنُ	to become clear, to become evident
تَصَوَّرَ / يَتَصَوَّرُ	to imagine, to think
حَسَّ / يَحِسُّ	to feel
رَأَى / يَرَى	to see, to view
شَعَرَ / يَشْعُرُ	to feel, to sense
شَكَّ / يَشُكُّ	to doubt
ظَنَّ / يَظُنُّ	to think, to suspect
ظَهَرَ / يَظْهَرُ	to appear, to surface
عَرَفَ / يَعْرِفُ	to know, to be familiar with
عَلِمَ / يَعْلَمُ	to know, to learn

عَنَى / يَعْنِي	to mean
فَهِمَ / يَفْهَمُ	to understand
قَدَّرَ / يُقَدِّرُ	to estimate, to guess
لاحَظَ / يُلاحِظُ	to observe
وَجَدَ / يَجِدُ	to find out, to discover

VERBS OF "MENTIONING," "HEARING," "REPORTING," ETC.

أَجابَ / يُجِيبُ	to answer, to respond
أَخْبَرَ / يُخْبِرُ	to inform, to tell
أشارَ إلى / يُشِيرُ إلى	to point to, to indicate
أَعْلَمَ / يُعْلِمُ	to inform
أَعْلَنَ / يُعْلِنُ	to announce, to declare
أفادَ / يُفِيدُ	to inform, to report
أوْضَحَ / يُوضِحُ	to clarify, to reveal
ذَكَرَ / يَذْكُرُ	to mention
رَدَّ / يَرُدُّ	to reply
رَدَّدَ / يُرَدِّدُ	to repeat
زَعَمَ / يَزْعُمُ	to allege, to claim
سَأَلَ / يَسْأَلُ	to ask
سَمِعَ / يَسْمَعُ	to hear
قَرَأَ / يَقْرَأُ	to read
كَتَبَ / يَكْتُبُ	to write, to record
كَرَّرَ / يُكَرِّرُ	to repeat, to reiterate
لَمَّحَ / يُلَمِّحُ	to hint, to imply
وَشَى / يَشِي	to inform against s.o.
وَضَّحَ / يُوَضِّحُ	to clarify

VERBS OF "ANGER," "SURPRISE," "HAPPINESS," "PRIDE"

أَدْهَشَ / يُدْهِشُ	to surprise
أَسْعَدَ / يُسْعِدُ	to please, to make s.o. happy
اِعْتَزَّ بِـ / يَعْتَزُّ بِـ	to take pride in
أَغْضَبَ / يُغْضِبُ	to annoy, to anger
اِفْتَخَرَ بِـ / يَفْتَخِرُ بِـ	to be proud of
أَفْرَحَ / يُفْرِحُ	to please, to make happy
أَقْلَقَ / يُقْلِقُ	to disturb, to distress
فاجَأَ / يُفاجِئُ	to surprise

VERBS OF "CONFIRMATION," "CERTAINTY"

أَثْبَتَ / يُثْبِتُ	to prove, to confirm
أَكَّدَ / يُؤَكِّدُ	to confirm, to ascertain, to assure
بَرْهَنَ / يُبَرْهِنُ	to prove
تَيَقَّنَ مِنْ / يَتَيَقَّنُ مِنْ	to be certain, to be sure
رَجَّحَ / يُرَجِّحُ	to think probable

Appendix G: phrases requiring the use of 'anna أَنَّ

لَوْ أَنَّ	were [he]
لَوْلا أَنَّ	had it not been for
بَيْدَ أَنَّ	although, whereas
غَيْرَ أَنَّ	except that, but, however
سِوَى أَنَّ	although
في حين أَنَّ	while
رَغْمَ أَنَّ	despite, in spite of, although
كَما أَنَّ	also, as well
عَلَى الرَّغْمِ (من) أَنَّ	despite, although
بالرَّغْمِ (مِنْ) أَنَّ	although, in spite of
لَيْسَ مِنْ شَكٍّ (في) أَنَّ	there is no doubt that
لا شَكَّ أَنَّ	there is no doubt that
مِنَ البَديهِيِّ أَنَّ	it is granted that
مِنَ الطَّبيعِيِّ أَنَّ	it is natural that
مِنَ المُفْتَرَضِ أَنَّ	it is assumed that
مِنَ الواضِح أَنَّ	it is clear that
مِنَ الطَّريفِ أَنَّ	it is interesting to note that
الطَّريفُ أَنَّ	it is interesting that
صَحيحٌ أَنَّ	it is true that
عِلْماً (بِ) أَنَّ	taking into consideration that
سِيَّما (و) أَنَّ	especially that
خاصَّةً (وَ) أَنَّ	especially that
لا جدالَ (في) أَنَّ	there is no argument that
مِنَ المَأْلوفِ أَنَّ	it is familiar that

Appendix H: phrases requiring the use of 'an أَنْ

مِنَ الرّاجِحِ أَنْ	it is more probable that
مِنَ الجائِزِ أَنْ	it is permissible that
مِنَ الـمَأْمول أَنْ	it is hoped that
مِنَ الـمُتَّفَق عَلَيْهِ أَنْ	it is agreed that
مِنَ العَجيب أَنْ	it is strange that
مِنَ الـمَطلوب أَنْ	it is required that
مِنَ الـمَعْقول أَنْ	it is reasonable that
مِنَ الـمُفْتَرَض أَنْ	it is assumed that
مِنَ الـمَفروض أَنْ	it is supposed that
مِنَ الـمُفيد أَنْ	it is beneficial that
مِنَ الـمَقْبول أَنْ	it is accepted that
مِنَ الـمُقَرَّر أَنْ	it is decided that
مِنَ الـمَرْغوب فيهِ أَنْ	it is desired that
مِنَ الـمَسْموح بِهِ أَنْ	it is permitted that

BIBLIOGRAPHY

ARABIC SOURCES

Al-Astrabadhi, Muhammad bin al-Hasan. 1982. *Sharh Shafiyat ibn al-Hajib.* 4 vols. Ed. Muhammad Nur al-Hasan, et al. Beirut: Dar al-Kutub al-Ilmiyya.

Al-Ghalayini, Mustafa. 1989. *Jaami ͨ al-Durus al-Arabiyya.* Sidon and Beirut: Al-Maktaba al-Asriyya.

Hasan, Abbas. 1975. *Al-Nahw al-Waafi.* 4 vols. Cairo: Dar al-Ma ͨarif (5th printing).

Ibn Hisham, Jamal al-Din. (d. 761). *Mughni al-Labib.* 2 vols. Ed. Muhammad Muhyi al-Din Abdul Hamid. Beirut: Dar Ihya' al-Turath al-Araby. n. d.

Ibn Jinni, Othman. 1972. *Kitab al-Luma ͨ fi al- ͨArabiyya.* Ed. Faiz Faris. Kuwait: Dar al-Kutub al-Thaqafiyya.

Ibn al-Sarraj, Muhammad bin Sahl. 1985. *Al-Usuul fi al-Nahw.* 3 vols. Ed. Abd al-Hussein Al-Fatli. Beirut: Mu'assast al-Risala.

Al- ͨUkburi, Ibn Burhan. 1984. *Sharh al-Luma ͨ.* 2 vols. Ed. Faiz Faris. Kuwait: Al-Silsila al-Turathiyya.

Sibawayhi, Amr bin Uthman. 1977. *Al-Kitaab.* Ed. Abdulsalam M. Haroun. Cairo: al-Hay'a al-Misriyya al- ͨAmma li al-Kitaab.

Al-Suyuti, Jalal al-Din. 1987. *Ham ͨ al-Hawaami ͨ.* 7 vols. Ed. Abdulsalam M. Haroun and Abd al- ͨAal Salem Makram. Beirut: Mu'assast al-Risala. 2nd printing.

Ibn Ya ͨish, Abu al-Baqa' Ya ͨish bin Ali. n. d. *Sharh al-Mufassal.* Cairo: al-Tiba ͨa al-Muniriyya (n.d.). Beirut: Dar Sader (reprod.).

Al-Zajjaji, Abdul Rahman. 1984. *Kitab al-Jumal fi al-Nahw.* Ed. Ali Tawfiq al-Hamad. Beirut: Mu'assasat al-Risala, and Irbid (Jordan): Dar al-Amal.

Al-Zamakhshari, Mahmoud bin Omar. 2001. *Al-Mufassal fi Sinaa ͨat al-'I ͨrab.* Beirut: Dar al-Kitab al-Lubnani, and Cairo: Dar al-Kitab al-Misri.

WESTERN LANGUAGE SOURCES

Badawi, Elsaid, M.G. Carter and Adrian Gully. 2004. *Modern Written Arabic: A Comprehensive Grammar.* London and New York: Routledge.

Brockelmann, Carl. 1985. *Arabische Grammatik.* Munich: Max Hueber Verlag.

Cantarino, Vincent. 1974. *Syntax of Modern Arabic Prose* (3 vols.). Bloomington/London: Indiana University Press.

Fischer, Wolfdietrich. 2002. *A Grammar of Classical Arabic*. Translated from German by Jonathan Rodgers. New Haven: Yale University Press (3rd edition).

Ryding, Karin C. 2005. *A Reference Grammar of Modern Standard Arabic*. Cambridge University Press.

Wright, William. 1975. *A Grammar of the Arabic Language*. Cambridge University Press (reprint).

DICTIONARIES

Abdul-Massih, George M. and Hani George Tabri. 1990. *Al-Khalil: A Dictionary of Arabic Grammar Terminology*. Beirut: Librairie du Liban.

Al-Bustani, Butrus. 1987. *Muhit al-Muhit*. Beirut: Librairie du Liban.

Esber, Muhammad Said and Bilal Junaidy. 1985. *Al-Shamil: Muʿjam fi ʿUlum al-lugha wa Mustalahatiha*. Beirut: Dar al-Awda.

Al-Firuzabadi, Muhammad bin Yaʿqub. 1986. *Al-Qaamuus al-Muhiit*. Beirut: Mu'assast al-Risala.

Ibn Manzur, Muhammad bin Mukarram. (d. 1311). 1968. *Lisan al-ʿArab*. Beirut: Dar Sader.

Al-Maʿlouf, Louis. 1975. *Al-Munjid fi al-Lugha wa al-'aʿlam*. Beirut: Dar al-Mashriq.

Wehr, Hans. 1979. *A Dictionary of Modern Written Arabic*. Wiesbaden: Otto Harrassouwitz (4th edition).

Index 1: English grammatical terms

Index 2: Arabic grammatical terms